Existentialism

Basic Writings

Existentialism

Basic Writings

Edited, with Introductions, by

CHARLES GUIGNON

and

DERK PEREBOOM

Hackett Publishing Company, Inc.

Indianapolis/Cambridge

Printed in the United States of America

00 99 98 97 96 95 1 2 3 4 5 6 7

For further information, please address

Hackett Publishing Company, Inc.
P.O. Box 44937
Indianapolis, Indiana 46244-0937

Design by Dan Kirklin

Production Coordinator: Elizabeth Shaw Editorial & Publishing Services

Library of Congress Cataloging-in-Publication Data

Existentialism: basic writings/edited, with introductions, by
    Charles Guignon and Derk Pereboom.
        p.   cm.
    ISBN 0-87220-215-1 (alk. paper).
    ISBN 0-87220-214-3 (pbk.: alk. paper)
    1. Existentialism.   I. Guignon, Charles B., 1944–
II. Pereboom, Derk, 1957–
8819.E865   1995
142'.78—dc20   94-48670
                                                CIP

The paper used in this publication meets the minimum requirements of American
National Standard for Information Sciences—Permanence of Paper for Printed
Library Materials, ANSI Z39.48-1984.

Contents

Nietzsche   85

Introduction:
    1. Life-Philosophy: The Dionysian and the Apollonian 85
    2. A New Kind of Science 88   3. The Death of God 93
    4. The Idea of the Eternal Recurrence of the Same 96
    5. Perspectivism 99   6. "The Great Health" and the Path
    to the Overman 103   7. Twilight of the Idols 106

Selections:

Heidegger   175

Introduction:
    1. The Question of Being 175   2. Human Being (Dasein)
    as Being-in-the-world 181   3. The Structure of Human
    Agency 188   4. Authenticity 195

Selections:

Preface

This book grew out of our shared feeling that there was a need for a collection of core works in the existentialist tradition for use in courses in philosophy, religion, literature, and film. In 1992, we joined forces to teach a seminar on existentialism at the University of Vermont using the texts collected in this volume. Through the input of the students in that class and through our own exchange of ideas in the seminar room, we worked out the view of existentialism that informs this book. We are very grateful to the students who participated in that seminar for their questions and contributions.

Although we each have an abiding interest in existentialism, we approach these ideas from somewhat different directions. Charles Guignon was trained in analytic philosophy at the University of California at Berkeley, but, under the influence of Professor Hubert L. Dreyfus, he shifted his attention to continental philosophy during his final years of graduate school. Most of his publications have been on Heidegger, though he has also written on such figures as Ludwig Wittgenstein, Richard Rorty, and Charles Taylor. Derk Pereboom wrote his dissertation on Immanuel Kant at the University of California at Los Angeles. He continues to teach and write on modern philosophy (Descartes to Kant) as well as on issues in current philosophy of mind. Pereboom also has a special interest in Kierkegaard, thanks largely to the influence of his teacher and friend, Professor Robert Adams, who is now at Yale.

Our common background in mainstream American philosophy has had an impact on the introductions to the readings in this volume. From the outset we agreed that our primary goal in presenting the ideas of existentialist thinkers would be to show how their thought continues to be highly relevant to important philosophical issues. That explains the central place given in our introductions to such issues as the nature of the self and agency, the problem of skepticism, the nature of the mental, the realism-antirealism debate, the place of faith in the modern world, and the problem of subjectivism in ethics. As a result of our focus, such existentialist themes as guilt, conscience, ennui, alienation, and so forth have been pushed into the background. Our hope is that most classes dealing with these texts today will find the issues we deal with to be those that are the most lasting contributions of existentialist philosophy. But we should point out that our introductions represent only one view of the figures whose works appear in this volume, and that very different emphases and orientations are possible. In the end, we decided to give our own interpretation of these authors rather than pre-sent remarks so general and banal that no one could possibly disagree.

Though we collaborated on all the introductions, Charles Guignon wrote most of the main introduction to the volume, as well as the introductions to the Nietzsche and Heidegger readings. Derk Pereboom wrote the introduc-tion to Kierkegaard, and we both worked on the Sartre introduction. In ad-dition, the new translation of section one of Nietzsche's *The Birth of Trag-edy* was done by Pereboom. For this translation we are indebted to the many thoughtful suggestions made by our former student, Hans Grünig.

This volume includes new translations by Richard Polt of parts of *The Gay Science* and *Twilight of the Idols.* In these translations, Polt set out to eliminate the sexist and archaic language found in earlier translations, and to break up sentences and paragraphs in a way that we hope will be more read-able for contemporary undergraduates and nonspecialists. We feel that the efforts represent a considerable improvement over the existing translations.

Many people contributed to the shaping of this volume. Dorothy Leland and Shari Starrett were extremely helpful in suggesting texts to be included. Leslie Fry, Graham Parkes, and Richard Polt read earlier drafts of some of our introductions and provided valuable suggestions for improvements. Fi-nally, we both want to thank our teachers, H. L. Dreyfus and Robert Adams, for introducing us to these ideas and shaping our thought about existential philosophy.

Charles Guignon
Derk Pereboom
The University of Vermont

Acknowledgments

For permission to reprint these selections, the authors are grateful to the following publishers and copyright holders:

PRINCETON UNIVERSITY PRESS   For the excerpts from *Fear and Trembling, The Sickness Unto Death*, by Søren Kierkegaard, translated by Walter Lowrie, and *Concluding Unscientific Postscript*, by Søren Kierkegaard, translated by D. Swenson and W. Lowrie. Copyright © 1941, 1954 by Princeton University Press. Reprinted by permission of the publishers.

HARPERCOLLINS PUBLISHERS   For selected excerpts from about 45 pages from *Being and Time*, by Martin Heidegger. Copyright © 1962 by SCM Press Ltd. Reprinted by permission of HarperCollins Publishers, Inc.

BLACKWELL PUBLISHERS   For excerpts from *Being and Time*, by Martin Heidegger, translated by John Macquarrie and Edward Robinson (for Canada). Copyright © 1962 by Blackwell Publishers. Reprinted by permission of the publishers.

PHILOSOPHICAL LIBRARY   For excerpts from *Existentialism and Human Emotions*, by Jean-Paul Sartre, translated by Bernard Frechtman. Copyright © 1957 by Philosophical Library. For excerpts from *Being and Nothingness*, by Jean-Paul Sartre, translated by Hazel E. Barnes, Copyright © 1956 by Philosophical Library. Reprinted by permission of the publisher and Regeen Najar.

HACKETT PUBLISHING COMPANY   For selections from Nietzsche, *The Gay Science*, and *The Twilight of the Idols*, translated by Richard Polt. Copyright © 1995 Hackett Publishing Company. Reprinted by permission of the translator and Hackett Publishing Company.

For selections from Nietzsche, *The Birth of Tragedy*, translated by Derk Pereboom. Copyright © 1995 by Hackett Publishing Company. Reprinted by permission of the translator and Hackett Publishing Company.

Introduction:
The Legacy of Existentialism

1. Existentialism Today

Nearly half a century has passed since existentialism first exploded on the European intellectual scene, setting the tone for Parisian café talk and creating a stir in such areas as psychoanalysis, theology, literature, theater, and film. By the 1950s and 1960s, the existentialist style and attitude had swept into the English-speaking world, and talk of anxiety, alienation, and absurdity provided a counterpoint to the mainstream thinking of the time. The "Outsider" and "the angry young man" presented alternatives to the prevailing "other-directed" personality type bent on making friends and influencing people. What made the post-war existentialist movement so attractive was its unflinching stance of resistance and refusal toward everything regarded as commonplace and beyond criticism in contemporary life.

Some of the ideas of that era have come to seem a bit dated. Deep existential themes like the search for a "reason for existing" are now satirized on late-night comedy shows, where advertisements for a new brand of cereal, *Raison d'Être,* promise 50 percent more raisons. At the same time that existentialism has lost some of its popular appeal, however, there has been a growing respect for some of the central thinkers who are generally regarded as representatives of the existentialist tradition. There has been a surge of interest in Friedrich Nietzsche's writings, fueled in part by the creative and contentious interpretations of his thought developed by such postmodern figures as Jacques Derrida and Michel Foucault. Interest in the thought of Martin Heidegger has been stirred up in the English-speaking world by influential writers such as Charles Taylor, H. L. Dreyfus, and Richard Rorty. And many debates about religious belief, free will, and ethics turn to the thought of Søren Kierkegaard and Jean-Paul Sartre for inspiration. Existentialist writers have important things to say about such current topics as the nature of the self, the realism-antirealism debate, computer models of the mind, and the relevance of care or local attachments to ethics. Whatever one makes of the post-war phenomenon called "existentialism," it is hard to ignore the figures who are seen as precursors and exponents of that movement.

Our goal in this volume is to gather together basic writings by four of the seminal thinkers associated with the existentialist movement: Kierkegaard, Nietzsche, Heidegger, and Sartre. There is, of course, some reason to be hesitant in calling all these thinkers "existentialists." Kierkegaard and Nietzsche, writing in the nineteenth century, lived long before the term "existentialism" came into use, and Heidegger in his later years went out of his way to deny he was an existentialist. But there is a long and well established tradition that groups these thinkers under the existentialist banner, and, we believe, for good reasons. Although the differences among these thinkers should not be obscured, we hope to show here that they have a great deal in common, and that together they can still be thought of as presenting a united front against standardized ways of thinking.

2. Existentialism and the Rise of the Modern Worldview

What is existentialism? The term is notoriously difficult to define, and no single definition will be adequate to fit all the works usually labeled "existentialist." But there are a number of features most existentialists have in common. We might start by saying that existentialism arises as a response to some of the major shifts that occurred with the emergence in the sixteenth and seventeenth centuries of what is called the modern worldview. This modern outlook results in part from the radically new view of reality created by the rise of modern science. The sociologist Max Weber described this shift as the "disenchantment of the world." In his view, traditional or premodern societies experienced the world as an "enchanted garden" in which nature is understood as a meaningful, value-filled order that determines the proper function and aim for each thing in advance. Thus, the ancient Greeks tended to assume that there is a built-in order of nature (the *cosmos*) that determines what things should be like and how people ought to live. In Medieval Europe when people understood themselves as God's creations they were inclined to see themselves as having a pregiven goal in life—the goal of realizing God's plan for them on earth. Even as late as the Renaissance people generally thought of reality as a "great chain of being" or a "ladder of being" in which each type of thing has a proper place.

For these earlier ways of understanding things, the world is regarded as a familiar home for humans, a place where everything is filled with meaning and significance. To say that the rise of modern science involved a "disenchantment" of the world, then, is to say that science undermines this sense of a pregiven meaning and value in things. The great achievements of the early scientists were made possible by their ability to set aside their belief in the inherent meaningfulness of things in order to look at the world as consisting of a vast aggregate of inherently meaningless entities: the material objects in causal relations posited by natural science.

We can see this new ability to see the universe as a totality of physical objects in some of Galileo's discoveries. Looking at the shadows on the moon, he made the shocking suggestion that they are caused by mountains and valleys like those on earth. This was considered shocking at the time because older views had regarded the moon as a radiant heavenly entity of a totally different type from things in the terrestrial sphere. Because each sphere was regarded as having a different meaning in the order of things, the entities in the different spheres should have different natures and principles. By brushing aside the older belief in the qualitative differences between the spheres, and by regarding the celestial as no different than the terrestrial, Galileo could treat the moon as basically a big rock not much different from the material objects found here on earth. But in doing so he set aside the older sense of the meanings of the different spheres that had been central to the premodern understanding of things.

To see things in this way requires the ability to "objectify" the world; that is to say, it calls for the ability to see the universe as a vast aggregate of meaningless brute objects, lacking any inherent value or significance. From this standpoint, however, the universe is no longer experienced as an "enchanted garden" where meanings and purposes are laid out for us in advance. Thanks to this new outlook, humans come to regard themselves as being merely one type of animal among others, as medium-sized creatures on a small planet at the outer edge of one among billions of galaxies. The religious thinker and proto-existentialist Blaise Pascal, writing soon after the scientifically oriented philosopher René Descartes, captured the sense of loneliness and homelessness accompanying this new outlook when he said, "The silence of these infinite spaces terrifies me." Existentialists start out from this feeling of homelessness even though they are quite critical of the scientific outlook that brought it into existence in the first place.

Another dimension of the rise of the modern worldview is the emergence of the new centralized state and the sense of the conception of the self as an individual set over against and distinct from society. Before the rise of the modern worldview, people generally found their identity in terms of having a place and function within small, relatively cohesive communities. Think, for example, of the film *The Return of Martin Guerre*. A man leaves his village and is later replaced by someone who looks quite different from him, yet is able to perform the same functions as the original man. To our astonishment, no one seems to notice that he is a different person. In such a world, there does not seem to be much of a sense of being an "individual," where this is understood in the modern way as an individuated, unique entity essentially distinct from others, whose identity swings free of the station he or she occupies in public. On the contrary, in the older worldview, a person is primarily defined by his or her place in a network of family and social relations.

With the shift to the modern outlook, there emerges a new way of understanding the relation of the self to the community. The sixteenth century marks the appearance of the concept of a "society" understood as an aggregate of essentially distinct individuals. Because a society is understood as a human creation, the result of some sort of social contract or agreement among initially unconnected individuals, there is no sense of there being any inbuilt or internal relations among individuals that are determined in advance by nature or by God. According to the emerging modern view, society is regarded as having "a life of its own, but not a human life," and so it is experienced as something "other" to the individual, opposing the individual's quest for fulfillment. Lionel Trilling argues that this new sense of society as essentially alien to the individual leads eventually to the profoundly modern ideal of "authenticity."[1] The concept of the individual, seen as caught in a constant struggle against an impersonal and dehumanizing society, is also at the root of much of the sense of alienation and isolation so central to the modern identity.

Nietzsche tries to convey a sense of how these shifts have led to a profound and irreversible breakdown of traditional ways of living in his well-known words, "God is dead." This remark does not just mean that people are less religious than they used to be. Instead, it means that the traditional conceptions of an "absolute" in the Western world—ideas about a transcendent basis of meaning and value in life, including the *cosmos* of the Greeks, the God of Christianity, the Humanism and Reason of the Enlightenment—all of these old absolutes have been found to be only transient human constructs with no binding force in telling us how we ought to act or what we ought to strive for. And where these old absolutes have failed, no new god-term seems to be in the offing. Nietzsche sees this loss of absolutes as quite terrifying. For as people become aware of the loss of a taken-for-granted basis for assessment and aspiration in Western civilization, he predicts, the outcome will be nihilism, the complete disbelief in all values.

Of course, other thinkers have been aware of the confusion and breakdown characteristic of the transition to modernity. But generally those thinkers have tended to suppose that the breakdown will lead to a new and better way of life (Hegel, Marx) or they have seen it as freeing us from a lot of pointless illusions so that we can lighten up and enjoy life (Camus, some

1. Lionel Trilling, *Sincerity and Authenticity* (Cambridge, Mass: Harvard University Press, 1971), 19–25.

scientific naturalists). In contrast, existentialists tend to regard this loss of traditional absolutes as a shattering event. For if God is dead, then we are left with no underlying grounds to legitimate our existence or define our aim in life. We find ourselves "abandoned," "forlorn," "thrown" into a world with no pregiven justifications or sense of direction. And though most of us cling to society for comfort and protection, the fact is that, at the deepest level, we are ultimately alone. We are basically isolated individuals who have to make sense of the world and find meaning for our lives on our own.

In their more dramatic moments, existentialists speak of a feeling of the "anguish," "anxiety," or "nausea" that comes from confronting a brute world of "being" devoid of any built-in design or purpose. In Heidegger's dramatic language, we find ourselves suspended over an "abyss of mean-inglessness," standing face to face with our own "being-toward-death," without worldly supports or guarantees. What these formulations point to is an awareness that there are no fixed foundations for our beliefs and practices, no pregiven "essences" that determine the proper goal of humans, so that it is up to each of us to give a determinate content and point to our own lives. With its clear-sighted recognition of our lack of absolutes in the modern age, existentialism makes explicit the understanding of our predicament that lies at the root a wide variety of recent challenges to the essentialism and foundationalism of traditional philosophy.

3. Human Existence

In attempting to understand our predicament in the modern age existentialists have formulated an insightful new way of thinking about human existence. In contrast to much of the philosophical tradition, which has sought to understand a human as a thing or an object of a particular sort (whether a mind or a body or some combination of the two), existentialists have characterized human existence as involving a profound tension or conflict, an ongoing struggle between opposing elements.

Though such a conception of human existence has roots in St. Augustine, Montaigne, Pascal, and even in Plato, the primary source of the modern existentialist version of this picture is G. W. F. Hegel. In his *Phenomenology of Spirit* (1807), Hegel distinguishes two dimensions or aspects that make up a human being. On the one hand, humans are natural organisms among others in nature, members of the animal kingdom, with needs and desires not much different from those of other animals. On the other hand, humans are also different from lower-order animals. Whereas birds and squirrels are limited to the immediate needs and drives of the life of nature and cannot transcend those limits in any way, the existence of consciousness (or self-awareness) in humans marks a qualitative difference from the lower orders of animals. As Hegel says, "Consciousness, however, is explicitly the notion of itself." In other words, as conscious beings, humans are capable of reflecting on themselves and evaluating themselves in the light of some overarching vision of what their lives are adding up to. And in this respect consciousness introduces a break into the order of nature. It embodies the ability to step back from its own dealings with the environment in order to question and assess those dealings. Hegel describes this by saying that consciousness "transcends its limits," and because these limits belong to it, "consciousness transcends its own self."[2]

Heidegger and Sartre capture this sense of transcendence by saying that what is unique to humans is that their being is "in question" or "at issue" for them. Humans are not content with simply satisfying their basic desires, for they care about what kinds of beings they are, and they therefore reflect on the worth of the things they desire. Because they are capable of having aspirations and striving for something beyond the immediacy of their basic needs and drives, they are capable of forming second-order desires about their basic desires and can regulate their immediate responses in the light of higher goals and purposes. Though I have a craving for rich desserts, for instance, I can reflect on that craving and I can monitor it in terms of some higher-level desires about what sort of person I want to be. But this means that, in reflecting on what we are, we can say "no" to our immediate inclinations. As a result, we introduce a "not" into the plenum of brute nature. We make a break with our mere factual givenness by *taking a stand* on it and taking it over in some way or other in the course of our active lives.

Thus, a rift or fissure, a "nothingness," is introduced into the fullness of being by human existence. Taking a stand on oneself creates the perpetual possibility of a "no" uttered to all that has been and now is. In this way, according to Hegel, "consciousness suffers . . . violence at its own hands; it spoils its own limited satisfaction." The gap opened up in the heart of being by consciousness leads to a perpetual *desire*: the constant craving to close up the rift by finally once and for all *realizing* the higher-order aspirations and ideals opened up by reflection. Thus, life is experienced as a lack or emptiness that strives to fill itself up. Human existence is constantly agitated by aspirations and strivings that go beyond its immediate needs and impressions, and so, Hegel says, "it can find no peace."

Hegel therefore presents us with a picture of human existence as a tension between two aspects of the self: the "in itself"—our "given," natural functions as finite, empirical beings—and the "for itself"—the reflective mo-

2. G. W. F. Hegel, *Phenomenology of Spirit,* trans. A. V. Miller (Oxford: Oxford University Press, 1979); all quotations are from paragraph 80 (translations modified).

ment that leads us to interpret and evaluate, and so to transcend or surpass our mere givenness. Kierkegaard, playing with Hegel's complicated language, tries to get at this structure of human existence in *The Sickness Unto Death* by saying that a self is "a relation that relates itself to itself." Nietzsche points to the duality at the core of human existence when he says that humans are both creatures and creators. And Heidegger and Sartre refer to humans as a duality consisting of "facticity" and "transcendence." For Heidegger, human being (which he calls "Dasein" or "being-there") consists of both "embodiment" and "freedom." As part of nature, he says, Dasein "is thrown, factical, thoroughly embedded in nature through its bodiliness." But, at the same time, "as transcending, Dasein is beyond nature"; that is to say, "although, as factical it remains environed by nature, . . . as transcending, i.e., as free, Dasein is something alien to nature."[3]

Hegel believed that the tension in consciousness between our creaturely givenness and our self-conscious strivings could eventually be resolved through a process of rational "dialectic." For existentialists, in contrast, such a tidy resolution of the tension is not so easy to come by. In their view, so long as we are alive and capable of reflection, we will always be more than what we are as mere factical entities, and so there will always be a gap between what is just "there" in our lives and what could or should be. Given the depth of this rift in the self, the most one can hope for is either to live in the tension with maximum lucidity and intensity (the view of secular existentialists like Sartre and Heidegger) or to find a meaning and content for one's life in a commitment (the view of a theistic existentialist like Kierkegaard).

When we think of the self as an ongoing struggle rather than as a static thing, it is natural to also think of ourselves as an unfolding event or happening. What defines my identity as a person of a specific sort is not some enduring set of properties I have through time, but is instead the "event of becoming" in which I struggle to find a resolution to the tension that defines my situation in the world. As an ongoing happening, I *am* what I make of myself throughout the course of my life as a whole.

This means that human existence has a particular sort of temporal structure. We do not just persist in existence like rocks or cauliflowers, occupying a position in the endless series of "nows" of time. Instead, human temporality has a kind of cumulativeness and goal-directedness that is different from the enduring presence of physical things. First, the temporal unfold-

---

3. Martin Heidegger, *Metaphysical Foundations of Logic*, trans. Michael Heim (Bloomington: Indiana University Press, 1984), 166.

ing of human existence has a distinctive "futural" character. As Hegel saw, we are relentlessly driven on by a desire to *be* something, to complete ourselves or to heal up the rift at the core of our being. As a result of this desire (which existentialists call "care" or "the desire to be God"), we are always directed forward into the future, moving toward realizing the fundamental projects that define our transcendence. Humans are futural beings, and their mode of relating to the future in turn defines the temporal modes of being of nonhuman things.

But, in addition, our own past shows up for us in a distinctive way because of the way it is shaped and colored by our future-directedness. I will interpret my past as a good preparation for what is to come or as a huge waste of time depending on what my plans for the future are at any given moment. We are "time-binding beings" in the sense that our goal-directedness or futurity leads us to gather up what has come before and carry it forward into the future as resources for our projects. Finally, our actions in the present occur as points of intersection between the cumulativeness of the past and the directionality of the future. In each of my actions, I seize on what came before for the purpose of realizing what I am out to achieve for my life as a whole. This is why, for existentialists generally, pure "presence" detached from past and future can never exist. We are always "out there," already beyond our being as mere entities in the present. Heidegger tries to capture this feature of human existence by emphasizing the etymology of the word "ex-ists," "standing outside."

To say that human temporality is cumulative is to say that every one of our actions is contributing to the constitution of our lives as a whole, right up to the end. In each thing I do, I am shaping the unique configuration of roles and traits I am becoming throughout the course of my life. If I go on procrastinating and missing deadlines, I am creating myself as an irresponsible person. This is the *identity* I am assuming for myself, regardless of what sorts of intentions I might have. For existentialists, then, we *are* what we *do* in the course of living out our active lives. We are self-creating or self-fashioning beings. We define our being through our ongoing choices in dealing with the world.

This conception of humans as self-creating beings explains Sartre's famous definition of existentialism as the view that "existence precedes essence." Sartre's point is that there is no fixed essential nature of humans that determines in advance how humans ought to live or inevitably will live. Instead, each of us decides his or her own definitive make up or essence (character, personality, individual lifestyle, and so on) through his or her own choices. For example, if I make a point of having an upbeat attitude toward things, always finding the good in everyone, then all things being equal I will come to *be* a person of that sort. As Aristotle saw, consistently acting in certain ways creates the corresponding character traits. Thus, my *being* or *essence* is something I make, not something I find. It is by taking up the capacities and traits I have and forming them into a particular configuration of life possibilities that I become a person of a particular sort. Whether I realize it or not, I am creating my own being or identity through what I do.

To say that "existence precedes essence," then, is to say that we first "exist"—we simply show up on the scene, we are just "there," initially having only inchoate potentialities and prospects—and that it is then up to us to take over what we are given and shape it into an "essence" that is definitive of who we are. For the existentialists, life is a task and a challenge. We can either recoil from our responsibility for our lives, pretending that we are forced to act in certain ways by circumstances beyond our control. Or we can embrace our responsibility for self-fashioning and seize on our lives with clarity, integrity, and courage. The fact that it is up to each of us to make something of our lives explains the age-old counsel, taken up by Nietzsche and Heidegger, that you should "become what you are."

4. Being-in-the-world

The existentialist insight into the "facticity" of human existence has important consequences for one of the core assumptions of traditional philosophy. Ever since Plato, philosophers have dreamed of finding an external vantage point outside of the cares and concerns of life, a position freed from all local emotions and interests, so that they could get a view of reality from the standpoint of eternity (*sub specie aeternitatis*). This was the aim, for example, of the British philosopher, Bertrand Russell, who recommends that we sever ourselves from everything local and particular in order to become purified, disengaged "citizens of the universe":

> Everything in contemplation that is personal or private, everything that depends upon habit, self-interest or desire, distorts the object, and hence impairs the union [with reality] which the intellect seeks. By thus making a barrier between subject and object, such personal and private things become a prison to the intellect. The free intellect will see as God might see, without a *here* and *now*, without hopes and fears, without the trammels of customary beliefs and traditional prejudices, calmly, dispassionately, in the sole and exclusive desire of knowledge—knowledge as impersonal, as purely contemplative, as it is possible for man to attain.[4]

In the view of existentialists, however, such a disengaged vantage point is impossible. We are always caught up in the midst of things, immersed in a

4. Bertrand Russell, *The Problems of Philosophy* (Oxford: Oxford University Press, 1969), 160–61.

particular context, with specific desires and commitments that affect our perception and thoughts. We must always start out from an "insider's perspective" on things, from a description of the world *as it appears to us*—to beings like ourselves who are participants in our forms of life, with our emotions, bodily orientation, and perceptual functions. We have no choice but to begin from an account of the thick and complex weave of our actual lives as they are experienced prior to abstraction and theorizing. And because there is no way to get beyond this insider's perspective, there is no way we can ever succeed in achieving a "God's-eye view" of the world, a "view from nowhere" that will give us a totally dispassionate, objective view of reality.

This emphasis on the priority of concrete, engaged existence is central to existentialist writers. One of Kierkegaard's main criticisms of Hegel was that he built a vast abstract system like a huge mansion with no doors or windows, while leaving the existing individual to live in a dog house out back. From his earliest writings Nietzsche insisted on the need to start out from the standpoint of life as it is lived prior to abstract reflection and rationalizing. In his *Untimely Meditations* he criticizes historians who try to adopt a rigorously objective point of view toward their subject matter— those "eternally objective ones" who "are themselves neither man nor woman, not even hermaphrodites, but always only neuters." For Nietzsche, objectivity in history acts as a solvent that bleaches out everything significant and valuable in the past, leaving only dusty antiquarian curiosities. In his view, it is not cool, impartial "detachment" that gives us genuine understanding in history, not "indifference parading as objectivity." On the contrary, *"Only from the standpoint of the highest strength of the present may you interpret the past"*; only on the basis of the most intense commitment "will you discern what is worthy of being known and preserved, what is great in the past."[5]

Heidegger and Sartre also insist on the importance of starting from a careful "phenomenology" of ordinary existence—a description of our day-to-day practical lives as they are before we adopt a theoretical attitude. What these descriptions reveal is that under normal circumstances we find ourselves up to our elbows in the midst of things, already "out there" in the familiar life world, caught up in day-to-day practical concerns and involvements with others. For Sartre, to say that our ordinary involvement with the world is "intentional" is to say that we are normally beyond the boundaries of what is traditionally regarded as the self: for the most part, we discover ourselves not as self-encapsulated "fields of consciousness" or as "thinking

5. Friedrich Nietzsche, *On the Advantage and Disadvantage of History for Life*, trans. Peter Preuss (Indianapolis & Cambridge: Hackett, 1980), 31, 37.

substances," but as bound up with things in the familiar life-world. When I am chasing a bus, for instance, my *self* appears not as a mental receptacle with beliefs and desires; rather, it is encountered as "out there," as a "running-toward-the-bus." In such cases my being is found not in my head, but with the bus. In a similar way, when I am absorbed in writing to a loved one who is far away, my being—my "self"—is closer to the other person— "a million miles away," as we say—than it is to the chair I sit in. For Sartre, it is only through a transformation of my ordinary stance toward things that I can experience myself as being a self-contained "mind" or "subject" who is collecting data, formulating beliefs, and having desires.

Existentialists generally tend to think that our existence as minds or fields of consciousness is derivative from and parasitic on a more fundamental way of being as agents and participants in the stream of life. The ability to see ourselves as subjects of experience is the result of a specialized stance we can take on ourselves, the stance of reflection. Instead of being something that accompanies all our activities, then, self-aware consciousness turns out to be a side-effect of some rather peculiar modes of comporting toward things. Consciousness (understood as a "field" of contents accompanied by self-awareness) is an achievement, not a given.

Heidegger expresses this idea by saying that what is "given" for the most part in our everyday lives is not a mind set distinct from a world of objects, but "the unified phenomenon of being-in-the-world." In our everyday activities, our being as agents is inseparable from the tools, workshops, and practical settings in which we find ourselves. For Heidegger, this absorption in familiar contexts of activity is prior to detached reflection in this sense. The purely reflective stance toward the world can be shown to be derivative from a more original way of being practically involved with things, whereas practical activities cannot be explained on the assumption that we are initially merely subjects contemplating the world.

It follows from this priority of the practical over the theoretical that the picture of reality we arrive at through detached, objective theorizing is not necessarily a "truer" or more accurate view of things than the tacit sense of the world we have in the midst of our practical interchange with things. For existentialists, the disengaged, dispassionate "spectator attitude" idealized by traditional philosophers actually tends to work as a distorting lens that conceals the richness and complexity of actual life in the world, giving us a one-sided and "privative" way of understanding the world. The standpoint of cool, disinterested inquiry pulls us out of the fabric of concrete existence where things show up as meaningful and value-laden, and it bleaches out crucial aspects of things while concealing the fact that this concealment is occurring. This is why Nietzsche considers the possibility that science might be "one of the *most stupid* of all possible interpretations of the world, meaning that it would be one of the poorest in meaning. . . . An essentially mechanistic world would be an essentially *meaningless* world."

In the view of existentialists, the problem with science is not that it is false, but that its objectifying approach to phenomena forces things into a particular framework of interpretation that blots out many of the most important things in the world as we actually encounter it. The scientific point of view on things, they contend, is just one optional outlook among others, and a rather narrow and misleading one at that. Because the stance of disengaged objectivity gives us a one-sided and distorted view of things, existentialists make an effort to try to hold on to the "passion" or "engagement" that normally makes manifest the significance and value of what we encounter in actual life. Kierkegaard, though he does not question the usefulness of a purely objective view of reality ("objective truth"), nevertheless suggests that there is a profound qualitative difference between mere objective belief and a passionate concern about what is believed ("subjective truth"). In certain areas of our life, subjective truth is superior to objective truth. Similarly Heidegger holds that it is only when we "care" about things and are fully absorbed in day-to-day practical concerns that we can arrive at a genuine understanding of the "being" of entities in the world. And, finally, it is precisely because the detached spectator attitude dims down reality and creates the impression of meaninglessness that Nietzsche is so critical of the Socratic and Platonic privileging of detached rationality over instinctual drives.

The existentialist conception of being-in-the-world tends to undermine some of the dualistic oppositions that have dominated so much of Western thought. From the existentialist's perspective, the traditional philosophical dualisms begin to look like high-level abstractions with no clear relevance for understanding our basic human predicament. This is the case, first of all, for the "mind-matter" dualism that has come down to us from Plato and Descartes. By showing us that our very being as selves is always inextricably tied up with a practical life-world, existentialists try to deflate the assumption that at a basic level we are "really" minds or fields of consciousness distinct from an "external" world of material objects. From this standpoint, the idea that reality must be understood as consisting of mental and material substances starts to look like an unwarranted prejudice handed down by the philosophical tradition.

Second, the idea that our primary condition is being-in-the-world tends to undermine the appeal of the subject-object model as a way of characterizing our relation to the world. Sartre makes fun of the traditional view of our predicament as trapped within a "veil of ideas," limited to representations that are "like flies bumping their noses on the window without being able to clear the glass."[6] If it is true that we are always already "out there" with things in the world as Sartre claims, then the idea that we never have access to the world except through the mediation of "sense data" or representations dissolves.

Finally, the view that our basic situation is being-in-the-world raises questions about the assumption that humans are essentially isolated individuals only contingently related to one another. Although existentialists are concerned with getting people to recognize their responsibility as individuals, they nevertheless emphasize the fact that the world in which we find ourselves initially is essentially a shared, public life-world, a realm of meanings constituted by our public practices. And this means that, as being-in-the-world, we are at the deepest level participants and place-holders within a social context. It is in terms of a shared "herd consciousness" or "they-self" that we pick up our initial sense of reality, and it is on the basis of our belongingness to the public that we can later strive to discover our identity as individuals. Thus, just as existentialists tend to think that consciousness is an achievement rather than a given, so they hold that our being as individuals is something we make rather than something we find.

5. Freedom

Our being enmeshed in a specific practical and social world with pregiven attachments and concerns is part of our "facticity" as humans. We are always "thrown" into a concrete context with determinate meanings and values laid out by the practices of a particular historical community. But this facticity is only one dimension of human existence, for, as we have seen, humans also have the ability to "transcend" their givenness. Our lives are "at stake" for us, which is to say that we are creatures who *care* about what we are. Because of this concern about our own being, each of us has taken a stand on his or her life by taking over some specific "sphere of existence" or configuration of meanings from the pool of options available in our world. As beings who transcend their mere givenness, each of us is shaping his or her own identity through what we do. In my actions I am constituting myself as a pleasure-loving aesthete, perhaps, or as a duty-bound, responsible citizen. To be human, then, is to go beyond one's facticity by taking it over, interpreting it, and trying to make something of it in the light of one's long-range projects.

This is the dimension of "transcendence" some existentialists talk about.

6. Jean-Paul Sartre, *Being and Nothingness*, trans. Hazel E. Barnes (New York: Philosophical Library, 1956), 100, quoted in David E. Cooper, *Existentialism: A Reconstruction* (Oxford: Blackwell, 1990), 48.

It is important to see that such re-evaluating and reinterpreting of a life often occurs quite "unconsciously" in the course of one's practical affairs. Generally, we just slide into some style of living currently deemed acceptable in the public world we live in. We are, as existentialists are inclined to say, "herd" animals or representatives of "the public" in most of our everyday activities.

But even though I am not aware that I am choosing to fall in with the crowd, it remains the case I am deciding my own life and identity in the course of my actions. If I refuse to get involved in politics and ignore what is going on in the public world, then I am choosing to create myself as an apathetic and apolitical individual. I am *assuming* this identity, even if I think I am doing nothing. Here, as William James says, even to refuse to make a choice is to make a choice. Because I *am* the totality of what I do (or fail to do) throughout my lifetime, there is no way to avoid the fact that I am choosing myself as a person of a particular sort through my actions and omissions.

This sense of the individual's choice in creating his or her own self is the basis for the central place the concept of freedom has in most existentialist writings.[7] To say that humans "transcend" their facticity is to say that we always stand out into an open range of possible courses of action for the future. According to existentialists, nothing compels us to choose one course of action over the others. For example, nothing forces a professor to persist in trying to build her career in academia. She shows up for work every day and takes care of her responsibilities, but at any moment she could walk away from the university and turn to a life of crime. What this shows is that if she continues to show up for her classes and perform her other duties in the university, then it is because she is choosing to do so. She is assuming this identity for herself. And if she feels that her character as a responsible person or her obligations to her family make it necessary for her to go on doing her job, then she is choosing to let her character or her family count as weighty for her in this way. As Sartre would say, everywhere she turns she encounters her freedom. She is "condemned to be free." No matter how she feels about what she is doing, according to Sartre, she is free in the sense that, for each of the choices she in fact makes, she could have chosen to act

7. It might seem that Nietzsche is an exception, because he often rails against the doctrine of "free will" as an insidious construct cooked up to make people feel guilty about what they do. But Nietzsche would most likely distinguish the Christian notion of free will that he criticizes from a healthier sense of freedom that is the basis on which we are able to transform our lives in the way Nietzsche envisions (which means also, of course, giving up that old, unhealthy concept of free will).

differently than she did, and for this reason she is responsible for her actions in the way required for moral responsibility. Thus, freedom is an inescapable component of human existence. Whether or not we acknowledge it, we are accountable for being the sorts of people we are.

But our freedom is not just limited to our ability to decide the direction of our own lives. For existentialists believe that we are also responsible for the way the world around us appears to us. To understand what this means, we need to see that existentialism is an heir to the way of thinking that has come down to us from Immanuel Kant. In his *Critique of Pure Reason* (1789), Kant argued that the world we encounter in our everyday lives is not the same as the world as it is in itself, independent of our ways of thinking and acting. On the contrary, Kant claimed, the familiar world that shows up for us is constituted and shaped by our own categories of thought and forms of perception. We encounter objects located in space and time and interacting causally not because space, time, and causality are constituents of reality as it is in itself, but because our minds generate a grid or template that makes things show up for us as spatial-temporal objects in causal relations. Thus, the world we experience is an orderly, spatial-temporal world of enduring objects not because of the way things are in themselves, but rather because of the ways our thinking and perceiving work over and give form to whatever we experience. For Kant, the ordinary world we see around us is coherent and knowable because it is largely a product of our own activities of articulating and conceptualizing.

Kant thought of his way of looking at things as a new "Copernican Revolution." Just as Copernicus accounted for a wide range of observations by saying that the earth rotates around the sun rather than the sun around the earth, so Kant was able to make sense of many features of our experience by saying that reality as we experience it is formed by the human mind. The existentialists follow Kant in saying that the world is constituted by humans, but they differ from Kant in two important ways. First, where Kant assumed that human constituting activity occurs "automatically" and is always the same for all humans, existentialists generally believe that it is our own freely chosen stance or orientation that determines how the world will show up for us. On their view, we can choose to interpret the world in different ways by shifting our stance toward things. Sartre and Merleau-Ponty, for example, talk about how we can bring about a "Gestalt-shift" when looking at an ambiguous figure (like a cube that can be seen as from above or from below) simply by shifting our perceptual orientation toward it. And, second, where Kant assumed that it is mental activity—the work of the transcendental ego—that transforms raw sensations into normal sorts of experiences, existentialists, following Hegel, tend to think that it is our concrete ways of dealing with things in practical contexts that give shape to the world we know.

The influence of the Kantian outlook is quite evident in the earlier existentialists, Kierkegaard and Nietzsche. Though each of these thinkers rejects Kant's assumption that there are unchanging, universal structures of experience built into our "human nature," both show Kant's influence in suggesting that the way reality shows up for a person depends upon that person's point of view or stance toward things. According to Kierkegaard, the way the world appears to someone is shaped by the particular sphere of existence that individual has entered into, for example, an aesthete who chooses to live for pleasure in the present might encounter the world as kind of playground, whereas the responsible citizen would see it as an arena of obligations and responsibilities. And Nietzsche holds that reality is accessible only under some "perspective" or other, with the result that there is no such thing as getting in touch with reality as it is in itself, independent of any point of view or framework of interpretation. Though he encourages us to multiply our perspectives in order to expand our ways of experiencing things, he does not believe there can be a pure, perspectiveless access to things.

Heidegger and Sartre were influenced not just by Kant, but also by the phenomenology of Edmund Husserl (1859–1938). Husserl emphasized the fact that all human experience has the quality of being directed toward objects (what is called "intentionality"). But, for Husserl, as for Kant, our encounters with things are never simply direct apprehensions of objects as they are in themselves, independent of our ways of encountering them. Instead, our experience is always mediated by our own meaning-giving activity. If I am afraid of bees, for example, I apprehend the bee circling my head as a terrifying, monstrous thing intent on harming me. When I take a moment to reflect on my experience, however, I realize that the threatening, vicious quality I perceive in the bee is less a characteristic of that noisy insect than it is something created and defined by my own fearfulness. This in turn can lead me to also see that my ability to label what I am experiencing as a "bee" (rather than as, say, a spiritual manifestation or a vector in a force field) presupposes a set of interpretations about natural kinds and living beings that I read into what I see. In fact, even my ability to apprehend what I encounter as a discrete, enduring object (rather than as, say, an event or a sequence of perceptual slices) depends on the meanings I give to my experience. What this Husserlian reflection is supposed to show is that the world given to my consciousness is always shaped and constituted by my own interpretations and meaning-giving activity. Thus, for Husserl, I am the source of the meaningful, coherent world I experience.

Heidegger and Sartre, following in Husserl's footsteps, try to lead us to see that the specific stand a person takes on his or her life defines in advance how the world will show up for that person. Heidegger describes how the world we encounter in the midst of our everyday practical dealings with equipment has a very different structure from that of the world encountered in detached, objective, theoretical reflection. And Sartre's writings are filled with vivid descriptions of how things in the world are colored and invested with significance by the particular stance of the individual dealing with those things.

For existentialists, there is a reciprocal interdependence between the factical situations in which we find ourselves and our own self-interpretations as agents within those situations. On the one hand, the situation has a meaning that defines in advance the range of choices and actions that will make sense in that context. At a semi-formal dinner party, for example, I can be a well-mannered guest or a clumsy boor, but not a third base coach. On the other hand, the specific meaning that the situation has is determined to some extent by the stance I take within that context. If I show up for a dinner party inappropriately dressed, I can make a self-deprecating joke about it and put everyone at ease, or I can sulk in the corner and make everyone uncomfortable. What this shows is that how the factual circumstances of my life *count* is something that depends on what I *do* in dealing with the situations I find myself in. And because there is no fixed limit on the number of ways I can respond to a particular context, there are indefinitely many possible meanings the situation can have for me.

Thus, although our facticity predefines the types of options available to us as agents, the actions we take in interpreting and handling our factical situations define the meaning those situations have. This does not mean, of course, that "thinking makes it so," that reality can be anything we want it to be. But it does mean that the way reality shows up for us is always endowed with a meaning through the stands we take in dealing with things. And, as a result, there is no way to drive in a wedge between the uninterpreted "given" in a situation and the meaning the situation has by virtue of our concrete ways of comporting ourselves in the world.

Husserl took this to mean that each of us is "absolutely responsible" for the way the world shows up for us in our activities. As he says, "I may owe much, perhaps almost everything, to others, but even they are, first of all, others for me who receive from me whatever meaning or validity they may have for me. They can be of assistance to me as fellow subjects only after they have received their meaning and validity from me. As transcendental ego I am thus the absolutely responsible subject of whatever has existential validity for me."[8] From this it is not too far to Sartre's claim that, although there are factors in my environment that seem to constrain my interpreting activities, they are ultimately only "opportunities" for me in the sense that it is up to me to decide what weight they are going to have for me. For Sartre, I never apprehend facts as they are in themselves, but only facts as I choose to interpret them. This means that I freely choose the meaning of all reality, including the meaning of the social world that I draw on for my interpretations of things. In Sartre's words, "facticity is everywhere, but inapprehensible: I never encounter anything except my responsibility. . . . Since others . . . are themselves only *opportunities* and *chances* [for my interpreting activity], the responsibility of the for-itself [i.e., my interpreting] extends to the entire world as a peopled-world." It is this awareness of our responsibility for the world that appears in the experience of "anguish." "It is precisely thus that the for-itself apprehends itself in anguish: that is, as a being . . . which is compelled to decide the meaning of being—within it and everywhere outside of it." Whether we realize it or not, we are deciding the meaning things have for us through our choices concerning how we relate to them.

Not all existentialists would put such an emphasis on the individual's freedom to choose the meaning of reality as Sartre does. In fact, disagreements about the nature and extent of freedom are central to existentialist philosophy. Kierkegaard, for instance, would say the extreme sort of freedom as "abstract possibility" envisioned by Sartre leads to a form of despair: the "despair of possibility" that is due to the "lack of necessity." But all existentialists tend to agree with the idea that reality is accessible to us only as interpreted (whether solely by individuals or by historical communities as well), so that it is always possible that we could encounter reality differently than we do.

The idea that we never encounter reality as it is in itself might suggest a way in which existentialists could try to respond to the traditional challenge to free will that seems to come from scientific determinism. Scientific determinists have claimed that science has demonstrated the truth of materialism: the view that the world consists solely of material objects governed by the deterministic laws posited by the physical sciences. Because humans in this view are themselves material objects, their actions must also be determined by these deterministic physical laws. In response to this, existentialists might grant that the scientific interpretation of reality has this conse-

---

8. Edmund Husserl, "Phenomenology and Anthropology," trans. Richard G. Schmitt, in Roderick M. Chisholm, ed., *Realism and the Background of Phenomenology* (Glencoe, Ill: The Free Press, 1960), 138.

quence. But, as we have seen, they also hold that this scientifically shaped outlook is just one interpretation among others, with no special claim to capturing the ultimate truth about things. If this is the case, they might argue, then there is no reason to assume that scientific discoveries must necessarily exclude the possibility of free will. Insofar as we choose the meaning of the contexts in which we find ourselves, existentialists might say, any attempt to think of ourselves as determined to act by those contexts would involve self-deception.

6. Authenticity

Existentialists are aware that people for the most part fail to see that they are self-creating beings, and that they generally try to avoid facing up to their own responsibility for their lives. In our day-to-day existence, we tend to drift along into the public ways of acting, doing what "one" does, and we assume that our lives are justified so long as we are conforming to the norms and conventions accepted in our social world. We are, in John Haugeland's catchy phrase, "censorious conformists."[9] We try to fit in with the crowd and we are quick to correct others when they step out of line (as is evident in our response when someone mispronounces a word). There is, in the modern world at least, an overwhelming pressure toward what Michel Foucault has called "normalization": the standardization of every region of life in order to produce and sustain a relatively regimented and manageable set of social practices. At the same time, the fact that we have to play many different roles in our complex society means that our lives lack coherence and focus. We are expected to be "all things to all people," capable of changing gears quickly as we move from family to work to our closest circle of friends. As a result, we tend to be dispersed and distracted, lacking any real cohesiveness and integrity as individuals.

Different existentialists characterize this tendency to fall into step with the crowd in different ways. Kierkegaard talks about the "public" and its way of leveling all differences among individuals. As everything exceptional is reduced to something commonplace, and as all meaningful distinctions in life are obliterated, it becomes increasingly difficult in the present age to find anything that has any real meaning in relation to our lives. When nothing stands out as genuinely *counting* for us, life becomes a dreary string of episodes with no cumulativeness or overarching direction. Life goes on "crabbedly like the writing in ancient manuscripts, without any punctuation

9. John Haugeland, "Heidegger on Being a Person," *Nous* 16 (March 1982), 6–26.

marks, one word, one sentence after another."[10] Yet despite Kierkegaard's harsh critique of the way contemporary life trivializes everything, he did not glorify the life of the anti-social rebel or outsider. On the contrary, he has a deep respect for "the ethical" (what Hegel calls *Sittlichkeit*) where everyone does his or her duty within a cohesive state. It is precisely because the call to be an individual *may* lead one to stand in opposition to this ethical way of life that the very idea of being an authentic individual is filled with such "fear and trembling."

The harshest indictment of contemporary social existence is found in Nietzsche's descriptions of the "herd." In his view, our existence as social animals tends to domesticate us. It covers over everything unique and creative in us, leading us to interpret ourselves purely in standardized, socially approved categories. We become mindless conformists who are tame and well behaved, with the result that we lose our capacity for creativity and originality. But even though Nietzsche is harshly critical of life in the herd, he does not reject communal existence as such. In a number of places he hints at older, more original ways of living together—the outgoing and creative "noble morality" of the ancient Greeks and Jews, for example—that he clearly regards as superior to our modern instrumentalist and self-absorbed lifestyle.

The writings of Heidegger and Sartre carry forward the existentialist critique of everyday social existence. Sartre ridicules the pompous "spirit of seriousness" of the bourgeoisie and is sharply critical of the effect of being brought within a "We." "The one who experiences himself as constituting an Us with other men feels himself trapped among an infinity of strange existences," he writes; "he is alienated radically and without recourse."[11] But even though Sartre's interpretation of social existence is almost entirely critical, his essay, "The Humanism of Existentialism," points to an image of an ideal society, similar to Kant's notion of a "kingdom of ends," characterized by reciprocity and mutuality among all its members. And, as we shall see in our introduction to the Sartre readings, Sartre and his co-worker Simone de Beauvoir both tried to formulate the idea of a just society characterized by recognition and liberty for all its members.

Finally, Heidegger criticizes the "tranquilization" and "alienation from

---

10. Søren Kierkegaard, *The Concept of Anxiety,* trans. Reidar Thomte and Albert B. Anderson (Princeton: Princeton University Press, 1980), 94, quoted in H. L. Dreyfus and Jane Rubin, "Kierkegaard, Division II, and Later Heidegger," appendix to H. L. Dreyfus, *Being-in-the-World: A Commentary on Heidegger's "Being and Time," Division I* (Cambridge, Mass: MIT Press, 1991). This essay provides valuable insights into Heidegger's debt to Kierkegaard.

11. Sartre, *Being and Nothingness,* 419.

one's own self" that is characteristic of our ordinary ways of "falling" into step with society. As "average everydayness," we tend to be interchangeable bits in the public mosaic, and we enact parts in various social dramas, guided by socially approved norms and conventions. The roles we fill and parts we play are anonymous in the sense that "anyone" could step in and take our place. As a result, for much of our lives we just *are* sets of anonymous roles and routines that anyone with comparable skills could fill. In our humdrum activities we simply do what "one" does, following the procedures laid out by the social world. Even when people rebel against social customs, they tend to do so in accordance with strictly defined norms (the flannel shirts of "grunge" musicians, for example, or the black leather and pierced ears of "punks"). In Heidegger's words, we exist as the "anyone" or the "they" (the German term *das Man* means "the one" as in "One doesn't do that here"). "We take pleasure and enjoy ourselves as *one* [*man*] takes pleasure; we read, see, and judge about literature and art as *one* sees and judges; likewise we shrink back from the 'masses of people' as *one* shrinks back; we find 'shocking' what *one* finds shocking." But, once again, this critical tone does not indicate an entirely negative estimation of social existence. On the contrary, for Heidegger, being the "they" or the "one" is a "*primordial phenomenon*" that "*belongs to [our] positive constitution.*"

What can free us from our complacent absorption in society, according to these authors, is not rational reflection or cognition, but rather a life-transforming insight resulting from a profound emotion or affective experience. Kierkegaard describes the "despair" accompanying our self-loss in humdrum, mundane existence, and he points to an experience of "dread" or "anxiety" that can wrench us away from our mindless drifting and force us to come to terms with our own lives. Heidegger, here clearly influenced by Kierkegaard, speaks of "anxiety" as a mood or form of "attunement" in which the public world no longer "speaks to us" in a meaningful way. In anxiety, we suddenly discover that we are "delivered over to ourselves" and that we are ultimately responsible for giving our lives a meaning. Nietzsche's description of the "madman's" experience of the death of God, together with his thought of the possibility of the "eternal recurrence" of everything that ever happens, is supposed to lead us to a shattering confrontation with nihilism. And Sartre speaks of the feeling of "nausea" through which being as such is revealed to us, and he refers to the "anguish" and sense of "abandonment" that leads to the recognition that we alone are responsible for how we interpret and define the world around us. For each of these writers, it turns out that the deepest grasp of our condition in the world occurs as a result of a noncognitive affect rather than through explicit, cognitive reflection.

What such intense emotional experiences reveal is the possibility of a transformed way of being. In *The Gay Science,* Nietzsche describes a new stance of "playfulness" opened up by the recognition that God is dead. For those who have faced up to nihilism and gotten past the initial reaction of bitterness about the breakdown of old beliefs, there is the possibility of playing naively yet seriously "with all that was hitherto called holy, good, untouchable, divine." This is a possibility that points to Nietzsche's conception of the "overman." Heidegger, in a quite different tone of voice, talks about the "sober joy" of an authentic existence in which, by facing up to one's own "being-toward-death," one resolutely appropriates one's own life by "repeating" the possibilities handed down by history. Though Sartre in *Being and Nothingness* says relatively little about authentic existence, he clearly believes it is possible to take over one's own freedom with clear-sightedness, intensity, and a kind of commitment that gives one's life a "fundamental project."

Finally, Kierkegaard, as a theistic or Christian existentialist, is unique among these four writers in holding that one cannot become an "existing individual" in the full sense of this term solely through one's own will. In his view, the highest realization of one's human existence—becoming a "knight of faith"—requires that one become grounded in a relation to the power that constitutes the self: "This then is the formula which describes the condition of the self when despair is completely eradicated: by relating itself to its own self, and by willing to be itself, the self is grounded transparently in the Power which constituted it."

The concept of authenticity does not necessarily have any ethical or political implications. The ideal of authenticity is supposed to call us back from our ordinary, inauthentic way of being distracted and dispersed in the world. It calls on us to live a more focused and intense life, a way of existing that integrates our feelings, desires, and beliefs into a unified whole. Because an authentic life is given focus by a "fundamental project" or an "ultimate concern," it has the kind of cumulativeness and directedness that is missing in ordinary inauthentic existence.

But there is no reason to believe that a person who is authentic necessarily will be a more benevolent or more principled person. For the most part, the ideal seems to be more concerned with the *style* of one's life rather than its content. It concerns the *how* rather than the *what*. The conception of authentic existence as a matter of giving one's life a focus appears in Nietzsche (who never actually uses the word "authenticity"). In a section called "One thing is needed" in *The Gay Science* he says that what is crucial is "to 'give style' to one's character," to survey all the strengths and weaknesses of [one's] nature and then fit them into an artistic plan. . . . In the end, when the work is finished, it becomes evident how the constraint of a single taste governed and formed everything large and small. Whether this taste was good or bad is less important than one might suppose, if only it was a single taste." As this quote makes clear, the main idea in authenticity is what we might call "self-focusing": giving coherence and integrity to one's life, creating oneself as a work of art, by imparting a unifying style to everything one does.

But even though the existentialist ideal does not have any immediate ethical consequences, it would be wrong to think that existentialists glorify some crude conception of the "outsider" or "rebel without a cause." For most existentialists, becoming authentic involves a double movement. First, by breaking away from ordinary complacent conformism and by lucidly facing up to the "death of God," one comes to confront one's own responsibility for one's life. The impact of this is that it leads people to understand their own role in creating their lives as "works of art." But, second, becoming authentic is supposed to push one into a transformed understanding of human relations and community. Heidegger, for instance, speaks of the sense of "authentic community" that arises when people understand their shared "destiny" together. Nietzsche envisions a new, stronger breed of humans that can be realized by abandoning the prevailing "slave morality" and creating new tables of values. And both Sartre and de Beauvoir understood their critique of bourgeois existence as pointing to an ideal of greater freedom for humankind. Thus, although embracing one's own being as an individual is central to existentialism, this does not necessarily exclude the possibility of authentic community.

7. Existentialism and Its Critics

Existentialism has been exposed to a number of powerful attacks over the past few decades, with the result that it is sometimes felt that existentialism is no longer a viable way of thinking. On closer inspection, however, it appears that many of these criticisms are directed either at some cartoonish caricature of existentialist thought with no resemblance to any actual figure's work, or at marginal figures who are unfairly regarded as representative of all existentialists. For example, it is often claimed that existentialists are in favor of some wild, "anything-goes" notion of freedom, or that existentialism is hung up on morbid worries about death, or that existentialists are too emotional, or that they are "irrationalist," or that they think everything is absurd. A close reading of the core existentialist texts shows, however, that these accusations are undeserved. It is indeed true that existentialists often set themselves up for such criticisms. Because they work on the assumption that people can be shaken out of their familiar, complacent ways of thinking only by highly dramatic or ironic formulations and ideas, existentialists often make jarring claims that look preposterous when taken out of context. But the richness and lasting significance of existentialist thought should be evident from recent works that develop its themes. One has only to think of such influential works as Robert C. Solomon's *The Passions* or Thomas Nagel's *Mortal Questions* to see how existentialist ideas can be developed in ways that speak to a wide audience of philosophers.

Nevertheless, there is an especially influential line of criticism we might explore in some depth. One way of putting this criticism is to say that existentialism reflects the point of view of a group of powerful and relatively affluent intellectuals whose worries about meaninglessness and isolation reveal more about their status as members of the bourgeoisie than about the human condition. This was the point of the criticisms launched by Marxists earlier in the century, and it reappears in recent arguments that existentialism masks or trivializes the concrete forms of suffering of oppressed people in the modern world by shifting attention from real problems to the worries of a cultural elite. Existentialism, these critics suggest, is a luxury only a group of comfortably ensconced academics can afford. Seen from this angle, the ideal of authenticity looks out of touch with the real needs of the majority of the earth's population. And the glorification of freedom in existentialism threatens to license a kind of self-indulgent capriciousness that might undermine moral obligation and political activism.

This line of criticism strikes us as extremely pressing for existentialists.[12] As we have seen, existentialism does not always have anything very substantive to add to discussions about normative ethics. We noted previously that the existentialist ideal of authenticity has no immediate implications for morality, and this seems to indicate that an authentic individual might conceivably turn out to be a serial killer or a Nazi. Of course, although existentialism does not rule out any particular moral or political position, neither does it entail any particular stance. Existentialists have occupied a variety of positions on the political spectrum, from Heidegger (who joined the Nazi party in 1933) to Sartre (a communist who dabbled in some extremist Maoist activities). What is so troubling, however, is the very idea that there could be an ideal like that of authenticity, which presumably points to a better or higher way of life yet may be consistent with the most monstrous ways of acting.

Though there is no way to eliminate this problem, we might note that the existentialist ideal of self-formation and self-fulfillment is part of a very old tradition in the Western world. In his last book, *The Care for the Self,* Michel

12. For a fuller version of this criticism see Charles Guignon, "Existentialist Ethics," in *New Directions in Ethics,* eds. Joseph P. DeMarco and Richard M. Fox (New York: Routledge, 1986), 73–91.

Foucault shows us how central the ideal of self-cultivation was in the ancient world. In the writings of the Stoics and Epicureans we find constant references to the idea that involvement in the public world must be accompanied by what Foucault calls an "art of existence," the cultivation of the self, if one is to avoid the kind of self-loss and fragmentation that makes meaningful action impossible. But this task of working on the self does not necessarily lead to self-absorption or egocentrism. As Foucault points out, this care for the self is "not an exercise in solitude, but a true social practice." The thinkers who emphasized self-cultivation in the ancient world were "quickest to denounce an attitude of laxity and self-satisfaction in practices of social withdrawal," and insisted most on "the need to fulfill one's obligations to mankind, to one's fellow-citizens, and to one's family."[13]

The idea that one can be an effective member of society only if one, so to speak, cleans one's own house and cultivates oneself is also central to modern existentialists. Though it is true that there is no particular moral or political theory entailed by existentialism, it does seem that the ideal of authenticity points to a set of character traits that might be seen as providing us with a better basis for making the first-order moral and political decisions we need to make in our active lives. Authenticity calls for a kind of clear-sightedness and honesty that would seem to rule out the possibility of hiding behind roles or remaining blind to the consequences of one's actions. Also, because authenticity involves the lucid awareness that our actions constitute our identity, it forces us to accept our responsibility for what we do. Moreover, authentic self-focusing calls for courage, steadiness, coherence, and integrity, character traits that seem essential to meaningful action. Finally, like the ancient arts of self-cultivation, most existentialists hold that, insofar as our facticity is shaped and defined by our embeddedness in a concrete historical community, we cannot avoid recognizing the fact that we have an obligation to work for the good of our own society. It is certainly true that attaining these sorts of "second-order values" will not be sufficient to lead an individual to be morally decent or to be a good citizen. But it might be argued that such character traits are necessary conditions for our being agents capable of making meaningful choices or engaging in effective social action at all.

The four thinkers gathered together in this volume offer some of the most compelling visions of what Foucault calls an "art of existence" in our modern age. The very fact that their ideas still seem risky and contentious is an indication of the enduring significance of their thought. What is perhaps

13. Michel Foucault, *The Care for the Self,* trans. Robert Hurley (New York: Random House, 1988), 42, 51.

most important to keep in mind is the fact that no existentialist ever asked for slavish, uncritical adherence to a particular "line" of thought. Each of these authors challenges you as an individual to think things through on your own, and to make a final decision using what Nietzsche calls "intellectual conscience." This emphasis on the individual's own responsibility is perhaps the most valuable and enduring contribution of existentialism to philosophy.

Kierkegaard

Søren Kierkegaard was born in Copenhagen, Denmark, in 1813, the youngest child of a large family. He was raised in a prosperous middle-class home, with the strictest devotion to church and religion. His father was a successful merchant and an avid reader of theology, and his mother had been his father's servant before she became his second wife. Kierkegaard had a hunchback, and this, according to some, is the "thorn in his flesh" he often mentions in his writings. He viewed his life as governed by a deep melancholy, which he self-consciously attempted to hide with wit and gaiety. An event of crucial importance for Kierkegaard was his breaking of his engagement to Regine Olsen in 1841. His reason for this action is an important but unsolved mystery in his life. First educated at home, he began university as a student of theology, but soon turned to literature and philosophy. Kierkegaard was especially steeped in the philosophy of Hegel, which he studied in Berlin. A dominant theme in his life was his opposition to official state Christianity, seen by him as encumbered by a passionless conformity to bourgeois respectability and stability. Instead, Kierkegaard advocated a life of intense religious commitment, free from superficiality and empty formalism. His works include *Either/Or* (1843), *Fear and Trembling* (1843), *Philosophical Fragments* (1844), *Concluding Unscientific Postscript* (1846), *The Sickness Unto Death* (1849), *Training in Christianity* (1851), and *The Attack Upon "Christendom"* (1854-55). His writings were largely ignored outside of Denmark up until the twentieth century, when they became very influential. Kierkegaard died in 1855, at the age of forty-two, after collapsing while carrying the last of his inheritance from the bank.

1. Kierkegaard's Aims

The overriding concern in Kierkegaard's religious and philosophical writings is to provide insight into the meaning and fulfillment of human life: to provide insight into what makes a human life worth living, and what makes it genuinely satisfying for the individual who is living it. He believed that in his own time both secular and religious people were especially unable to attain the meaning and fulfillment of which they are capable. In *The Present Age*, he describes his own culture as having lost an agreed-upon sense of qualitative distinctions accepted within society as a whole. People no longer make a clear distinction, for example, between fine art and schlock art, or

1

between great writers and hacks. As a result, there is no longer a basis for experiencing things as genuinely worthwhile or significant in life. As such distinctions are leveled down, Kierkegaard claims, the possibility of finding meaning and fulfillment in our lives is diminished. We would then lose any generally accepted bases for making the kinds of commitments that would give our lives a point and a sense of direction.

In his characteristically existentialist view, Kierkegaard believes that achieving meaning in life is not something simply given to us, something that comes with just being alive. Rather, it depends on the choices we make. It is by our decisions, by the stands we take, that we can impart a meaning to our lives. This is why our choices are a matter of the greatest seriousness. In Kierkegaard's view, we only genuinely come to exist as human selves through the life-defining choices we make.

Unlike the other existentialists discussed in this volume, however, Kierkegaard does not believe that we are ultimately on our own in making the best possible choice for our lives. His final recommendations are religious, and he argues that the best decision we can make is one in which we are dependent on God. Hence he is called a religious or Christian existentialist, in contrast to such figures as Nietzsche and Sartre, who are often designated secular existentialists.

As a religious thinker, Kierkegaard has been extremely influential, especially in the twentieth century. But his original views also had an especially profound effect on secular existentialist thinkers, like Heidegger. Many of the major themes in secular existentialism were first developed by Kierkegaard. First, he holds that everyday life tends to be deeply unfulfilling. Second, he claims that human existence involves a profound tension or conflict between two dimensions, facticity and transcendence, that is, between what we always already are and the capacity we have to transcend this existence. Third, Kierkegaard holds that the meaning we find in life is not something that simply comes to us, but is something we attain through struggle, by means of our choices and commitments. And finally, he formulates the view that certain kinds of decisions lead to more fulfilling lives than do others, and that these decisions express and constitute what we truly are. On his view, then, we are, to a certain extent, self-constructing beings: we are what we make of ourselves by means of our decisions.

2. The Human Situation

Though Kierkegaard was an exceptionally original thinker, he was familiar with Hegel's thought and often reacted to it. According to Hegel, the development of reality through history must be understood as following a *dialectical* process. The term 'dialectical' is etymologically related to the word 'dialogue'. Socrates and Plato originally thought of a dialectical process as like a conversation between two people who, starting from opposing perspectives on an issue, eventually arrive at a position that preserves the insights of each and on which both can rationally agree. Hegel believed that history generates opposing forces and principles, like subject and object, or the immanent and the transcendent, and that these opposites are reconciled in history by a rational, dialectical process.

Schematically, the process of dialectic begins with an *immediacy*, something that is a *particular* aspect of reality and is just given independent of conceptual reflection. For example, Hegel thinks of our particular sensations, prior to conceptual reflection, as immediate. For example, one might have a sensation of a particular redness independently of thinking of it as similar to or different from other color sensations. Another example of immediacy is a person's particular desires and urges conceived independently of conceptual reflection. One might have particular sexual urges, for example, independently of any reflection on how they fit into one's conception of oneself as a moral and responsible agent.

In the dialectical process, according to Hegel, immediacy comes to be *mediated* through reflection. This reflection always involves *universal* or general considerations, which serve to transform our understanding of the immediacy in experience. For example, we would think of a particular color sensation differently if we understood it as falling into a general class, such as the class of red sensations, conceived as distinct from the class of orange or of yellow sensations. Similarly, we would think of our immediate sexual desires differently if we understood ourselves, together with these desires, as having a role in a community of rational beings with shared interests and a common culture. Furthermore, it is crucial to Hegel's view that this process of rational reflection not only influences our ways of thinking about things, but that this influence also transforms our behavior, our projects, and our institutions. When rational reflection changes how we think about our sexual desires, we will come to respect other people's feelings and sensibilities, and we will set up institutions such as marriage as a publicly recognized exclusive relationship.

The mediation Hegel has in mind always preserves the essential content of the aspects of immediacy. The aspects of immediacy are *aufgehoben*, that is, superseded but yet preserved by the dialectical process. The outcome of the dialectical process usually functions as a "higher immediacy," and a new process of mediation can then be brought to bear on this new immediacy. As this rational process continues, the result becomes more and more rational until reality is conceived as and becomes maximally rational. At this point the *Absolute* has been reached, and the rational is the real and the real is the rational.

Like Hegel, Kierkegaard conceives of human reality as a clash of opposites, but he does not believe that these disparities can always be resolved through rational mediation. One set of opposites plays a particularly important role throughout Kierkegaard's thought. In his view, a self is a tension between the finite and the infinite, which he also characterizes as a tension between the temporal and the eternal. For Kierkegaard the notion of the temporal signifies the events of our lives considered as immediate and distinct from one another, as separate particular moments. As temporal beings, we are no different from the other animals, having sensations and trying to satisfy desires. By contrast, the notion of the eternal signifies the overarching unity that these events can have just for humans. This unity has the potential of providing the separate moments of our lives with the kind of meaning and significance they lack without this unity. What is distinctive about humans is their ability to give their lives an enduring meaning.

Kierkegaard denies that the disparity between the temporal and eternal aspects of our lives can be resolved by a rational, dialectical process, and this disagreement with Hegel is fundamental to his view of human reality. In Kierkegaard's thought there is a deep and unresolvable distinction between (1) the abstract speculative outlook on reality found in Hegel's philosophy and (2) the concrete circumstances of a person who is attempting to find meaning in her life—"the existential situation." In the existential situation we find ourselves to be finite, temporal beings who are confronted with the demand to impart a meaning to our lives that goes beyond the transitory and local—the demand to achieve an eternal and infinite significance for our existence. From the existential point of view, these confrontations cannot be resolved by rational dialectic. In fact, it is not clear that the tension can be resolved at all by our efforts. We experience ourselves as finite and temporal, and we sense an impassable divide between what we are at this level and the infinite and the eternal, which stand as demands and ideals for us.

The crucial tension at the core of human existence cannot be resolved by rational thought. A kind of resolution of this tension is expressed in the idea, fundamental to Christian belief, that the eternal can exist in time, that the infinite can be incarnate as a finite being. Yet as thinkers, the most we can do is to become acutely aware of this paradox—that "the eternal has come into being in time," which for Christians means that God has become a temporal human being. Such a paradox cannot even be understood as a genuine possibility: "there is nothing for speculation to do except to arrive at an understanding of this impossibility."[1] Thus, whereas Hegel posits a rational reconciliation of all opposition in reality, Kierkegaard believes that

1. Søren Kierkegaard, *Concluding Unscientific Postscript*, trans. David F. Swenson and Walter Lowrie (Princeton: Princeton University Press, 1941), 187.

existential reality exhibits a fundamental and irreconcilable conflict. This conflict is something with which the individual must struggle in taking a stand on his or her life. In effect, Kierkegaard stands in sharp disagreement with Hegelian rationalist optimism. This is no doubt one of the reasons that his views became so influential after European faith in rational progress was so badly shaken as a result of the First World War.

3. Three Kinds of Life

A good way to begin to understand Kierkegaard's positive views is by looking at his threefold classification of the ways we humans can attempt to achieve fulfillment. In his view there are three main "spheres of existence" or modes of life: the aesthetic, the ethical, and the religious.[2] Sometimes Kierkegaard portrays these lives as a sequence of steps, each of which we must take on the path to meaning and fulfillment. Kierkegaard presents these three modes of life as advocated by several different pseudonymous authors. For example, the putative author of *Concluding Unscientific Postscript*, in which the religious life is discussed, is Johannes Climacus, a philosophically inclined religious writer. The aesthetic, *Either* part of *Either/Or* is presented as written by "A," the ethical, *Or* part by "B," and the entire book as edited by Victor Eremita. Kierkegaard's reason for presenting a mode of life through the device of a fictitious author might be to detach the ideas from his own authorial position, and thereby to encourage the reader to decide for himself or herself whether such a life is genuinely worthy of choice.[3]

Kierkegaard uses the word 'aesthetic' in a sense closely related to its Greek origin, *aisthesis*, which means sensation, and especially feeling. An aesthetic person is someone who lives for sensations, and in particular, for feelings. The most fundamental characteristic of the person living the aesthetic life is that his purposes are exhausted by the satisfaction of desires for momentary or short-term fulfillments. An obvious example of an aesthetic person is someone whose purpose in life is solely to satisfy desires for "peak experiences," such thrills as those achieved from, say, bungee-jumping or doing cocaine. But another example of an aesthetic life would be the professor who is so elated whenever she obtains a new result or makes an exciting discovery that she lives just for those rushes of intense pleasure she gets

2. See C. Stephen Evans, *Kierkegaard's Fragments and Postscript: The Religious Philosophy of Johannes Climacus* (Atlantic Highlands, N.J.: Humanities Press, 1983), 33–54.

3. This type of view is developed by Louis Mackey in *Kierkegaard: A Kind of Poet* (Philadelphia: University of Pennsylvania Press, 1971), in chapter 6, 241–46.

in such moments. The aesthetic life can also be lived with different levels of reflective attention. An unreflective person might simply strive for moments of pleasure without any plan designed to secure them, whereas a strategist like the seducer described in *Either* devises elaborate designs to ensure frequent moments of satisfaction and infrequent moments of frustration.

Kierkegaard believes that the aesthetic option will always fail as a route to fulfillment. One reason for this failure is internal to the nature of the aesthetic life. An aesthetic person aims at the satisfaction of desires for momentary pleasures, but whether such satisfactions are actually secured often depends on circumstances beyond his control. An experience of intimacy can be thwarted by another's lack of inclination, a sudden loss of confidence can ruin a chance for a gold medal, and the difficulty of an issue can hinder an inquirer from gaining philosophical insight into it. This is so no matter how well crafted one's strategies are for achieving one's aesthetic goals. Success in the aesthetic life, therefore, is dependent on fortune.[4] Moreover, even if one often succeeds in one's aesthetic endeavors, one will always be gripped by the anxiety that some misfortune will result in failure in future ventures. This anxiety undermines the sense of well-being that is the aim of the aesthetic life, and hence robs the aesthetic life of genuine success.

At a deeper level, both the attraction and the failure of the aesthetic life can be explained by the fact that human beings are a synthesis of the temporal and the eternal. Most abstractly, this means that though our lives are constituted by a series of separate moments in time, we are also beings whose existence can transcend the disunity of these moments. Put more existentially, this means that though we are beings governed by basic passions and desires, aiming at momentary satisfactions, we are also beings who can make life something more coherent and unified, something more than just a series of fragmented projects aimed at transitory enjoyments.

But why should this reflection on the metaphysics of a human life have any implications for what kind of life is best for us? And how, in particular, can it help to explain why the aesthetic life is doomed to be unfulfilling? To answer these questions, we need to examine a current in the thought of the Romantic period that Charles Taylor has called *expressivism*.[5] Expressivism is the view that in order to achieve fulfillment in life we need to express who and what we are. In this view, which has its roots in German Romanticism and was richly developed by Hegel, human beings have a certain nature or essence, and the best kind of life is one in which that nature or essence is expressed. In Hegel's view, for instance, as history proceeds the nature of human beings is progressively expressed in the arts and sciences, and in cul-

4. Kierkegaard, *Concluding Unscientific Postscript*, 388.
5. Charles Taylor, *Hegel* (Cambridge: Cambridge University Press, 1975), chapter 1.

tural institutions such as marriage, civil society, and the state. As the expression of human nature becomes more comprehensive, human life becomes increasingly more fulfilled.

Kierkegaard (or at least Johannes Climacus, the pseudonymous author of *Concluding Unscientific Postscript*) is also an expressivist, but with an emphasis that differs from Hegel's. "The task of the subjective thinker," he writes, "is to transform himself into an instrument that clearly and definitely expresses in existence whatever is essentially human."[6] The feature of human nature that he believes most crucially requires expression is our existence as a synthesis of the temporal and the eternal. It is fairly easy to express the temporal aspect: as a rule, we have little difficulty taking on a series of projects whose sole aim is momentary satisfaction. Expressing the eternal side, however, is much more difficult, and it comes only with a struggle. But if we can express the eternal within us, such expression provides a unity, an overarching purpose or theme, for our entire lives. This realization of a unifying structure for one's life is the task of every human: "To have been young, and then to grow older, and finally to die, is a very mediocre form of human existence; this merit belongs to every animal. But the unification of the different stages of life . . . is the task set for human beings."[7]

Kierkegaard believes that this overarching unity can be achieved only by means of a decisive, continuously renewed choice. In other words, it calls for a commitment, a "leap," that will unify one's life. Such a commitment might be to another person in marriage, or to God in a religious life. Here Kierkegaard sets out for the first time what is perhaps the most fundamental theme in existentialism: the idea that we can achieve meaning for our lives only through a decisive, life-defining commitment. In fact, only a person who aims to attain unity in this way can properly be called an *existing* individual. Existence, in this sense, is not a final state or a finished product. This is why Kierkegaard says "existence itself, the act of existing, is a striving."[8] To be an existing individual is to engage oneself in a difficult process aimed at expressing what one is, a project that never ends so long as one is alive, but must be continuously taken up and pursued.

Accordingly, the deeper reason the aesthetic life fails is that it expresses only one side of the self, the temporal aspect of our nature, while ignoring the eternal aspect. This failure manifests itself concretely in the aesthetic life. Whenever the aesthetic person achieves the momentary fulfillment she was seeking, and the moment of fulfillment has ended, she must start anew, and the moment of fulfillment loses the meaning it had. "Yea, so long as

6. Kierkegaard, *Concluding Unscientific Postscript*, 318.

7. Ibid., 311.

8. Ibid., 84.

every nerve in you is aquiver . . . then you feel that you are living. But when the battle is won . . . when the swift thoughts report that the victory is yours—then, in fact, you know nothing, you know not how to begin; for then, for the first time, you are at the beginning."[9] We remain unsatisfied in this type of life, because meaning and fulfillment require a commitment that pulls the various moments of our lives together, and that imparts a significance to our existence by giving these moments an overall coherence.

4. Despair, Subjectivity, and Resignation

In *Sickness unto Death*, Kierkegaard discusses various ways one might attempt to confront the most basic predicament for human existence: the need to express both one's temporal and one's eternal nature. There he describes three unsuccessful ways of managing this predicament, three stances he calls forms of *despair*. The first stance is to be unaware of the problem and thus to live a life of indifference to the most fundamental tension in one's being.[10] This type of life he describes as "not being conscious of having a self." If one is in despair in this sense, one does not even feel that one is in despair, and accordingly Kierkegaard calls this state "despair improperly so-called." For example, an aesthetic devotee of the momentary pleasures of partying and revelry may never realize that there is an eternal side to his nature that he is not expressing. He may feel that he is living well, but Kierkegaard holds that he is in fact in the worst form of despair.

The second stance is to recognize, perhaps as a result of a blow of fate, or by self-reflection, that one is not only temporal but also eternal, and then attempt to resolve the tension between these two aspects by repudiating the eternal and immersing oneself in the temporal.[11] For example, an aesthetic person who is aware of her eternal nature might resolutely attempt to disavow her eternal aspect and persevere in living for the momentary pleasures of sport or social life. Because this stance involves denial of a part of the self, Kierkegaard calls it "despair at not willing to be oneself." Such a stance may range from trying to drive consciousness of one's despair into the background and ignoring one's sense of the eternal as much as possible to nourishing a distinct consciousness of one's despair. Someone who is distinctly conscious of his despair may fully "understand that it is weakness to take the earthly so much to heart," but as a result may be "more deeply absorbed in his despair and despair over his weakness."[12]

9. Ibid., 90.

10. Søren Kierkegaard, *Fear and Trembling and The Sickness unto Death*, trans. Walter Lowrie (Princeton: Princeton University Press, 1941), 175–80.

11. Ibid., 180–200, esp. 185–89, 195.

12. Ibid., 189, 195.

The third type of despair Kierkegaard describes is one that results from trying to express the fundamental tension through one's own power. It is characterized by the attempt to express the eternal through one's own will alone, while "detaching the self from every relation to the Power which posited it."[13] Kierkegaard calls this type of response "despair of willing to be oneself." He cites the Stoic attitude as representative of this sort of despair. In this outlook one attempts to control oneself, to detach oneself psychologically from any potential cause of distress, and to be content with the events of one's life no matter how bad they may seem, all by one's own power.

In the second part of *Either/Or* Kierkegaard describes a kind of life, the ethical, that might be thought of as an instance of this third type of despair. The mark of the ethical life is a constantly renewed decision, made by one's own will alone, to live in accord with ethical duty. For Kierkegaard marriage can be an example of the ethical life, for in marriage one can make the decision to commit oneself to another human being by one's own power, and by renewing this commitment continuously, one can attempt to provide a unity to the various moments in one's life that expresses one's eternal nature. Although *Either/Or* does not describe the ethical life as one that involves despair, *The Sickness unto Death* characterizes the striving to express the eternal through one's own will alone as the most agonizing, albeit the highest form of despair. Kierkegaard calls the attempt to express the eternal aspect of the self by one's own will alone "defiance." In his view, or at least in the view of Anti-Climacus, the pseudonymous author of *The Sickness unto Death*, this attempt is bound to fail. Of the despairing self who actively attempts to express the eternal he says: "no derived self [i.e. no created self] can by regarding itself give itself more than it is. . . . Hence the self in its despairing effort to will to be itself labors itself into the direct opposite, it becomes really no self."[14] For the secular existentialists like Heidegger and Sartre, however, a stance of defiance is the highest level of authenticity we human beings can hope to achieve. Indeed, Camus in *The Myth of Sisyphus* treats defiant, lucid self-awareness as the only realistic response to the absurdity of life.

But for Kierkegaard there is a better solution, which is to be found in the religious life (or at least in one kind of religious life). Religiousness is discussed in *Fear and Trembling, Edifying Discourses, Philosophical Fragments,* and *Concluding Unscientific Postscript.* The last of these works represents Kierkegaard's most thorough and most systematic effort to explain his views on religion. Perhaps the single most important theme of the *Postscript* is the claim that *truth is subjectivity.* With this claim Kierkegaard does not mean to

13. Ibid., 200–207; the quotation is at p. 201.
14. Ibid., 202.

deny that there are objective facts, that is, facts that are independent of our modes of representing and our ways of coming to know the world.[15] Rather, "truth is subjectivity" means that, when issues regarding meaning and fulfillment in one's life are at stake, one's attitude towards the object of one's concerns takes precedence over the issue of whether one is actually right about some fact:

> When the question of truth is raised in an objective manner, reflection is directed objec-tively to the truth, as an object to which the knower is related. Reflection is not focused on the relationship, however, but on the question of whether it is the truth to which the knower is related. If only the object to which he is related is the truth, the subject is ac-counted to be in the truth.[16]

We might clarify this passage by thinking about two ways a person might be said to have arrived at the truth. First, someone might master all of the true sentences about something that is genuinely important, while con-stantly maintaining a detached, theoretical stance. Imagine, for example, a psychologist who develops a theory about human relationships so accurate and insightful that it has changed the lives of millions of people. But sup-pose further that as a scientist she has developed so detached an attitude to-wards the world that she is unable to live in accordance with her theory in her own relationships, with the result that her life is very empty and un-fulfilled. Such a person possesses the truth objectively, but not subjectively.

By contrast, another person might deeply and passionately live her rela-tionships in accord with her insights. She would be in the truth subjectively. In Kierkegaard's view, when finding meaning and fulfillment for one's life is at issue, what is most important is the nature of one's relationship, not being right: "*When the question of truth is raised subjectively, reflection is directed sub-jectively to the nature of the individual's relationship; if only the mode of this relationship is in the truth, the individual is in the truth even if he should happen to be related to what is not true.*"[17] According to Kierkegaard, one is in the truth subjectively when the degree of passion in one's relationship expresses the nature of the thing or person to which one relates oneself. Thus, in his view, if one is attempting to relate oneself to God, the infinite being, the appropriate kind of relationship is one of infinite intensity. To illustrate these claims about truth, Kierkegaard argues that a pagan praying with in-

15. See Robert Adams, "Truth and Subjectivity," in *Reasoned Faith: Essays in Philo-sophical Theology in Honor of Norman Kretzmann*, ed. Eleanor Stump (Ithaca: Cornell University Press, 1993): 15–41.

16. Kierkegaard, *Concluding Unscientific Postscript*, 178.

17. Ibid.

finite passion, "although his eyes rest on the image of an idol," has a more appropriate relationship to the truth, or is more "in the truth," than someone who has fewer false beliefs and more true beliefs about religion, but holds them without deep feeling.

> If one who lives in the midst of Christendom goes up to the house of God, the house of the true God, with the true conception of God in his knowledge, and prays, but prays in a false spirit; and one who lives in an idolatrous community prays with the entire passion of the infinite, although his eyes rest upon the image of an idol: where is there more truth? The one prays in truth to God though he worships an idol; the other prays falsely to the true God, and hence worships in fact an idol.[18]

In his philosophical writings about religion, Kierkegaard distinguishes between two different sorts of religious life. The first, which he calls "Religiousness A," is characterized by an attempt to relate oneself to God by means of a continuously repeated commitment, but solely by means of one's own power. This sort of religiousness can be characterized by three different modes of self-expression, or as Kierkegaard calls them, simply "expressions." The first of these is *resignation.* An attempt to express the infinite in one's life requires that one be willing to renounce all temporal and finite things in order to achieve a relation to the eternal and infinite. As he says, "if for any individual an eternal happiness is his highest good, this will mean that all finite satisfactions are voluntarily relegated to the status of what may have to be renounced in favor of an eternal happiness."[19] This does not necessarily suggest that one must stop eating food, for example, but rather that one must psychologically detach oneself from all such finite things so that one does not rely on them for fulfillment in life. One must, however, be willing to give them up altogether if one's relationship to the infinite is at issue. Moreover, as Robert Adams points out, resignation does not involve indifference.[20] On the contrary, it requires the intensification of one's desire for the finite, and in the paradigm case, a concentration of all of one's desire for the finite into a desire for a single finite thing. (This concentration is required, Kierkegaard says, so that the soul will not be "dispersed in the multifarious," as the aesthetic person's is.) Then, while one's desire for this finite thing is the greatest it can be, one, *while maintaining this desire,* resigns that thing.

In *Fear and Trembling* Kierkegaard provides two illustrations of infinite

18. Ibid., 179–80.

19. Ibid., 350.

20. Robert Adams, "The Knight of Faith," *Faith and Philosophy* 7 (October 1990): 383–95, 387–90.

resignation.[21] The first involves "a young swain" who falls in love with a princess. Kiekegaard says that "the whole content of his life consists in this love, and yet the situation is such that it is impossible for it to be realized." But he does not give up his love: "He is not cowardly, he is not afraid of letting love creep into his most secret, most hidden thoughts, to let it twine in innumerable coils about every ligament of his consciousness—if the love becomes unhappy love, he will never be able to tear himself loose from it." When he comes to terms with the impossibility of his having a relationship with the princess, rather than give up his love, he becomes a "knight of infinite resignation." This involves two "movements:" first, that he "concentrate the whole content of life and the whole significance of reality in one single wish," his wish to have a relationship with the princess he loves, and second, that at the very same time he uses all of his strength to sacrifice having a relationship with her. In the process of resignation, the knight never relinquishes his love and this is of crucial significance. It is by focusing all his love for the finite and temporal into one wish, while at the very same time sacrificing the possibility of attaining that wish, that the knight expresses the eternal aspect of his nature. And thus, "love for that princess became for him the expression for an eternal love, assumed a religious character," and it "was transfigured into a love for the Eternal Being."

Kierkegaard also illustrates infinite resignation by the story of Abraham, the great biblical father of faith. Abraham and his wife Sarah have lived long and prosperous lives, but despite their ardent wish, they have never had a child together. But when Abraham is ninety-nine years old, and Sarah is ninety, God promises them a son (Genesis 17: 15–19). Abraham laughs when he hears this, because he thinks that they are too old to have a child, and then God tells him to name the child, whom they soon have, "Isaac," which means "(one) will laugh." As Isaac is growing up, however, God one day says to Abraham: "take your son, your only son Isaac, whom you love, and go to the land of Moriah, and offer him there as a burnt offering upon one of the mountains of which I shall tell you" (Genesis 22: 2). Abraham, in obedience to God, takes his son to Moriah and prepares to sacrifice him. In Kierkegaard's analysis, when God asks him to sacrifice his son, Abraham fully intends to do so, even though Isaac continues to mean as much to him as anything in the finite world could possibly mean to anyone. And thus, while concentrating his love for the finite in Isaac, he at the same time performs the movement of resignation by agreeing to sacrifice him.

The second expression of Religiousness A is *suffering*. Suffering arises in

---

21. All quotations from *Fear and Trembling* are taken from Søren Kierkegaard, *Fear and Trembling and The Sickness Unto Death,* trans. Walter Lowrie (Princeton: Princeton University Press, 1941). All subsequent quotations from *Fear and Trembling* are reprinted below.

this kind of religious person because of the difficulty involved in psychologically detaching oneself from finite things—"this process is a dying away from the immediate."[22] Because attachment to finite things comes naturally to us, genuine detachment requires a continuously renewed decision and causes us intense psychological pain. Kierkegaard actually demeans those who flagellate themselves in order to express their devotion to God, because the suffering caused by renunciation is much more intense, he believes, than the physical suffering inflicted by the whip.

The third expression reveals why, just as in the case of the aesthetic life, Religiousness A is in some sense deeply unfulfilling. This third expression Kierkegaard calls *guilt*. The guilt he has in mind here is not the familiar moral attitude, but a special kind of religious guilt. In our attempt to express the infinite by our own efforts, we come to the realization that our expression inevitably will be negative. Guilt "is the expression for the relationship [with an eternal happiness] by reason of the fact that it expresses the incompatibility or disrelationship."[23] To express the infinite we can only renounce the finite—there is no positive expression of the infinite that is within our power. The theologian Paul Tillich makes the same point in terms of his categories of *ultimacy* and *concreteness*. In religious life, Tillich claims, we desire to express the ultimate, but for us there is no concrete content—an object, event, or act—that can adequately express the infinite.[24] Similarly, Kierkegaard argues that the highest expression possible within the confines of Religiousness A is an eternal or perpetual recollection of guilt, a constant awareness that one's own powers are insufficient to express infinitude.

5. Faith

Kierkegaard's characterization of Religiousness A makes room for another possibility, a type of religion in which one does not rely solely on one's own powers. In the *Philosophical Fragments,* he contrasts Religiousness A, or as he calls it here, "Socratic Religion," with Christianity. In Socratic Religion, the truth is not held to come to a person from an outside source, but rather to come from inside a person, as an innate (inborn) idea, and it becomes conscious by a process of remembering what one knew more clearly. The moment at which one recollects is not of particular significance, for there is a sense in which one possesses the truth all along; Socratic religion is one of human self-sufficiency. By contrast, in Christianity, or "Religiousness B" as

22. Kierkegaard, *Concluding Unscientific Postscript,* 432.

23. Ibid., 473.

24. Paul Tillich, *Systematic Theology* (Chicago: University of Chicago Press, 1951) 1:211. See Robert Adams discussion of Tillich's relationship to Kierkegaard in "Truth and Subjectivity," 37.

it is called in the *Postscript,* we do not possess the truth all along. Instead, we are initially in error. Furthermore, we do not arrive at the truth by discovering something already in us, but rather by being taught by God as teacher. The moment at which one realizes the truth is therefore of decisive significance, because before this moment one had no grasp of the truth at all.

Furthermore, Christianity supplies concrete content for religious expression. The Truth that we are taught is a Person: the Incarnation, God who has become human while remaining God. The God who has become human is the ultimate paradox—the finite and the infinite, the temporal and the eternal in a single being. As we have seen, Kierkegaard does not believe that the resolution of the most fundamental oppositions in reality can be achieved by means of a Hegelian rational dialectic. Instead, he argues that the ultimate paradox—that the eternal has been in time—in virtue of its very nature defies understanding. Kierkegaard maintains that this incomprehensibility is an asset, for this paradox is precisely the sort of thing that can inspire passion of the kind required for an expression of the infinite. "Subjectivity culminates in passion, Christianity is the paradox, paradox and passion are a mutual fit, and the paradox is altogether suited to one whose situation is to be in the extremity of existence."[25] Thus, to be a Christian requires continuously reaffirmed commitment to the deepest paradox conceivable, and this requires the greatest possible passion. This passion is expressed in a *leap* of faith, in taking a stand on a religious commitment that is absurd, and thus cannot be rationally established or explained. One who has faith is condemned to *silence.*

In *Fear and Trembling,* Kierkegaard illustrates a further characteristic of Religiousness B by the example of the knight of faith. Kierkegaard contrasts this knight with the knight of infinite resignation who, as we have seen, concentrates all of his desire for the finite into his love for the princess and then sacrifices the possibility of a relationship with her in order to express the infinite. The knight of faith is similar to the knight of infinite resignation in that he also goes through these two movements in order to express the infinite. But he is unique in making an additional move. *At the very same time* that he resigns the finite he receives and accepts it back "by virtue of the absurd." After making the movement of resignation, Kierkegaard says, the knight of faith "makes still another movement more wonderful than all." The knight says about the princess he loves, but from whom he has psychologically distanced himself in the process of infinite resignation: "I believe nevertheless that I shall get her, in virtue, that is, of the absurd, in virtue of the fact that with God all things are possible."

For Kierkegaard, Abraham is the paradigmatic example of the knight of

---

25. Kierkegaard, *Concluding Unscientific Postscript,* 206.

faith. In the biblical account, as he takes the knife to sacrifice his son, an angel calls to Abraham from heaven: "Do not lay your hand on the lad or do anything to him; for now I know that you fear God, seeing that you have not withheld your son, your only son, from me" (Genesis 22: 12). Abraham then sees a ram whose horns are caught in a thicket, and sacrifices it instead of his son. In Kierkegaard's interpretation, Abraham resigns Isaac by agreeing to sacrifice him in obedience to God, and then accepts him back when God provides a ram for the sacrifice. For Kierkegaard it is crucial that when Abraham accepts Isaac back, he does not relinquish the movements involved in infinite resignation. Instead, he maintains his intense love, his resignation, and his acceptance, all at the same time.

In Kierkegaard's view, the movement of faith is extremely difficult to make. Kierkegaard imagines the knight accepting a relationship with the princess while preserving the movements of infinite resignation. Speaking through the pseudonymous author of *Fear and Trembling,* Johannes de Silentio, he says, "but by faith, says that marvelous knight, by faith I shall get her in virtue of the absurd. But this movement I am unable to make. As soon as I would begin to make it everything turns around dizzily, and I flee back to the pain of resignation. I can swim in existence, but for that mystical soaring I am too heavy." (Kierkegaard seems to be reflecting on his own relationship with Regine Olsen here.) In Adams' view, the movement of faith is so difficult because the "taking back of what one is still giving up with all one's force is a practical . . . contradiction," and this contradiction is "the absurd by virtue of which the knight of faith says the princess is to be won."[26] (A practical contradiction arises when an agent cannot perform an action due to conflicting factors within its specification.) For Kierkegaard, the complex attitude of Abraham, and of the knight of faith who accepts the princess back while at the same time maintaining infinite resignation, is an expression of the ultimate paradox—the unity of the temporal and eternal, of the finite and infinite. Abraham resigns Isaac in expression of the infinite, and accepts him back in expression of the finite, and maintains both attitudes at once, thereby expressing the ultimate paradox.

The notion that one can maintain an attitude of resignation toward something and at the same time an attitude of accepting it back is the most central idea in Kierkegaard's conception of faith. Adams argues that in developing this account of the knight of faith, Kierkegaard is presenting a solution to a psychological problem that arises for the religious life, and for any life which involves deep, all-embracing commitments.[27] If I am committed to

26. Adams, "The Knight of Faith," 385. See also Evans, *Kierkegaard's Fragments and Postscript,* 212–45.

27. Adams, "Truth and Subjectivity," 35–41, and in conversation.

expressing my relationship with God in my entire life, how am I to be related to such features of everyday finitude as my ordinary physical and psychological needs? The solution of Religiousness A is that I should resign them, but this strategy involves agonizing psychological distress. By advocating Religiousness B, Kierkegaard is recommending a different solution, one that combines psychological detachment with acceptance. According to this solution, I should not consider these finite elements as the aim of my search for ultimate fulfillment, yet I accept them as integrated into a life devoted to this quest. But although a life lived in accordance with this conception escapes the anguish of the three expressions of Religiousness A, it nevertheless involves embracing the ultimate paradox, an act of acceptance that, in Kierkegaard's view, poses an immense challenge.

6. The Teleological Suspension of the Ethical

One of the deepest problems that Kierkegaard raises for faith in *Fear and Trembling* is whether the requirements of the religious life can ever override the requirements of the ethical life. In Hegel's conception, this could never happen, because ethical requirements are expressions of the universality essential to all rational reflection and agency, and nothing can supersede what is rational and universal. Kierkegaard, in contrast, thinks ethical requirements can sometimes be superseded. To show this, he focuses his discussion of this issue on the divine command for Abraham to sacrifice Isaac. This sacrifice, Kierkegaard assumes, is ethically wrong, because it requires making of oneself, as a particular individual, an exception to rational and universal principles. His point is not that all human sacrifice is ethically wrong. On the contrary, he suggests that if the Greeks would be saved by Agamemnon's sacrifice of Iphigenia, these acts of human sacrifice might have an ethical, universal justification. But no such ethical justification applies in Abraham's situation. In this case, Kierkegaard holds, feeling an impulse to make oneself an exception to universal ethical requirements is "temptation": "Whenever the individual after he has entered the universal feels an impulse to assert himself as the particular, he is in temptation." Nevertheless, Abraham's religious faith requires him to sacrifice his son.

By Kierkegaard's account, faith, in which "the individual as particular stands in an absolute relation to the absolute," is a relationship of a particular person to a particular God. Thus, faith stands in opposition to the rational and the universal. Kierkegaard's crucial claim, then, is that religious faith, as a particular thing, *supersedes* the universal; in Hegelian terms, it is a "higher immediacy." "Faith," he says, "is precisely this paradox, that the individual as particular is higher than the universal." But faith does not *do away* with the ethical; rather it supersedes it while preserving its essential content. This is manifest in Abraham's *struggle* with the command to sacrifice his son. Having faith is not like being an outlaw who rejects ethical principles altogether. If Abraham's faith did away with the ethical, there would be no need for him to struggle with God's command.

Yet, in addition, faith does not supersede the ethical in a way that is rationally comprehensible. Abraham cannot express his faith in language, for language is limited to the expression of universal concepts, the means we have for rational comprehension. Rather, the relationship between faith and the ethical remains a paradox. We can become acutely aware of this paradox, we can passionately struggle with it, but we can never rationally grasp it: "it is and remains to all eternity a paradox, inaccessible to thought." In Kierkegaard's view, then, there is a dimension of humanity, expressed in an individual relationship with God, that is independent of one's relationships and obligations to humanity, and that cannot be rationally comprehended but only passionately appropriated. And thus, for the knight of faith, life does not become meaningful through rational acceptance of a coherent system of ethical principles. Rather, it becomes meaningful through a passionate struggle to live in accord with the fundamental and irresolvable paradox that lies at the heart of human existence.[28]

28. We are grateful to Robert Adams and Oliver Carling for enlightening discussion of issues in this section.

Fear and Trembling

A Dialectical Lyric

by Johannes de Silentio

PREFACE

Not merely in the realm of commerce but in the world of ideas as well our age is organizing a regular clearance sale. Everything is to be had at such a bargain that it is questionable whether in the end there is anybody who will want to bid. Every speculative price-fixer who conscientiously directs attention to the significant march of modern philosophy, every *Privatdocent,* tutor, and student, every crofter and cottar in philosophy, is not content with doubting everything but goes further. Perhaps it would be untimely and ill-timed to ask them where they are going, but surely it is courteous and unobtrusive to regard it as certain that they have doubted everything, since otherwise it would be a queer thing for them to be going further. This preliminary movement they have therefore all of them made, and presumably with such ease that they do not find it necessary to let drop a word about the how; for not even he who anxiously and with deep concern sought a little enlightenment was able to find any such thing, any guiding sign, any little dietetic prescription, as to how one was to comport oneself in supporting this prodigious task. "But Descartes[1] did it." Descartes, a venerable, humble and honest thinker, whose writings surely no one can read without the deepest emotion, did what he said and said what he did. Alas, alack, that is a great rarity in our times! Descartes, as he repeatedly affirmed, did not doubt in matters of faith. Remembering, however, as I have already said, that the natural light is to be trusted only in so far as nothing to the contrary is revealed by God Himself. . . . Moreover, it must be fixed in one's memory as the highest rule, that what has been revealed to us by God is to be believed as

1. The Preface is aimed at the Danish Hegelian Hans Lassen Martensen's review of J. L. Heiberg's "Introductory Lectures to Speculative Logic," *Danske Maanedskrift,* No. 16 for 1836, pp. 515*ff.* Descartes is mentioned here because Martensen made appeal to him in that article.

the most certain of all things; and even though the light of reason should seem most clearly to suggest something else, we must nevertheless give credence to the divine authority only, rather than to our own judgment. (*Principia philosophiae, pars prima* 28 and 76.) He did not cry, "Fire!" nor did he make it a duty for everyone to doubt; for Descartes was a quiet and solitary thinker, not a bellowing night-watchman; he modestly admitted that his method had importance for him alone and was justified in part by the bungled knowledge of his earlier years. Let no one think that I am here about to propound a method which everyone ought to follow in order to govern his reason aright; for I have merely the intention of expounding the method I myself have followed. . . . But no sooner had I finished the course of study at the conclusion of which one is ordinarily adopted into the ranks of the learned, than I began to think of something very different from that. For I became aware that I was involved in so many doubts, so many errors, that all efforts to learn were, as I saw it, of no other help to me than that I might more and more discover my ignorance (*Dissertatio de methodo*, pp. 2 and 3).

What those ancient Greeks (who also had some understanding of philosophy) regarded as a task for a whole lifetime, seeing that dexterity in doubting is not acquired in a few days or weeks, what the veteran combatant attained when he had preserved the equilibrium of doubt through all the pitfalls he encountered, who intrepidly denied the certainty of sense-perception and the certainty of the processes of thought, incorruptibly defied the apprehensions of self-love and the insinuations of sympathy—that is where everybody begins in our time.

In our time nobody is content to stop with faith but wants to go further. It would perhaps be rash to ask where these people are going, but it is surely a sign of breeding and culture for me to assume that everybody has faith, for otherwise it would be queer for them to be . . . going further. In those old days it was different, then faith was a task for a whole lifetime, because it was assumed that dexterity in faith is not acquired in a few days or weeks. When the tried oldster drew near to his last hour, having fought the good fight and kept the faith, his heart was still young enough not to have forgotten that fear and trembling which chastened the youth, which the man indeed held in check, but which no man quite outgrows . . . except as he might succeed at the earliest opportunity in going further. Where these revered figures arrived, that is the point where everybody in our day begins to go further.

The present writer is nothing of a philosopher, he has not understood the System, does not know whether it actually exists, whether it is completed; already he has enough for his weak head in the thought of what a prodigious head everybody in our day must have, since everybody has such a prodigious thought. Even though one were capable of converting the whole content of faith into the form of a concept, it does not follow that one has adequately conceived faith and understands how one got into it, or how it got into one. The present writer is nothing of a philosopher; he is, *poetice et eleganter*, an amateur writer who neither writes the System nor *promises*[2] of the System, who neither subscribes to the System nor ascribes anything to it. He writes because for him it is a luxury which becomes the more agreeable and more evident, the fewer there are who buy and read what he writes. He can easily foresee his fate in an age when passion has been obliterated in favor of learning, in an age when an author who wants to have readers must take care to write in such a way that the book can easily be perused during the afternoon nap, and take care to fashion his outward deportment in likeness to the picture of that polite young gardener in the advertisement sheet,[3] who with hat in hand, and with a good certificate from the place where he last served, recommends himself to the esteemed public. He foresees his fate—that he will be entirely ignored. He has a presentiment of the dreadful event, that a jealous criticism will many a time let him feel the birch; he trembles at the still more dreadful thought that one or another enterprising scribe, a gulper of paragraphs, who to rescue learning is always willing to do with other peoples' writings what Trop[4] "to preserve good taste" magnanimously resolved to do with a book called *The Destruction of the Human Race*—that is, he will slice the author into paragraphs, and will do it with the same inflexibility as the man who in the interest of the science of punctuation divided his discourse by counting the words, so that there were fifty words for a period and thirty-five for a semicolon.

 I prostrate myself with the profoundest deference before every systematic "bag-peerer" at the custom house, protesting, "This is not the System, it has nothing whatever to do with the System." I call down every blessing upon the System and upon the Danish shareholders in this omnibus—for a tower it is hardly likely to become. I wish them all and sundry good luck and all prosperity.

Respectfully,

Johannes DE SILENTIO

2. Martensen gave such "promises" in the article referred to in note 1.

3. S. K.'s contemptuous way of referring to the *Berlingske Tidende*, a newspaper owned and edited by his *bête noire*, the wholesale merchant Nathanson. This advertisement attracted particular attention because the enterprising young gardener accompanied it with a sketch of himself in the ingratiating attitude here described.

4. In J. L. Heiberg's *The Reviewer and the Beast*, Trop tears his own tragedy, *The Destruction of the Human Race*, into two equal pieces, remarking, "Since it doesn't cost more to preserve good taste, why shouldn't we do it?"

Abraham's faith

A PANEGYRIC UPON ABRAHAM

Praise vs. treatise (admiration, amo)

If there were no eternal consciousness in a man, if at the foundation of all
there lay only a wildly seething power which writhing with obscure passions
produced everything that is great and everything that is insignificant, if a
bottomless void never satiated lay hidden beneath all—what then would life
be but despair? If such were the case, if there were no sacred bond which
united mankind, if one generation arose after another like the leafage in the
forest, if the one generation replaced the other like the song of birds in the
forest, if the human race passed through the world as the ship goes through
the sea, like the wind through the desert, a thoughtless and fruitless activity,
if an eternal oblivion were always lurking hungrily for its prey and there was
no power strong enough to wrest it from its maw—how empty then and
comfortless life would be! But therefore it is not thus, but as God created
man and woman, so too He fashioned the hero and the poet or orator. The
poet cannot do what that other does, he can only admire, love and rejoice in
the hero. *Abraham's* Yet he too is happy, and not less so, for the hero is as it were his
better nature, with which he is in love, rejoicing in the fact that this after all
is not himself, that his love can be admiration. He is the genius of recollection, can do nothing except call to mind what has been done, do nothing but
admire what has been done; he contributes nothing of his own, but is jealous
of the intrusted treasure. He follows the option of his heart, but when he
has found what he sought, he wanders before every man's door with his song
and with his oration, that all may admire the hero as he does, be proud of
the hero as he is. This is his achievement, his humble work, this is his faithful service in the house of the hero. If he thus remains true to his love, he
strives day and night against the cunning of oblivion which would trick him
out of his hero, then he has completed his work, then he is gathered to the
hero, who has loved him just as faithfully, for the poet is as it were the hero's
better nature, powerless it may be as a memory is, but also transfigured as a
memory is. Hence no one shall be forgotten who was great, and though time
tarries long, though a cloud[5] of misunderstanding takes the hero away, his
lover comes nevertheless, and the longer the time that has passed, the more
faithfully will he cling to him.

No, not one shall be forgotten who was great in the world. But each was
great in his own way, and each in proportion to the greatness of that which
he *loved.* For he who loved himself became great by himself, and he who
loved other men became great by his selfless devotion, but he who loved God
became greater than all. Everyone shall be remembered, but each became

5. Alluding to various passages in Homer (e.g. *Iliad* III 381) where a divinity saves a
hero by enveloping him in a cloud and carrying him away. We discover additional
pathos in this picture of the "lover" when we remember that at the end of *The Point
of View* (pp. 62*f.* and 100*ff.*) S. K. looks for the coming of his poet, his lover.

great in proportion to his *expectation*. One became great by expecting the possible, another by expecting the eternal, but he who expected the impossible became greater than all. Everyone shall be remembered, but each was great in proportion to the greatness of that with which he *strove*. For he who strove with the world became great by overcoming the world, and he who strove with himself became great by overcoming himself, but he who strove with God became greater than all. So there was strife in the world, man against man, one against a thousand, but he who strove with God was greater than all. So there was strife upon earth: there was one who overcame all by his power, and there was one who overcame God by his impotence. There was one who relied upon himself and gained all, there was one who secure in his strength sacrificed all, but he who believed God was greater than all. There was one who was great by reason of his power, and one who was great by reason of his wisdom, and one who was great by reason of his hope, and one who was great by reason of his love; but Abraham was greater than all, great by reason of his power whose strength is impotence, great by reason of his wisdom whose secret is foolishness, great by reason of his hope whose form is madness, great by reason of the love which is hatred of oneself.

By faith Abraham went out from the land of his fathers and became a sojourner in the land of promise. He left one thing behind, took one thing with him: he left his earthly understanding behind and took faith with him—otherwise he would not have wandered forth but would have thought this unreasonable. By faith he was a stranger in the land of promise, and there was nothing to recall what was dear to him, but by its novelty everything tempted his soul to melancholy yearning—and yet he was God's elect, in whom the Lord was well pleased! Yea, if he had been disowned, cast off from God's grace, he could have comprehended it better; but now it was like a mockery of him and of his faith. There was in the world one too who lived in banishment[6] from the fatherland he loved. He is not forgotten, nor his Lamentations when he sorrowfully sought and found what he had lost. There is no song of Lamentations by Abraham. It is human to lament, human to weep with them that weep, but it is greater to believe, more blessed to contemplate the believer.

By faith Abraham received the promise that in his seed all races of the world would be blessed. Time passed, the possibility was there, Abraham believed; time passed, it became unreasonable, Abraham believed. There was in the world one who had an expectation, time passed, the evening drew nigh, he was not paltry enough to have forgotten his expectation, therefore he too shall not be forgotten. Then he sorrowed, and sorrow did not deceive

---

6. It is evident from the sequel that Jeremiah is meant.

him as life had done, it did for him all it could, in the sweetness of sorrow he possessed his delusive expectation. It is human to sorrow, human to sorrow with them that sorrow, but it is greater to believe, more blessed to contemplate the believer. There is no song of Lamentations by Abraham. He did not mournfully count the days while time passed, he did not look at Sarah with a suspicious glance, wondering whether she were growing old, he did not arrest the course of the sun, that Sarah might not grow old, and his expectation with her. He did not sing lullingly before Sarah his mournful lay. Abraham became old, Sarah became a laughingstock in the land, and yet he was God's elect and inheritor of the promise that in his seed all the races of the world would be blessed. So were it not better if he had not been God's elect? What is it to be God's elect? It is to be denied in youth the wishes of youth, so as with great pains to get them fulfilled in old age. But Abraham believed and held fast the expectation. If Abraham had wavered, he would have given it up. If he had said to God, "Then perhaps it is not after all Thy will that it should come to pass, so I will give up the wish. It was my only wish, it was my bliss. My soul is sincere, I hide no secret malice because Thou didst deny it to me"—he would not have been forgotten, he would have saved many by his example, yet he would not be the father of faith. For it is great to give up one's wish, but it is greater to hold it fast after having given it up, it is great to grasp the eternal, but it is greater to hold fast to the temporal after having given it up.

Then came the fulness of time. If Abraham had not believed, Sarah surely would have been dead of sorrow, and Abraham, dulled by grief, would not have understood the fulfillment but would have smiled at it as at a dream of youth. But Abraham believed, therefore he was young; for he who always hopes for the best becomes old, and he who is always prepared for the worst grows old early, but he who believes preserves an eternal youth. Praise therefore to that story! For Sarah, though stricken in years, was young enough to desire the pleasure of motherhood, and Abraham, though gray-haired, was young enough to wish to be a father. In an outward respect the marvel consists in the fact that it came to pass according to their expectation, in a deeper sense the miracle of faith consists in the fact that Abraham and Sarah were young enough to wish, and that faith had preserved their wish and therewith their youth. He accepted the fulfillment of the promise, he accepted it by faith, and it came to pass according to the promise and according to his faith—for Moses smote the rock with his rod, but he did not believe.

Then there was joy in Abraham's house, when Sarah became a bride on the day of their golden wedding.

But it was not to remain thus. Still once more Abraham was to be tried. He had fought with that cunning power which invents everything, with that alert enemy which never slumbers, with that old man who outlives all things—he had fought with Time and preserved his faith. Now all the terror of the strife was concentrated in one instant. "And God tempted Abraham and said unto him, Take Isaac, thine only son, whom thou lovest, and get thee into the land of Moriah, and offer him there for a burnt offering upon the mountain which I will show thee."

So all was lost—more dreadfully than if it had never come to pass! So the Lord was only making sport of Abraham! He made miraculously the preposterous actual, and now in turn He would annihilate it. It was indeed foolishness, but Abraham did not laugh at it like Sarah when the promise was announced. All was lost! Seventy years of faithful expectation, the brief joy at the fulfillment of faith. Who then is he that plucks away the old man's staff, who is it that requires that he himself shall break it? Who is he that would make a man's gray hairs comfortless, who is it that requires that he himself shall do it? Is there no compassion for the venerable oldling, none for the innocent child? And yet Abraham was God's elect, and it was the Lord who imposed the trial. All would now be lost. The glorious memory to be preserved by the human race, the promise in Abraham's seed—this was only a whim, a fleeting thought which the Lord had had, which Abraham should now obliterate. That glorious treasure which was just as old as faith in Abraham's heart, many, many years older than Isaac, the fruit of Abraham's life, sanctified by prayers, matured in conflict—the blessing upon Abraham's lips, this fruit was now to be plucked prematurely and remain without significance. For what significance had it when Isaac was to be sacrificed? That sad and yet blissful hour when Abraham was to take leave of all that was dear to him, when yet once more he was to lift up his head, when his countenance would shine like that of the Lord, when he would concentrate his whole soul in a blessing which was potent to make Isaac blessed all his days—this time would not come! For he would indeed take leave of Isaac, but in such a way that he himself would remain behind; death would separate them, but in such a way that Isaac remained its prey. The old man would not be joyful in death as he laid his hands in blessing upon Isaac, but he would be weary of life as he laid violent hands upon Isaac. And it was God who tried him. Yea, woe, woe unto the messenger who had come before Abraham with such tidings! Who would have ventured to be the emissary of this sorrow? But it was God who tried Abraham.

Yet Abraham believed, and believed for this life. Yea, if his faith had been only for a future life, he surely would have cast everything away in order to hasten out of this world to which he did not belong. But Abraham's faith was not of this sort, if there be such a faith; for really this is not faith but the furthest possibility of faith which has a presentiment of its object at the extremest limit of the horizon, yet is separated from it by a yawning abyss within which despair carries on its game. But Abraham believed precisely for this life, that he was to grow old in the land, honored by the people, blessed in his generation, remembered forever in Isaac, his dearest thing in life, whom he embraced with a love for which it would be a poor expression to say that he loyally fulfilled the father's duty of loving the son, as indeed is evinced in the words of the summons, "the son whom thou lovest." Jacob had twelve sons, and one of them he loved; Abraham had only one, the son whom he loved.

Yet Abraham believed and did not doubt, he believed the preposterous. If Abraham had doubted—then he would have done something else, something glorious; for how could Abraham do anything but what is great and glorious! He would have marched up to Mount Moriah, he would have cleft the fire-wood, lit the pyre, drawn the knife—he would have cried out to God, "Despise not this sacrifice, it is not the best thing I possess, that I know well, for what is an old man in comparison with the child of promise; but it is the best I am able to give Thee. Let Isaac never come to know this, that he may console himself with his youth." He would have plunged the knife into his own breast. He would have been admired in the world, and his name would not have been forgotten; but it is one thing to be admired, and another to be the guiding star which saves the anguished.

But Abraham believed. He did not pray for himself, with the hope of moving the Lord—it was only when the righteous punishment was decreed upon Sodom and Gomorrha that Abraham came forward with his prayers.

We read in those holy books: "And God tempted Abraham, and said unto him, Abraham, Abraham, where art thou? And he said, Here am I." Thou to whom my speech is addressed, was such the case with thee? When afar off thou didst see the heavy dispensation of providence approaching thee, didst thou not say to the mountains, Fall on me, and to the hills, Cover me? Or if thou wast stronger, did not thy foot move slowly along the way, longing as it were for the old path? When a call was issued to thee, didst thou answer, or didst thou not answer perhaps in a low voice, whisperingly? Not so Abraham: joyfully, buoyantly, confidently, with a loud voice, he answered, "Here am I." We read further: "And Abraham rose early in the morning"—as though it were to a festival, so he hastened, and early in the morning he had come to the place spoken of, to Mount Moriah. He said nothing to Sarah, nothing to Eleazar. Indeed who could understand him? Had not the temptation by its very nature exacted of him an oath of silence? He cleft the wood, he bound Isaac, he lit the pyre, he drew the knife. My hearer, there was many a father who believed that with his son he lost everything that was dearest to him in the world, that he was deprived of every hope for the future, but yet there was none that was the child of promise in the sense that Isaac was for Abraham. There was many a father who lost his child; but then it was God, it was the unalterable, the unsearchable will of the Almighty, it was His hand took the child. Not so with Abraham. For him was reserved a harder trial, and Isaac's fate was laid along with the knife in Abraham's hand. And there he stood, the old man, with his only hope! But he did not doubt, he did not look anxiously to the right or to the left, he did not challenge heaven with his prayers. He knew that it was God the Almighty who was trying him, he knew that it was the hardest sacrifice that could be required of him; but he knew also that no sacrifice was too hard when God required it—and he drew the knife.

Who gave strength to Abraham's arm? Who held his right hand up so that it did not fall limp at his side? He who gazes at this becomes paralyzed. Who gave strength to Abraham's soul, so that his eyes did not grow dim, so that he saw neither Isaac nor the ram? He who gazes at this becomes blind.—And yet rare enough perhaps is the man who becomes paralyzed and blind, still more rare one who worthily recounts what happened. We all know it—it was only a trial.

If Abraham when he stood upon Mount Moriah had doubted, if he had gazed about him irresolutely, if before he drew the knife he had by chance discovered the ram, if God had permitted him to offer it instead of Isaac— then he would have betaken himself home, everything would have been the same, he has Sarah, he retained Isaac, and yet how changed! For his retreat would have been a flight, his salvation an accident, his reward dishonor, his future perhaps perdition. Then he would have borne witness neither to his faith nor to God's grace, but would have testified only how dreadful it is to march out to Mount Moriah. Then Abraham would not have been forgotten, nor would Mount Moriah, this mountain would then be mentioned, not like Ararat where the Ark landed, but would be spoken of as a consternation, because it was here that Abraham doubted.

Venerable Father Abraham! In marching home from Mount Moriah thou hadst no need of a panegyric which might console thee for thy loss; for thou didst gain all and didst retain Isaac. Was it not so? Never again did the Lord take him from thee, but thou didst sit at table joyfully with him in thy tent, as thou dost in the beyond to all eternity. Venerable Father Abraham! Thousands of years have run their course since those days, but thou hast need of no tardy lover to snatch the memorial of thee from the power of oblivion, for every language calls thee to remembrance—and yet thou dost reward thy lover more gloriously than does any other; hereafter thou dost make him blessed in thy bosom; here thou dost enthral his eyes and his heart by the marvel of thy deed. Venerable Father Abraham! Second Father of the human race! Thou who first wast sensible of and didst first bear witness to that prodigious passion which disdains the dreadful conflict with the rage of the elements and with the powers of creation in order to strive with God; thou

From ethics to faith (religious stage)
Knight of infinite resignation (their hero)

who first didst know that highest passion, the holy, pure and humble expression of the divine madness[7] which the pagans admired—forgive him who would speak in praise of thee, if he does not do it fittingly. He spoke humbly, as if it were the desire of his own heart, he spoke briefly, as it becomes him to do, but he will never forget that thou hadst need of a hundred years to obtain a son of old age against expectation, that thou didst have to draw the knife before retaining Isaac; he will never forget that in a hundred and thirty years thou didst not get further than to faith.

← not beyond faith

PROBLEMATA:
PRELIMINARY EXPECTORATION

to cast out of the breast heart

An old proverb fetched from the outward and visible world says: "Only the man that works gets the bread." Strangely enough this proverb does not aptly apply in that world to which it expressly belongs. For the outward world is subjected to the law of imperfection, and again and again the experience is repeated that he too who does not work gets the bread, and that he who sleeps gets it more abundantly than the man who works. In the outward world everything is made payable to the bearer, this world is in bondage to the law of indifference, and to him who has the ring, the spirit of the ring is obedient, whether he be Noureddin or Aladdin,[8] and he who has the world's treasure, has it, however he got it. It is different in the world of spirit. Here an eternal divine order prevails, here it does not rain both upon the just and upon the unjust, here the sun does not shine both upon the good and upon the evil, here it holds good that only he who works gets the bread, only he who was in anguish finds repose, only he who descends into the underworld rescues the beloved, only he who draws the knife gets Isaac. He who will not work does not get the bread but remains deluded, as the gods deluded Orpheus with an airy figure in place of the loved one, deluded him because he was effeminate, not courageous, because he was a cithara-player, not a man. Here it is of no use to have Abraham for one's father, nor to have seventeen ancestors—he who will not work must take note of what is written about the maidens of Israel,[9] for he gives birth to wind, but he who is willing to work gives birth to his own father.

must go thru fear + trembly for Gods grace

There is a knowledge which would presumptuously introduce into the world of spirit the same law of indifference under which the external world sighs. It counts it enough to think the great—other work is not necessary.

7. Cf. Plato's *Phaedrus*, 22 and 37.

8. In Oelenschläger's play *Aladdin* the hero is contrasted with Noureddin the representative of darkness.

9. Isaiah 26:18.

But therefore it doesn't get the bread, it perishes of hunger, while everything is transformed into gold. And what does it really know? There were many thousands of Greek contemporaries, and countless numbers in subsequent generations, who knew all the triumphs of Miltiades, but only one[10] was made sleepless by them. There were countless generations which knew by rote, word for word, the story of Abraham—how many were made sleepless by it?

Now the story of Abraham has the remarkable property that it is always glorious, however poorly one may understand it; yet here again the proverb applies, that all depends upon whether one is willing to labor and be heavy laden. But they will not labor, and yet they would understand the story. They exalt Abraham—but how? They express the whole thing in perfectly general terms: "The great thing was that he loved God so much that he was willing to sacrifice to Him the best." That is very true, but "the best" is an indefinite expression. In the course of thought, as the tongue wags on, Isaac and "the best" are confidently identified, and he who meditates can very well smoke his pipe during the meditation, and the auditor can very well stretch out his legs in comfort. In case that rich young man who Christ encountered on the road had sold all his goods and given to the poor, we should extol him, as we do all that is great, though without labor we would not understand him—and yet he would not have become an Abraham, in spite of the fact that he offered his best. What they leave out of Abraham's history is dread; for to money I have no ethical obligation, but to the son the father has the highest and most sacred obligation. Dread, however, is a perilous thing for effeminate natures, hence they forget it, and in spite of that they want to talk about Abraham. So they talk—in the course of the oration they use indifferently the two terms, Isaac and "the best." All goes famously. However, if it chanced that among the auditors there was one who suffered from insomnia—then the most dreadful, the profoundest tragic and comic misunderstanding lies very close. He went home, he would do as Abraham did, for the son is indeed "the best."

If the orator got to know of it, he perhaps went to him, he summoned all his clerical dignity, he shouted, "O abominable man, offscouring of society, what devil possessed thee to want to murder thy son?" And the parson, who had not been conscious of warmth or perspiration in preaching about Abraham, is astonished at himself, at the earnest wrath which he thundered down upon that poor man. He was delighted with himself, for he had never spoken with such verve and unction. He said to himself and to his wife, "I am an orator. What I lacked was the occasion. When I talked about Abraham on Sunday I did not feel moved in the least." In case the same orator had a little

10. Themistocles, as related in Plutarch's *Themistocles*, 3, 3.

Abraham's dread (contradiction between ethics + faith ...)

superabundance of reason which might be lost, I think he would have lost it if the sinner were to say calmly and with dignity, "That in fact is what you yourself preached on Sunday." How could the parson be able to get into his head such a consequence? And yet it was so, and the mistake was merely that he didn't know what he was saying. Would there were a poet who might resolve to prefer such situations, rather than the stuff and nonsense with which comedies and novels are filled! The comic and the tragic here touch one another at the absolute point of infinity. The parson's speech was perhaps in itself ludicrous enough, but it became infinitely ludicrous by its effect, and yet this consequence was quite natural. Or if the sinner, without raising any objection, were to be converted by the parson's severe lecture, if the zealous clergyman were to go joyfully home, rejoicing in the consciousness that he not only was effective in the pulpit, but above all by his irresistible power as a pastor of souls, who on Sunday roused the congregation to enthusiasm, and on Monday like a cherub with a flaming sword placed himself before the man who by his action wanted to put to shame the old proverb, that "things don't go on in the world as the parson preaches."*

If on the other hand the sinner was not convinced, his situation is pretty tragic. Presumably he would be executed or sent to the lunatic asylum, in short, he would have become unhappy in relation to so-called reality—in another sense I can well think that Abraham made him happy, for he that labors does not perish.

How is one to explain the contradiction illustrated by that orator? Is it because Abraham had a prescriptive right to be a great man, so that what he did is great, and when another does the same it is sin, a heinous sin? In that case I do not wish to participate in such thoughtless eulogy. If faith does not make it a holy act to be willing to murder one's son, then let the same condemnation be pronounced upon Abraham as upon every other man. If a man perhaps lacks courage to carry his thought through, and to say that Abraham was a murderer, then it is surely better to acquire this courage, rather than waste time upon undeserved eulogies. The ethical expression for what Abraham did is, that he would murder Isaac; the religious expression is, that he would sacrifice Isaac; but precisely in this contradiction consists the dread which can well make a man sleepless, and yet Abraham is not what he is without this dread. Or perhaps he did not do at all what is related, but something altogether different, which is accounted for by the circumstances of his times—then let us forget him, for it is not worth while to remember

---

*In the old days they said, "What a pity things don't go on in the world as the parson preaches"—perhaps the time is coming, especially with the help of philosophy, when they will say, "Fortunately things don't go on as the parson preaches; for after all there is some sense in life, but none at all in his preaching."

that past which cannot become a present. Or had perhaps that orator forgotten something which corresponds to the ethical forgetfulness of the fact that Isaac was the son? For when faith is eliminated by becoming null or nothing, then there only remains the crude fact that Abraham wanted to murder Isaac—which is easy enough for anyone to imitate who has not faith, the faith, that is to say, which makes it hard for him.

For my part I do not lack the courage to think a thought whole. Hitherto there has been no thought I have been afraid of; if I should run across such a thought, I hope that I have at least the sincerity to say, "I am afraid of this thought, it stirs up something else in me, and therefore I will not think it. If in this I do wrong, the punishment will not fail to follow." If I had recognized that it was the verdict of truth that Abraham was a murderer, I do not know whether I would have been able to silence my pious veneration for him. However, if I had thought that, I presumably would have kept silent about it, for one should not initiate others into such thoughts. But Abraham is no dazzling illusion, he did not sleep into renown, it was not a whim of fate.

Can one then speak plainly about Abraham without incurring the danger that an individual might in bewilderment go ahead and do likewise? If I do not dare to speak freely, I will be completely silent about Abraham, above all I will not disparage him in such a way that precisely thereby he becomes a pitfall for the weak. For if one makes faith everything, that is, makes it what it is, then, according to my way of thinking, one may speak of it without danger in our age, which hardly extravagates in the matter of faith, and it is only by faith one attains likeness to Abraham, not by murder. If one makes love a transitory mood, a voluptuous emotion in a man, then one only lays pitfalls for the weak when one would talk about the exploits of love. Transient emotions every man surely has, but if as a consequence of such emotions one would do the terrible thing which love has sanctified as an immortal exploit, then all is lost, including the exploit and the bewildered doer of it.

So one surely can talk about Abraham, for the great can never do harm when it is apprehended in its greatness; it is like a two-edged sword which slays and saves. If it should fall to my lot to talk on the subject, I would begin by showing what a pious and God-fearing man Abraham was, worthy to be called God's elect. Only upon such a man is imposed such a test. But where is there such a man? Next I would describe how Abraham loved Isaac. To this end I would pray all good spirits to come to my aid, that my speech might be as glowing as paternal love is. I hope that I should be able to describe it in such a way that there would not be many a father in the realms and territories of the King who would dare to affirm that he loved his son in such a way. But if he does not love like Abraham, then every thought of

offering Isaac would be not a trial but a base temptation [*Anfechtung*]. On
this theme one could talk for several Sundays, one need be in no haste. The
consequence would be that, if one spoke rightly, some few of the fathers
would not require to hear more, but for the time being they would be joyful
if they really succeeded in loving their sons as Abraham loved. If there was
one who, after having heard about the greatness, but also about the dreadfulness of Abraham's deed, ventured to go forth upon that road, I would saddle
my horse and ride with him. At every stopping place till we came to Mount
Moriah I would explain to him that he still could turn back, could repent the
misunderstanding that he was called to be tried in such a conflict, that he
could confess his lack of courage, so that God Himself must take Isaac, if
He would have him. It is my conviction that such a man is not repudiated
but may become blessed like all the others. But in time he does not become
blessed. Would they not, even in the great ages of faith, have passed this
judgment upon such a man? I knew a person who on one occasion could
have saved my life if he had been magnanimous. He said, "I see well enough
what I could do, but I do not dare to. I am afraid that later I might lack
strength and that I should regret it." He was not magnanimous, but who for
this cause would not continue to love him?

Having spoken thus and moved the audience so that at least they had
sensed the dialectical conflict of faith and its gigantic passion, I would not
give rise to the error on the part of the audience that "he then has faith in
such a high degree that it is enough for us to hold on to his skirts." For I
would add, "I have no faith at all, I am by nature a shrewd pate, and every
such person always has great difficulty in making the movements of faith—
not that I attach, however, in and for itself, *any value to this difficulty which
through the overcoming of it brought the clever head further than the point which
the simplest and most ordinary man reaches more easily.*"

After all, in the poets love has its priests, and sometimes one hears a voice
which knows how to defend it; but of faith one hears never a word. Who
speaks in honor of this passion? Philosophy goes further. Theology sits
rouged at the window and courts its favor, offering to sell her charms to philosophy. It is supposed to be difficult to understand Hegel, but to understand Abraham is a trifle. To go beyond Hegel is a miracle, but to get beyond
Abraham is the easiest thing of all. I for my part have devoted a good deal of
time to the understanding of the Hegelian philosophy, I believe also that I
understand it tolerably well, but when in spite of the trouble I have taken
there are certain passages I cannot understand, I am foolhardy enough to
think that he himself has not been quite clear. All this I do easily and naturally, my head does not suffer from it. But on the other hand when I have to
think of Abraham, I am as though annihilated. I catch sight every moment
of that enormous paradox which is the substance of Abraham's life, every

moment I am repelled, and my thought in spite of all its passion cannot get a hairs-breadth further. I strain every muscle to get a view of it—that very instant I am paralyzed.

I am not unacquainted with what has been admired as great and noble in the world, my soul feels affinity with it, being convinced in all humility that it was in my cause the hero contended, and the instant I contemplate his deed I cry out to myself, *jam tua res agitur.*[11] I *think* myself *into* the hero, but into Abraham I cannot think myself; when I reach the height I fall down, for what I encounter there is the paradox. I do not however mean in any sense to say that faith is something lowly, but on the contrary that it is the highest thing, and that it is dishonest of philosophy to give something else instead of it and to make light of faith. Philosophy cannot and should not give faith, but it should understand itself and know what it has to offer and take nothing away, and least of all should fool people out of something as if it were nothing. I am not unacquainted with the perplexities and dangers of life, I do not fear them, and I encounter them buoyantly. I am not unacquainted with the dreadful, my memory is a faithful wife, and my imagination is (as I myself am not) a diligent little maiden who all day sits quietly at her work, and in the evening knows how to chat to me about it so prettily that I must look at it, though not always, I must say, is it landscapes, or flowers, or pastoral idyls she paints. I have seen the dreadful before my own eyes, I do not flee from it timorously, but I know very well that, although I advance to meet it, my courage is not the courage of faith, nor anything comparable to it. I am unable to make the movements of faith, I cannot shut my eyes and plunge confidently into the absurd, for me that is an impossibility . . . but I do not boast of it. I am convinced that God is love, this thought has for me a primitive lyrical validity. When it is present to me, I am unspeakably blissful, when it is absent, I long for it more vehemently than does the lover for his object; but I do not believe, this courage I lack. For me the love of God is, both in a direct and in an inverse sense, incommensurable with the whole of reality. I am not cowardly enough to whimper and complain, but neither am I deceitful enough to deny that faith is something much higher. I can well endure living in my way, I am joyful and content, but my joy is not that of faith, and in comparison with that it is unhappy. I do not trouble God with my petty sorrows, the particular does not trouble me, I gaze only at my love, and I keep its virginal flame pure and clear. Faith is convinced that God is concerned about the least things. I am content in this life with being married to the left hand, faith is humble enough to demand the right hand—for that this is humility I do not deny and shall never deny.

11. Quoted from Horace's *Letters,* I, 18, 84: "It's your affair when the neighbor's house is afire."

Abraham's movement of faith (dialectic) —→
losing the finite — regaining the
(reaching to the infinite) finite

But really is everyone in my generation capable of making the movements of faith, I wonder? Unless I am very much mistaken, this generation is rather inclined to be proud of making what they do not even believe I am capable of making, viz. incomplete movements. It is repugnant to me to do as so often is done, namely, to speak inhumanly about a great deed, as though some thousands of years were an immense distance; I would rather speak humanly about it, as though it had occurred yesterday, letting only the greatness be the distance, which either exalts or condemns. So if (*in the quality of a tragic hero,* for I can get no higher) I had been summoned to undertake such a royal progress to Mount Moriah, I know well what I would have done. I would not have been cowardly enough to stay at home, neither would I have laid down or sauntered along the way, nor have forgotten the knife, so that there might be a little delay—I am pretty well convinced that I would have been there on the stroke of the clock and would have had everything in order, perhaps I would have arrived too early in order to get through with it sooner. But I also know what else I would have done. The very instant I mounted the horse I would have said to myself, "Now all is lost. God requires Isaac, I sacrifice him, and with him my joy—yet God is love and continues to be that for me; for in the temporal world God and I cannot talk together, we have no language in common." Perhaps one or another in our age will be foolish enough, or envious enough of the great, to want to make himself and me believe that if I really had done this, I would have done even a greater deed than Abraham; for my prodigious resignation was far more ideal and poetic than Abraham's narrow-mindedness. And yet this is the greatest falsehood, for my prodigious resignation was the surrogate for faith, nor could I more than make the infinite movement, in order to find myself and again repose in myself. In that case I would not have loved Isaac as Abraham loved. That I was resolute in making the movement might prove my courage, humanly speaking; that I loved him with all my soul is the presumption apart from which the whole thing becomes a crime, but yet I did not love like Abraham, for in that case I would have held back even at the last minute, though not for this would I have arrived too late at Mount Moriah. Besides, by my behavior I would have spoiled the whole story; for if I had got Isaac back again, I would have spoiled the whole story; for if I had got Isaac back again, I would have been in embarrassment. What Abraham found easiest, I would have found hard, namely to be joyful again with Isaac; for he who with all the infinity of his soul, *propio motu et propiis auspiciis* [by his own power and on his own responsibility], has performed the infinite movement [of resignation] and cannot do more, only retains Isaac with pain.

But what did Abraham do? He arrived neither too soon nor too late. He mounted the ass, he rode slowly along the way. All that time he believed—he believed that God would not require Isaac of him, whereas he was willing nevertheless to sacrifice him if it was required. He believed by virtue of the

Dialectic of the absurd in faith

absurd; for there could be no question of human calculation, and it was indeed the absurd that God who required it of him should the next instant recall the requirement. He climbed the mountain, even at the instant when the knife glittered he believed . . . that God would not require Isaac. He was indeed astonished at the outcome, but by a double-movement he had reached his first position, and therefore he received Isaac more gladly than the first time. Let us go further. We let Isaac be really sacrificed. Abraham believed. He did not believe that some day he would be blessed in the beyond, but that he would be happy here in the world. God could give him a new Isaac, could recall to life him who had been sacrificed. He believed by virtue of the absurd; for all human reckoning had long since ceased to function. That sorrow can derange a man's mind, that we see, and it is sad enough. That there is such a thing as strength of will which is able to haul up so exceedingly close to the wind that it saves a man's reason, even though he remains a little queer, that too one sees. I have no intention of disparaging this; but to be able to lose one's reason, and therefore the whole of finiteness of which reason is the broker, and then by virtue of the absurd to gain precisely the same finiteness—that appalls my soul, but I do not for this cause say that it is something lowly, since on the contrary it is the only prodigy. Generally people are of the opinion that what faith produces is not a work of art, that it is coarse and common work, only for the more clumsy natures; but in fact this is far from the truth. The dialectic of faith is the finest and most remarkable of all; it possesses an elevation, of which indeed I can form a conception, but nothing more. I am able to make from the springboard the great leap whereby I pass into infinity, my back is like that of a tight-rope dancer, having been twisted in my childhood,[12] hence I find this easy; with a one-two-three! I can walk about existence on my head; but the next thing I cannot do, for I cannot perform the miraculous, but can only be astonished by it. Yes, if Abraham the instant he swung his leg over the ass's back had said to himself, "Now, since Isaac is lost, I might just as well sacrifice him here at home, rather than ride the long way to Moriah"— then I should have no need of Abraham, whereas now I bow seven times before his name and seventy times before his deed. For this indeed he did not do, as I can prove by the fact that he was glad at receiving Isaac, heartily glad, that he needed no preparation, no time to concentrate upon the finite and its joy. If this had not been the case with Abraham, then perhaps he might have loved God but not believed; for he who loves God without faith reflects upon himself, he who loves God believingly reflects upon God.

Upon this pinnacle stands Abraham. The last stage he loses sight of is the infinite resignation. He really goes further, and reaches faith; for all these

12. S. K. attributed his spinal curvature to a fall from a tree when he was a child.

caricatures of faith, the miserable lukewarm indolence which thinks, "There surely is no instant need, it is not worth while sorrowing before the time," the pitiful hope which says, "One cannot know what is going to happen . . . it might possibly be after all"—these caricatures of faith are part and parcel of life's wretchedness, and the infinite resignation has already consigned them to infinite contempt.

Abraham I cannot understand, in a certain sense there is nothing I can learn from him but astonishment. If people fancy that by considering the outcome of this story they might let themselves be moved to believe, they deceive themselves and want to swindle God out of the first movement of faith, the infinite resignation. They would suck worldly wisdom out of the paradox. Perhaps one or another may succeed in that, for our age is not willing to stop with faith, with its miracle of turning water into wine, it goes further, it turns wine into water.

Would it not be better to stop with faith, and is it not revolting that everybody wants to go further? When in our age (as indeed is proclaimed in various ways) they will not stop with love, where then are they going? To earthy wisdom, to petty calculation, to paltriness and wretchedness, to everything which can make man's divine origin doubtful. Would it not be better that they should stand still at faith, and that he who stands should take heed lest he fall? For the movements of faith must constantly be made by virtue of the absurd, yet in such a way, be it observed, that one does not lose the finite but gains it every inch. For my part I can well describe the movements of faith, but I cannot make them. When one would learn to make the motions of swimming one can let oneself be hung by a swimming-belt from the ceiling and go through the motions (describe them, so to speak, as we speak of describing a circle), but one is not swimming. In that way I can describe the movements of faith, but when I am thrown into the water, I swim, it is true (for I don't belong to the beach-waders), but I make other movements, I make the movements of infinity, whereas faith does the opposite: after having made the movements of infinity, it makes those of finiteness. Hail to him who can make those movements, he performs the marvellous, and I shall never grow tired of admiring him, whether he be Abraham or a slave in Abraham's house; whether he be a professor of philosophy or a servant-girl, I look only at the movements. But at them I do look, and do not let myself be fooled, either by myself or by any other man. The knights of the infinite resignation are easily recognized: their gait is gliding and assured. Those on the other hand who carry the jewel of faith are likely to be delusive, because their outward appearance bears a striking resemblance to that which both the infinite resignation and faith profoundly despise . . . to Philistinism. *Crass ind. guided by material rather than spiritual value*

I candidly admit that in my practice I have not found any reliable example of the knight of faith, though I would not therefore deny that every second man may be such an example. I have been trying, however, for several years to get on the track of this, and all in vain. People commonly travel around the world to see rivers and mountains, new stars, birds of rare plumage, queerly deformed fishes, ridiculous breeds of men—they abandon themselves to the bestial stupor which gapes at existence, and they think they have seen something. This does not interest me. But if I knew where there was such a knight of faith, I would make a pilgrimage to him on foot, for this prodigy interests me absolutely. I would not let go of him for an instant, every moment I would watch to see how he managed to make the movements, I would regard myself as secured for life, and would divide my time between looking at him and practising the exercises myself, and thus would spend all my time admiring him. As was said, I have not found any such person, but I can well think him. Here he is. Acquaintance made, I am introduced to him. The moment I set eyes on him I instantly push him from me, I myself leap backwards, I clasp my hands and say half aloud, "Good Lord, is this the man? Is it really he? Why, he looks like a tax-collector!" However, it is the man after all. I draw closer to him, watching his least movements to see whether there might not be visible a little heterogeneous fractional telegraphic message from the infinite, a glance, a look, a gesture, a note of sadness, a smile, which betrayed the infinite in its heterogeneity with the finite. No! I examine his figure from tip to toe to see if there might not be a cranny through which the infinite was peeping. No! He is solid through and through. His tread? It is vigorous, belonging entirely to finiteness; no smartly dressed townsman who walks out to Fresberg on a Sunday afternoon treads the ground more firmly, he belongs entirely to the world, no Philistine more so. One can discover nothing of that aloof and superior nature whereby one recognizes the knight of the infinite. He takes delight in everything, and whenever one sees him taking part in a particular pleasure, he does it with the persistence which is the mark of the earthly man whose soul is absorbed in such things. He tends to his work. So when one looks at him one might suppose that he was a clerk who had lost his soul in an intricate system of book-keeping, so precise is he. He takes a holiday on Sunday. He goes to church. No heavenly glance or any other token of the incommensurable betrays him; if one did not know him, it would be impossible to distinguish him from the rest of the congregation, for his healthy and vigorous hymn-singing proves at the most that he has a good chest. In the afternoon he walks to the forest. He takes delight in everything he sees, in the human swarm, in the new omnibuses, in the water of the Sound; when one meets him on the Beach Road one might suppose he was a shopkeeper taking his fling, that's just the way he disports himself, for he is not a poet, and I have sought in vain to detect in him the poetic incommensurability. Toward eve-

Faith: The infinite in the finite

ning he walks home, his gait is as indefatigable as that of the postman. On his way he reflects that his wife has surely a special little warm dish prepared for him, e.g. a calf's head roasted, garnished with vegetables. If he were to meet a man like-minded, he could continue as far as East Gate to discourse with him about that dish, with a passion befitting a hotel chef. As it happens, he hasn't four pence to his name, and yet he fully and firmly believes that his wife has that dainty dish for him. If she had it, it would then be an invidious sight for superior people and an inspiring one for the plain man, to see him eat; for his appetite is greater than Esau's. His wife hasn't it—strangely enough, it is quite the same to him. On the way he comes past a building site and runs across another man. They talk together for a moment. In the twinkling of an eye he erects a new building, he has at his disposition all the powers necessary for it. The stranger leaves him with the thought that he certainly was a capitalist, while my admired knight thinks, "Yes, if the money were needed, I dare say I could get it." He lounges at an open window and looks out on the square on which he lives; he is interested in everything that goes on, in a rat which slips under the curb, in the children's play, and this with the nonchalance of a girl of sixteen. And yet he is no genius, for in vain I have sought in him the incommensurability of genius. In the evening he smokes his pipe; to look at him one would swear that it was the grocer over the way vegetating in the twilight. He lives as carefree as a ne'er-do-well, and yet he buys up the acceptable time at the dearest price, for he does not do the least thing except by virtue of the absurd. And yet, and yet—actually I could become furious over it, for envy if for no other reason—this man has made and every instant is making the movements of infinity. With infinite resignation he has drained the cup of life's profound sadness, he knows the bliss of the infinite, he senses the pain of renouncing everything, the dearest things he possesses in the world, and yet finiteness tastes to him just as good as to one who never knew anything higher, for his continuance in the finite did not bear a trace of the cowed and fearful spirit produced by the process of training; and yet he has this sense of security in enjoying it, as though the finite life were the surest thing of all. And yet, and yet the whole earthly form he exhibits is a new creation by virtue of the absurd. He resigned everything infinitely, and then he grasped everything again by virtue of the absurd. He constantly makes the movements of infinity, but he does this with such correctness and assurance that he constantly gets the finite out of it, and there is not a second when one has a notion of anything else. It is supposed to be the most difficult task for a dancer to leap into a definite posture in such a way that there is not a second when he is grasping after the posture, but by the leap itself he stands fixed in that posture. Perhaps no dancer can do it—that is what this knight does. Most people live dejectedly in worldly sorrow and joy; they are the ones who

sit along the wall and do not join in the dance. The knights of infinity are
dancers and possess elevation. They make the movements upward, and fall
down again; and this too is no mean pastime, nor ungraceful to behold. But
whenever they fall down they are not able at once to assume the posture,
they vacillate an instant, and this vacillation shows that after all they are
strangers in the world. This is more or less strikingly evident in proportion
to the art they possess, but even the most artistic knights cannot altogether
conceal this vacillation. One need not look at them when they are up in the
air, but only the instant they touch or have touched the ground—then one
recognizes them. But to be able to fall down in such a way that the same
second it looks as if one were standing and walking, to transform the leap of
life into a walk, absolutely to express the sublime in the pedestrian—that
only the knight of faith can do—and this is the one and only prodigy.

But since the prodigy is so likely to be delusive, I will describe the movements in a definite instance which will serve to illustrate their relation to reality, for upon this everything turns. A young swain falls in love with a princess, and the whole content of his life consists in this love, and yet the
situation is such that it is impossible for it to be realized, impossible for it to
be translated from ideality into reality.* The slaves of paltriness, the frogs in
life's swamp, will naturally cry out, "Such a love is foolishness. The rich
brewer's widow is a match fully as good and respectable." Let them croak in
the swamp undisturbed. It is not so with the knight of infinite resignation,
he does not give up his love, not for all the glory of the world. He is no fool.
First he makes sure that this really is the content of his life, and his soul is
too healthy and too proud to squander the least thing upon an inebriation.
He is not cowardly, he is not afraid of letting love creep into his most secret,
his most hidden thoughts, to let it twine in innumerable coils about every
ligament of his consciousness—if the love becomes an unhappy love, he will
never be able to tear himself loose from it. He feels a blissful rapture in letting love tingle through every nerve, and yet his soul is as solemn as that of
the man who has drained the poisoned goblet and feels how the juice perme-
ates every drop of blood—for this instant is life and death. So when he has
thus sucked into himself the whole of love and absorbed himself in it, he
does not lack courage to make trial of everything and to venture everything.
He surveys the situation of his life, he convokes the swift thoughts, which

---

*Of course any other instance whatsoever in which the individual finds that for him
the whole reality of actual existence is concentrated, may, when it is seen to be unre-
alizable, be an occasion for the movement of resignation. However, I have chosen a
love experience to make the movement visible, because this interest is doubtless
easier to understand, and so relieves me from the necessity of making preliminary
observations which in a deeper sense could be of interest only to a few.

like tame doves obey his every bidding, he waves his wand over them, and they dart off in all directions. But when they all return, all as messengers of sorrow, and declare to him that it is an impossibility, then he becomes quiet, he dismisses them, he remains alone, and then he performs the movements. If what I am saying is to have any significance, it is requisite that the movement come about normally.* So for the first thing, the knight will have power to concentrate the whole content of life and the whole significance of reality in one single wish. If a man lacks this concentration, this intensity, if his soul from the beginning is dispersed in the multifarious, he never comes to the point of making the movement, he will deal shrewdly in life like the capitalists who invest their money in all sorts of securities, so as to gain on the one what they lose on the other—in short, he is not a knight. In the next place the knight will have the power to concentrate the whole result of the operations of thought in one act of consciousness. If he lacks this intensity, if his soul from the beginning is dispersed in the multifarious, he will never get time to make the movements, he will be constantly running errands in life, never enter into eternity, for even at the instant when he is closest to it he will suddenly discover that he has forgotten something for which he must go back. He will think that to enter eternity is possible the next instant, and that also is perfectly true, but by such considerations one never reaches the point of making the movements, but by their aid one sinks deeper and deeper into the mire.

So the knight makes the movement—but what movement? Will he forget the whole thing? (For in this too there is indeed a kind of concentration.) No! For the knight does not contradict himself, and it is a contradiction to forget the whole content of one's life and yet remain the same man. To become another man he feels no inclination, nor does he by any means regard this as greatness. Only the lower natures forget themselves and become

---

*To this end passion is necessary. Every movement of infinity comes about by passion, and no reflection can bring a movement about. This is the continual leap in existence which explains the movement, whereas mediation is a chimera which according to Hegel is supposed to explain everything, and at the same time this is the only thing he has never tried to explain. Even to make the well-known Socratic distinction between what one understands and what one does not understand, passion is required, and of course even more to make the characteristic Socratic movement, the movement, namely, of ignorance. What our age lacks, however, is not reflection but passion. Hence in a sense our age is too tenacious of life to die, for dying is one of the most remarkable leaps, and a little verse of a poet has always attracted me much, because, after having expressed prettily and simply in five or six preceding lines his wish for good things in life, he concludes thus:

Ein seliger Sprung in die Ewigkeit ["A blissful leap into eternity."]

something new. Thus the butterfly has entirely forgotten that it was a cater-
pillar, perhaps it may in turn so entirely forget it was a butterfly that it becomes a fish. The deeper natures never forget themselves and never become
anything else than what they were. So the knight remembers everything,
but precisely this remembrance is pain, and yet by the infinite resignation he
is reconciled with existence. Love for that princess became for him the expression for an eternal love, assumed a religious character, was transfigured
into a love for the Eternal Being, which did to be sure deny him the fulfillment of his love, yet reconciled him again by the eternal consciousness of its
validity in the form of eternity, which no reality can take from him. Fools
and young men prate about everything being possible for a man. That, however, is a great error. Spiritually speaking, everything is possible, but in the
world of the finite there is much which is not possible. This impossible,
however, the knight makes possible by expressing it spiritually, but he expresses it spiritually by waiving his claim to it. The wish which would carry
him out into reality, but was wrecked upon the impossibility, is now bent
inward, but it is not therefore lost, neither is it forgotten. At one moment it
is the obscure emotion of the wish within him which awakens recollections,
at another moment he awakens them himself; for he is too proud to be willing that what was the whole content of his life should be the thing of a fleeting moment. He keeps this love young, and along with him it increases in
years and in beauty. On the other hand, he has no need of the intervention
of the finite for the further growth of his love. From the instant he made the
movement the princess is lost to him. He has no need of those erotic tin-
glings in the nerves at the sight of the beloved etc., nor does he need to be
constantly taking leave of her in a finite sense, because he recollects her in
an eternal sense, and he knows very well that the lovers who are so bent
upon seeing "her" yet once again, to say farefell for the last time, are right in
being bent upon it, are right in thinking that it is the last time, for they forget one another the soonest. He has comprehended the deep secret that also
in loving another person one must be sufficient unto oneself. He no longer
takes a finite interest in what the princess is doing, and precisely this is proof
that he has made the movement infinitely. Here one may have an opportunity to see whether the movement on the part of a particular person is
true or fictitious. There was one who also believed that he had made the
movement; but lo, time passed, the princess did something else, she
married—a prince, let us say—then his soul lost the elasticity of resignation.
Thereby he knew that he had not made the movement rightly; for he who
has made the act of resignation infinitely is sufficient unto himself. The
knight does not annul his resignation, he preserves his love just as young as
it was in its first moment, he never lets it go from him, precisely because he
makes the movements infinitely. What the princess does, cannot disturb

him, it is only the lower natures which find in other people the law for their actions, which find the premises for their actions outside themselves. If on the other hand the princess is like-minded, the beautiful consequence will be apparent. She will introduce herself into that order of knighthood into which one is not received by balloting, but of which everyone is a member who has courage to introduce himself, that order of knighthood which proves its immortality by the fact that it makes no distinction between man and woman. The two will preserve their love young and sound, she also will have triumphed over her pains, even though she does not, as it is said in the ballad, "lie every night beside her lord." These two will to all eternity remain in agreement with one another, with a well-timed *harmonia praestabilita*,[13] so that if ever the moment were to come, the moment which does not, however, concern them finitely (for then they would be growing older), if ever the moment were to come which offered to give love its expression in time, then they will be capable of beginning precisely at the point where they would have begun if originally they had been united. He who understands this, be he man or woman, can never be deceived, for it is only the lower natures which imagine they were deceived. No girl who is not so proud really knows how to love; but if she is so proud, then the cunning and shrewdness of all the world cannot deceive her.

In the infinite resignation there is peace and rest; every man who wills it, who has not abased himself by scorning himself (which is still more dreadful than being proud), can train himself to make this movement which in its pain reconciles one with existence. Infinite resignation is that shirt we read about in the old fable. The thread is spun under tears, the cloth bleached with tears, the shirt sewn with tears; but then too it is a better protection than iron and steel. The imperfection in the fable is that a third party can manufacture this shirt. The secret in life is that everyone must sew it for himself, and the astonishing thing is that a man can sew it fully as well as a woman. In the infinite resignation there is peace and rest and comfort in sorrow—that is, if the movement is made normally. It would not be difficult for me, however, to write a whole book, were I to examine the various misunderstandings, the preposterous attitudes, the deceptive movements, which I have encountered in my brief practice. People believe very little in spirit, and yet making this movement depends upon spirit, it depends upon whether this is or is not a one-sided result of a *dira necessitas*, and if this is present, the more dubious it always is whether the movement is normal. If one means by this that the cold, unfruitful necessity must necessarily be present, one thereby affirms that no one can experience death before he

13. "The pre-established harmony" was a fundamental concept of Leibniz's philosophy.

actually dies, and that appears to me a crass materialism. However, in our time people concern themselves rather little about making pure movements. In case one who was about to learn to dance were to say, "For centuries now one generation after another has been learning positions, it is high time I drew some advantage out of this and began straightway with the French dances"—then people would laugh at him; but in the world of spirit they find this exceedingly plausible. What is education? I should suppose that education was the curriculum one had to run through in order to catch up with oneself, and he who will not pass through this curriculum is helped very little by the fact that he was born in the most enlightened age.

The infinite resignation is the last stage prior to faith, so that one who has not made this movement has not faith; for only in the infinite resignation do I become clear to myself with respect to my eternal validity, and only then can there be any question of grasping existence by virtue of faith.

Now we will let the knight of faith appear in the rôle just described. He makes exactly the same movements as the other knight, infinitely renounces claim to the love which is the content of his life, he is reconciled in pain; but then occurs the prodigy, he makes still another movement more wonderful than all, for he says, "I believe nevertheless that I shall get her, in virtue, that is, of the absurd, in virtue of the fact that with God all things are possible." The absurd is not one of the factors which can be discriminated within the proper compass of the understanding: it is not identical with the improbable, the unexpected, the unforeseen. At the moment when the knight made the act of resignation, he was convinced, humanly speaking, of the impossibility. This was the result reached by the understanding, and he had sufficient energy to think it. On the other hand, in an infinite sense it was possible, namely, by renouncing it; but this sort of possessing is at the same time a relinquishing, and yet there is no absurdity in this for the understanding, for the understanding continued to be in the right in affirming that in the world of the finite where it holds sway this was and remained an impossibility. This is quite as clear to the knight of faith, so the only thing that can save him is the absurd, and this he grasps by faith. So he recognizes the impossibility, and that very instant he believes the absurd; for, if without recognizing the impossibility with all the passion of his soul and with all his heart, he should wish to imagine that he has faith, he deceives himself, and his testimony has no bearing, since he has not even reached the infinite resignation.

Faith therefore is not an aesthetic emotion but something far higher, precisely because it has resignation as its presupposition; it is not an immediate instinct of the heart, but is the paradox of life and existence. So when in spite of all difficulties a young girl still remains convinced that her wish will surely be fulfilled, this conviction is not the assurance of faith, even if she was brought up by Christian parents, and for a whole year perhaps has been catechized by the parson. She is convinced in all her childish naïveté and innocence, this conviction also ennobles her nature and imparts to her a preternatural greatness, so that like a thaumaturge she is able to conjure the finite powers of existence and make the very stones weep, while on the other hand in her flurry she may just as well run to Herod as to Pilate and move the whole world by her tears. Her conviction is very lovable, and one can learn much from her, but one thing is not to be learned from her, one does not learn the movements, for her conviction does not dare in the pain of resignation to face the impossibility.

So I can perceive that it requires strength and energy and freedom of spirit to make the infinite movement of resignation, I can also perceive that it is feasible. But the next thing astonishes me, it makes my head swim, for after having made the movement of resignation, then by virtue of the absurd to get everything, to get the wish whole and uncurtailed—that is beyond human power, it is a prodigy. But this I can perceive, that the young girl's conviction is mere levity in comparison with the firmness faith displays notwithstanding it has perceived the impossibility. Whenever I essay to make this movement, I turn giddy, the very instant I am admiring it absolutely a prodigious dread grips my soul—for what is it to tempt God? And yet this movement is the movement of faith and remains such, even though philosophy, in order to confuse the concepts, would make us believe that it has faith, and even though theology would sell out faith at a bargain price.

For the act of resignation faith is not required, for what I gain by resignation is my eternal consciousness, and this is a purely philosophical movement which I dare say I am able to make if it is required, and which I can train myself to make, for whenever any finiteness would get the mastery over me, I starve myself until I can make the movement, for my eternal consciousness is my love to God, and for me this is higher than everything. For the act of resignation faith is not required, but it is needed when it is the case of acquiring the very least thing more than my eternal consciousness, for this is the paradoxical. The movements are frequently confounded, for it is said that one needs faith to renounce the claim to everything, yea, a stranger thing than this may be heard, when a man laments the loss of his faith, and when one looks at the scale to see where he is, one sees, strangely enough, that he has only reached the point where he should make the infinite movement of resignation. In resignation I make renunciation of everything, this movement I make by myself, and if I do not make it, it is because I am cowardly and effeminate and without enthusiasm and do not feel the significance of the lofty dignity which is assigned to every man, that of being his own censor, which is a far prouder title than that of Censor General to the whole Roman Republic. This movement I make by myself, and what I gain is myself in my eternal consciousness, in blissful agreement with my love for the Eternal Being. By faith I make renunciation of nothing, on the contrary, by faith I acquire everything, precisely in the sense in which it is said that he who has faith like a grain of mustard can remove mountains. A purely human courage is required to renounce the whole of the temporal to gain the eternal; but this I gain, and to all eternity I cannot renounce it—that is a self-contradiction. But a paradoxical and humble courage is required to grasp the whole of the temporal by virtue of the absurd, and this is the courage of faith. By faith Abraham did not renounce his claim upon Isaac, but by faith he got Isaac. By virtue of resignation that rich young man should have given away everything, but then when he had done that, the knight of faith should have said to him, "By virtue of the absurd thou shalt get every penny back again. Canst thou believe that?" And this speech ought by no means to have been indifferent to the aforesaid rich man, for in case he gave away his goods because he was tired of them, his resignation was not much to boast of.

It is about the temporal, the finite, everything turns in this case. I am able by my own strength to renounce everything, and then to find peace and repose in pain. I can stand everything—even though that horrible demon, more dreadful than death, the king of terrors, even though madness were to hold up before my eyes the motley of the fool, and I understood by its look that it was I who must put it on, I still am able to save my soul, if only it is more to me than my earthly happiness that my love to God should triumph in me. A man may still be able at the last instant to concentrate his whole soul in a single glance toward that heaven from which cometh every good gift, and his glance will be intelligible to himself and also to Him whom it seeks as a sign that he nevertheless remained true to his love. Then he will calmly put on the motley garb. He whose soul has not this romantic enthusiasm has sold his soul, whether he got a kingdom for it or a paltry piece of silver. But by my own strength I am not able to get the least of the things which belong to finiteness, for I am constantly using my strength to renounce everything. By my own strength I am able to give up the princess, and I shall not become a grumbler, but shall find joy and repose in my pain; but by my own strength I am not able to get her again, for I am employing all my strength to be resigned. But by faith, says that marvellous knight, by faith I shall get her in virtue of the absurd.

So this movement I am unable to make. As soon as I would begin to make it everything turns around dizzily, and I flee back to the pain of resignation. I can swim in existence, but for this mystical soaring I am too heavy. To exist in such a way that my opposition to existence is expressed as the most beautiful and assured harmony with it, is something I cannot do. And yet it must be glorious to get the princess, that is what I say every instant, and the knight of resignation who does not say it is a deceiver, he has not had only one wish, and he has not kept the wish young by his pain. Perhaps there was one who thought it fitting enough that the wish was no longer vivid, that the barb of pain was dulled, but such a man is no knight. A free-born soul who caught himself entertaining such thoughts would despise himself and begin over again, above all he would not permit his soul to be deceived by itself. And yet it must be glorious to get the princess, and yet the knight of faith is the only happy one, the heir apparent to the finite, whereas the knight of resignation is a stranger and a foreigner. Thus to get the princess, to live with her joyfully and happily day in and day out (for it is also conceivable that the knight of resignation might get the princess, but that his soul had discerned the impossibility of their future happiness), thus to live joyfully and happily every instant by virtue of the absurd, every instant to see the sword hanging over the head of the beloved, and yet not to find repose in the pain of resignation, but joy by virtue of the absurd—this is marvellous. He who does it is great, the only great man. The thought of it stirs my soul, which never was niggardly in the admiration of greatness.

In case then everyone in my generation who will not stop at faith is really a man who has comprehended life's horror, who has understood what Daub[14] means when he says that a soldier who stands alone at his post with a loaded gun in a stormy night beside a powder-magazine . . . will get strange thoughts into his head—in case then everyone who will not stop at faith is a man who had strength of soul to comprehend that the wish was an impossibility, and thereupon gave himself time to remain alone with this thought, in case everyone who will not stop at faith is a man who is reconciled in pain and is reconciled to pain, in case everyone who will not stop at faith is a man who in the next place (and if he has not done all the foregoing, there is no need of his troubling himself about faith)—in the next place did the marvellous thing, grasped the whole of existence by virtue of the absurd . . . then what I write is the highest eulogy of my contemporaries by one of the lowliest among them, who was able only to make the movement of resignation. But why will they not stop at faith, why does one sometimes hear that people are ashamed to acknowledge that they have faith? This I cannot comprehend. If ever I contrive to be able to make this movement, I shall in the future ride in a coach and four.

If it is really true that all the Philistinism I behold in life (which I do not permit my word but my actions to condemn) is not what it seems to be—is it the miracle? That is conceivable, for the hero of faith had in fact a striking resemblance to it—for that hero of faith was not so much an ironist or a

14. See Rosenkranz, *Erinnerungen an Karl Daub* (Berlin 1837), p. 2. Cf. *Journal* IV A 92.

humorist, but something far higher. Much is said in our age about irony and humor, especially by people who have never been capable of engaging in the practice of these arts, but who nevertheless know how to explain everything. I am not entirely unacquainted with these two passions, I know a little more about them than what is to be found in German and German-Danish compendiums. I know therefore that these two passions are essentially different from the passion of faith. Irony and humor reflect also upon themselves, and therefore belong within the sphere of the infinite resignation, their elasticity is due to the fact that the individual is incommensurable with reality.

The last movement, the paradoxical movement of faith, I cannot make (be that a duty or whatever it may be), in spite of the fact that I would do it more than gladly. Whether a man has a right to make this affirmation, must be left to him, it is a question between him and the Eternal Being who is the object of faith whether in this respect he can hit upon an amicable compromise. What every man can do is to make the movement of infinite resignation, and I for my part would not hesitate to pronounce everyone cowardly who wishes to make himself believe he can not do it. With faith it is a different matter. But what every man has not a right to do, is to make others believe that faith is something lowly, or that it is an easy thing, whereas it is the greatest and the hardest.

People construe the story of Abraham in another way. They extol God's grace in bestowing Isaac upon him again—the whole thing was only a trial. A trial—that word may say much or little, and yet the whole thing is over as quickly as it is said. One mounts a winged horse, the same instant one is at Mount Moriah, the same instant one sees the ram; one forgets that Abraham rode only upon an ass, which walks slowly along the road, that he had a journey of three days, that he needed some time to cleave the wood, to bind Isaac, and to sharpen the knife.

And yet they extol Abraham. He who is to deliver the discourse can very well sleep till a quarter of an hour before he has to preach, the auditor can well take a nap during the discourse, for all goes smoothly, without the least trouble from any quarter. If there was a man present who suffered from insomnia, perhaps he then went home and sat in a corner and thought: "It's an affair of a moment, this whole thing; if only you wait a minute, you see the ram, and the trial is over." If the orator were to encounter him in this condition, he would, I think, confront him with all his dignity and say, "Wretched man, that thou couldst let thy soul sink into such foolishness! No miracle occurs. The whole of life is a trial." In proportion as the orator proceeds with his outpouring, he would get more and more excited, would become more and more delighted with himself, and whereas he had noticed no congestion of the blood while he talked about Abraham, he now felt how the vein swelled in his forehead. Perhaps he would have lost his breath as well as his tongue if the sinner had answered calmly and with dignity, "But it was about this you preached last Sunday."

Let us then either consign Abraham to oblivion, or let us learn to be dismayed by the tremendous paradox which constitutes the significance of Abraham's life, that we may understand that our age, like every age, can be joyful if it has faith. In case Abraham is not a nullity, a phantom, a show one employs for a pastime, then the fault can never consist in the fact that the sinner wants to do likewise, but the point is to see how great a thing it was that Abraham did, in order that man may judge for himself whether he has the call and the courage to be subjected to such a test. The comic contradiction in the behavior of the orator is that he reduced Abraham to an insignificance, and yet would admonish the other to behave in the same way.

Should not one dare then to talk about Abraham? I think one should. If I were to talk about him, I would first depict the pain of his trial. To that end I would like a leech suck all the dread and distress and torture out of a father's sufferings, so that I might describe what Abraham suffered, whereas all the while he nevertheless believed. I would remind the audience that the journey lasted three days and a good part of the fourth, yea, that these three and a half days were infinitely longer than the few thousand years which separate me from Abraham. Then I would remind them that, in my opinion, every man dare still turn around ere he begins such an undertaking, and every instant he can repentantly turn back. If one does this, I fear no danger, nor am I afraid of awakening in people an inclination to be tried like Abraham. But if one would dispose of a cheap edition of Abraham, and yet admonish everyone to do likewise, then it is ludicrous.

It is now my intention to draw out from the story of Abraham the dialectical consequences inherent in it, expressing them in the form of *problemata*, in order to see what a tremendous paradox faith is, a paradox which is capable of transforming a murder into a holy act well-pleasing to God, a paradox which gives Isaac back to Abraham, which no thought can master, because faith begins precisely there where thinking leaves off.

PROBLEM I

Is There Such a Thing as a Teleological Suspension of the Ethical?

The ethical as such is the universal, and as the universal it applies to everyone, which may be expressed from another point of view by saying that it applies every instant. It reposes immanently in itself, it has nothing without itself which is its *telos*,[15] but is itself *telos* for everything outside it, and when

15. A Greek word meaning "end" or "goal."

Individual
In Sub...
Universal

this has been incorporated by the ethical it can go no further. Conceived immediately as physical and psychical, the particular individual is the individual who has his *telos* in the universal, and his ethical task is to express himself constantly in it, to abolish his particularity in order to become the universal. As soon as the individual would assert himself in his particularity over against the universal he sins, and only by recognizing this can he again reconcile himself with the universal. Whenever the individual after he has entered the universal feels an impulse to assert himself as the particular, he

ethical
task
subjection
to
Universal

is in temptation (*Anfechtung*), and he can labor himself out of this only by penitently abandoning himself as the particular in the universal. If this be the highest thing that can be said of man and of his existence, then the ethical has the same character as man's eternal blessedness, which to all eternity and at every instant is his *telos,* since it would be a contradiction to say that this might be abandoned (i.e. teleologically suspended), inasmuch as this is no sooner suspended than it is forfeited, whereas in other cases what is suspended is not forfeited but is preserved precisely in that higher thing which is its *telos.*

If such be the case, then Hegel is right when in his chapter on "The Good and the Conscience,"[16] he characterizes man merely as the particular and regards this character as "a moral form of evil" which is to be annulled in the teleology of the moral, so that the individual who remains in this stage is either sinning or subjected to temptation (*Anfechtung*). On the other hand, Hegel is wrong in talking of faith, wrong in not protesting loudly and

Paradox

clearly against the fact that Abraham enjoys honor and glory as the father of faith, whereas he ought to be prosecuted and convicted of murder.

faith
ind. superor

For faith is this paradox, that the particular is higher than the universal— yet in such a way, be it observed, that the movement repeats itself, and that consequently the individual, after having been in the universal, now as the particular isolates himself as higher than the universal. If this be not faith, then Abraham is lost, then faith has never existed in the world . . . because it has always existed. For if the ethical (i.e. the moral) is the highest thing, and if nothing incommensurable remains in man in any other way but as the evil (i.e. the particular which has to be expressed in the universal), then one needs no other categories besides those which the Greeks possessed or which by consistent thinking can be derived from them. This fact Hegel ought not to have concealed, for after all he was acquainted with Greek thought.

One not infrequently hears it said by men who for lack of losing themselves in studies are absorbed in phrases, that a light shines upon the Christian world whereas a darkness broods over paganism. This utterance has al-

16. Cf. *Philosophie des Rechts,* [*Philosophy of Right*] 2nd ed. (1840) §§129–41 and Table of Contents p. xix.

ways seemed strange to me, inasmuch as every profound thinker and every serious artist is even in our day rejuvenated by the eternal youth of the Greek race. Such an utterance may be explained by the consideration that people do not know what they ought to say but only that they must say something. It is quite right for one to say that paganism did not possess faith, but if with this one is to have said something, one must be a little clearer about what one understands by faith, since otherwise one falls back into such phrases. To explain the whole of existence and faith along with it, without having a conception of what faith is, is easy, and that man does not make the poorest calculation in life who reckons upon admiration when he possesses such an explanation; for, as Boileau says, "*un sot trouve toujours un plus sot qui l'admire.*" ["a fool always finds a bigger fool to admire him."]

Faith is precisely this paradox, that the individual as the particular is higher than the universal, is justified over against it, is not subordinate but superior—yet in such a way, be it observed, that it is the particular individual who, after he has been subordinated as the particular to the universal, now through the universal becomes the individual who as the particular is superior to the universal, for the fact that the individual as the particular stands in an absolute relation to the absolute. This position cannot be mediated, for all mediation comes about precisely by virtue of the universal; it is and remains to all eternity a paradox, inaccessible to thought. And yet faith is this paradox—or else (these are the logical deductions which I would beg the reader to have *in mente* at every point, though it would be too prolix for me to reiterate them on every occasion)—or else there never has been faith . . . precisely because it always has been. In other words, Abraham is lost.

That for the particular individual this paradox may easily be mistaken for a temptation (*Anfechtung*) is indeed true, but one ought not for this reason to conceal it. That the whole constitution of many persons may be such that this paradox repels them is indeed true, but one ought not for this reason to make faith something different in order to be able to possess it, but ought rather to admit that one does not possess it, whereas those who possess faith should take care to set up certain criteria so that one might distinguish the paradox from a temptation (*Anfechtung*).

Now the story of Abraham contains such a teleological suspension of the ethical. There have not been lacking clever pates and profound investigators who have found analogies to it. Their wisdom is derived from the pretty proposition that at bottom everything is the same. If one will look a little more closely, I have not much doubt that in the whole world one will not find a single analogy (except a later instance which proves nothing), if it stands fast that Abraham is the representative of faith, and that faith is normally expressed in him whose life is not merely the most paradoxical that

absurd

no mediato

not tragic hero

ethical relation of duty to son

can be thought but so paradoxical that it cannot be thought at all. He acts by virtue of the absurd, for it is precisely absurd that he as the particular is higher than the universal. This paradox cannot be mediated; for as soon as he begins to do this he has to admit that he was in temptation (*Anfechtung*), and if such was the case, he never gets to the point of sacrificing Isaac, or, if he has sacrificed Isaac, he must turn back repentantly to the universal. By virtue of the absurd he gets Isaac again. Abraham is therefore at no instant a tragic hero but something quite different, either a murderer or a believer. The middle term which saves the tragic hero, Abraham has not. Hence it is that I can understand the tragic hero but cannot understand Abraham, though in a certain crazy sense I admire him more than all other men.

Abraham's relation to Isaac, ethically speaking, is quite simply expressed by saying that a father shall love his son more dearly than himself. Yet within its own compass the ethical has various gradations. Let us see whether in this story there is to be found any higher expression for the ethical such as would ethically explain his conduct, ethically justify him in suspending the ethical obligation toward his son, without in this search going beyond the teleology of the ethical. *no*

tragic hero

Agamenon + Menelaos appear Souls

When an undertaking in which a whole nation is concerned is hindered,[17] when such an enterprise is brought to a standstill by the disfavor of heaven, when the angry deity sends a calm which mocks all efforts, when the seer performs his heavy task and proclaims that the deity demands a young maiden as a sacrifice—then will the father heroically make the sacrifice. He will magnanimously conceal his pain, even though he might wish that he were "the lowly man who dares to weep,"[18] not the king who must act royally. And though solitary pain forces its way into his breast, he has only three confidants among the people, yet soon the whole nation will be cognizant of his pain, but also cognizant of his exploit, that for the welfare of the whole he was willing to sacrifice her, his daughter, the lovely young maiden. O charming bosom! O beautiful cheeks! O bright golden hair! (v.687). And the daughter will affect him by her tears, and the father will turn his face away, but the hero will raise the knife.—When the report of this reaches the ancestral home, then will the beautiful maidens of Greece blush with enthusi-

---

17. The Trojan war. When the Greek fleet was unable to set sail from Aulis because of an adverse wind the seer Calchas announced that King Agamemnon had offended Artemis and that the goddess demanded his daughter Iphigenia as a sacrifice of expiation.

18. See Euripides, *Iphigenia* in *Aulis*, v. 448 in Wilster's translation. Agamemnon says, "How lucky to be born in lowly station where one may be allowed to weep." The confidants mentioned below are Menelaus, Calchas and Ulysses. Cf. v. 107.

asm, and if the daughter was betrothed, her true love will not be angry but be proud of sharing in the father's deed, because the maiden belonged to him more feelingly than to the father.

When the intrepid judge[19] who saved Israel in the hour of need in one breath binds himself and God by the same vow, then heroically the young maiden's jubilation, the beloved daughter's joy, he will turn to sorrow, and with her all Israel will lament her maiden youth; but every free-born man will understand, and every stout-hearted woman will admire Jephtha, and every maiden in Israel will wish to act as did his daughter. For what good would it do if Jephtha were victorious by reason of his vow if he did not keep it? Would not the victory again be taken from the nation?

When a son is forgetful of his duty,[20] when the state entrusts the father with the sword of justice, when the laws require punishment at the hand of the father, then will the father heroically forget that the guilty one is his son, he will magnanimously conceal his pain, but there will not be a single one among the people, not even the son, who will not admire the father, and whenever the law of Rome is interpreted, it will be remembered that many interpreted it more learnedly, but none so gloriously as Brutus.

If, on the other hand, while a favorable wind bore the fleet on with swelling sails to its goal, Agamemnon had sent that messenger who fetched Iphigenia in order to be sacrificed; if Jephtha, without being bound by any vow which decided the fate of the nation, had said to his daughter, "Bewail now thy virginity for the space of two months, for I will sacrifice thee"; if Brutus had had a righteous son and yet would have ordered the lictors to execute him—who would have understood them? If these three men had replied to the query why they did it by saying, "It is a trial in which we are tested," would people have understood them better?

When Agamemnon, Jephtha, Brutus at the decisive moment heroically overcome their pain, have heroically lost the beloved and have merely to accomplish the outward sacrifice, then there never will be a noble soul in the world who will not shed tears of compassion for their pain and of admiration for their exploit. If, on the other hand, these three men at the decisive moment were to adjoin to their heroic conduct this little word, "But for all that it will not come to pass," who then would understand them? If as an explanation they added, "This we believe by virtue of the absurd," who would understand them better? For who would not easily understand that it was absurd, but who would understand that one could then believe it?

19. Jephtha. Judges 11:30–40.

20. The sons of Brutus, while their father was Consul, took part in a conspiracy to restore the king Rome had expelled, and Brutus ordered them to be put to death.

The difference between the tragic hero and Abraham is clearly evident. The tragic hero still remains within the ethical. He lets one expression of the ethical find its *telos* in a higher expression of the ethical; the ethical relation between father and son, or daughter and father, he reduces to a sentiment which has its dialectic in its relation to the idea of morality. Here there can be no question of a teleological suspension of the ethical itself.

With Abraham the situation was different. By his act he overstepped the ethical entirely and possessed a higher *telos* outside of it, in relation to which he suspended the former. For I should very much like to know how one would bring Abraham's act into relation with the universal, and whether it is possible to discover any connection whatever between what Abraham did and the universal . . . except the fact that he transgressed it. It was not for the sake of saving a people, not to maintain the idea of the state, that Abraham did this, and not in order to reconcile angry deities. If there could be a question of the deity being angry, he was angry only with Abraham, and Abraham's whole action stands in no relation to the universal, is a purely private undertaking. Therefore, whereas the tragic hero is great by reason of his moral virtue, Abraham is great by reason of a purely personal virtue. In Abraham's life there is no higher expression for the ethical than this, that the father shall love his son. Of the ethical in the sense of morality there can be no question in this instance. In so far as the universal was present, it was indeed cryptically present in Isaac, hidden as it were in Isaac's loins, and must therefore cry out with Isaac's mouth, "Do it not! Thou art bringing everything to naught."

Why then did Abraham do it? For God's sake, and (in complete identity with this) for his own sake. He did it for God's sake because God required this proof of his faith; for his own sake he did it in order that he might furnish the proof. The unity of these two points of view is perfectly expressed by the word which has always been used to characterize this situation: it is a trial, a temptation (*Fristelse*). A temptation—but what does that mean? What ordinarily tempts a man is that which would keep him from doing his duty, but in this case the temptation is itself the ethical . . . which would keep him from doing God's will. But what then is duty? Duty is precisely the expression for God's will.

Here is evident the necessity of a new category if one would understand Abraham. Such a relationship to the deity paganism did not know. The tragic hero does not enter into any private relationship with the deity, but for him the ethical is the divine, hence the paradox implied in his situation can be mediated in the universal.

Abraham cannot be mediated, and the same thing can be expressed also by saying that he cannot talk. So soon as I talk I express the universal, and if

I do not do so, no one can understand me. Therefore if Abraham would express himself in terms of the universal, he must say that his situation is a temptation (*Anfechtung*), for he has no higher expression for that universal which stands above the universal which he transgresses.

Therefore, though Abraham arouses my admiration, he at the same time appalls me. He who denies himself and sacrifices himself for duty gives up the finite in order to grasp the infinite, and that man is secure enough. The tragic hero gives up the certain for the still more certain, and the eye of the beholder rests upon him confidently. But he who gives up the universal in order to grasp something still higher which is not the universal—what is he doing? Is it possible that this can be anything else but a temptation (*Anfechtung*)? And if it be possible . . . but the individual was mistaken—what can save him? He suffers all the pain of the tragic hero, he brings to naught his joy in the world, he renounces everything . . . and perhaps at the same instant debars himself from the sublime joy which to him was so precious that he would purchase it at any price. Him the beholder cannot understand nor let his eye rest confidently upon him. Perhaps it is not possible to do what the believer proposes, since it is indeed unthinkable. Or if it could be done, but if the individual had misunderstood the deity—what can save him? The tragic hero has need of tears and claims them, and where is the envious eye which would be so barren that it could not weep with Agamemnon; but where is the man with a soul so bewildered that he would have the presumption to weep for Abraham? The tragic hero accomplishes his act at a definite instant in time, but in the course of time he does something not less significant, he visits the man whose soul is beset with sorrow, whose breast for stifled sobs cannot draw breath, whose thoughts pregnant with tears weigh heavily upon him, to him he makes his appearance, dissolves the sorcery of sorrow, loosens his corslet, coaxes forth his tears by the fact that in his sufferings the sufferer forgets his own. One cannot weep over Abraham. One approaches him with a *horror religiosus,* as Israel approached Mount Sinai.—If then the solitary man who ascends Mount Moriah, which with its peak rises heaven-high above the plain of Aulis, if he be not a somnambulist who walks securely above the abyss while he who is stationed at the foot of the mountain and is looking on trembles with fear and out of reverence and dread dare not even call to him—if this man is disordered in his mind, if he had made a mistake! Thanks and thanks again to him who proffers to the man whom the sorrows of life have assaulted and left naked—proffers to him the fig-leaf of the word with which he can cover his wretchedness. Thanks be to thee, great Shakespeare, who art able to express everything, absolutely everything, precisely as it is—and yet why didst thou never pronounce this pang? Didst thou perhaps reserve it to thyself—like the loved one whose name one cannot endure that the world should mention? For the poet purchases the power of words, the power of uttering all the dread secrets of others, at the price of a little secret he is unable to utter . . . and a poet is not an apostle, he casts out devils only by the power of the devil.

But now when the ethical is thus teleologically suspended, how does the individual exist in whom it is suspended? He exists as the particular in opposition to the universal. Does he then sin? For this is the form of sin, as seen in the idea. Just as the infant, though it does not sin, because it is not as such yet conscious of its existence, yet its existence is sin, as seen in the idea, and the ethical makes its demands upon it every instant. If one denies that this form can be repeated [in an adult] in such a way that it is not sin, then the sentence of condemnation is pronounced upon Abraham. How then did Abraham exist? He believed. This is the paradox which keeps him upon the sheer edge and which he cannot make clear to any other man, for the paradox is that he as the individual puts himself in an absolute relation to the absolute. Is he justified in doing this? His justification is once more the paradox; for if he is justified, it is not by virtue of anything universal, but by virtue of being the particular individual.

How then does the individual assure himself that he is justified? It is easy enough to level down the whole of existence to the idea of the state or the idea of society. If one does this, one can also mediate easily enough, for then one does not encounter at all the paradox that the individual as the individual is higher than the universal—which I can aptly express also by the thesis of Pythagoras, that the uneven numbers are more perfect than the even. If in our age one occasionally hears a rejoinder which is pertinent to the paradox, it is likely to be to the following effect: "It is to be judged by the result." A hero who has become a σκανδαλον[21] to his contemporaries because they are conscious that he is a paradox who cannot make himself intelligible, will cry out defiantly to his generation, "The result will surely prove that I am justified." In our age we hear this cry rather seldom, for as our age, to its disadvantage, does not produce heroes, it has also the advantage of producing few caricatures. When in our age one hears this saying, "It is to be judged according to the result," a man is at once clear as to who it is he has the honor of talking with. Those who talk thus are a numerous tribe, whom I will denominate by the common name of *Docents*.[22] In their thoughts they

21. This is the Scriptural word which we translate by "offense" or "stumbling block." [e.g., I. Corinthians 1:23]

22. *Docents* and *Privatdocents* (both of them German titles for subordinate teachers in the universities) were very frequently the objects of S. K.'s satire. He spoke more frequently of "the professor" after Martensen had attained that title.

live secure in existence, they have a *solid* position and *sure* prospects in a well-ordered state, they have centuries and even millenniums between them and the concussions of existence, they do not fear that such things could recur—for what would the police say to that! and the newspapers! Their lifework is to judge the great, and to judge them according to the result. Such behavior toward the great betrays a strange mixture of arrogance and misery: of arrogance because they think they are called to be judges; of misery because they do not feel that their lives are even in the remotest degree akin to the great. Surely a man who possesses even a little *erectioris ingenii* [of the higher way of thinking] has not become entirely a cold and clammy mollusk, and when he approaches what is great it can never escape his mind that from the creation of the world it has been customary for the result to come last, and that, if one would truly learn anything from great actions, one must pay attention precisely to the beginning. In case he who should act were to judge himself according to the result, he would never get to the point of beginning. Even though the result may give joy to the whole world, it cannot help the hero, for he would get to know the result only when the whole thing was over, and it was not by this he became a hero, but he was such for the fact that he began.

Moreover, the result (inasmuch as it is the answer of finiteness to the infinite query) is in its dialectic entirely heterogeneous with the existence of the hero. Or is it possible to prove that Abraham was justified in assuming the position of the individual with relation to the universal . . . for the fact that he got Isaac by *miracle?* If Abraham had actually sacrificed Isaac, would he then have been less justified?

But people are curious about the result, as they are about the result in a book—they want to know nothing about dread, distress, the paradox. They flirt aesthetically with the result, it comes just as unexpectedly but also just as easily as a prize in the lottery; and when they have heard the result they are edified. And yet no robber of temples condemned to hard labor behind iron bars, is so base a criminal as the man who pillages the holy, and even Judas who sold his Master for thirty pieces of silver is not more despicable than the man who sells greatness.

It is abhorrent to my soul to talk inhumanly about greatness, to let it loom darkly at a distance in an indefinite form, to make out that it is great without making the human character of it evident—wherewith it ceases to be great. For it is not what happens to me that makes me great, but it is what I do, and there is surely no one who thinks that a man became great because he won the great prize in the lottery. Even if a man were born in humble circumstances, I would require of him nevertheless that he should not be so inhuman toward himself as not to be able to think of the King's castle except at a remote distance, dreaming vaguely of its greatness and wanting at the same time to exalt it and also to abolish it by the fact that he exalted it meanly. I require of him that he should be man enough to step forward confidently and worthily even in that place. He should not be unmanly enough to desire impudently to offend everybody by rushing straight from the street into the King's hall. By that he loses more than the King. On the contrary, he should find joy in observing every rule of propriety with a glad and confident enthusiasm which will make him frank and fearless. This is only a symbol, for the difference here remarked upon is only a very imperfect expression for spiritual distance. I require of every man that he should not think so inhumanly of himself as not to dare to enter those palaces where not merely the memory of the elect abides but where the elect themselves abide. He should not press forward impudently and impute to them kinship with himself; on the contrary, he should be blissful every time he bows before them, but he should be frank and confident and always be something more than a charwoman, for if he will not be more, he will never gain entrance. And what will help him is precisely the dread and distress by which the great are tried, for otherwise, if he has a bit of pith in him, they will merely arouse his justified envy. And what distance alone makes great, what people would make great by empty and hollow phrases, that they themselves reduce to naught.

Who was ever so great as that blessed woman, the Mother of God, the Virgin Mary? And yet how do we speak of her? We say that she was highly favored among women. And if it did not happen strangely that those who hear are able to think as inhumanly as those who talk, every young girl might well ask, "Why was not I too the highly favored?" And if I had nothing else to say, I would not dismiss such a question as stupid, for when it is a matter of favor, abstractly considered, everyone is equally entitled to it. What they leave out is the distress, the dread, the paradox. My thought is as pure as that of anyone, and the thought of the man who is able to think such things will surely become pure—and if this be not so, he may expect the dreadful; for he who once has evoked these images cannot be rid of them again, and if he sins against them, they avenge themselves with quiet wrath, more terrible than the vociferousness of ten ferocious reviewers. To be sure, Mary bore the child miraculously, but it came to pass with her after the manner of women, and that season is one of dread, distress and paradox. To be sure, the angel was a ministering spirit, but it was not a servile spirit which obliged her by saying to the other young maidens of Israel, "Despise not Mary. What befalls her is the extraordinary." But the Angel came only to Mary, and no one could understand her. After all, what woman was so mortified as Mary? And is it not true in this instance also that one whom God blesses He curses in the same breath? This is the spirit's interpretation of Mary, and she is not (as it shocks me to say, but shocks me still more to think that they have thoughtlessly and coquettishly interpreted her thus)—she is not a fine lady who sits in state and plays with an infant god. Nevertheless, when she says, "Behold the handmaid of the Lord"—then she is great, and I think it will not be found difficult to explain why she became the Mother of God. She has no need of worldly admiration, any more than Abraham has need of tears, for she was not a heroine, and he was not a hero, but both of them became greater than such, not at all because they were exempted from distress and torment and paradox, but they became great through these.

It is great when the poet, presenting his tragic hero before the admiration of men, dares to say, "Weep for him, for he deserves it." For it is great to deserve the tears of those who are worthy to shed tears. It is great that the poet dares to hold the crowd in check, dares to castigate men, requiring that every man examine himself whether he be worthy to weep for the hero. For the waste-water of blubberers is a degradation of the holy.—But greater than all this it is that the knight of faith dares to say even to the noble man who would weep for him, "Weep not for me, but weep for thyself."

One is deeply moved, one longs to be back in those beautiful times, a sweet yearning conducts one to the desired goal, to see Christ wandering in the promised land. One forgets the dread, the distress, the paradox. Was it so easy a matter not to be mistaken? Was it not dreadful that this man who walks among the others—was it not dreadful that He was God? Was it not dreadful to sit at table with Him? Was it so easy a matter to become an Apostle? But the result, eighteen hundred years—that is a help, it helps to the shabby deceit wherewith one deceives oneself and others. I do not feel the courage to wish to be contemporary with such events, but hence I do not judge severely those who were mistaken, nor think meanly of those who saw aright.

I return, however, to Abraham. Before the result, either Abraham was every minute a murderer, or we are confronted by a paradox which is higher than all mediation.

The story of Abraham contains therefore a teleological suspension of the ethical. As the individual he became higher than the universal. This is the paradox which does not permit of mediation. It is just as inexplicable how he got into it as it is inexplicable how he remained in it. If such is not the position of Abraham, then he is not even a tragic hero but a murderer. To want to continue to call him the father of faith, to talk of this to people who do not concern themselves with anything but words, is thoughtless. A man can become a tragic hero by his own powers—but not a knight of faith. When a man enters upon the way, in a certain sense the hard way of the tragic hero, many will be able to give him counsel; to him who follows the narrow way of faith no one can give counsel, him no one can understand.

Faith is a miracle, and yet no man is excluded from it; for that in which all human life is unified is passion,* and faith is a passion.

PROBLEM II

Is There Such a Thing as an Absolute Duty Toward God?

The ethical is the universal, and as such it is again the divine. One has therefore a right to say that fundamentally every duty is a duty toward God; but if one cannot say more, then one affirms at the same time that properly I have no duty toward God. Duty becomes duty by being referred to God, but in duty itself I do not come into relation with God. Thus it is a duty to love one's neighbor, but in performing this duty I do not come into relation with God but with the neighbor whom I love. If I say then in this connection that it is my duty to love God, I am really uttering only a tautology, inasmuch as "God" is in this instance used in an entirely abstract sense as the divine, i.e. the universal, i.e. duty. So the whole existence of the human race is rounded off completely like a sphere, and the ethical is at once its limit and its content. God becomes an invisible vanishing point, a powerless thought, His power being only in the ethical which is the content of existence. If in any way it might occur to any man to want to love God in any other sense than that here indicated, he is romantic, he loves a phantom which, if it had merely the power of being able to speak, would say to him, "I do not require your love. Stay where you belong." If in any way it might occur to a man to want to love God otherwise, this love would be open to suspicion, like that of which Rousseau speaks, referring to people who love the Kaffirs instead of their neighbors.

*Lessing has somewhere given expression to a similar thought from a purely aesthetic point of view. What he would show expressly in this passage is that sorrow too can find a witty expression. To this end he quotes a rejoinder of the unhappy English king, Edward II. In contrast to this he quotes from Diderot a story of a peasant woman and a rejoinder of hers. Then he continues: "That too was wit, and the wit of a peasant at that; but the situation made it inevitable. Consequently one must not seek to find the excuse for the witty expressions of pain and of sorrow in the fact that the person who uttered them was a superior person, well educated, intelligent, and witty withal, *for the passions make all men again equal*—but the explanation is to be found in the fact that in all probability everyone would have said the same thing in the same situation. The thought of a peasant woman a queen could have had and must have had, just as what the king said in that instance a peasant too would have been able to say and doubtless would have said." Cf. *Sämtliche Werke*, XXX. p. 223.[23]

23. In *Auszüge aus den Literatur-Briefen*, 81st letter, in Maltzahn's ed. Vol. vi, pp. 205*ff.*

So in case what has been expounded here is correct, in case there is no incommensurability in a human life, and what there is of the incommensurable is only such by an accident from which no consequences can be drawn, in so far as existence is regarded in terms of the idea, Hegel is right; but he is not right in talking about faith or in allowing Abraham to be regarded as the father of it; for by the latter he has pronounced judgment both upon Abraham and upon faith. In the Hegelian philosophy *das Äussere* (*die Entäusserung*) is higher than *das Innere*.[24] This is frequently illustrated by an example. The child is *das Innere,* the man *das Äussere.* Hence it is that the child is defined by the outward, and conversely, the man, as *das Äussere,* is defined precisely by *das Innere.* Faith, on the contrary, is the paradox that inwardness is higher than outwardness—or, to recall an expression used above, the uneven number is higher than the even.

In the ethical way of regarding life it is therefore the task of the individual to divest himself of the inward determinants and express them in an outward way. Whenever he shrinks from this, whenever he is inclined to persist in or to slip back again into the inward determinants of feeling, mood, etc., he sins, he is in a temptation (*Anfechtung*). The paradox of faith is this, that there is an inwardness which is incommensurable for the outward, an inwardness, be it observed, which is not identical with the first but is a new inwardness. This must not be overlooked. Modern philosophy[25] has permitted itself without further ado to substitute in place of "faith" the immediate. When one does that it is ridiculous to deny that faith has existed in all ages. In that way faith comes into rather simple company along with feeling, mood, idiosyncrasy, vapors, etc. To this extent philosophy may be right in saying that one ought not to stop there. But there is nothing to justify philosophy in using this phrase with regard to faith. Before faith there goes a movement of infinity, and only then, unexpected, by virtue of the absurd, faith enters upon the scene. This I can well understand without maintaining on that account that I have faith. If faith is nothing but what philosophy makes it out to be, then Socrates already went further, much further, whereas the contrary is true, that he never reached it. In an intellectual respect he made the movement of infinity. His ignorance is infinite resignation. This task in itself is a match for human powers, even though people in

---

24. E.g. Hegel's *Logik*, ii, Book 2, Sect. 3, Cap. C (*Werke* IV, pp. 177*ff.*; *Encyclopedie* I §140 (*Werke* VI, pp. 275*ff.*) ["*das Äussere*" means "the outward"; *Entäusserung* means "the making outward"; "*das Innere*" means "the inward."]

25. It appears from the *Journal* (I A 273) that S. K. had in mind Schleiermacher's "Theology of Feeling," and also (with not so obvious a justification) the dogmatists of the Hegelian school. The Danish editors refer to Marheineke, *Dogmatik*, 2nd ed. §§70, 71, 86.

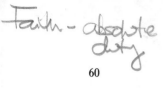

our time disdain it; but only after it is done, only when the individual has evacuated himself in the infinite, only then is the point attained where faith can break forth.

The paradox of faith is this, that the individual is higher than the universal, that the individual (to recall a dogmatic distinction now rather seldom heard) determines his relation to the universal by his relation to the absolute, not his relation to the absolute by his relation to the universal. The paradox can also be expressed by saying that there is an absolute duty toward God; for in this relationship of duty the individual as an individual stands related absolutely to the absolute. So when in this connection it is said that it is a duty to love God, something different is said from that in the foregoing; for if this duty is absolute, the ethical is reduced to a position of relativity. From this, however, it does not follow that the ethical is to be abolished, but it acquires an entirely different expression, the paradoxical expression— that, for example, love to God may cause the knight of faith to give his love to his neighbor the opposite expression to that which, ethically speaking, is required by duty.

If such is not the case, then faith has no proper place in existence, then faith is a temptation (*Anfechtung*), and Abraham is lost, since he gave in to it.

This paradox does not permit of mediation, for it is founded precisely upon the fact that the individual is only the individual. As soon as this individual [who is aware of a direct command from God] wishes to express his absolute duty in [terms of] the universal [i.e. the ethical, and] is sure of his duty in that [i.e. the universal or ethical precept], he recognizes that he is in temptation [i.e. a trial of faith], and, if in fact he resists [the direct indication of God's will], he ends by not fulfilling the absolute duty so called [i.e. what here has been called the absolute duty]; and, if he doesn't do this, [i.e. doesn't put up a resistance to the direct intimation of God's will], he sins, even though *realiter* his deed were that which it was his absolute duty to do.*
So what should Abraham do? If he would say to another person, "Isaac I

---

*The translator has ventured to render this muddy sentence very liberally (though he has bracketed his explanatory additions), in order to bring out the meaning this sentence must have if it is to express the anguishing paradox of a "teleological suspension of the ethical." This is the meaning Niels Thulstrup gets out of it, and he tells me that this is the translation of Emanuel Hirsch. As S.K.'s sentence stands, without explanatory additions, it reminds me of a rigmarole I have often recited to the mystification of my hearers: "If a man were to signify, which he were not, if he had the power, which being denied him, he were to endeavor anyhow—merely because he don't, would you?" Much as I love Kierkegaard, I sometimes hate him for keeping me awake at night. Only between sleeping and waking am I able to unravel some of his most complicated sentences.

Faith — immediacy + intelligibility

love more dearly than everything in the world, and hence it is so hard for me to sacrifice him"; then surely the other would have shaken his head and said, "Why will you sacrifice him then?"—or if the other had been a sly fellow, he surely would have seen through Abraham and perceived that he was making a show of feelings which were in strident contradiction to his act.

In the story of Abraham we find such a paradox. His relation to Isaac, ethically expressed, is this, that the father should love the son. This ethical relation is reduced to a relative position in contrast with the absolute relation to God. To the question, "Why?" Abraham has no answer except that it is a trial, a temptation (*Fristelse*)—terms which, as was remarked above, express the unity of the two points of view: that it is for God's sake and for his own sake. In common usage these two ways of regarding the matter are mutually exclusive. Thus when we see a man do something which does not comport with the universal, we say that he scarcely can be doing it for God's sake, and by that we imply that he does it for his own sake. The paradox of faith has lost the intermediate term, i.e. the universal. On the one side it has the expression for the extremest egoism (doing the dreadful thing it does for one's own sake); on the other side the expression for the most absolute self-sacrifice (doing it for God's sake). Faith itself cannot be mediated into the universal, for it would thereby be destroyed. Faith is this paradox, and the individual absolutely cannot make himself intelligible to anybody. People imagine maybe that the individual can make himself intelligible to another individual in the same case. Such a notion would be unthinkable if in our time people did not in so many ways seek to creep slyly into greatness. The one knight of faith can render no aid to the other. Either the individual becomes a knight of faith by assuming the burden of the paradox, or he never becomes one. In these regions partnership is unthinkable. Every more precise explication of what is to be understood by Isaac the individual can give only to himself. And even if one were able, generally speaking, to define ever so precisely what should be intended by Isaac (which moreover would be the most ludicrous self-contradiction, i.e. that the particular individual who definitely stands outside the universal is subsumed under universal categories precisely when he has to act as the individual who stands outside the universal), the individual nevertheless will never be able to assure himself by the aid of others that this application is appropriate, but he can do so only by himself as the individual. Hence even if a man were cowardly and paltry enough to wish to become a knight of faith on the responsibility of an outsider, he will never become one; for only the individual becomes a knight of faith as the particular individual, and this is the greatness of this knighthood, as I can well understand without entering the order, since I lack courage; but this is also its terror, as I can comprehend even better.

Absolute love of God does not entail hatred

In Luke 14:26, as everybody knows, there is a striking doctrine taught about the absolute duty toward God: "If any man cometh unto me and hateth not his own father and mother and wife and children and brethren and sisters, yea, and his own life also, he cannot be my disciple." This is a hard saying, who can bear to hear it? For this reason it is heard very seldom. This silence, however, is only an evasion which is of no avail. Nevertheless, the student of theology learns to know that these words occur in the New Testament, and in one or another exegetical aid he finds the explanation that μισεῖν [hate] in this passage and a few others is used in the sense of μείσειν [diminish], signifying *minus diligo* [love less], *posthabeo* [put aside], *non colo* [be indifferent to], *nihili facio* [disregard]. However, the context in which these words occur does not seem to strengthen this tasteful explanation. In the verse immediately following there is a story about a man who desired to build a tower but first sat down to calculate whether he was capable of doing it, lest people might laugh at him afterwards. The close connection of this story with the verse here cited seems precisely to indicate that the words are to be taken in as terrible a sense as possible, to the end that everyone may examine himself as to whether he is able to erect the building.

In case this pious and kindly exegete, who by abating the price thought he could smuggle Christianity into the world, were fortunate enough to convince a man that grammatically, linguistically and κατ᾽ ἀναλογίαν [analogically] this was the meaning of that passage, it is to be hoped that the same moment he will be fortunate enough to convince the same man that Christianity is one of the most pitiable things in the world. For the doctrine which in one of its most lyrical outbursts, where the consciousness of its eternal validity swells in it most strongly, has nothing else to say but a noisy word which means nothing but only signifies that one is to be less kindly, less attentive, more indifferent; the doctrine which at the moment when it makes as if it would give utterance to the terrible ends by driveling instead of terrifying—that doctrine is not worth taking off my hat to.

The words are terrible, yet I fully believe that one can understand them without implying that he who understands them has courage to do them. One must at all events be honest enough to acknowledge what stands written and to admit that it is great, even though one has not the courage for it. He who behaves thus will not find himself excluded from having part in that beautiful story which follows, for after all it contains consolation of a sort for the man who had not courage to begin the tower. But we must be honest, and not interpret this lack of courage as humility, since it is really pride, whereas the courage of faith is the only humble courage.

One can easily perceive that if there is to be any sense in this passage, it must be understood literally. God it is who requires absolute love. But he who in demanding a person's love thinks that this love should be proved also by becoming lukewarm to everything which hitherto was dear—that man is not only an egoist but stupid as well, and he who would demand such love signs at the same moment his own death-warrant, supposing that his life was bound up with this coveted love. Thus a husband demands that his wife shall leave father and mother, but if he were to regard it as a proof of her extraordinary love for him that she for his sake became an indolent, lukewarm daughter etc., then he is the stupidest of the stupid. If he had any notion of what love is, he would wish to discover that as daughter and sister she was perfect in love, and would see therein the proof that she would love him more than anyone else in the realm. What therefore in the case of a man one would regard as a sign of egoism and stupidity, that one is to regard by the help of an exegete as a worthy conception of the Deity.

But how hate them? I will not recall here the human distinction between loving and hating—not because I have much to object to in it (for after all it is passionate), but because it is egoistic and is not in place here. However, if I regard the problem as a paradox, then I understand it, that is, I understand it in such a way as one can understand a paradox. The absolute duty may cause one to do what ethics would forbid, but by no means can it cause the knight of faith to cease to love. This is shown by Abraham. The instant he is ready to sacrifice Isaac the ethical expression for what he does is this: he hates Isaac. But if he really hates Isaac, he can be sure that God does not require this, for Cain and Abraham are not identical. Isaac he must love with his whole soul; when God requires Isaac he must love him if possible even more dearly, and only on this condition can he *sacrifice* him; for in fact it is this love for Isaac which, by its paradoxical opposition to his love for God, makes his act a sacrifice. But the distress and dread in this paradox is that, humanly speaking, he is entirely unable to make himself intelligible. Only at the moment when his act is in absolute contradiction to his feeling is his act a sacrifice, but the reality of his act is the factor by which he belongs to the universal, and in that aspect he is and remains a murderer.

Moreover, the passage in Luke must be understood in such a way as to make it clearly evident that the knight of faith has no higher expression of the universal (i.e. the ethical) by which he can save himself. Thus, for example, if we suppose that the Church requires such a sacrifice of one of its members, we have in this case only a tragic hero. For the idea of the Church is not qualitatively different from that of the State, in so far as the individual comes into it by a simple mediation, and in so far as the individual comes into the paradox he does not reach the idea of the Church; he does not come out of the paradox, but in it he must find either his blessedness or his perdition. Such an ecclesiastical hero expresses in his act the universal, and there will be no one in the Church—not even his father and mother etc.—who fails to understand him. On the other hand, he is not a knight of faith, and he has also a different answer from that of Abraham: he does not say that it is a trial or a temptation in which he is tested.

People commonly refrain from quoting such a text as this in Luke. They are afraid of giving men a free rein, are afraid that the worst will happen as soon as the individual takes it into his head to comport himself as the individual. Moreover, they think that to exist as the individual is the easiest thing of all, and that therefore people have to be compelled to become the universal. I cannot share either this fear or this opinion, and both for the same reason. He who has learned that to exist as the individual is the most terrible thing of all will not be fearful of saying that it is great, but then too he will say this in such a way that his words will scarcely be a snare for the bewildered man, but rather will help him into the universal, even though his words do to some extent make room for the great. The man who does not dare to mention such texts will not dare to mention Abraham either, and his notion that it is easy enough to exist as the individual implies a very suspicious admission with regard to himself; for he who has a real respect for himself and concern for his soul is convinced that the man who lives under his own supervision, alone in the whole world, lives more strictly and more secluded than a maiden in her lady's bower. That there may be some who need compulsion, some who, if they were free-footed, would riot in selfish pleasures like unruly beasts, is doubtless true; but a man must prove precisely that he is not of this number by the fact that he knows how to speak with dread and trembling; and out of reverence for the great one is bound to speak, lest it be forgotten for fear of the ill effect, which surely will fail to eventuate when a man talks in such a way that one knows it for the great, knows its terror—and apart from the terror one does not know the great at all.

Let us consider a little more closely the distress and dread in the paradox of faith. The tragic hero renounces himself in order to express the universal, the knight of faith renounces the universal in order to become the individual. As has been said, everything depends upon how one is placed. He who believes that it is easy enough to be the individual can always be sure that he is not a knight of faith, for vagabonds and roving geniuses are not men of faith. The knight of faith knows, on the other hand, that it is glorious to belong to the universal. He knows that it is beautiful and salutary to be the individual who translates himself into the universal, who edits as it were a pure and elegant edition of himself, as free from errors as possible and which everyone can read. He knows that it is refreshing to become intelligible to oneself in the universal so that he understands it and so that every individual who understands him understands through him in turn the universal, and both rejoice in the security of the universal. He knows that it is beautiful to be born as the individual who has the universal as his home, his friendly abiding-place, which at once welcomes him with open arms when he would tarry in it. But he knows also that higher than this there winds a solitary path, narrow and steep; he knows that it is terrible to be born outside the universal, to walk without meeting a single traveller. He knows very well where he is and how he is related to men. Humanly speaking, he is crazy and cannot make himself intelligible to anyone. And yet it is the mildest expression, to say that he is crazy. If he is not supposed to be that, then he is a hypocrite, and the higher he climbs on this path, the more dreadful a hypocrite he is.

The knight of faith knows that to give up oneself for the universal inspires enthusiasm, and that it requires courage, but he also knows that security is to be found in this, precisely because it is for the universal. He knows that it is glorious to be understood by every noble mind, so glorious that the beholder is ennobled by it, and he feels as if he were bound; he could wish it were this task that had been allotted to him. Thus Abraham could surely have wished now and then that the task were to love Isaac as becomes a father, in a way intelligible to all, memorable throughout all ages; he could wish that the task were to sacrifice Isaac for the universal, that he might incite the fathers to illustrious deeds—and he is almost terrified by the thought that for him such wishes are only temptations and must be dealt with as such, for he knows that it is a solitary path he treads and that he accomplishes nothing for the universal but only himself is tried and examined. Or what did Abraham accomplish for the universal? Let me speak humanly about it, quite humanly. He spent seventy years in getting a son of his old age. What other men get quickly enough and enjoy for a long time he spent seventy years in accomplishing. And why? Because he was tried and put to the test. Is not that crazy? But Abraham believed, and Sarah wavered and got him to take Hagar as a concubine—but therefore he also had to drive her away. He gets Isaac, then he has to be tried again. He knew that it is glorious to express the universal, glorious to live with Isaac. But this is not the task. He knew that it is a kingly thing to sacrifice such a son for the universal, he himself would have found repose in that, and all would have reposed in the commendation of his deed, as a vowel reposes in its consonant,[26] but that is not the task—he is tried. That Roman general who is

26. The Hebrew consonants *yodh* and *vav* originally indicated vowel sounds, and when the vowel sounds came to be written below the consonants these letters became superfluous in this respect and were said to repose (*hvile*) in the vowel. So S. K. understood the situation in his *Journal* II A 406, but here he has inverted it.

celebrated by his name of Cunctator[27] checked the foe by procrastination—but what a procrastinator Abraham is in comparison with him! . . . yet he did not save the state. That is the content of one hundred and thirty years. Who can bear it? Would not his contemporary age, if we can speak of such a thing, have said of him, "Abraham is eternally procrastinating. Finally he gets a son. That took long enough. Now he wants to sacrifice him. So is he not mad? And if at least he could explain why he wants to do it—but he always says that it is a trial." Nor could Abraham explain more, for his life is like a book placed under a divine attachment and which never becomes *publici juris* [public property].

   This is the terrible thing. He who does not see it can always be sure that he is no knight of faith, but he who sees it will not deny that even the most tried of tragic heroes walks with a dancing step compared with the knight of faith, who comes slowly creeping forward. And if he has perceived this and assured himself that he has not courage to understand it, he will at least have a presentiment of the marvellous glory this knight attains in the fact that he becomes God's intimate acquaintance, the Lord's friend, and (to speak quite humanly) that he says "Thou" to God in heaven, whereas even the tragic hero only addresses Him in the third person.

   The tragic hero is soon ready and has soon finished the fight, he makes the infinite movement and then is secure in the universal. The knight of faith, on the other hand, is kept sleepless, for he is constantly tried, and every instant there is the possibility of being able to return repentantly to the universal, and this possibility can just as well be a temptation as the truth. He can derive evidence from no man which it is, for with that query he is outside the paradox.

   So the knight of faith has first and foremost the requisite passion to concentrate upon a single factor the whole of the ethical which he transgresses, so that he can give himself the assurance that he really loves Isaac with his whole soul.* If he cannot do that, he is in temptation (*Anfechtung*). In the

---

27. Fabius Maximus who in 217 B.C. conducted the war against Hannibal and received the appellation of Cunctator for his successful strategy of delay or procrastination.

*I would elucidate yet once more the difference between the collisions which are encountered by the tragic hero and by the knight of faith. The tragic hero assures himself that the ethical obligation [i.e., the lower ethical obligation, which he puts aside for the higher; in the present case, accordingly, it is the obligation to spare his daughter's life] is totally present in him by the fact that he transforms it into a wish. Thus Agamemnon can say, "The proof that I do not offend against my parental duty is that my duty is my only wish." So here we have wish and duty face to face with one another. The fortunate chance in life is that the two correspond, that my wish is my

next place, he has enough passion to make this assurance available in the twinkling of an eye and in such a way that it is as completely valid as it was in the first instance. If he is unable to do this, he can never budge from the spot, for he constantly has to begin all over again. The tragic hero also concentrated in one factor the ethical which he teleologically surpassed, but in this respect he had support in the universal. The knight of faith has only himself alone, and this constitutes the dreadfulness of the situation. Most men live in such a way under an ethical obligation that they can let the sorrow be sufficient for the day, but they never reach this passionate concentration, this energetic consciousness. The universal may in a certain sense help the tragic hero to attain this, but the knight of faith is left all to himself. The hero does the deed and finds repose in the universal, the knight of faith is kept in constant tension. Agamemnon gives up Iphigenia and thereby has found repose in the universal, then he takes the step of sacrificing her. If Agamemnon does not make the infinite movement, if his soul at the decisive instant, instead of having passionate concentration, is absorbed by the common twaddle that he had several daughters and *vielleicht* [perhaps] the *Ausserordentliche* [extraordinary] might occur—then he is of course not a hero but a hospital-case. The hero's concentration Abraham also has, even though in his case it is far more difficult, since he has no support in the universal; but he makes one more movement by which he concentrates his soul upon the miracle. If Abraham did not do that, he is only an Agamemnon—if in any way it is possible to explain how he can be justified in sacrificing Isaac when thereby no profit accrues to the universal.

Whether the individual is in temptation (*Anfechtung*) or is a knight of faith only the individual can decide. Nevertheless it is possible to construct from the paradox several criteria which he too can understand who is not within the paradox. The true knight of faith is always absolute isolation, the false knight is sectarian. This sectarianism is an attempt to leap away from the narrow path of the paradox and become a tragic hero at a cheap price. The tragic hero expresses the universal and sacrifices himself for it. The sectarian punchinello, instead of that, has a private theatre, i.e. several good

---

duty and vice versa, and the task of most men in life is precisely to remain within their duty and by their enthusiasm to transform it into their wish. The tragic hero gives up his wish in order to accomplish his duty. For the knight of faith wish and duty are also identical, but he is required to give up both. Therefore when he would resign himself to giving up his wish he does not find repose, for that is after all his duty. If he would remain within his duty and his wish, he is not a knight of faith, for the absolute duty requires precisely that he should give them up. The tragic hero apprehended a higher expression of duty but not an absolute duty.

friends and comrades who represent the universal just about as well as the beadles in *The Golden Snuffbox*[28] represent justice. The knight of faith, on the contrary, is the paradox, is the individual, absolutely nothing but the individual, without connections or pretensions. This is the terrible thing which the sectarian manikin cannot endure. For instead of learning from this terror that he is not capable of performing the great deed and then plainly admitting it (an act which I cannot but approve, because it is what I do) the manikin thinks that by uniting with several other manikins he will be able to do it. But that is quite out of the question. In the world of spirit no swindling is tolerated. A dozen sectaries join arms with one another, they know nothing whatever of the lonely temptations which await the knight of faith and which he dares not shun precisely because it would be still more dreadful if he were to press forward presumptuously. The sectaries deafen one another by their noise and racket, hold the dread off by their shrieks, and such a hallooing company of sportsmen think they are storming heaven and think they are on the same path as the knight of faith who in the solitude of the universe never hears any human voice but walks alone with his dreadful responsibility.

The knight of faith is obliged to rely upon himself alone, he feels the pain of not being able to make himself intelligible to others, but he feels no vain desire to guide others. The pain is his assurance that he is in the right way, this vain desire he does not know, he is too serious for that. The false knight of faith readily betrays himself by this proficiency in guiding which he has acquired in an instant. He does not comprehend what it is all about, that if another individual is to take the same path, he must become entirely in the same way the individual and have no need of any man's guidance, least of all the guidance of a man who would obtrude himself. At this point men leap aside, they cannot bear the martyrdom of being uncomprehended, and instead of this they choose conveniently enough the worldly admiration of their proficiency. The true knight of faith is a witness, never a teacher, and therein lies his deep humanity, which is worth a good deal more than this silly participation in others' weal and woe which is honored by the name of sympathy, whereas in fact it is nothing but vanity. He who would only be a witness thereby avows that no man, not even the lowliest, needs another man's sympathy or should be abased that another may be exalted. But since he did not win what he won at a cheap price, neither does he sell it out at a cheap price, he is not petty enough to take men's admiration and give them

---

28. A play by Olussen, which in Act ii, Scene 10 and elsewhere speaks of "two witnesses" but not of beadles (*Stokkemændene*) i.e. four men appointed to attend legal proceedings as witnesses.

in return his silent contempt, he knows that what is truly great is equally accessible to all.

Either there is an absolute duty toward God, and if so it is the paradox here described, that the individual as the individual is higher than the universal and as the individual stands in an absolute relation to the absolute/or else faith never existed, because it has always existed, or, to put it differently, Abraham is lost, or one must explain the passage in the fourteenth chapter of Luke as did that tasteful exegete, and explain in the same way the corresponding passages and similar ones.[29]

29. The corresponding passages are Deut. 13:6*f.* and 33:9; Matt. 10:37; 19:29. In the manuscript 1 Cor. 7:11 is spoken of as a "similar" passage, but not with good reason.

The Sickness unto Death

A Christian Psychological Exposition for Edification and Awakening

by Anti-Climacus
Edited by S. Kierkegaard

Part First
1. That Despair is the Sickness Unto Death

A. DESPAIR IS A SICKNESS IN THE SPIRIT, IN THE SELF, AND SO IT MAY ASSUME A TRIPLE FORM: IN DESPAIR AT NOT BEING CONSCIOUS OF HAVING A SELF (DESPAIR IMPROPERLY SO CALLED); IN DESPAIR AT NOT WILLING TO BE ONESELF; IN DESPAIR AT WILLING TO BE ONESELF.

Man is spirit. But what is spirit? Spirit is the self. But what is the self? The self is a relation which relates itself to its own self, or it is that in the relation [which accounts for it] that the relation relates itself to its own self; the self is not the relation but [consists in the fact] that the relation relates itself to its own self. Man is a synthesis of the infinite and the finite, of the temporal and the eternal, of freedom and necessity, in short he is a synthesis. A synthesis is a relation between two factors. So regarded, man is not yet a self.

In the relation between two, the relation is the third term as a negative unity, and the two relate themselves to the relation, and in the relation to the relation; such a relation is that between soul and body, when man is regarded as soul. If on the contrary the relation relates itself to its own self, the relation is then the positive third term, and this is the self.

Such a relation which relates itself to its own self (that is to say, a self) must either have constituted itself or have been constituted by another.

If this relation which relates itself to its own self is constituted by another, the relation doubtless is the third term, but this relation (the third term) is in turn a relation relating itself to that which constituted the whole relation.

Such a derived, constituted, relation is the human self, a relation which relates itself to its own self, and in relating itself to its own self relates itself to another. Hence it is that there can be two forms of despair properly so called. If the human self had constituted itself, there could be a question only of one form, that of not willing to be one's own self, of willing to get rid of oneself, but there would be no question of despairingly willing to be oneself. This formula [i.e. that the self is constituted by another] is the expression for the total dependence of the relation (the self namely), the expression for the fact that the self cannot of itself attain and remain in equilibrium and rest by itself, but only by relating itself to that Power which constituted the whole relation. Indeed, so far is it from being true that this second form of despair (despair at willing to be one's own self) denotes only a particular kind of despair, that on the contrary all despair can in the last analysis be reduced to this. If a man in despair is as he thinks conscious of his despair, does not talk about it meaninglessly as of something which befell him (pretty much as when a man who suffers from vertigo talks with nervous self-deception about a weight upon his head or about its being like something falling upon him, etc., this weight and this pressure being in fact not something external but an inverse reflection from an inward experience), and if by himself and by himself only he would abolish the despair, then by all the labor he expends he is only laboring himself deeper into a deeper despair. The disrelationship of despair is not a simple disrelationship but a disrelationship in a relation which relates itself to its own self and is constituted by another, so that the disrelationship in that self-relation reflects itself infinitely in the relation to the Power which constituted it.

This then is the formula which describes the condition of the self when despair is completely eradicated: by relating itself to its own self and by willing to be itself the self is grounded transparently in the Power which posited it.

B. POSSIBILITY AND ACTUALITY OF DESPAIR

Is despair an advantage or a drawback? Regarded in a purely dialectical way it is both. If one were to stick to the abstract notion of despair, without thinking of any concrete despairer, one might say that it is an immense advantage. The possibility of this sickness is man's advantage over the beast, and this advantage distinguishes him far more essentially than the erect posture, for it implies the infinite erectness or loftiness of being spirit. The pos-

sibility of this sickness is man's advantage over the beast; to be sharply
observant of this sickness constitutes the Christian's advantage over the
natural man; to be healed of this sickness is the Christian's bliss.

So then it is an infinite advantage to be able to despair; and yet it is not
only the greatest misfortune and misery to be in despair; no, it is perdition.
Ordinarily there is no such relation between possibility and actuality; if it is
an advantage to be able to be this or that, it is a still greater advantage to be
such a thing. That is to say, being is related to the ability to be as an ascent.
In the case of despair, on the contrary, being is related to the ability to be as
a fall. Infinite as is the advantage of the possibility, just so great is the measure of the fall. So in the case of despair the ascent consists in not being in
despair. Yet this statement is open to misunderstanding. The thing of not
being in despair is not like not being lame, blind, etc. In case the not being in
despair means neither more nor less than not being this, then it is precisely
to be it. The thing of not being in despair must mean the annihilation of the
possibility of being this; if it is to be true that a man is not in despair, one
must annihilate the possibility every instant. Such is not ordinarily the relation between possibility and actuality. Although thinkers say that actuality is
the annihilated possibility, yet this is not entirely true; it is the fulfilled, the
effective possibility. Here, on the contrary, the actuality (not being in despair), which in its very form is a negation, is the impotent, annihilated possibility; ordinarily, actuality in comparison with possibility is a confirmation, here it is a negation.

Despair is the disrelationship in a relation which relates itself to itself. But
the synthesis is not the disrelationship, it is merely the possibility, or, in the
synthesis is latent the possibility of the disrelationship. If the synthesis were
the disrelationship, there would be no such thing as despair, for despair
would then be something inherent in human nature as such, that is, it would
not be despair, it would be something that befell a man, something he suffered passively, like an illness into which a man falls, or like death which is
the lot of all. No, this thing of despairing is inherent in man himself; but if
he were not a synthesis, he could not despair, neither could he despair if the
synthesis were not originally from God's hand in the right relationship.

Whence then comes despair? From the relation wherein the synthesis relates itself to itself, in that God who made man a relationship lets this go as
it were out of His hand, that is, in the fact that the relation relates itself to
itself. And herein, in the fact that the relation is spirit, is the self, consists
the responsibility under which all despair lies, and so lies every instant it exists, however much and however ingeniously the despairer, deceiving himself and others, may talk of his despair as a misfortune which has befallen
him, with a confusion of things different, as in the case of vertigo aforemen-
tioned, with which, though it is qualitatively different, despair has much in

common, since vertigo is under the rubric soul what despair is under the rubric spirit, and is pregnant with analogies to despair.

So when the disrelationship—that is, despair—has set in, does it follow as a matter of course that it continues? No, it does not follow as a matter of course; if the disrelationship continues, it does not follow as a consequence of the disrelation but as a consequence of the relation which relates itself to itself. That is to say, every time the disrelation expresses itself, and every instant it exists, it is to the relation one must revert. Observe that we speak of a man contracting a disease, maybe through carelessness. Then the illness sets in, and from that instant it affirms itself and is now an *actuality*, the origin of which recedes more and more into the past. It would be cruel and inhuman if one were to continue to say incessantly, "This instant thou, the sick man, art contracting this disease"; that is, if every instant one were to resolve the actuality of the disease into its possibility. It is true that he did contract the disease, but this he did only once; the continuance of the disease is a simple consequence of the fact that he once contracted it, its progress is not to be referred every instant to him as the cause; he contracted it, but one cannot say that he *is contracting* it. Not so with despair: every actual instant of despair is to be referred back to possibility, every instant the man in despair is *contracting* it, it is constantly in the present tense, nothing comes to pass here as a consequence of a bygone actuality superseded; at every actual instant of despair the despairer bears as his responsibility all the foregoing experience in possibility as a present. This comes from the fact that despair is a qualification of spirit, that it is related to the eternal in man. But the eternal he cannot get rid of, no, not to all eternity; he cannot cast it from him once for all, nothing is more impossible; every instant he does not possess it he must have cast it or be casting it from him—but it comes back, every instant he is in despair he contracts despair. For despair is not a result of the disrelationship but of the relation which relates itself to itself. And the relation to himself a man cannot get rid of, any more than he can get rid of himself, which moreover is one and the same thing, since the self is the relationship to onself.

C. DESPAIR IS "THE SICKNESS UNTO DEATH."

The concept of the sickness unto death must be understood, however, in a peculiar sense. Literally it means a sickness the end and outcome of which is death. Thus one speaks of a mortal sickness as synonymous with a sickness unto death. In this sense despair cannot be called the sickness unto death. But in the Christian understanding of it death itself is a transition unto life. In view of this, there is from the Christian standpoint no earthly, bodily sickness unto death. For death is doubtless the last phase of the sickness, but death is not the last thing. If in the strictest sense we are to speak of a sickness unto death, it must be one in which the last thing is death, and death the last thing. And this precisely is despair.

Yet in another and still more definite sense despair is the sickness unto death. It is indeed very far from being true that literally understood, one dies of this sickness, or that this sickness ends with bodily death. On the contrary, the torment of despair is precisely this, not to be able to die. So it has much in common with the situation of the moribund when he lies and struggles with death, and cannot die. So to be sick *unto* death is, not to be able to die—yet not as though there were hope of life; no, the hopelessness in this case is that even the last hope, death, is not available. When death is the greatest danger, one hopes for life; but when one becomes acquainted with an even more dreadful danger, one hopes for death. So when the danger is so great that death has become one's hope, despair is the disconsolateness of not being able to die.

It is in this last sense that despair is the sickness unto death, this agonizing contradiction, this sickness in the self, everlastingly to die, to die and yet not to die, to die the death. For dying means that it is all over, but dying the death means to live to experience death; and if for a single instant this experience is possible, it is tantamount to experiencing it forever. If one might die of despair as one dies of a sickness, then the eternal in him, the self, must be capable of dying in the same sense that the body dies of sickness. But this is an impossibility; the dying of despair transforms itself constantly into a living. The despairing man cannot die; no more than "the dagger can slay thoughts" can despair consume the eternal thing, the self, which is the ground of despair, whose worm dieth not, and whose fire is not quenched. Yet despair is precisely *self*-consuming, but it is an impotent self-consumption which is not able to do what it wills; and this impotence is a new form of self-consumption, in which again, however, the despairer is not able to do what he wills, namely, to consume himself. This is despair raised to a higher potency, or it is the law for the potentiation. This is the hot incitement, or the cold fire in despair, the gnawing canker whose movement is constantly inward, deeper and deeper, in impotent self-consumption. The fact that despair does not consume him is so far from being any comfort to the despairing man that it is precisely the opposite, this comfort is precisely the torment, it is precisely this that keeps the gnawing pain alive and keeps life in the pain. This precisely is the reason why he despairs—not to say despaired—because he cannot consume himself, cannot get rid of himself, cannot become nothing. This is the potentiated formula for despair, the rising of the fever in the sickness of self.

A despairing man is in despair over *something*. So it seems for an instant, but only for an instant; that same instant the true despair manifests itself, or despair manifests itself in its true character. For in the fact that he despaired of *something*, he really despaired of himself, and now would be rid of himself. Thus when the ambitious man whose watchword was "Either Caesar or nothing"[1] does not become Caesar, he is in despair thereat. But this signifies something else, namely, that precisely because he did not become Caesar he now cannot endure to be himself. So properly he is not in despair over the fact that he did not become Caesar, but he is in despair over himself for the fact that he did not become Caesar. This self which, had he become Caesar, would have been to him a sheer delight (though in another sense equally in despair), this self is now absolutely intolerable to him. In a profounder sense it is not the fact that he did not become Caesar which is intolerable to him, but the self which did not become Caesar is the thing that is intolerable; or, more correctly, what is intolerable to him is that he cannot get rid of himself. If he had become Caesar he would have been rid of himself in desperation, but now that he did not become Caesar he cannot in desperation get rid of himself. Essentially he is equally in despair in either case, for he does not possess himself, he is not himself. By becoming Caesar he would not after all have become himself but have got rid of himself, and by not becoming Caesar he falls into despair over the fact that he cannot get rid of himself. Hence it is a superficial view (which presumably has never seen a person in despair, not even one's own self) when it is said of a man in despair, "He is consuming himself." For precisely this it is he despairs of, and to his torment it is precisely this he cannot do, since by despair fire has entered into something that cannot burn, or cannot burn up, that is, into the self.

So to despair over something is not yet properly despair. It is the beginning, or it is as when the physician says of a sickness that it has not yet declared itself. The next step is the declared despair, despair over oneself. A young girl is in despair over love, and so she despairs over her lover, because he died, or because he was unfaithful to her. This is not a declared despair; no, she is in despair over herself. This self of hers, which, if it had become "his" beloved, she would have been rid of in the most blissful way, or would have lost, this self is now a torment to her when it has to be a self without "him"; this self which would have been to her her riches (though in another sense equally in despair) has now become to her a loathsome void, since "he" is dead, or it has become to her an abhorrence, since it reminds her of the fact that she was betrayed. Try it now, say to such a girl, "Thou art consuming thyself," and thou shalt hear her reply, "Oh, no, the torment is precisely this, that I cannot do it."

To despair over oneself, in despair to will to be rid of oneself, is the formula for all despair, and hence the second form of despair (in despair at will-

---

1. *Aut Caesar aut nullus* was the motto of Caesar Borgia.

ing to be oneself) can be followed back to the first (in despair at willing to be oneself), just as in the foregoing we resolved the first into the second (cf.I). A despairing man wants despairingly to be himself. But if he despairingly wants to be himself, he will not want to get rid of himself. Yes, so it seems; but if one inspects more closely, one perceives that after all the contradiction is the same. That self which he despairingly wills to be is a self which he is not (for to will to be that self which one truly is, is indeed the opposite of despair); what he really wills is to tear his self away from the Power which constituted it. But notwithstanding all his despair, this he is unable to do, notwithstanding all the efforts of despair, that Power is the stronger, and it compels him to be the self he does not will to be. But for all that he wills to be rid of himself, to be rid of the self which he is, in order to be the self he himself has chanced to choose. To be *self* as he wills to be would be his delight (though in another sense it would be equally in despair), but to be compelled to be *self* as he does not will to be is his torment, namely, that he cannot get rid of himself.

Socrates proved the immortality of the soul from the fact that the sickness of the soul (sin) does not consume it as sickness of the body consumes the body. So also we can demonstrate the eternal in man from the fact that despair cannot consume his self, that this precisely is the torment of contradiction in despair. If there were nothing eternal in a man, he could not despair; but if despair could consume his self, there would still be no despair.

Thus it is that despair, this sickness in the self, is the sickness unto death. The despairing man is mortally ill. In an entirely different sense that can appropriately be said of any disease, we may say that the sickness has attacked the noblest part; and yet the man cannot die. Death is not the last phase of the sickness, but death is continually the last. To be delivered from this sickness by death is an impossibility, for the sickness and its torment . . . and death consist in not being able to die.

This is the situation in despair. And however thoroughly it eludes the attention of the despairer, and however thoroughly the despairer may succeed (as in the case of that kind of despair which is characterized by unawareness of being in despair) in losing himself entirely, and losing himself in such a way that it is not noticed in the least—eternity nevertheless will make it manifest that his situation was despair, and it will so nail him to himself that the torment nevertheless remains that he cannot get rid of himself, and it become manifest that he was deluded in thinking that he succeeded. And thus it is eternity must act, because to have a self, to be a self, is the greatest concession made to man, but at the same time it is eternity's demand upon him.

Concluding Unscientific Postscript:

A Mimic-Pathic-Dialectic Composition, an Existential Contribution

by Johannes Climacus

The Subjective Truth, Inwardness; Truth is Subjectivity

Whether truth is defined more empirically, as the conformity of thought and being, or more idealistically, as the conformity of being with thought, it is, in either case, important carefully to note what is meant by being. And in formulating the answer to this question it is likewise important to take heed lest the knowing spirit be tricked into losing itself in the indeterminate, so that it fantastically becomes a something that no existing human being ever was or can be, a sort of phantom with which the individual occupies himself upon occasion, but without making it clear to himself in terms of dialectical intermediaries how he happens to get into this fantastic realm, what significance being there has for him, and whether the entire activity that goes on out there does not resolve itself into a tautology within a recklessly fantastic venture of thought. . . .

Since the inquirer stresses precisely the fact that he is an existing individual, then one of the above two ways which especially accentuates existence would seem to be especially worthy of commendation.

The way of objective reflection makes the subject accidental, and thereby transforms existence into something indifferent, something vanishing. Away from the subject the objective way of reflection leads to the objective truth, and while the subject and his subjectivity become indifferent, the truth also becomes indifferent, and this indifference is precisely its objective validity; for all interest, like all decisiveness, is rooted in subjectivity. The way of objective reflection leads to abstract thought, to mathematics, to historical knowledge of different kinds; and always it leads away from the subject, whose existence or non-existence, and from the objective point of view quite rightly, becomes infinitely indifferent. . . .

The subjective reflection turns its attention inwardly to the subject, and desires in this intensification of inwardness to realize the truth. And it proceeds in such fashion that, just as in the preceding objective reflection, when the objectivity had come into being, the subjectivity had vanished, so here the subjectivity of the subject becomes the final stage, and objectivity a vanishing factor. Not for a single moment is it forgotten that the subject is an existing individual, and that existence is a process of becoming, and that therefore the notion of the truth as identity of thought and being is a chimera of abstraction, in its truth only an expectation of the creature; not because the truth is not such an identity, but because the knower is an existing individual for whom the truth cannot be such an identity as long as he lives in time. Unless we hold fast to this, speculative philosophy will immediately transport us into the fantastic realism of the I-am-I,[1] which modern speculative thought has not hesitated to use without explaining how a particular individual is related to it; and God knows, no human being is more than such a particular individual.

If an existing individual were really able to transcend himself, the truth would be for him something final and complete; but where is the point at which he is outside himself? The I-am-I is a mathematical point which does not exist, and in so far there is nothing to prevent everyone from occupying this standpoint; the one will not be in the way of the other. It is only momentarily that the particular individual is able to realize existentially a unity of the infinite and the finite which transcends existence. This unity is realized in the moment of passion. Modern philosophy has tried anything and everything in the effort to help the individual to transcend himself objectively, which is a wholly impossible feat; existence exercises its restraining influence, and if philosophers nowadays had not become mere scribblers in the service of a fantastic thinking and its preoccupation, they would long ago have perceived that suicide was the only tolerable practical interpretation of its striving. But the scribbling modern philosophy holds passion in contempt; and yet passion is the culmination of existence for an existing individual—and we are all of us existing individuals. In passion the existing subject is rendered infinite in the eternity of the imaginative representation,

1. As in Fichte's philosophy, *Werke*, Vol. I, p. 98.

and yet he is at the same time most definitely himself. The fantastic I-am-I is not an identity of the infinite and the finite, since neither the one nor the other is real; it is a fantastic rendezvous in the clouds,[2] an unfruitful embrace, and the relationship of the individual self to this mirage is never indicated.

All essential knowledge relates to existence, or only such knowledge as has an essential relationship to existence is essential knowledge. All knowledge which does not inwardly relate itself to existence, in the reflection of inwardness, is, essentially viewed, accidental knowledge; its degree and scope is essentially indifferent. That essential knowledge is essentially related to existence does not mean the above-mentioned identity which abstract thought postulates between thought and being; nor does it signify, objectively, that knowledge corresponds to something existent as its object. But it means that knowledge has a relationship to the knower, who is essentially an existing individual, and that for this reason all essential knowledge is essentially related to existence. Only ethical and ethico-religious knowledge has an essential relationship to the existence of the knower.

Mediation is a mirage, like the I-am-I. From the abstract point of view everything is and nothing comes into being. Mediation can therefore have no place in abstract thought, because it presupposes *movement*. Objective knowledge may indeed have the existent for its object; but since the knowing subject is an existing individual, and through the fact of his existence in process of becoming, philosophy must first explain how a particular existing subject is related to a knowledge of mediation. It must explain what he is in such a moment, if not pretty nearly *distrait*; where he is, if not in the moon? There is constant talk of mediation and mediation; is mediation then a man, as Peter Deacon[3] believes that *Imprimatur* is a man? How does a human being manage to become something of this kind? Is this dignity, this great *philosophicum*, the fruit of study, or does the magistrate give it away, like the office of deacon or grave-digger? Try merely to enter into these and other such plain questions of a plain man, who would gladly become mediation if it could be done in some lawful and honest manner, and not either by saying abracadabra, or by forgetting that he is himself an existing human being, for whom existence is therefore something essential, and an ethico-religious existence a suitable *quantum satis* [sufficiency]. A speculative philosopher may perhaps find it in bad taste to ask such questions. But it is important not to direct the polemic to the wrong point, and hence not to begin in a fantastic objective manner to discuss *pro* and *contra* whether there is a mediation or not, but to hold fast what it means to be a human being.

2. As when Axion sought to embrace Juno and found that he was embracing a cloud.
3. As in Holberg's comedy *Erasmus Montanus*, Act III, Scene 3.

In an attempt to make clear the difference of way that exists between an objective and a subjective reflection, I shall now proceed to show how a subjective reflection makes its way inwardly in inwardness. Inwardness in an existing subject culminates in passion; corresponding to passion in the subject the truth becomes a paradox; and the fact that the truth becomes a paradox is rooted precisely in its having a relationship to an existing subject. Thus the one corresponds to the other. By forgetting that one is an existing subject, passion goes by the board and the truth is no longer a paradox; the knowing subject becomes a fantastic entity rather than a human being, and the truth becomes a fantastic object for the knowledge of this fantastic entity.

When the question of truth is raised in an objective manner, reflection is directed objectively to the truth, as an object to which the knower is related. Reflection is not focussed upon the relationship, however, but upon the question of whether it is the truth to which the knower is related. If only the object to which he is related is the truth, the subject is accounted to be in the truth. When the question of the truth is raised subjectively, reflection is directed subjectively to the nature of the individual's relationship; if only the mode of this relationship is in the truth, the individual is in the truth even if he should happen to be thus related to what is not true. Let us take as an example the knowledge of God. Objectively, reflection is directed to the problem of whether this object is the true God; subjectively, reflection is directed to the question whether the individual is related to a something in such a manner that his relationship is in truth a God-relationship. On which side is the truth now to be found? Ah, may we not here resort to a mediation, and say: It is on neither side, but in the mediation of both? Excellently well said, provided we might have it explained how an existing individual manages to be in a state of mediation. For to be in a state of mediation is to be finished, while to exist is to become. Nor can an existing individual be in two places at the same time—he cannot be an identity of subject and object. When he is nearest to being in two places at the same time he is in passion; but passion is momentary, and passion is also the highest expression of subjectivity.

The existing individual who chooses to pursue the objective way enters upon the entire approximation-process by which it is proposed to bring God to light objectively. But this is in all eternity impossible, because God is a subject, and therefore exists only for subjectivity in inwardness. The existing individual who chooses the subjective way apprehends instantly the entire dialectical difficulty involved in having to use some time, perhaps a long

*The reader will observe that the question here is about essential truth, or about the truth which is essentially related to existence, and that it is precisely for the sake of clarifying it as inwardness or as subjectivity that this contrast is drawn.

time, in finding God objectively; and he feels this dialectical difficulty in all its painfulness, because every moment is wasted in which he does not have God.* That very instant he has God, not by virtue of any objective deliberation, but by virtue of the infinite passion of inwardness. The objective inquirer, on the other hand, is not embarrassed by such dialectical difficulties as are involved in devoting an entire period of investigation to finding God—since it is possible that the inquirer may die tomorrow; and if he lives he can scarcely regard God as something to be taken along if convenient, since God is precisely that which one takes *a tout prix,* which in the understanding of passion constitutes the true inward relationship to God.

It is at this point, so difficult dialectically, that the way swings off for everyone who knows what it means to think, and to think existentially; which is something very different from sitting at a desk and writing about what one has never done, something very different from writing *de omnibus dubitandum* [everything is to be doubted] and at the same time being as credulous existentially as the most sensuous of men. Here is where the way swings off, and the change is marked by the fact that while objective knowledge rambles comfortably on by way of the long road of approximation without being impelled by the urge of passion, subjective knowledge counts every delay a deadly peril, and the decision so infinitely important and so instantly pressing that it is as if the opportunity had already passed.

Now when the problem is to reckon up on which side there is most truth, whether on the side of one who seeks the true God objectively, and pursues the approximate truth of the God-idea; or on the side of one who, driven by the infinite passion of his need of God, feels an infinite concern for his own relationship to God in truth (and to be at one and the same time on both sides equally, is as we have noted not possible for an existing individual, but is merely the happy delusion of an imaginary I-am-I): the answer cannot be in doubt for anyone who has not been demoralized with the aid of science. If one who lives in the midst of Christendom goes up to the house of God, the house of the true God, with the true conception of God in his knowledge, and prays, but prays in a false spirit; and one who lives in an idolatrous community prays with the entire passion of the infinite, although his eyes rest upon the image of an idol: where is there most truth? The one prays in truth

---

*In this manner God certainly becomes a postulate, but not in the otiose manner in which this word is commonly understood. It becomes clear rather that the only way in which an existing individual comes into relation with God, is when the dialectical contradiction brings his passion to the point of despair, and helps him to embrace God with the "category of despair" (faith). Then the postulate is so far from being arbitrary that it is precisely a life-necessity. It is then not so much that God is a postulate, as that the existing individual's postulation of God is a necessity.

to God though he worships an idol; the other prays falsely to the true God, and hence worships in fact an idol.

When one man investigates objectively the problem of immortality, and another embraces an uncertainty with the passion of the infinite: where is there most truth, and who has the greater certainty? The one has entered upon a never-ending approximation, for the certainty of immortality lies precisely in the subjectivity of the individual; the other is immortal, and fights for his immortality by struggling with the uncertainty. Let us consider Socrates.[4] Nowadays everyone dabbles in a few proofs; some have several such proofs, others fewer. But Socrates! He puts the question objectively in a problematic manner: *if* there is an immortality. He must therefore be accounted a doubter in comparison with one of our modern thinkers with the three proofs? By no means. On this "if" he risks his entire life, he has the courage to meet death, and he has with the passion of the infinite so determined the pattern of his life that it must be found acceptable—*if* there is an immortality. Is any better proof capable of being given for the immortality of the soul? But those who have the three proofs do not at all determine their lives in conformity therewith; if there is an immortality it must feel disgust over their manner of life: can any better refutation be given of the three proofs? The bit of uncertainty that Socrates had, helped him because he himself contributed the passion of the infinite; the three proofs that the others have do not profit them at all, because they are dead to spirit and enthusiasm, and their three proofs, in lieu of proving anything else, prove just this. A young girl may enjoy all the sweetness of love on the basis of what is merely a weak hope that she is beloved, because she rests everything on this weak hope; but many a wedded matron more than once subjected to the strongest expressions of love, has in so far indeed had proofs, but strangely enough has not enjoyed *quod erat demonstrandum* [what was to be demonstrated]. The Socratic ignorance, which Socrates held fast with the entire passion of his inwardness, was thus an expression for the principle that the eternal truth is related to an existing individual, and that this truth must therefore be a paradox for him as long as he exists; and yet it is possible that there was more truth in the Socratic ignorance as it was in him, than in the entire objective truth of the System, which flirts with what the times demand and accommodates itself to *Privatdocents*.

The objective accent falls on WHAT is said, the subjective accent on HOW it is said. This distinction holds even in the aesthetic realm, and receives definite expression in the principle that what is in itself true may in the mouth of such and such a person become untrue. In these times this distinction is par-

---

4. The reference is doubtless to Plato's *Apology* and to his *Phaedrus*, though in neither is to be found exactly what S. K. says here.

ticularly worthy of notice, for if we wish to express in a single sentence the difference between ancient times and our own, we should doubtless have to say: "In ancient times only an individual here and there knew the truth; now all know it, except that the inwardness of its appropriation stands in an inverse relationship to the extent of its dissemination.* Aesthetically the contradiction that truth becomes untruth in this or that person's mouth, is best construed comically: In the ethico-religious sphere, accent is again on the "how." But this is not to be understood as referring to demeanor, expression, or the like; rather it refers to the relationship sustained by the existing individual, in his own existence, to the content of his utterance. Objectively the interest is focussed merely on the thought-content, subjectively on the inwardness. At its maximum this inward "how" is the passion of the infinite, and the passion of the infinite is the truth. But the passion of the infinite is precisely subjectivity, and thus subjectivity becomes the truth. Objectively there is no infinite decisiveness, and hence it is objectively in order to annul the difference between good and evil, together with the principle of contradiction, and therewith also the infinite difference between the true and the false. Only in subjectivity is there decisiveness, to seek objectivity is to be in error. It is the passion of the infinite that is the decisive factor and not its content, for its content is precisely itself. In this manner subjectivity and the subjective "how" constitute the truth.

But the "how" which is thus subjectively accentuated precisely because the subject is an existing individual, is also subject to a dialectic with respect to time. In the passionate moment of decision, where the road swings away from objective knowledge, it seems as if the infinite decision were thereby realized. But in the same moment the existing individual finds himself in the temporal order, and the subjective "how" is transformed into a striving,

---

Stages on Life's Way, Note on p. 426. Though ordinarily not wishing an expression of opinion on the part of reviewers, I might at this point almost desire it, provided such opinions, so far from flattering me, amounted to an assertion of the daring truth that what I say is something that everybody knows, even every child, and that the cultured know infinitely much better. If it only stands fast that everyone knows it, my standpoint is in order, and I shall doubtless make shift to manage with the unity of the comic and the tragic. If there were anyone who did not know it I might perhaps be in danger of being dislodged from my position of equilibrium by the thought that I might be in a position to communicate to someone the needful preliminary knowledge. It is just this which engages my interest so much, this that the cultured are accustomed to say: that everyone knows what the highest is. This was not the case in paganism, nor in Judaism, nor in the seventeen centuries of Christianity. Hail to the nineteenth century! Everyone knows it. What progress has been made since the time when only a few knew it. To make up for this, perhaps, we must assume that no one nowadays does it.

a striving which receives indeed its impulse and a repeated renewal from the decisive passion of the infinite, but is nevertheless a striving.

When subjectivity is the truth, the conceptual determination of the truth must include an expression for the antithesis to objectivity, a memento of the fork in the road where the way swings off; this expression will at the same time serve as an indication of the tension of the subjective inwardness. Here is such a definition of truth: *An objective uncertainty held fast in an appropriation-process of the most passionate inwardness is the truth*, the highest truth attainable for an *existing* individual. At the point where the way swings off (and where this is cannot be specified objectively, since it is a matter of subjectivity), there objective knowledge is placed in abeyance. Thus the subject merely has, objectively, the uncertainty; but it is this which precisely increases the tension of that infinite passion which constitutes his inwardness. The truth is precisely the venture which chooses an objective uncertainty with the passion of the infinite. I contemplate the order of nature in the hope of finding God, and I see omnipotence and wisdom; but I also see much else that disturbs my mind and excites anxiety. The sum of all this is an objective uncertainty. But it is for this very reason that the inwardness becomes as intense as it is, for it embraces this objective uncertainty with the entire passion of the infinite. In the case of a mathematical proposition the objectivity is given, but for this reason the truth of such a proposition is also an indifferent truth.

But the above definition of truth is an equivalent expression for faith. Without risk there is no faith. Faith is precisely the contradiction between the infinite passion of the individual's inwardness and the objective uncertainty. If I am capable of grasping God objectively, I do not believe, but precisely because I cannot do this I must believe. If I wish to preserve myself in faith I must constantly be intent upon holding fast the objective uncertainty, so as to remain out upon the deep, over seventy thousand fathoms of water, still preserving my faith.

Nietzsche

Friedrich Nietzsche was born in a small town in Prussia in 1844. His father, a Lutheran pastor, died when he was only four, and he was raised in a household of five very religious women. His work as a student at the universities of Bonn and Leipzig was so outstanding that at the age of twenty-four he was appointed professor of classical philology at the University of Basel. While at Basel he immersed himself in Greek philosophy and in the works of Schopenhauer. For several years he was enthralled by the composer Richard Wagner, whose work he regarded as capable of bringing Germany to the level of greatness formerly achieved by ancient Greece. Shy and withdrawn by nature, Nietzsche was subject to migraine headaches and generally racked by poor health. In 1879 he stepped down from his position at Basel, citing chronic illness as the reason. During the next ten years, he wrote the main body of works that make up his mature philosophy. These include *The Gay Science* (1882, with a new preface and a fifth book in 1887), *Thus Spoke Zarathustra* (1883–85), *Beyond Good and Evil* (1886), *Genealogy of Morals* (1887), and *Twilight of the Idols* and *The Antichrist* (both published in 1889). For a short time in 1882 he was swept away by a brilliant young woman, Lou Salomé, but it seems that nothing came of the relationship in the end. He was forty-four years old when he suffered a complete mental collapse from which he remained an invalid until his death in 1900. Although his insanity was almost certainly caused by syphilis, it is a matter of debate, given his withdrawn and chaste life, how he might have contracted the disease.

1. Life-Philosophy: The Dionysian and the Apollonian

It would be hard to think of a philosopher whose writings have been subjected to a wider range of interpretations than Nietzsche. Thanks to the influence of his sister and literary executor, Elizabeth, Nietzsche was regarded for several decades as a proto-Nazi and anti-Semite—as if a Nazi might believe that a "master race" could be created through "race mixture!"[1] After the Second World War it became increasingly clear that Nietzsche was nei-

1. *The Will to Power*, trans. Walter Kaufmann (New York: Random House, 1968), see secs. 862 and 960. See also *The Gay Science* § 377 for Nietzsche's critique of "the mendacious racial self-admiration and racial indecency" in Germany.

ther an ultra-nationalist nor an anti-Semite.[2] More recently, his writings
have been appropriated by a number of French authors, most notably
Jacques Derrida and Michel Foucault, whose works have laid a foundation
for the movement called postmodernism.[3] So influential has Nietzsche been
in this movement, in fact, that some people (mostly critics) refer to postmodernism in general as "neo-Nietzscheanism."

   But it is worth noting that when Nietzsche's writings first began to be recognized at the end of the nineteenth century, they were treated as part of
the influential philosophical movement of the time known as life-
philosophy.[4] Life-philosophy, then associated with the names of Henri
Bergson and Wilhelm Dilthey among others, started from the assumption
that philosophy had become excessively technical and abstract, and that it
had lost contact with its point of origin, the concrete reality of *life* as it is
actually lived. Dilthey, for example, criticizes the view of the self as a
"knowing subject" in traditional theory of knowledge: "No real blood flows
in the veins of the knowing subject constructed by Locke, Hume, and
Kant," he says, "only the diluted juice of reason."[5] To make sense of humans and their world, Dilthey claims, we need to recover a sense of the dynamic life-process and of the "willing, feeling, representing" totality, the
human being as a whole. In his words, "Life is the fundamental fact which

2. The current respect for Nietzsche as a philosopher is much indebted to such clas-
sic works as Walter Kaufmann's *Nietzsche: Philosopher, Psychologist, Antichrist* 3rd
edition (Princeton: Princeton University Press, 1968), Arthur C. Danto's *Nietzsche as
Philosopher* (New York: Macmillan, 1965), and Robert C. Solomon's *From Rational-
ism to Existentialism: The Existentialists and Their Nineteenth-Century Backgrounds*
(New York: Harper & Row, 1972).

3. For a good collection of writings reflecting this reading of Nietzsche, see Da-
vid B. Allison, ed., *The New Nietzsche: Contemporary Styles of Interpretation*
(Cambridge, Mass.: MIT Press, 1985). Bernd Magnus, Stanley Stewart, and Jean-
Pierre Mileur's *Nietzsche's Case: Philosophy as/and Literature* (New York: Routledge,
1993) provides a postmodernist reading of Nietzsche written from an interdisciplin-
ary perspective. Michel Foucault's "Nietzsche, Genealogy, History," reprinted in
The Foucault Reader, ed. Paul Rabinow (New York: Pantheon, 1984), shows how
Nietzsche's writings pave the way to postmodernist trends.

4. Herbert Schnädelbach, in *Philosophy in Germany: 1831–1933* (Cambridge: Cambridge University Press, 1984), 139–60, shows the direct line of succession extending from life-philosophy through the *Existenzphilosophie* developed by Karl Jaspers
to what came to be called "existentialism" in the middle of the twentieth century.

5. Wilhelm Dilthey, *An Introduction to the Human Studies* (1883), in *Dilthey: Selected
Writings*, ed. and trans. H. P. Rickman (Cambridge: Cambridge University Press,
1976), 162.

determines the outcome of philosophy. It is that which is known from within, that behind which one cannot go. Life cannot be brought before the tribunal of reason."[6] In a similar vein, Bergson tried to make sense of life as a dynamic, unfolding *élan vital* that is more basic to us as humans than observation and theorizing.

Nietzsche's early work, *The Birth of Tragedy* (1872), reflects this concern with recovering a sense of the origins of our experience in the dynamism of raw, pre-theoretical life. It starts out by reflecting on the origin of tragedy, that magnificent art form created by the Greeks. The word "tragedy" in Greek means "goat-song," and scholars have long suspected that tragedy originated from satyr plays presented in honor of Dionysus, the god associated with intoxication, sensuality, and revelry. Nietzsche takes this to indicate that tragedy first emerged as part of the ancient Dionysian mystery religion whose frenzied orgies celebrated the fertility and abundance of nature and the participation of humans in the divine.

The claim of *The Birth of Tragedy* is that tragedy originated in the droning music, frenzied dancing, and ecstatic choral chanting of Dionysian worship. Under the spell of Richard Wagner's operas, and influenced by Schopenhauer's aesthetic theory, Nietzsche describes music as an overpowering, flowing groundswell of sound that brings to expression the raw undercurrent of life itself.[7] The mystical sense of life as a unified flux of energy, experienced in the rapture and intoxication of the ancient celebration of Dionysus, is called the "Dionysian." This term refers to the primal totality of nature, where nature is understood as a creative, dynamic life force that exists prior to all division and articulation into individual forms. It is the "Primordial Oneness," the "substrate of the universe," that underlies and makes possible the familiar world of discrete phenomena we encounter in everyday life. Nietzsche's notion of the Dionysian draws on Schopenhauer's view that reality at its deepest level is a seething cauldron of raw "Will," an undifferentiated totality of energy that spews out individual forms, sustains them for a brief time, and then swallows them up once again into the primal oneness.

The Dionysian is contrasted with a form-giving, individuating force called the "Apollonian." The god Apollo is the patron of reason, control, and stability, and his formative influence is seen in such "plastic," visual arts as architecture, painting, and sculpture (for example, the magnificent Classi-

6. Dilthey's notes for a 1909 lecture, in Dilthey's *Gesammelte Schriften*, Vol. 7 (Stuttgart: Teubner, 1958), 359.

7. *The Birth of Tragedy*, sec. 2, in *The Birth of Tragedy and the Genealogy of Morals*, trans. Francis Golffing (Garden City, N.Y.: Doubleday, 1956).

cal Greek sculptures portraying idealized human bodies) but also in the measured, controlled cadences and imagery of epic poetry. Just as Schopenhauer had claimed that the familiar world of stable, individual forms we see around us is ultimately an illusion concealing the primal reality of "Will," so Nietzsche portrays the Apollonian world of articulated shapes we encounter in ordinary life as a world of dreams or phantasms. The Apollonian makes manifest and gives form to the Dionysian undercurrent, but ultimately it creates illusions. With its "principle of individuation," it lets us believe that the world is a manageable world of discrete material objects and individual people, a world that is stable, enduring, and therefore intelligible to the human mind. But this is all just a veil of comforting illusion. Nietzsche says that nature "bemoans her fragmentation, her decomposition into separate individuals," and desires "to tear asunder the veil of Maya ["illusion" in Hinduism], to sink back into the original oneness of nature." In this recovery of overflowing life, the "mystical jubilation of Dionysus . . . breaks the spell of individuation and opens a path to the maternal womb of being."[8]

Nietzsche's thesis in *The Birth of Tragedy* is that, at its deepest level, art is a tension or *agon* (the Greek word for a contest or struggle) between the opposing forces of the Dionysian and the Apollonian. The Apollonian, form-giving moment of the work of art is necessary because it protects us from total self-loss in the "rapture" of the Dionysian. Nietzsche says that the unfolding of the initially inchoate ground-rhythm of life into enduring, beautiful forms "redeems" the Dionysian. "The Apollonian illusion . . . saves us from the direct identification with Dionysian music" by interposing a "medium" between us and the Dionysian.[9] But it remains the case that the Apollonian is merely an illusion—a smoke screen of shapes and images that conceals the underlying truth about life. When the veil of Apollonian illusion is torn asunder through the experience of music, the illusory fragmentation of nature into discrete individuals falls away, and it becomes possible for humans to experience once again their oneness with the human community and with the universe as a whole.

2. A New Kind of Science   *Important to see n*

The writings of Nietzsche's middle period shift away from the point of view of the earlier works. This shift is evident in the title of what is perhaps Nietzsche's most representative philosophical work, *The Gay Science*

critiques positivism too !

8. Ibid., secs. 2 and 16.
9. Ibid., sec. 24.

(1882).[10] Though the subtitle of the work, *"la gaya scienza,"* alludes to a style of medieval poetry, it is clear that the title also expresses a very upbeat perspective on the great accomplishments of nineteenth-century science. The preface to the second edition, added in 1887 along with the fifth book, describes *The Gay Science* as reflecting the high spirits that accompany the author's recovery from a debilitating illness. The sickness he has recovered from, we find, is the *"nausea* that had gradually grown out of a careless and pampering spiritual diet, known as Romanticism." The implication here is that Nietzsche's earlier works, such as *The Birth of Tragedy*, had been caught up in an unhealthy Romanticism. What is unhealthy about Romanticism, it seems, is its nostalgic longing for a bygone "Golden Age," a time when people were still in touch with a primordial origin—the "ground of being," as it was called in *The Birth of Tragedy*. By glorifying an imagined time of origins, Romanticism spawns the kind of discouragement with the present and the yearning for "the good old days" that cuts people off from a healthy concern with building for the future by acting in the here and now. When the past is used as a stick to beat the present, the result is a gloomy view of both the current world and the prospects for the future.

In *The Gay Science*, in contrast, the emphasis is clearly on the present and the prospects for the future. But it is also clear that the pivotal concept of "life" has not been abandoned. Nietzsche is still concerned with recovering a full and healthy life for people, but his view of what constitutes such a life has been transformed. Where *The Birth of Tragedy* had treated life as a deep, dark current beneath the surface play of appearances, *The Gay Science* treats the very opposition between surface appearance and concealed reality as itself the main source of sickness. The shift seems to be due in part to what in *Twilight of the Idols* is called the "first yawn of reason," the "cock's crow of positivism." Positivism, a late nineteenth-century conception of science, rejects the distinction between phenomena and reality, and treats the phenomena, the surface appearances themselves, as the only reality. On this view, the idea that we need to posit the existence of underlying forces to explain phenomena is pointless. It has no real cash value in science.

In line with this new view of science, *The Gay Science* denies the distinction between perceivable appearances on the one hand and a concealed, underlying reality on the other. In this respect it marks a break with much of

10. Richard Schacht says of *The Gay Science*, "If there is any one of his published works in which 'the essential philosophical Nietzsche' is to be found, it would seem to me to be this one." See his essay "Nietzsche's *Gay Science*, or, How to Naturalize Cheerfully," in *Reading Nietzsche*, ed. Robert C. Solomon and Kathleen M. Higgins (New York: Oxford University Press, 1988), 70–71.

Western philosophy. Ever since the time of Plato, there has been a tendency in metaphysics to draw a distinction between the way things *appear*, which is treated as something derivative, secondary, and inferior, and the way things *really are*, which is seen as original, primary, and superior. This sort of hierarchically arranged binary opposition, with its invidious contrast between "mere" appearance and "genuine" reality, has cropped up again and again in Western thought, so much so, in fact, that all Western philosophy has been called "Platonism." By attacking various forms of this dualism, then, Nietzsche puts in question one of the most fundamental tenets of Western thinking.

The dualistic opposition between appearance and reality paves the way for a particular conception of our task as humans. There is a tendency to believe that we are currently caught in a veil of mere appearance, out of touch with reality, and that it is our task to extricate ourselves from this illusion and distortion in order to get in touch with what is real. Thus, metaphysical thinking tends to assume that we can rise "above" or "beyond" our current state and finally arrive at the truth about reality. As Nietzsche now sees it, however, it is precisely this belief in a better world to come that is the source of our sickness. What causes illness, he says, is "every metaphysics and physics that knows of a *finale*, a final state of any sort, every . . . longing for an elsewhere, a beyond, an outside, an above." In other words, sickness results from dreaming of a better way of life we might achieve in the future, a superior state of affairs in contrast to which our present condition seems inferior or worthless.

This kind of fantasizing about a better future, with its accompanying distaste for the present, is deeply ingrained in our thinking. It presupposes a teleological picture of our history that is expressed in a particular sort of story line we use in making sense of where we are now and where we are going. The general structure of this story line is the traditional "redemption myth" that has been so central to Western thought. It assumes that the course of events is guided by a particular "sending" that determines in advance the goal or purpose we ought to be trying to reach. In terms of this idea of a shared sending and purpose we have as a historical people, it holds that we are currently "falling" away from that goal, though we have the ability to get back on track again if we change our ways.

This sort of teleological "metanarrative" or narrative schema is found in a wide range of the stories we tell ourselves to make sense of our situation. Consider these stories: "Once we were in a Garden, but we sinned and now are falling, but there is the promise that we can be saved and return to the Garden if we repent and do God's will." Or: "Once people were spontaneous, childlike, and free, but then society came along and distorted their nature; still, there is the hope that we can achieve a better kind of society where people again will be pure and free." Or: "Once people were altruistic and shared among themselves, but along came capitalism and private property and people became alienated from one another; nevertheless, there is the promise that class warfare will bring a new world order in which everyone will live happily and share freely." Or: "Once people had initiative and took responsibility, but then along came liberals and welfare and taxes, and now the world is a mess; but there is the hope. . . ." What these stories have in common is a belief in an underlying teleology or purposiveness running through history. They all assume that our culture's history embodies a "sending" that determines in advance what our proper purpose is on earth, and that we have the prospects for achieving a better life—some correlate of "salvation"—if we are willing to change our ways and make sacrifices for the sake of the future.

The teleological metanarrative seems to be linked to a two-tiered vision of our culture's history. It assumes a distinction between our *actuality*—our current state of existence, which is seen as falling or deceived or wicked—and our *potentiality*—the truer, better, happier, more beautiful world that we could achieve if we realized the aims built into our original sending on earth. This kind of story line therefore goes hand in hand with what Nietzsche calls an "ascetic ideal": the faith that our sufferings ultimately make sense because they are necessary for achieving some bright, shining ideal we can attain in the future. Such stories tell us we should be willing to work harder and suffer more because we have before us the prospect of achieving some totality of knowledge or justice or happiness that will make it all worthwhile. Finally, the two-tiered view of history, with its distinction between our actual state and our potential *telos* or goal, has often been tied to a distinction between two worlds: the concrete, material world in which we currently find ourselves, and a better, perhaps more "spiritual" world that is presently beyond our reach but is promised for those willing to work for it.

It is this kind of teleological metanarrative that "those who teach the goals of existence" use in trying to motivate people to behave in the ways they want them to behave. According to section 1 of *The Gay Science*, the ethical teacher "invents a second and different existence, and with his new machinery lifts the common old existence off its common old hinges." Teleological narratives always make a negative judgment about life, because they assume that there is something bad or lacking in our ordinary existence that needs to be rectified by discipline and sacrifice. All talk of "progress," "improvement," "betterment," "development," and "goals" presupposes this essentially negative assessment of life as it is in the here and now. Nevertheless, such stories are immensely appealing, because they offer us the comfort of letting us believe that our lives are nested in the wider story of the "sending" of our culture as a whole. Thus, they tell us that our sufferings are not in vain, for they contribute to a greater historical project that legitimates them and gives them a meaning. The fact that what we do is part of a larger world-historical story assures us that life is not a tale told by an idiot signifying nothing.

The Gay Science sets out to undermine the traditional teleological narratives of the West. In the preface to the second edition, Nietzsche attacks many of the aspirations that have been central to Western thought. He characterizes "the will to truth," which has been central to religion and science, as a "will to closure" that aims at freezing over culture by putting an end to all inquiry. The will to truth, he suggests, is really a will to the end, a will to death. Because our understanding of the importance of truth is shaped by a bunch of metaphors usually regarded as beyond criticism in our culture, Nietzsche tries to shake us out of our complacent self-assurance by challenging those metaphors. When he asks, "What if truth is a woman?" for example, he seems to be suggesting that the age-old masculine imagery of truth as driving home a point or being penetrating is totally inappropriate to what we need, and that we might do well to substitute new metaphors of fertility and breadth for the old metaphors of incisiveness and making points.

The new, exuberant science Nietzsche has in mind will abandon the old, hierarchically arranged oppositions of surface and depth, darkness and light, appearance and reality, image and original, fiction and truth, and ignorance and knowledge. Instead of tearing asunder veils to get at the hidden truth, this science will be content to live at the level of the surfaces and appearances. The real greatness of the early, pre-Platonic Greeks, Nietzsche now suggests, was precisely their ability to live without such invidious distinctions. The ancient Greek tragedians and myth-makers lived totally at the level of what shows up in the sensory world, at the level of *physis* understood as what emerges into presence, with no illusions about another world "behind" or "above" this world. They were able to embrace life on its own terms, with its ceaseless ebb and flow, its risks and uncertainties, and they did so with neither nostalgia for a Garden that never was nor fantasies about a future that can never be. The Greeks were great because they could deal with this world on its own terms, embracing even what is most terrible and frightening about life. It is this ability to accept every aspect of life with intensity and joy that defines the life-affirming, "yes-saying" quality of Greek tragedy. It is because the tragic affirmation of life is the opposite of teleological story lines with their emphasis on what ought to be that Nietzsche takes as both the end and beginning of *The Gay Science* the words, *Incipit tragoedia*, "Now begins the tragedy."

3. The Death of God

We can read much of *The Gay Science* as an attempt to undermine traditional teleological narratives and the dualistic oppositions they presuppose. Metanarratives about progress and improvement make sense only on the assumption that there is something genuinely worth striving for, some end or goal that is genuinely superior to the way things are in the present. And this sort of ranking of things into "better" and "worse" assumes the existence of standards and values that are regarded as transcendent and objective, that is, not merely transient products of human feeling or practice. In other words, it assumes the existence of *absolutes*, where these are regarded as timeless, unchanging, objective bases for assessment and aspiration.

To undermine this belief in absolutes, Nietzsche looks at how an attitude of skepticism has gained power over the course of Western history. The really corrosive effects of doubt, Nietzsche notes, began with Christianity's faith that "the truth shall make you free." It was Christianity's uncompromising critique of pagan superstition and its quest for truth that began to shatter older, taken-for-granted ways of thinking. This method of doubt was later intensified by the emergence of science and scientific procedure in the modern age, with the result that modern Western people are losing their capacity for uncritical belief. Thus, at this stage in the history of skepticism in the West, it has become increasingly difficult to believe in a transcendent ground for values and belief. God, Reason, the cosmos, providence, divine rights, the noumenal realm, *Geist*, Humanity, History—all these conceptions of the ultimate foundation for our beliefs and practices have been shown up for what they are: human constructs, expressions of our own hopes and needs, with no basis in a transcendent reality beyond our ways of thinking and acting. The "self-grounding grounds" that traditionally were used to legitimate beliefs and institutions now appear as products of our own "craving for metaphysical comfort," as symptoms of our wishful thinking rather than as foundation stones of reality.

The upshot of this process of doubt is the recognition that there are no longer any absolutes in the West. There is no fixed source of order and direction beneath the flux of events in the world, no "spider of purpose and morality behind the great captious web of causality."[11] This is the significance of the statement, made by "the madman" in section 125 of *The Gay Science*, that "God is dead." The tone of this passage makes it clear that Nietzsche sees nothing funny about the thought of the death of God. If the

---

11. Nietzsche, *On the Genealogy of Morals*, III, 9, in *On the Genealogy of Morals and Ecce Homo*, ed. and trans. Walter Kaufmann (New York: Viking, 1969), 113.

development of Western culture has led to the point that there is no firm foundation for our lives, no agreed-upon belief in a transcendent basis for our values and beliefs, then it seems that there are no longer any guidelines to give direction to our aspirations or provide a basis for our assessments. Nietzsche tries to capture the sense of *weightlessness* or free-fall that results from this awareness with images of falling endlessly into a dark, cold abyss and of the earth being unchained from the sun and spinning madly out of control. For if there is nothing that is universally accepted as an absolute in our culture, if there is no basis for consensus about what is right or wrong, good or bad, then this opens the door to *nihilism*, the complete disbelief in all values.

The initial reaction to nihilism, Nietzsche believes, will be an attempt to find a new absolute—a new god-term in science or history or art—to fill the hole left by the collapse of absolutes. To do away with these "shadows" of God, he criticizes various attempts to "deify nature" in our contemporary, scientific age. Scientific realists, for example, with their faith that natural science is discovering the truth about the world, are turning their conception of nature into a new absolute or surrogate god-term. In response to such realists, Nietzsche drives home the insight, rooted in Kant, that what presents itself to us as "reality" is largely a product of our own modes of apprehension and interpretation. What we call "hard facts" about the real world, Nietzsche suggests, are mainly products of some optional metaphors cooked up at earlier points in Western history, metaphors that have been deposited in our language and have been repeated so often through the course of history that they come to seem beyond criticism.

In some ingenious analyses, Nietzsche tries to get us to consider the possibility that such notions as substance, causality, unity, duration, stability, and even consciousness itself are products of our own ways of categorizing and perceiving, projections of our own need for order rather than features of the world as it is in itself. For example, the idea that the world is broken up into neat "natural kinds" tailor-made to the standards of our own intellects is subjected to doubt. The idea that the world consists of discrete, reidentifiable things is portrayed as a product of the requirements of our logical systems rather than a fact of nature. And the assumption that events follow one another in a neat, linear causal ordering is treated as something we impose onto experience rather than something we discover from experience.

Nietzsche also suggests that such concepts as "stability," "order," "lawfulness," "cause and effect," and "regularity" are anthropomorphisms, concepts derived from our own social arrangements and normative principles. Ascribing such concepts to nonhuman phenomena might be totally inappropriate. For all we know, *our* distinctions between necessity and accident, lawfulness and lawlessness, order and disorder, may be quite out of place in trying to describe the world as it is in itself. Nietzsche toys with the idea that what exists "out there" in reality, the ultimate "truth" about the world, might be what we would regard as *chaos*, that is, the complete absence of what we consider order and manageability. In the end, we really have no reason to suppose that reality must be designed in such a way as to satisfy our craving for intellectual mastery. If we seem to find such a design, then that is more likely a product of our ways of creating categories than it is a discovery about the true structure of reality. Nietzsche suggests that our senses and modes of interpretation act more like filters that remove what is painful or recalcitrant than like receptors that convey to us the full, unembellished truth about reality.

To say that God is dead, then, is to say that we should give up the assumption that we can gain access to a "self-grounding ground" or an ultimate basis of intelligibility of the sort imagined by philosophers when they spoke of a *causa sui* (a self-causing cause, such as the Prime Mover or First Cause). It may be that the complexity of phenomena will never be reducible to a few easily managed, inherently intelligible principles. Nature is under no obligation to measure up to our intellectual standards.

And if there is no ultimate grounding for our beliefs, then it would seem to follow that not just our scientific theories, but our moral values as well are our own constructs and have no firm basis in the order of things. They are ultimately matters of choice and preference rather than injunctions issuing from some transcendent source. Nietzsche suggests that moral codes are expressions of a community's needs and drives that have been raised to the status of timeless truths and instilled in individuals in order to domesticate and socialize them. Their sole function is to insure the preservation of the herd. As people become aware of the death of God and the loss of any basis for a shared consensus about values, however, morality will begin to look like a sucker's game with no binding force for us.

Nietzsche sees this impending breakdown of morality as a terrifying turn of events, for it will lead to the breakdown of culture as we have known it. It could lead people to recoil in horror from the awareness of the abyss surrounding them, so that they turn into "little men" who go about their business mindlessly singing, "Don't worry, be happy." Or it could lead to a life-negating, reactive form of nihilism, where people, obsessed with the feeling that something has been lost, run amok in a frenzy of destructiveness similar to that portrayed in Dostoevsky's *The Possessed*. But Nietzsche envisions another possible outcome of this event. At the end of the initial period of confusion, European civilization might succeed in passing through the stage of reactive, "transitional" nihilism (as it is called in *The Will to Power*), and pass on to a creative form of nihilism that appropriates the death of God in a positive way and uses it as a basis for creating a new form of cultural life.

Such an active, life-affirming nihilism would be the "nihilation of nihilism." Much of *The Gay Science* could be thought of as an experiment designed to see what that might be like.

4. The Idea of the Eternal Recurrence of the Same

The effect of the death of God is a sense of the "weightlessness" of all things. With no absolutes to justify our actions or prop up our beliefs, life seems to lose its center of gravity and everything seems to be up for grabs. The old teleological narratives lose their power, for there is no longer any basis for saying that some potential future condition is genuinely superior to the way things are now. If we no longer have the assurance that there is some future state that is really worth striving for, then we seem to be simply drifting through life with no sense of purpose or justification. With the loss of any background "metanarrative" to serve as a ground for our existence, life becomes a meaningless series of episodes without any cumulativeness, coherence, or direction.

The doctrine of the "eternal recurrence of the same" is introduced in the section called "The heaviest weight," and it might be thought of as an attempt to provide an antidote to the sense of weightlessness that results from the death of God. The idea of eternal recurrence was an ancient Stoic doctrine, which held that a finite number of elements governed by a fixed number of necessary connections will, over an infinite amount of time, repeat the same patterns over and over again.[12] Nietzsche was fascinated with this idea of the eternal recurrence of the same, and in different places he considers the possibility that everything that has ever happened, is happening, and will happen in a person's lifetime has already happened before in earlier incarnations of our universe, and will happen again and again, an infinite number of times, throughout all eternity. It is not clear whether Nietzsche actually believed in this doctrine, but it turns out not to be very important for the purposes of *The Gay Science* whether or not it is a reasonable view. For in this work he never assumes that the doctrine is actually true. Instead, he presents the idea of the eternal recurrence of the same as a thought experiment, an exercise in the kind of "transfiguration" he feels authentic philosophy ought to achieve.[13]

12. See A. A. Long and D. N. Sedley, *The Hellenistic Philosophers* (Cambridge: Cambridge University Press, 1987), Vol 1, sec. 52, "Everlasting Recurrence," for texts and commentary on the Stoic doctrine.

13. The best account of the eternal recurrence is Bernd Magnus's *Nietzsche's Existential Imperative* (Bloomington: Indiana University Press, 1978). Magnus has modified his views in interesting ways lately. See his "Perfectibility and Attitude in Nietzsche's *Übermensch*," *The Review of Metaphysics* 36 (March 1983): 633–60.

To understand the role of the idea of the eternal recurrence in *The Gay Science*, we need to look carefully at what Nietzsche says. Section 341 begins, "What if one day or one night a demon . . . said to you: 'This life, as you live it now and as you have lived it, you will have to live once more and countless times more; and there will be nothing new about it, . . . and everything unspeakably small and great in your life must come back to you, and all in the same series and sequence.'" Note that the idea of the eternal repetition of the same is presented here as a hypothesis we are to entertain: it says "what if" rather than "it is the case that." The aim of this passage, it seems, is to encourage you to consider something so unsettling that even the thought of its being true might bring about a radical transformation in your life. *What if* you had to live every detail of your life over and over again in exactly the same way? *What if* your life story was to be repeated an infinite number of times? To take such a thought seriously could have a devastating effect on you: "If that thought took control of you," Nietzsche says, "it would change you as you are, and maybe shatter you."

Why would this thought have such an effect? The answer seems to be that the idea of an eternal recurrence of the same would totally shatter any sense of teleology in life. Life for most of us tends to be goal-directed and future-oriented: we see our action as directed toward achieving certain short-range and long-term goals we take as definitive for our lives. You go to school to get a degree, you get a degree to succeed in a career. You set aside money in order to have a comfortable retirement. You work in order to save up in order to take a vacation in order to have fun. And so on. What gives our lives cumulativeness and direction is precisely the feeling that we are accomplishing something, that things are adding up for us as a whole.

But if everything we do is something we have done innumerable times before, and is something we will do over and over again for all eternity, then that sense of getting somewhere or achieving something through our actions is undermined. There is no final culmination or realization that would give our actions a point. We would be like Sisyphus in Greek mythology, whose punishment in the afterlife was to push the same rock up a hill and then watch it roll to the bottom where he had to begin pushing it up again, over and over for all eternity. Or we would be like the character in the movie *Groundhog Day*, who goes through the same events day after day, except that we would not even have any recollection of earlier lives, and we would not be able to introduce any variations into our life stories. In Nietzsche's thought experiment, it would be exactly the same set of events and actions occurring in exactly the same way for all eternity: "The eternal hourglass of existence is turned over again and again—and you with it, you mote of dust!"

It is not hard to see why this thought might shatter you. All planning and goal-setting would suddenly seem pointless, mere exercises in futility, since they would never get you anywhere except where you would have been anyway and where you have already been innumerable times before. But even though this thought could shatter you, it could also transform you. Nietzsche suggests that facing up to the thought of eternal recurrence might impart a new and greater weightiness to your life, for it would lead you to ask this "question in each and every thing, 'Do you will this once more and countless times more'?" And this question, he says, "would lie as the heaviest weight upon your acts."

It seems that what Nietzsche is suggesting here is that if we were to will that our lives be repeated innumerable times exactly as they are, with no embellishments or changes, then this would give a kind of "weight" to our existence. For it would force us to embrace our own lives and to affirm for all eternity every event in our lives, even while accepting the fact that there is no underlying teleology to life that gives what we do some overarching sense. And, because Nietzsche believes that everything an individual does is tied up with everything else that happens in the universe (since everything is interconnected in the whole), to affirm your own life in all its details is also to affirm everything that has happened and ever will happen in the universe—the important and the trivial, the good and the bad, everything!

Nietzsche asks you to consider "how benevolent [you would] have to become toward yourself and toward life in order to *long for nothing more ardently* than for this ultimate eternal sanction and seal." To will the eternal repetition of every tiny event in your life, to will it ardently, would require the ability to completely embrace your own life as it is, without any regrets or longing for something different. If you could do this, you would be freed from the need to see your life as part of a wider cosmic story about our purpose on earth, and you would be able to appropriate the events in your own life without worrying about how they contribute to realizing some greater *telos*. As a result, you would be able to live fully and intensely in each moment, being totally present to your own life. In giving your life an ultimate "sanction and seal" in this way, you would achieve the kind of life-affirming, "yes-saying" stance toward life Nietzsche hoped to find after the demise of the old teleological metanarratives.

This conception of a life-affirming stance toward all existence is found in the ideal of *amor fati*, "loving one's fate." In Nietzsche's words, "My formula for greatness in a human being is *amor fati*: that one wants nothing to be different, not forward, not backward, not in all eternity. Not merely bear what is necessary, still less conceal it . . . but *love* it."[14] The important thing

---

14. *Ecce Homo*, "Why I Am So Clever," 10, in *On the Genealogy of Morals and Ecce Homo*, ed. and trans. Walter Kaufmann (New York: Viking, 1969), 258.

is to make your life your own by *willing* it. When we give up on the idea of an overarching purpose to life, ordinary existence can seem dispersed and disconnected, lacking any cohesiveness or continuity. It is only when we take over all that has happened and appropriate it by willing it, Nietzsche claims, that our lives begin to have coherence and form. As Nietzsche says, "All 'it was' is a fragment, a riddle, a dreadful accident—until the creative will says to it, 'But thus I willed it'."[15] This ideal of embracing all your life by willing all you have been and will be—willing both backward into the past as well as forward into the future—"annihilates nihilism" to the extent that it grounds your life, imparting the eternal seal of a "Yes" to everything you have done, are doing, and will do. Only by accepting your own life story as it is can you be liberated from the craving for some sort of large-scale tele-ological legitimation for your existence.

5. Perspectivism   Relate ₹ Plato !

To say that God is dead is to say that there is no prospect of finding a fixed source of order and direction beneath the flux of events in the world. Old notions of reality, order, the good, the true, the beautiful—all these ideas turn out to be social constructions invented by people to try to satisfy their "craving for metaphysical comfort." They are products of dogmatic systems of belief that are no longer tenable in the modern world.

To show the contingent nature of traditional dogmas, Nietzsche looks at how such systems of belief get started in the first place. In section 353 of *The Gay Science*, he proposes an account of the origin of a particular set of religious beliefs, Christianity. What was given initially, he claims, was a form of life occurring alongside other forms of life, that of a small group of people living a modest existence alongside other peoples in a dusty corner of the Roman Empire. The practices of these people embodied a tacit background sense of what life is all about, but that background understanding was still inchoate and had no particular significance. The religious belief system first begins to take shape, according to Nietzsche, when someone comes along and bestows on the community's form of life "an *interpretation* thanks to which it seems to be lit up by the highest value so that now it becomes a good for which one struggles and, under certain circumstances, gives up one's life." Thus "Jesus (or Paul)" interpreted the impoverished lives of the subjected people in such a way as to read into them the "highest meaning and value." Through their formulation of the significance of this way of life, what had previously looked base and slavish—meekness, humility, chas-

15. *Thus Spoke Zarathustra*, II, "On Redemption," in *The Portable Nietzsche*, ed. and trans. Walter Kaufmann (New York: Viking, 1960), 253.

tity, mercy—is made to look like the best possible way of living, whereas the lifestyle of the Roman masters—with their strength, pride, sensuality, and retaliation—begins to look harsh, brutal, and "evil." Eventually the new interpretation is crystalized and enshrined in the texts and institutions of an established Church. As it gains control over people's imaginations, it begins to seem self-evidently true, an expression of God's will that only insensitive brutes could fail to acknowledge and bow down to.

This account of the formation of a religion could serve as a model for Nietzsche's general account of how belief systems come into existence. According to this story, a tacit background sense of things, embodied in a community's practices, comes to be formulated and made explicit, and those interpretations then come to be passed down from generation to generation. Eventually people forget that this interpretation is just one take on things among others, and it comes to be treated as a timeless, self-evident truth.

What this account implies, however, is that the beliefs treated as obviously true by a people are really only calcified interpretations that took shape in the past and have been passed down through history. And this means that our sense of reality is ultimately "interpretation all the way down": There are only interpretations of interpretations, commentaries on commentaries, texts about texts, redescriptions of descriptions, with no bedrock of "facts" underlying the play of interpretations that have emerged through the millennia. In Jacques Derrida's well-known phrase, "There is nothing outside the text." What we call the "truth," Nietzsche says, is "a mobile army of metaphors . . . in short, a sum of human relations, which have been enhanced, transposed, and embellished poetically and rhetorically, and which after long use seem firm, canonical, and obligatory to a people: truths are illusions about which one has forgotten that this is what they are; metaphors which are worn out and without sensuous power."[16] Even science is based on a set of ungrounded metaphors to the extent that it uncritically assumes that there are enduring substances, temporal sequences, spatial relations, and causal interactions. Science is just one more interpretation among others, and it is a "prejudice" to the extent that it treats its own view of things as the ultimate "truth" about reality.

In Section 354 of *The Gay Science*, "On the 'genius of the species'," Nietzsche suggests that even our most treasured possession, our vaunted *consciousness* as subjects of knowledge and choice, is a side-effect of social interactions that conceals our real nature as selves. His claim is that consciousness first arises as a result of the need for cooperation with others. As social animals, we need to work together, and for that purpose language

16. "On Truth and Lie in an Extra-Moral Sense," in *The Portable Nietzsche*, 47.

comes into existence as a common medium of exchange. Consciousness in turn results from this linguistic and cooperative social practice. As a result, consciousness is essentially pragmatic and linguistic. But that means that what goes on in our conscious minds is always only the commonplace, public interpretation of things circulating in our public world. What we become aware of through consciousness is not our own thoughts and feelings (which are always unconscious), but rather ways of thinking dictated by the "metaphysics" or "mythology" built into the grammar of our public language. In Nietzsche's words, "everything that becomes conscious *becomes*, by the same token, shallow, thin, relatively stupid, general, a sign, a signal of the herd; . . . all becoming conscious is bound up with a great and radical perversion, falsification, superficialization, and generalization." As conscious beings, then, each of us exists as a commentary on the public text laid out by our historical culture. And that implies that, in our conscious lives, we are precisely *not* ourselves, but are bearers or representatives of the lowest common denominator of the herd mentality.

If our sense of reality and even our own identities as humans are constructed by cultural interpretations that have evolved through history, does that mean that Nietzsche is some sort of pragmatist who equates "truth" with "what is useful" in helping us cope with life? Nietzsche rejects such a suggestion. Pragmatists assume that we can check to see whether our interpretations help us cope with reality. But if we always operate within the framework of some interpretation or other, then there is no way we can compare our interpretations with an uninterpreted reality to see whether they are really helping us cope with that reality. In fact, by our lights it might seem to us that we are coping quite well, while all along we have been slowly destroying ourselves: "and even what is here called 'usefulness' is in the end just another belief, a product of the imagination, and perhaps is precisely that most dangerous stupidity that will someday ruin us."

From this picture of reality as a play of socially constructed interpretations Nietzsche derives his "perspectivism," the view that we have access only to our own perspectives on things, with the result that we can never exit from our perspectives to know reality as it is in itself. This perspectivist outlook is formulated in section 374, "Our new 'infinite'," where Nietzsche claims that we can see things only from "our own corner." What this means is that the world we encounter is always shaped in advance by particular points of view or grids of interpretation that have taken shape as a result of thousands of years of human development. Note that this is not the claim that each person sees things differently, but rather that all humans will tend to see things in specific ways due to their shared heritage and historical formation. This is what Nietzsche implies in Section 54 when he says it is not I alone who thinks and interprets, but rather "the human and animal of past ages, in fact the whole prehistory and past of all sentient being, [which] goes on fabricating, loving, hating, and drawing conclusions within me."[17]

Thus, Nietzsche's perspectivism holds that our shared heritage has created us in such a way that we will encounter the world through a specific range of possible perspectives, and that given this repertoire of possible perspectives, we now have the ability to shift our outlook from, say, the cool, objective outlook of theoretical inquiry to the intense outlook of religious fervor. What is important to see is that there is no way we can step outside of all human perspectives in order to get a view of reality as it is in itself, independent of our perspectives. That is why we cannot get out of our own corner. And since there is no way to stand outside our own perspectives to compare them to reality as it is in itself, there is no way we can distinguish what is the result of our interpretations from what is supposed to be just "there" in our experience.

A common objection to perspectivism is to say that if we can make no sense of other, radically different perspectives, we simply ought to accept our own perspectives as *the* truth about reality. Our human perspectives are, one might say, as true as anything can get for us. But Nietzsche is not impressed by this objection. It would be a "laughable presumption," he says, to decree "from our corner that one is *allowed* to have perspectives only from this corner." The fact that we humans have created a variety of perspectives and continue to create new perspectives gives us a basis for assuming that there can be an unlimited number of perspectives reflecting the interests and needs of different forms of life. Even if we humans can never quite imagine what it is like to be a bat, for example, we have every reason to think that there is such a thing as "what it is like to be a bat," and that a batty type of experience (involving echo location and flying at night) is very different from our human experience. Thus, even if we cannot really make sense of alternative perspectives or modes of experience, it would be ridiculous immodesty to say they do not exist.

The suspicion that there might be innumerable perspectives can lead to "a great horror," Nietzsche says. For the idea of an infinite number of perspectives might seem to lead us back to the traditional idea of "the Infinite." This is the idea (found in Spinoza and Hegel among others) of an all-embracing, self-contained totality that embodies all possible aspects and interpretations. The idea of the "Infinite" has been used as a surrogate god-term by philosophers, because it seems to imply the possibility of the Un-

17. In his book, *Composing the Soul: Reaches of Nietzsche's Psychology* (Chicago: University of Chicago Press, 1994), Graham Parkes shows how all interpretation is grounded in a shared perspective determined by our human heritage.

known One who has (or could have) an ultimate God's-eye view of all perspectives, and so would be able to comprehend all that is. In other words, it seems to presuppose a new concept of Totality, and this threatens to resuscitate the traditional idea of the all-embracing One that contains all that is True and Good and Beautiful. But Nietzsche makes it clear that his "new infinite" does not give us any basis for positing a new god-term. For, as he says, there are "too many *ungodly* possibilities of interpretation comprised in this unknown," too much of what is *not* true or good or beautiful, for anyone to be tempted to *deify* this new unknown.

6. "The Great Health" and the Path to the Overman

Though there is no explicit discussion of the ideal of the Overman (*Übermensch*) in *The Gay Science*, there are a number of clues to what Nietzsche took to be the most authentic form of life for humans after the death of God. First, the section called "One thing is needful" (290) suggests that Nietzsche's vision of an ideal way of life is concerned with the *style* one imparts to one's existence rather than with its content. We are told that what is important is fitting one's traits into "an artistic plan, until each thing appears as art and reason, and even the weakness charms the eye." In the end what is decisive is that "it was the compulsion of a single taste that was ruling and forming, in things both great and small. Whether the taste was a good or a bad one means less than one thinks—it is enough that it is *one* taste."

The ideal of giving one's life a personal style is coupled with the injunction, "Become who you are." Though this counsel dates back to Pindar, it might seem rather puzzling coming from Nietzsche. For it is natural to suppose that this injunction is telling us that we ought to realize our inbuilt potential or essence. Yet Nietzsche has told us that we have no pregiven "essence" or "potentiality." In fact, in one of his earliest writings he suggests that our true nature is a yet-undefined possibility that we might achieve through self-overcoming: "Your true nature lies, not concealed deep within you, but immeasurably high above you, or at least above that which you usually take yourself to be."[18] More importantly, Nietzsche has told us that there really is no "self" understood as a self-encapsulated consciousness or mind that is a center of experience and action. The conscious self, as we have seen, is merely the lowest common denominator of the everyday social world. If this is the case, however, then it is not at all clear what self you should become when you become who you are.

18. "Schopenhauer as Educator," in *Untimely Meditations*, trans. R. J. Hollingdale (Cambridge: Cambridge University Press, 1983), 129.

Alexander Nehamas has suggested a way of making sense of the idea of becoming what you are that draws on what Nietzsche says in different contexts about the eternal recurrence and the need for style. Nehamas recommends that we think of the self as a life story or narrative an individual is composing throughout the course of his or her life. If we assume that the doctrine of eternal recurrence is true, then what gives continuity to such a life cannot be its being directed toward realizing some set of goals. And if that is the case, then the best way to make sense of the idea of becoming what we are is to think of it as meaning that we should embrace all the events of our lives by owning up to (and thereby owning) all we have been, are, and will be. The aim is to shape one's life story into a coherent narrative by imparting a unique, personal style to everything one does. On this way of describing Nietzsche's ideal, becoming the person you are is not so much a matter of realizing a pregiven potential as it is of creating yourself in such a way that you can fully *assume* the identity you create for yourself. This self-creation, according to Nehamas, "involves accepting everything that we have done and, in the ideal case, blending it into a perfectly coherent whole." The goal is "to appropriate and to organize as my own all that I have done, or at least that I know I have done, into a coherent whole. It is simply to become able to accept all such things, good and evil, as things I have done."[19] Though Nehamas' description of Nietzsche's aesthetic ideal helps us make sense of the notion of "becoming what you are," we should note that "accepting" yourself sounds too much like the banal pop psychology idea of "self-acceptance." It is not accepting oneself that Nietzsche has in mind, but joyfully *embracing* one's own existence, *affirming* all that one is, and *loving* one's fate.

The ideal of the Overman is inseparable from the concept of the "will to power." A lot of confusion has surrounded this idea over the years. It is tempting to think that the will to power involves being on a power trip or trying to control others. But a close reading of Nietzsche's texts shows that this is not at all what he has in mind. In a number of places he tries to clarify what he means by the will to power by contrasting this notion with a plausible view about what constitutes the motivating force behind all life forms. Nietzsche says that Spinoza had formulated a "law of self-preservation," according to which all living things strive to preserve themselves and their own species.[20] But Nietzsche thinks that such a "law of preservation" can-

19. Alexander Nehamas, *Nietzsche: Life as Literature* (Cambridge, Mass.: Harvard University Press, 1985), 188–89, 190.

20. In section 349 of *The Gay Science*, Nietzsche suggests that the same conception of evolution in nature is found in "Darwinism with its unbelievably one-sided doctrine of the 'struggle for existence'."

not be the truth about what motivates living things, for if it were true, then when a life form had reached the point where it could survive, it would stop developing and not grow anymore. But it is easy to see that just the opposite is true: "every living thing does everything it can not to preserve itself but to become *more*."[21] A tree in an open pasture, for example, does not just spread its foliage and sink its roots to the minimum degree needed in order to survive. On the contrary, the tree keeps on growing, spreading its branches out, and digging its roots deeper and deeper into the soil. The tree keeps striving for greater and greater energy and strength long after it has satisfied the bare conditions for mere survival.

What we see in living organisms generally, according to Nietzsche, is not just a will to survive, but a will to flourish, to thrive, to realize ever greater possibilities and powers. Living things throughout nature press onward, trying to exceed all limits and constraints in order to achieve superabundance and overflowing life. Instead of resting content with what they are, natural beings strive to go beyond what they have achieved and to be more than what they currently are.

This idea of the will to power in all nature explains Nietzsche's view of the fundamental force motivating humans. Humans, like all living things, are driven by a will to achieve ever greater power and abundance, to "go beyond" what they are at any given time. This will to flourish and "become *more*" can take two forms. It takes a weak and sickly form when it is merely reactive, intent simply on negating something else. This unhealthy form of the will to power is motivated by resentment and it is always "nay-saying" and negative. But the will to power takes an active, positive form when it spontaneously goes beyond all apparent boundaries in a quest for greater strength and expanded possibilities. This active, "yes-saying" form of the will to power is central to Nietzsche's concept of the most healthy, life-affirming way of life.

An image of such a life is presented in the penultimate section of *The Gay Science* called "the great health." Here Nietzsche speaks of "free spirits" who understand their rootedness in the background interpretations passed down by their historical culture, but who also understand that those interpretations are ultimately metaphors with no absolutely binding significance for us. Such people are able to take up the interpretations handed down by the tradition in a new way. Nietzsche speaks of "the ideal of a spirit that plays naively, that is, not deliberately but from overflowing fullness and power, with all that up to now was called holy, good, untouchable, divine." In other words, it is the ideal of someone who can take up the perspectives handed down by the past and work them over into new, original perspectives

21. Nietzsche, *The Will to Power*, 688.

expressing a unique, creative intent. For such a person, the ideals and beliefs of the past are treated as something to play with in a free-ranging, experimental approach to things.

This passage shows how Nietzsche thinks that the death of God might ultimately lead to the "nihilation of nihilism." Those who have confronted the loss of all absolutes, and have gotten over yearning for new absolutes to fill the hole left by the death of God, are now in a position to see everything that has been called holy in older, traditional perspectives as material on hand for creative reinterpretation and reformulation. Such a person will joyfully play in the ruins of the collapsed traditions, making of things what he or she will, without any illusion that there are objective criteria, constraints, or guidelines determining what one ought to be. This kind of experimentalism seems to require some rigorous preparation if it is not to lead to mere anarchy. In section 283, Nietzsche describes a transitional type of human who prepares the way for the coming of the Overman. These are people who have the courage to struggle against everything taken as settled and beyond dispute, who are proud and willing to command, and who seek in all things that which is "*to be overcome.*" For those who have undergone the discipline to become this new sort of person, however, a way of life becomes possible that is spontaneous and creative, in which the only goals are self-expansion, the multiplication of perspectives, and the ceaseless drive to overcome everything that has come to seem "self-evident" and beyond dispute.

7. Twilight of the Idols

Twilight of the Idols (1889), written at the very end of Nietzsche's productive life, presents many of Nietzsche's most mature thoughts in an incredibly compressed form. The title (a play on Wagner's *Twilight of the Gods*) suggests that many of the concepts central to Western thought have turned out to be hollow idols we would do well to discard. The main text begins with a rather shocking attack on Socrates, perhaps the most venerated figure in the history of Western philosophy. Socrates was a notoriously homely person who wandered through Athens talking to people, trying to get them to seek the truth instead of accepting received opinions. Through his student, Plato, he introduced into Western culture an uncompromising insistence on reason, the ideal of finding the truth through rational discussion or "dialectic," and the conviction that a happy, virtuous life is one in which reason governs the appetites and drives. Condemned to death for "corrupting the youth," Socrates calmly drank the poison his executioners gave him, expressing his belief that a better life awaited him in the other world.

Nietzsche's strategy in dealing with Socrates and Plato is not to present arguments against their views, but to propose a sort of thought experiment designed to shake up our uncritical faith that the introduction of Socratic rationality and dialectical method has represented a genuine gain for Western culture. Instead of thinking of Socrates as the apex of Greek culture, he suggests, we might think of him as a symptom of decadence and decline in contrast to the great heroic Greeks described by Homer. Looked at in this way, Socrates' glorification of reason would be a kind of sour grapes: the response of a misfit who, unable to measure up to the Greek ideals of beauty and strength, tries to look better than others by claiming he has something special that no one else has. From this point of view, dialectic is just the pathetic rationalizing of a loser who is too weak to stand up for his own views, and the fascination with reason is the sign of an unhealthy person who is unable to satisfy his normal, healthy drives.

This picture of Socrates is supposed to soften us up for Nietzsche's diagnosis of what he calls the "prejudice of reason" that has dominated so much of Western thought. This prejudice results, he says, from a particular idiosyncrasy common to philosophers: their fear of change, "their hatred of the very notion of becoming." Of course, everyone is uncomfortable with change, but Nietzsche suggests that philosophers are people who have a morbid, almost pathological fear of change.

It is philosophers' hatred of any form of becoming and process, according to this story, that leads to their contempt for the constantly changing material world in which we actually live. In order to avoid dealing with the ever-changing material world, they focus not on the concrete objects we discover through sensory perception, but on their own abstract *concepts* of things. Thus, philosophers in the Platonic tradition have instructed us to focus not on this or that particular triangle, with its unique characteristics, but rather on what all triangles have in common—on triangularity as such—in trying to understand the truths of geometry. Analogously, we should try to grasp not this or that instance of beauty, but Beauty itself—what all beautiful things have in common.

Nietzsche's claim is that this tendency to dwell on one's own concepts of things rather than on the things themselves is due to fear of loss and change. Philosophers deal with concepts because such abstractions do not come and go as particular things do. The fateful move for philosophy occurs, however, when philosophers start to regard their own concepts as giving them access to a "higher," "truer" reality distinct from our world—an "other" world known not through the senses but through pure conceptualizing. Because concepts are general and relatively stable, it is assumed that the other world must consist of nonmaterial entities that are perfect and unchanging.

The belief in a higher reality correlated with our abstract concepts is the source of the belief in timeless "absolutes" so pervasive in the West. The tendency to treat concepts as if they referred to something real is also the source of the dualism of appearance and reality that shows up in the Platonic distinction between our material world, which is labeled mere "appearance," and an "other," perfect world of Forms identified as true "reality." This Platonic opposition between appearance and reality gets taken up again and again throughout Western history. Nietzsche sees it as the source of the Christian distinction between earth and heaven, which explains why he calls Christianity "Platonism for the masses." It recurs in Kant's distinction between "phenomena," the world as it appears to us, and the "thing-in-itself," reality as it is independent of our perception and thought. And it influences even those contemporary scientists who make a distinction between observable data and the unobservable, underlying forces that are posited to explain those data.

Nietzsche's own view stands in stark contrast to all these traditional dualisms. He holds that the changing world of material objects we perceive by means of our senses is the only world there is. There is simply no point to positing an "other" world distinct from our world. Views about "higher" types of entities correlated with our abstract concepts—such things as substance, materiality, duration, stability, causality, unity, and so on—are merely projections of our own prejudices onto what we experience. The idea that there is an "other" world beyond our world of flux and change arises only as a result of hatred for the actual world we live in. Nietzsche suggests that it is a product of nay-saying and negativity, a symptom of the resentment of individuals who cannot live fully in the actual world.

In an extraordinary tour de force, Nietzsche traces the entire history of the West, treating it as one vast "history of an error." Nietzsche assumes that in the earlier, pre-Platonic period of Western history, as is evident in the Homeric Greeks and ancient Jews, people lived fully and intensely in the here and now, with no illusions about an "other" world. But beginning with Socrates and Plato, the idea of an other, "true" world distinct from our "apparent" world came to be insinuated into Western thought. This idea was relatively innocuous in its first forms. But as it spread throughout theology and philosophy and created greater distrust in our world here and now, it gradually became more insidious and life-negating.

The first break in the history of the error occurs with positivism and the claim that belief in an "other" world distinct from the phenomena is pointless for the purposes of science. When positivism first appears on the scene, according to Nietzsche, the response will be the feeling that something has been lost, and this feeling of a *lack* or *absence* will lead people to feel that now everything is permitted. The result is the stage of anarchy and confusion, the "pandemonium of all free spirits," that Nietzsche calls "transitional nihilism."

But to assume that the rejection of the other world, the so-called "true" world, means that there now is "only" the veil of "appearance" is not to have thought this through to its logical conclusion. For, as Nietzsche points out, in binary oppositions like those of appearance and reality or becoming and being, each term gains its meaning solely from its contrast with the opposing term. Once we understand this, however, we will also understand that to get rid of one of the terms of a binary opposition is not just to affirm the other term. It is to get rid of the binary opposition altogether. We might see why this is so by considering the binary opposition used to describe people as "tall" and "short." For us right now, people who are 6'6" are regarded as tall. But suppose that through some accident of nature all people became 6'6" tall. Would we then still say that people who are 6'6" are tall? Perhaps at first we would. But eventually it would become clear that the invidious contrast between "short" and "tall" had become meaningless. When everyone is the same height, no one is "tall" (or "short"). In the same way, if we get rid of the idea of the "true" world, that does not mean that there is now only appearance. It means that the entire philosophical distinction between the "true" and the "apparent" no longer makes any sense.

In the end, there is only *the* world we find around us. We need to get over the idea that this implies that we have *lost* anything or that there is a hole or gap to be filled after we get rid of the "true" world. By affirming our world as it is, we put an end to reactive, "transitional" nihilism, and we pave the way to the kind of active, creative nihilism envisioned in Nietzsche's *Thus Spoke Zarathustra*. This is why the "History of an Error" ends with the words, "Enter Zarathustra."

The reader of *Twilight of the Idols* might feel that with this work Nietzsche's thought has gone full circle. For, as in *The Birth of Tragedy*, he refers here to the tragic artist and the Dionysian as his highest ideals. But these ideals have undergone a considerable change in the intervening years. In Nietzsche's final writings, the Dionysian has nothing to do with the ecstatic intoxication and revelry that tears asunder the veil of appearance to reveal the "primal Oneness" beyond our world. Instead, the Dionysian is now thought of as the spontaneous but disciplined mode of life that both has confronted the death of God and also has gotten over the feeling that something is *missing* when God dies. Freed from the craving for metaphysical comfort, such a life is restored to the "innocence of becoming."

And the tragic artist is not so much someone who makes contact with a deep hidden truth as someone who is able to embrace life as it is in the here and now: someone who "says *Yes* to everything," even to things that are terrifying and painful, without passing judgment or longing for something different. Nietzsche now posits as his ideal the person who is freed from the very idea of hidden depths distinct from surfaces, who has engaged in enough self-discipline to create a unique "style" in all he or she does, and who is able to embrace whatever shows up as raw materials for artistic creativity. The tragic artist is someone who, finally freed from the longing for absolutes, yet having a firm sense of "fate,"[22] can play in the wreckage left by shattered absolutes.

22. This qualification is necessary, for Nietzsche explicitly says in *Twilight of the Idols* that "Dionysus" is the name of the person who has a "joyful and trusting fatalism" and feels that "in the totality everything is redeemed and affirmed" ("Expeditions of an Untimely Man," § 49, in *Twilight of the Idols and The Antichrist,* trans. R. J. Hollingdale [Baltimore: Penguin, 1975]).

The Birth of Tragedy

SECTION I

We will secure much for the study of aesthetics if we grasp, not only by logical insight, but also by the immediate certainty of intuition, that the development of art is bound to the duality of the *Apollonian* and the *Dionysian*, in a manner similar to the way procreation depends on the duality of the sexes—with continuous struggle and only periodic intervening reconciliations. We borrow these names from the Greeks, who make intelligible the profound mysteries of their vision of art to those with insight, not by concepts, but by the vividly clear figures of their world of gods. It is in relation to Apollo and Dionysus, the two art-gods, that we understand the world of the Greeks as displaying, in origin and goals, an immense opposition between the form-giving arts [i.e. the visual, plastic arts, such as sculpture and painting], the Apollonian, and the nonpictorial art of music, that of Dionysus.

These very different forces go side by side, usually in open conflict with each other. They mutually stimulate each other incessantly to new and more vigorous productions, in which the struggle of this opposition will be continued—a struggle that is only apparently bridged by the word they have in common, 'art'—until at last through a metaphysical miracle of Hellenic "will" they appear paired with each other, and in this pairing they at last engender that work of art which is equally Dionysian and Apollonian, Attic tragedy.

To bring these two forces closer, let us consider them as the separated art-worlds of *dream* and *intoxication*. Between these physiological phenomena there is a contrast comparable to that found between the Apollonian and the Dionysian. Lucretius held that it is in dreams that the magnificent figures of the gods first appeared to human souls, and in dreams the great sculptor[1] first saw the beautiful organic unity of the body of superhuman beings. The Hellenic poet, if asked about the secrets of poetic inspiration, would also be reminded of dreams, and would provide an account similar to that of Hans Sachs in the *Meistersinger*:

Selections from Nietzsche, *The Birth of Tragedy*, translated by Derk Pereboom, © 1995, Hackett Publishing Company. Reprinted by permission of the translator and Hackett Publishing Company.

1. Phidias was considered the great sculptor of classical Greece.

My friend, this is the poet's task:
His dreams to interpret and observe.
Trust me, a person's truest fantasy
Will be disclosed to him in dreams:
All poetic craft and poetry
Is but interpretation of prophetic dream.

The fair appearance of the dream world, in whose production each person is the master artist, is presupposed by all form-giving arts, and also, as we shall see, by a significant part of poetry. We enjoy an immediate grasp of figure (*Gestalt*); all forms speak to us; there is nothing indifferent and unnecessary. Still, even in the most intense experience of this dream reality we have, glimmering through it, a sense that it is only *appearance*. This, at least, is my experience, and for its frequency or even its normality I could produce much evidence, and the sayings of the poets. Those who are philosophically inclined have a prior sense that there lies hidden a second, very different world beneath this reality in which we live and exist, and that therefore this reality is also an appearance. In fact, Schopenhauer says that the mark of philosophical ability is the gift of occasionally having all persons and things seem to be mere phantoms or dream images.

As the philosopher stands to the reality of existence, so the person susceptible to artistic inspiration stands to the reality of the dream. He observes readily and keenly, for on the basis of these images he interprets life, and by these events he trains himself for life. And it may not be only the pleasant and friendly images that he experiences in himself with such thorough comprehension. The serious, the sad, the sorrowful, the dark, the sudden obstructions, the irritations of fortune, the apprehensive anticipations, in short the entire "Divine Comedy" of life, including the Inferno,[2] also passes before him, not merely like a shadow play—for he lives and suffers in these scenes—and yet not at the same time without that fleeting sense of appearance. Perhaps many will remember as I do crying out at times in the dangers and fears of the dream, reassuringly and with success, "It's a dream! I want to dream on!" I have been told of people who could carry on the causal chain of one and the same dream for three or more consecutive nights. These facts clearly show that our innermost being, the common ground of all of us, experiences dreams with profound delight and joyful urgency.

This joyful urgency of dream experience is likewise expressed by the Greeks in their [god] Apollo. Apollo, as the god of all form-giving powers, is at the same time the soothsaying god. He, who by the root of his name is the

2. Dante's *Divine Comedy* included three books: *Inferno* (Hell), *Purgatory*, and *Paradise*.

"shining one," the god of light, also rules the fair appearance of the inner world of imagination. The higher truth, the perfection of these states, contrasts with only partially understandable everyday reality, and thus the deep consciousness of nature, healing and helping in sleep and dream, is at the same time the symbolic analogue of soothsaying ability, and in general of the arts, through which life is made possible and worth living.

But in addition, there is a fine line that the dream image may not overstep if it is to avoid having a pathological effect (for otherwise appearance would deceive us as coarse reality). This fine line cannot be inadequate to the image of Apollo: that sober restriction, that freedom from the wilder impulses, that sagacious tranquility of the form-giving god. His eye must be "sunlike" in conformity with his origin. Even when it is angry and looks displeased, the solemnity of his fair appearance remains. And so what Schopenhauer says of people wrapped in the veil of Maya might also hold in a special sense for Apollo (*The World as Will and Representation*, Book IV ¶63): "Just as the boatman sits in his small boat, trusting his frail craft in a stormy sea that is boundless in every direction, with howling, mountainous waves, so in the midst of a world full of suffering and misery the individual calmly sits, supported by and trusting the principle of individuation (*principium individuationis*)" [E. F. J. Payne translation]. Indeed, one might say of Apollo that in him the unperturbed faith in that principle and the calm repose of the person wrapped in it has had its most exalted expression. One might characterize Apollo as the magnificent divine image of the principle of individuation, from whose demeanor and look all the delight, wisdom, and beauty of "appearance" speak to us.

In the same work Schopenhauer has portrayed for us that tremendous *horror* that grips a person when he suddenly loses his faith in the forms of knowledge of appearance because the principle of sufficient reason, in any one of its forms, seems to have an exception.[3] When we add to this horror the joyful rapture that arises from the innermost ground of the person, indeed from nature, at this shattering of the principle of individuation, we may glimpse the essence of the *Dionysian*, which we can best understand by the analogy of *intoxication*. These Dionysian impulses are awakened either through the influence of a narcotic potion, about which all primordial peoples and tribes speak in hymns, or through the powerful approach of spring, which penetrates all of nature with delight. As these impulses intensify, everything subjective vanishes into complete self-forgetfulness.

In the German Middle Ages, ever-expanding throngs reeled from place to

---

3. In Book II of *The World as Will and Representation* Schopenhauer discusses the effect of discovering phenomena that contradict the Principle of Sufficient Reason (the principle that everything that exists must have a reason, cause, or explanation for its existence).

place, singing and dancing, under the same Dionysian power. In these Saint John and Saint Vitus dancers we recognize the Bacchic choruses of the Greeks, together with their antecedents in Asia Minor, dating back to Babylon and the orgiastic Sacaea. There are those who, due to inexperience or dullness, spurn with derision or pity such phenomena as "folk-illnesses," while assured of their own health. Of course these poor souls fail to suspect how pallid and ghostly their "health" appears when the radiant vitality of the Dionysian multitudes rushes by them.

Under the spell of the Dionysian, not only is the bond between person and person re-established, but estranged, hostile, and subdued nature also celebrates anew its reconciliation feast with its prodigal son, humanity. The earth freely presents her gifts, and beasts of prey draw near from rocks and desert. The chariot of Dionysus is covered with flowers and wreaths, and under his yoke panther and tiger stride. Were one to transform Beethoven's "Ode to Joy" into a painting, and to refuse to restrain one's imagination as the awe-struck millions bow down into the dust, one might come closer to the Dionysian in this way.

Now the slave is free; now all the rigid, hostile barriers that necessity, whim, or "insolent fashion" have set up between people collapse. Now, with the evangelism of world harmony, each not only feels united, reconciled, merged with his neighbor, but also as one, as if the veil of Maya had been torn and now only flutters about in shreds before the mysterious Primordial Oneness. Singing and dancing, the person manifests himself as a member of a higher community. He has unlearned walking and speaking, and as he dances he is about to take flight into the sky. His demeanor bespeaks enchantment. As the animals now speak, and the earth yields milk and honey, so something supernatural reverberates from him. He feels like a god; he now walks about just as enraptured and elated as he saw the gods walk about in dreams. The person is no longer an artist; he has become a work of art. The artistic power of all nature, to the highest blissful satisfaction of the Primordial One, here reveals itself in the thrill of intoxication. Here humanity, made of the most precious clay and the most expensive marble, is kneaded and cut, and to the chisel blows of the Dionysian world-artist resounds the Eleusian mystery call: "Do you prostrate yourselves, O millions? Do you discern the Creator, O world?"

The Gay Science

PREFACE TO THE SECOND EDITION

1

This book, perhaps, requires more than just a *single* preface, and in the end it will always remain doubtful whether prefaces can bring anyone closer to the *experiences* of this book who has not experienced something similar. It seems to have been written in the language of a warm spring breeze: in it there is overconfidence, agitation, contradiction, April weather, so that one is constantly reminded both of the winter's nearness and of the *victory* over winter which is coming, must come, maybe has already come.

Gratitude pours out without pause, as if the most unexpected event had come to pass, the gratitude of one who is healing—for the *healing* was this most unexpected event. "Gay science": that refers to the saturnalia of a spirit who has patiently withstood a terribly long oppression—patiently, rigorously, coldly, without giving in, but without hope—and who now is struck by hope all at once, by hope for health, by the *drunkenness* of healing. Small wonder that much that is irrational and foolish comes to light in this process, much mischievous tenderness that is spent even on problems that have a rough coat and hence are unsuited to be petted and coaxed. This whole book is nothing but a festivity after a long period of deprivation and powerlessness—the jubilation of returning strength, of the newly awakened belief in a tomorrow and a day after, of the sudden perception and premonition of a future, of imminent adventures, of reopened seas, of goals that are allowed again, believed in again.

And look at all that lay behind me! This desolate stretch of exhaustion, disbelief, and frost in the middle of my youth, this senility inserted at the wrong point; this tyranny of pain, surpassed, however, by the tyranny of pride, which rejected the *implications* of pain—and implications are consolations; this radical isolation as self-defense against a disdain for humanity that had grown unhealthily clear-sighted; this confinement on principle to what is bitter, sharp, and hurtful in knowledge, as prescribed by a *nausea* that had gradually grown out of a careless and pampering spiritual diet, known as

Selections from Nietzsche, *The Gay Science*, translated by Richard Polt, © 1995, Hackett Publishing Co. Reprinted by permission.

romanticism—oh, who could share my experience of all that? But anyone who could would certainly forgive more than my little bit of foolishness, wildness, "gay science"—for instance, the handful of songs that are attached to the book this time around, songs in which a poet makes fun of all poets in a way that is hard to forgive.—Ah, it is not only the poets and their beautiful "lyrical feelings" on whom this resurrected author must vent his malice; who knows what sort of victim he's searching out for himself, what monstrous object of parody will soon appeal to him? "*Incipit tragoedia*,"[1] it says at the end of this dubiously undoubting book; one should be on one's guard! Something exceedingly nasty and malicious announces itself: *incipit parodia* [now begins the parody], there's no doubt.

2

—But let us leave Herr Nietzsche; what difference does it make to us that Herr Nietzsche got well again? . . . Psychologists know few questions as compelling as the question of the relation between health and philosophy, and if they happen to get sick themselves, they bring all their scientific curiosity with them into their sickness. For, assuming that one is a person, one also has the philosophy proper to that person. But there is an important distinction to be made here. In some, it is their defects that philosophize; in others, their riches and strengths. The former *need* their philosophy, be it as a crutch, a tranquilizer, medication, salvation, exaltation, or distancing from themselves; for the latter, it is only a beautiful luxury, and at its best, the sensuality of a triumphant thankfulness, which must ultimately inscribe itself in cosmic capital letters on the conceptual sky. But in the first, more typical case, when it is one's needs that philosophize, as in all sick thinkers—and perhaps sick thinkers are predominant in the history of philosophy—what will become of the thought itself that is brought forth under the *pressure* of sickness?

It is with this question that the psychologist is concerned, and here, it is possible to experiment. We philosophers do just as travelers do who plan to wake up at a certain hour, and then calmly give in to sleep: if it should happen that we get sick, we give ourselves over in body and soul to the sickness for a while—we shut our eyes, as it were. And just as those travelers know that something is *not* asleep, that something is counting off the hours and will wake them up, we also know that the decisive moment will find us awake—that something springs up then and catches the spirit *in the act*, I mean in weakness or retreat or surrender or stiffening or gloominess, and

1. "Now begins the tragedy": the title of §342, which was the last section of the first edition.

whatever other sickly conditions of the spirit you can name, which on healthy days are opposed by the spirit's *pride* (for the old saw holds true: "Proud spirits, peacocks, and stallions are the proudest beasts on earth"). After a self-interrogation, self-temptation, of this sort, one learns to look with a keener eye at everything that has been philosophized at all up to now. One discerns better than before the involuntary detours, side streets, resting spots, *sunny* spots of thought to which the suffering thinkers, precisely as sufferers, are led and seduced. One also knows where the sick *body* and its needs unconsciously drive the spirit, pushing it and enticing it—to sun, calm, mildness, patience, medication, balm in any sense. Every philosophy that puts peace higher than war, every ethics with a negative appraisal of the concept of happiness, every metaphysics and physics that knows of a finale, a final state of any sort, every predominantly aesthetic or religious longing for an elsewhere, a beyond, an outside, an above, allows one to ask whether it was not sickness that inspired the philosopher.

The unconscious disguise of physiological needs under the mantle of the objective, the ideal, the purely spiritual, takes place to a shocking extent—and often enough, I have asked myself whether on the whole, philosophy up to now has not simply been an interpretation of the body, and a *misunderstanding of the body*. Behind the highest value-judgments by which the history of thought has been guided up to now, there lie hidden certain misunderstandings of the bodily constitution—be it of the individual, or of classes, or of entire races. One may, to begin with, see all those daring delusions of metaphysics, in particular their answers to the question of the *value of existence*, as symptoms of particular bodies. And if these types of wholesale world-affirmation or world-negation contain not a grain of significance when measured scientifically, they nevertheless give the historian and the psychologist glimpses which are all the more valuable—when they are taken, as I said, as symptoms of the body, of its happiness and mishaps, of its fullness, powerfulness, self-mastery in history, or of its limitations, exhaustion, impoverishment, of its premonition of the end, its will to the end. I am still waiting for a philosophical *physician* in the exceptional sense of the word—one who has to pursue the problem of the total health of a people, an age, a race, humanity—who will finally have the courage to bring my suspicion to a head and risk the statement: all philosophizing up to now was not about "truth," but about something else, let us say about health, future, growth, power, life.

3

As you can guess, I would not like to take my leave ungratefully from that period of difficult affliction, whose profit is not yet exhausted for me even today—I am well aware of all the advantages my variable health gives me over all hardy, hulking spirits. A philosopher who has passed and continues to pass through many states of health has also passed through just as many philosophies; he *can* do nothing but transpose his every condition into the most spiritual form and distance—for this art of transfiguration *is* philosophy. We philosophers are not free to disconnect soul and body, as the masses do; we are even less free to disconnect soul and spirit. We are no thinking frogs, no objectifying and registering devices with refrigerated guts; we must constantly give birth to our thoughts from our pain and, like mothers, give them everything we have in us in the way of blood, heart, fire, desire, passion, torment, conscience, destiny and doom. To live—that means, for us philosophers, constantly to transform everything we are into light and flame; everything that affects us, too—we *can* do nothing else.

And as for sickness: aren't we almost seduced into asking whether it isn't altogether indispensable for us? It is only great pain that is the ultimate liberator of the spirit, the teacher of the *great suspicion* that makes out of every U an X, a real and genuine X, that is, the penultimate of the letters before the ultimate. . . .[2] It is only great pain—that slow, sustained pain that takes its time, in which we are, as it were, burned with smoldering green firewood—that forces us philosophers to sink to our ultimate profundity and to do away with all the trust, everything good-natured, veil-imposing, mild and middling, on which we may have previously based our humanity. I doubt that such a pain makes us "better"—but I know that it makes us *deeper*. Whether we learn to oppose to this pain our pride, our contempt, our willpower, and act like American Indians, who, as badly as they may be tormented, pay back their tormentors with the spite of their tongues; whether we draw back from pain into that oriental nothingness—it is called Nirvana—into mute, stiff, deaf self-surrender, self-oblivion, self-dissolution; one emerges from such long, dangerous exercises of self-mastery as another person, with a few question marks more, above all with the *will* from now on to question more persistently, deeply, strictly, rigorously, evilly, quietly, than one had up to now. Trust in life is gone; life itself has become a *problem*.

But please don't believe that this necessarily makes one morose! Even love of life is still possible—one just loves differently. It is the love for a woman who makes us doubt. . . . But the charm of everything problematic, the joy in the X, is too great in such more spiritual and more spiritualized human beings for this joy not to break all at once like a bright glow over every crisis

2. "To make a U into an X" (i.e., to make a five, V, into a ten, X) means, in German, to try to pass something off as more valuable than it is. But Nietzsche is also playing on the use of "x" to represent something unknown or "problematic," as is clear later in this section.

[Marginal notes: soul not detached; pain liberates from illusion of knowingly mystery life = X underlying unknown; problem not given new challenge here joy]

of the problematic, over every danger of insecurity, even over a lover's jealousy. We know a new happiness. . . .

4 *(vs. Plato's conception of appearance)*

Finally, lest what is most essential go unsaid: one comes back from such abysses, from such a difficult affliction, even from the affliction of difficult suspicion, *newborn*—one's skin is shed, one is more ticklish and malicious, one's taste for joy is finer, one's tongue for good things is more tender, at once more childlike and a hundredfold more subtle than one ever was before. And oh, how disgusting pleasure is to one now—crass, stuffy, drab pleasure, as it is understood by those who try to give themselves pleasure, our "cultured" people, our rich and ruling people! And how maliciously we now listen to the big county-fair boom-boom with which the "cultured people" and cosmopolitans let themselves be raped by art, books and music for purposes of "spiritual pleasure," with the aid of alcoholic spirits! How the theatrical screech of passion hurts our ears now; how foreign to our taste has grown the whole Romantic uproar and sensory mishmash which the cultured rabble loves, along with its aspirations after the sublime, the exalted, the overwrought!

No, if we who are recovering from sickness still need an art at all, it is a *different* art—a joking, light, flighty, divinely undisturbed, divinely artful art, which comes blazing like a bright flame into a cloudless sky! Above all: an art for artists, for artists only! After our sickness, we better understand the primary requirement for *this* art—cheerfulness, *any* cheerfulness, my friends!—also as artists. I would like to prove this. We now know a few things too well, we knowing ones; oh, how we are now learning to forget well, to *not*-know well, as artists!

And as for our future, one will hardly find us back on the path of those Egyptian youths who make temples unsafe at night, wrapping their arms around statues, and in general uncovering and tearing the veil away from everything that, with good reasons, is kept covered—they want to put it into bright light.[3] No, this bad taste, this will to truth, to "truth at any price,"

---

3. An allusion to Friedrich Schiller's poem "The Veiled Image of Sais," in which a youth full of "burning thirst for knowledge" hears that a statue in an Egyptian temple, concealed by a veil which it is forbidden to raise, is Truth itself. He steals to the temple at night and lifts the veil—and in the morning is found "senseless and pale" on the ground. "His life's cheerfulness was gone forever, / a deep grief brought him to an early grave. / "Woe," was his word of warning / when impetuous questions assailed him, / "Woe to him who reaches truth by guilt, / She will nevermore be pleasant to him."

this juvenile lunacy in the love of truth has been spoiled for us; we are too experienced for that, too serious, too playful, too burned, too deep. We no longer believe that truth remains truth when one snatches its veils away; we have lived too much to believe this. For us today it is a matter of decorum that one not wish to see everything in the nude, not wish to witness everything, to understand and "know" it all. "Is it true that the dear Lord is everywhere?" a little girl asked her mother; "But I think that's indecent"—a hint to philosophers! We should have greater respect for the *modesty* with which nature has hidden itself behind riddles and colorful uncertainties. Perhaps truth is a woman who has grounds for not letting her grounds be seen? Perhaps her name is, to speak in Greek, Baubo?[4]

Oh, those Greeks! They understood how to *live*: for that, it is necessary to remain steadfastly on the surface, the fold, the skin, to worship appearance, to believe in forms, tones, words, the entire Olympus of appearance! Those Greeks were superficial—*because they were deep!* And isn't that just what we are coming back to, we daredevils of the spirit, who have scaled the highest and most dangerous peak of contemporary thought and have looked around from there, we who have *looked down* from there? Are we not precisely thereby—Greeks? Worshipers of forms, of tones, of words? And precisely therefore—artists?

Ruta, near Genoa,
Autumn 1886

---

4. A divinity which was originally a personification of the female genitals.

1

Teachers of the aim of existence.—Whether I look at human beings with a good or an evil eye, I always find them busy at a *single* task, each and every one of them: doing what serves the preservation of the human species. And, truth be told, they do it not out of a feeling of love for this species, but simply because nothing in them is older, stronger, more unrelenting, more insuperable than this instinct—because this instinct is in fact *the essence* of our type and herd.

We are in the habit of neatly and quickly separating our neighbors, with the usual short-sightedness, from just five paces away, into useful and harmful, good and evil people. But upon a large-scale accounting, upon a longer reflection on the whole, we become suspicious of this neatness and this separation, and finally give it up. Even the most harmful people are perhaps the most useful of all, as regards the preservation of the species, for they maintain in themselves, or by their effect on others, drives without which humanity would long ago have become sluggish or decayed. Hatred, malicious gloating, the ambition to rob and rule, and anything else called evil belongs to the amazing economy of the preservation of the species, which, to be sure, is a costly, spendthrift, and on the whole most foolish economy—but which has *demonstrably* preserved our kind up to now.

I do not know anymore whether you, my dear fellow human being and neighbor, *can* at all live detrimentally to the species, that is, "irrationally" and "badly." Whatever could have harmed the species may have died out many millennia ago, and now may be one of those things that are no longer possible even for God. Indulge your best or your worst desires, and even—do yourself in! In either case, you are probably still furthering and benefiting humanity somehow, and are entitled to your eulogists—and your mockers, too!

But you will never find anyone who could know how to mock you fully—you, the individual, even at your best—anyone who could drive home to your mind your limitless, flylike, froglike misery, so as to do justice to the truth! To laugh at oneself in the way one would have to laugh in order to laugh *from the whole truth*—up to now, the best have not had enough sense of the truth to do this, and the most gifted have had far too little genius! Maybe laughter too still has a future! When the axiom, "The species is all, one person is no one," has incorporated itself into humanity, when this ultimate liberation and irresponsibility is accessible to everyone at every time, maybe laughter will then have allied itself to wisdom, maybe there will be only "gay science" then.

For now, things are still quite different; for now, the comedy of existence has not yet "become conscious" of itself; for now, it is still the time of tragedy, the time of moralities and religions. What is the significance of the constant reappearance of those founders of moralities and religions, those originators of the struggle for moral assessments, those who teach the pangs of conscience and religious wars? What is the significance of these heroes on this stage?—For up to now, they *have been* this stage's heroes, and everything else, which at times was all that we could see and was all too close, has always served only to prepare for the entrance of these heroes, whether it was serving as machinery and side stage, or in the role of confidants and valets. (The poets, for instance, were always the valets of some morality or other.)

It is self-evident that these tragedians also work in the interest of the *species*, even if they may believe they are working in the interest of God and as God's agents. They, too, further the life of the race, *by furthering faith in life.* "It is worthwhile to live," every one of them cries, "there is something to this life. Life has something behind it, beneath it. Watch out!" That drive that holds sway in the highest as much as in the commonest human beings, the drive to preserve the species, breaks out from time to time as reason and passion of the *mind*. It is then surrounded by a dazzling entourage of grounds to justify it, and it wants to use all its force to make us forget that at its ground, it is drive, instinct, foolishness, groundlessness. Life *ought* to be loved, *because* . . . ! Human beings *ought* to improve themselves and their neighbors, *because* . . . ! And whatever form all these oughts and becauses take, and may take in the future!

In order that what happens necessarily and always, on its own, and without any aim at all, may from now on appear to be done for an aim, and may strike people as reason and an ultimate command—this is why the ethical teachers come forward, as the teachers of the aim of existence. This is why they invent a second and different existence, and with their new machinery lift the common old existence off its common old hinges. They do not want us to *laugh* at existence at all, oh no, nor at ourselves—nor at them. For them, one is always one, something first and last and colossal; for them there are no species, no sums, no zeroes. As foolish and fanatical as their inventions and assessments may be, as much as they may misunderstand the course of nature and deny its preconditions—and all ethics up to now have been foolish and anti-natural, to the point that humanity would have perished if any of them had conquered humanity—nevertheless, every time "the hero" stepped onto the stage, something new was attained, the horrible antithesis of laughter, that deep tremor felt by many individuals at the thought, "Yes, it is worthwhile to live! Yes, I am worthy of living!"—Life and I and you and all of us together became *interesting* to ourselves again for some time.

It cannot be denied that *in the long run* laughter and reason and nature have mastered every single one of these great teachers of an aim. In the end, the brief tragedy always turned back into the eternal comedy of existence, and the "waves of uncountable laughter," to use Aeschylus' expression,[5] must finally crash over even the greatest of these tragedians. But despite all this corrective laughing, human nature has nevertheless been changed, on the whole, by this constant reappearance of these teachers of the aim of existence: human nature now has one more need, the need for the constant reappearance of such teachers and teachings of the "aim." Human beings have gradually become fantastic animals who have to satisfy one more precondition of existence than any other animals do: human beings *have* to believe from time to time, to know, *why* they exist—their race cannot flourish without periodically trusting in life, without believing in *reason in life!* And the human race will decree from time to time, again and again, "There is something that it is absolutely forbidden to laugh at anymore!" And the most careful friend of humanity will add, "Not only laughter and gay wisdom, but also the tragic with all its sublime unreason, belongs to the means and necessities of preserving the species!"

And consequently! Consequently! Consequently! Oh, do you understand me, my friends? Do you understand this new law of ebb and flow? We, too, have our own time!

54

The consciousness of appearance.—What a wonderful and new, and at the same time dreadful and ironic situation I feel my knowledge has put me into in relation to existence as a whole! I have *discovered* for myself that the human and animal of past ages, in fact the whole prehistory and past of all sentient being, goes on fabricating, loving, hating, and drawing conclusions within me. I have suddenly awakened in the midst of this dream, but only to the consciousness that I *am* dreaming, and that I *have to* keep on dreaming, so as not to perish—as the sleepwalker has to keep on dreaming so as not to fall down. What is "appearance" for me now? Truly not the opposite of any essence—what can I say about any essence, except to list the predicates of its appearance? Truly not a dead mask which one could place upon an unknown X, and just as well take away! Appearance is, for me, what is itself at work and alive, what goes so far in its self-ridicule that it makes me feel that here there is appearance, and will-o'-the-wisp,[6] and spirit-dance, and nothing

5. Cf. *Prometheus Bound*, lines 89–90.
6. *Irrlicht*: etymologically, "deceptive light."

else—that among all these dreamers, I, too, the "knower," am dancing my dance; that the knower is a means of prolonging the earthly dance, and hence is one of the masters of ceremonies of existence; and that the sublime consistency and connectedness of all knowledge is and will be, perhaps, the highest means of *maintaining the universality of the dreaming*, and the universal, mutual intelligibility of all these dreamers, and thereby *the duration of the dream*.

57

To the realists.—You sober people, who feel that you are armed against passion and fantasy and would gladly make your emptiness into a point of pride and a decoration, you call yourselves realists and imply that the world is really constituted as it appears to you. Before you alone does reality stand unveiled, and perhaps you yourselves are the best part of it—oh, you dear images of Sais![7] But aren't you, even in your most unveiled condition, still extremely passionate and obscure beings in comparison to fish, and still all too similar to an artist in love? And what is "reality" to an artist in love? You still carry around with you ways of assessing things whose origin lies in the passions and loves of earlier centuries! A secret and indelible drunkenness is still incorporated in your sobriety! Your love of "reality," for instance—oh, that is an old, a primordial love! In every feeling, in every sense-impression, there is a part of this old love. And it has also been worked on and woven by some fantasy, some prejudice, some irrationality, some incomprehension, some fear, and whatever else! That mountain over there! That cloud! What is "real" about them anyway? Remove the phantasm and all the human contribution from them, you sober ones! Aye, if you could do *that*! If you could forget your heritage, your past, your prior training—your entire humanity and animality! For us, there is no "reality"—and not for you either, you sober ones. We are not nearly as foreign to each other as you think, and maybe our good will to get beyond drunkenness is just as respectable as your belief that you are altogether *incapable* of drunkenness.

58

Only as creators!—This has given me the greatest difficulty and goes on being my greatest difficulty: to recognize that unspeakably more depends on *what things are called* than on what they are. The fame, name, and appearance of a thing, what it counts as, its customary measure and weight—

7. As at the end of the Preface, Nietzsche is alluding to Schiller's "The Veiled Image of Sais."

which in the beginning is an arbitrary error for the most part, thrown over things like a garment and alien to their essence, even to their skin—due to the continuous growth of belief in it from generation to generation, this gradually grows, as it were, onto and into the thing, and turns into its very body. The initial appearance almost always becomes the essence in the end and *acts* as essence! But only a fool would think it was enough to point to this beginning and to this misty mantle of illusion in order to *destroy* the world that counts as essential, so-called "*reality*!" Only as creators can we destroy! But we also should not forget this: creating new names and assessments and apparent truths is eventually enough to create new "things."

108

New struggles.—After Buddha was dead, his shadow was still displayed in a cave for centuries—a colossal, horrible shadow. God is dead. But as is the way of human beings, there may still be caves for millennia in which his shadow is displayed. And we—we must still defeat even his shadow!

109

Let us beware!—Let us beware of thinking that the world is a living thing. In what direction is it supposed to expand? What is it supposed to feed on? How could it grow and reproduce? We do know more or less what the organic is—and we are supposed to take what is unbelievably derivative, late, rare, and accidental, which we perceive only on the crust of the Earth, and reinterpret it into the essential, universal, and eternal, as do those who call the universe an organism? That makes me sick.

Let us even beware of believing that the universe is a machine; it is certainly not constructed for any purpose, and with the word "machine" we do it far too great an honor. Let us beware of supposing that something as regular as the cyclical motion of our neighboring stars occurs universally and everywhere: a mere look into the Milky Way raises doubts about whether there may not be far cruder and more contradictory motions there, as well as stars with eternally straight courses and the like. The astral order in which we live is an exception; this order and the relative stability for which it is responsible have, in turn, made possible the exception of all exceptions—the formation of the organic.

In contrast, the overall character of the world is, for all eternity, chaos—not in the sense that it lacks necessity, but rather in the sense that it lacks order, articulation, form, beauty, wisdom, and whatever else our aesthetic anthropomorphisms might say. As judged by our reason, the unlucky casts of the dice are by far the rule, the exceptions are not the secret purpose, and the whole music box eternally replays its tune, which may never be called a melody—and in the end, even the expression "unlucky cast" is already an anthropomorphism that implies blame. But how could we be allowed to blame or praise the universe? Let us beware of ascribing heartlessness and irrationality, or their opposites, to it; it is neither perfect, nor beautiful, nor noble, and does not want to be any of these—it does not at all try to imitate humanity! It is not grasped at all by any of our aesthetic and moral judgments! It also has no drive for self-preservation, and no drives at all. It also knows no laws. Let us beware of saying that there are laws in nature. There are only necessities. There is no one there who commands, no one who obeys, no one who transgresses. When you know that there are no aims, you also know that there is no accident, for only in relation to a world of aims does the word "accident" have any meaning.

Let us beware of saying that death is contrary to life. What is living is only a subset of what is dead, and a very rare subset. Let us beware of thinking that the world eternally creates the new. There are no eternally lasting substances; matter is an error, just like the God of the Eleatics.[8]

But when will we come to an end with our cares and cautions? When will all these shadows of God no longer darken us? When will we have completely de-deified nature? When will we be allowed to begin to *naturalize* humanity through the pure, newly found, newly redeemed nature?

110

Origin of knowledge.—For immense stretches of time, the intellect gave rise to nothing but errors. A few of these turned out to be useful and preserved the species; those who ran across them or received them through inheritance had greater luck in their struggle for themselves and their offspring. Such erroneous propositions taken on faith, which were inherited continuously and finally almost turned into the basic components of the human species, include, for example, these: that there are enduring things; that there are identical things; that there are things, substances, bodies; that a thing is what it appears to be; that our will is free; that what is good for me is also good in and of itself.

It was much later that those who denied and doubted such propositions came on the scene—it was much later that truth came on the scene, as the feeblest form of knowledge. It seemed that one could not live with truth, for our organism was adapted for the opposite; all its higher functions, the perceptions of the senses and every sort of feeling in general, cooperated with

8. Followers of Parmenides of Elea (ca. 475 B.C.E.), who asserted that what really exists is unchangeable, unitary, and uniform.

those anciently embodied fundamental errors. Not only that, but those propositions became, even within knowledge, the norms according to which one established the "true" and the "untrue"—even in the most abstruse fields of pure logic. Thus, the *strength* of our knowledge does not lie in its degree of truth but in its age, its embodiment, its character as a condition of life. Wherever life and knowledge seemed to contradict each other, there was never any serious struggle: in such cases, denial and doubt amounted to madness.

Those exceptional thinkers, such as the Eleatics,[9] who in spite of this, affirmed and clung to the opposites of the natural errors, believed that it was also possible to *live* this contrary position. They invented the sage as the person who was unchangeable, impersonal, and had universal intuition, who was one and all simultaneously, with a special capacity for this reversed knowledge. They were of the belief that their knowledge was at the same time the principle of *life*. But in order to be able to assert all this, they had to *deceive* themselves about their own condition. They had to impute impersonality and changeless duration to themselves; they had to overlook the essence of the knower, deny the force exercised in knowledge by our drives, and in general conceive of reason as fully free activity which originates from itself. They closed their eyes to the fact that they also had arrived at their propositions through contradicting ordinary beliefs, or through longing for calm, or for sole possession, or for domination.

The subtler development of honesty and skepticism finally made these people, too, impossible; their life and judgments, too, turned out to be dependent on ancient drives and fundamental errors of all sentient existence. That subtler honesty and skepticism originated wherever two opposing propositions appeared to be *applicable* to life, because both were compatible with the fundamental errors, and thus a conflict became possible regarding the greater or lesser degree of *usefulness* for life. They also originated wherever new propositions, though not shown to be useful, at least did not seem to be harmful either: they were expressions of an intellectual play impulse, and were innocent and happy, like all play. Gradually, the human brain filled up with such judgments and convictions, and in this tangle there arose ferment, struggle, and lust for power. Not only usefulness and desire, but every sort of drive took sides in the struggle over "truths." The intellectual struggle became an occupation, an enticement, a profession, a duty, a thing of dignity—and finally, knowing and striving for the truth took their place as needs among the other needs. From then on, not only belief and conviction, but testing, denial, mistrust, contradiction became a *power*. All "evil" instincts were subordinated to knowledge and placed in its service,

9. See the footnote to §109.

and they acquired the glamor of the permitted, the honored, the useful, and finally even the luster and innocence of the *good*.

Knowledge thus became an element of life itself, and as life, it became an ever-growing power—until finally, our knowledge and those ancient fundamental errors ran up against each other, both being life and power, both within the same person. The thinker—that is now the being in whom the drive to truth and those life-preserving errors are fighting their first fight, after the drive to truth has also *proved* to be a life-preserving power. In comparison to the importance of this fight, everything else is irrelevant. The ultimate question about the condition of life is being posed here, and here the first attempt is being made to answer this question by experiment. How far does truth tolerate embodiment?—That is the question, that is the experiment.

111

Source of the logical.—From where in the human head did logic arise? Certainly from the illogical, whose domain must originally have been tremendous. Countless beings who drew conclusions in ways other than we do now were destroyed, yet their ways might have been truer nonetheless! The animal, for instance, who did not know how to find the "same" often enough regarding food or regarding animals who were hostile to it—the animal who thus classified things too slowly, or was too careful in classifying—had a poorer chance of survival than the one who immediately guessed that whatever was similar was the same. But the predominant inclination to treat the similar as the same, an illogical inclination—for there is nothing that in itself is the same—was what first created all the foundations of logic. Likewise, in order for the concept of substance to arise—a concept which is indispensable to logic, although strictly speaking it corresponds to nothing actual—for a long time the changing aspects of things had to go unseen, unperceived. Those beings who did not see accurately had an edge over those who saw everything "in flux."

Every high degree of caution in drawing conclusions, every skeptical inclination, is in itself already a great danger to life. No living things would have survived were it not for the fact that the opposite inclination—the inclination to make assertions rather than to suspend judgment, to be mistaken and to fabricate rather than to take one's time, to agree rather than to deny, to pass judgment rather than to be fair—was cultivated with extraordinary strength. The flow of logical thoughts and conclusions in our brain today reflects the process of a battle among drives which by themselves are each very illogical and unfair. Ordinarily we experience only the result of the battle; that is how quickly and covertly this age-old mechanism plays itself out in us now.

112

Cause and effect.—We call it "explanation," but it is "description" that differentiates us from older phases of knowledge and science. We describe better; we explain no more than those who came before. We have discovered a manifold succession where the naive person and the researchers of older cultures saw only two separate things—"cause" and "effect," as the expression went. We have perfected the image of becoming, but we have done nothing to get beyond or behind the image. In each case, the sequence of "causes" stands before us more completely, and we infer that such and such must first precede so that the other thing may follow—but with this, we have *comprehended* nothing at all. Quality—for instance, in every chemical process—appears, both now and earlier, as a "miracle," as does every locomotion; nobody has "explained" thrust. How *could* we explain anything? We operate with things that simply don't exist: with lines, planes, bodies, atoms, divisible times, divisible spaces. How should explanation even be possible if we first make everything into an *image*, our own image! It is enough to consider science as the most faithful humanization of things that is possible; we are constantly learning to describe ourselves better by describing things and their succession.

Cause and effect—there probably never is such a duality. In truth, a continuum stands before us from which we isolate a couple of pieces, just as we always perceive a motion only as isolated points—that is, we really do not see it, but infer it. The suddenness with which many effects take place leads us astray, but it is a suddenness only for us. There is an infinite set of events in this second of suddenness that escapes us. An intellect that saw cause and effect as a continuum, not with our sort of arbitrary division and fragmentation, an intellect that saw the flux of events, would throw aside the concept of cause and effect and deny all determination.

113

On the theory of poisons.—So much must come together in order for a scientific way of thinking to arise, and all these necessary powers have had to be separately discovered, practiced, and cultivated! But when they were separate, they very often had an effect completely different from the one they have now when they are integrated and keep each other in line within scientific thinking. Before they worked as poisons. Consider, for instance, the doubting drive, the denying drive, the postponing drive, the collecting drive, the unraveling drive. Many hecatombs of human beings were sacrificed before these drives learned to grasp their interrelation and to feel themselves to be functions of one organizing force in one human being! And how far we are still from the time when artistic forces and the practical wisdom of living will also find their way into scientific thinking—when a higher organic system will develop itself, in comparison to which the scholar, the doctor, the artist, and the lawmaker, such as we now know them, will necessarily look like poor antiquities!

116

Herd instinct.—Wherever we run across a morality, we find an assessment and ranking of human drives and actions. These assessments and rankings always express the needs of a community and herd: whatever profits *it* in the first place—and in the second and third—is also the supreme measure of the value of all individuals. By means of morality, individuals are led to be functions of the herd and to attribute value to themselves merely as functions. Since the conditions of the survival of one community have been very different from the conditions of another community, there have been very different moralities. And in view of the essential transformations of the herds and communities, states, and societies that still lie ahead, one can prophesy that there will still be very diverse moralities. Morality is herd instinct in the individual.

117

The herd's pang of conscience.—During the longest and most remote eras of humanity, there was a pang of conscience that was completely different from today's. Today one feels responsible only for what one wills and does oneself, and one has one's pride within oneself; all our law professors begin with the single person's sense of self and sense of pleasure, as if this had always been the source from which law had sprung. But throughout the longest era of humanity, there was nothing more frightful than feeling single. Being alone, perceiving as a single person, neither obeying nor ruling, constituting an individual—that was no pleasure then, but a punishment; one was condemned "to being individual." Freedom of thought counted as discontentment itself. Whereas we perceive law and order as coercion and renunciation, at that time one perceived egoism as a painful thing, as a veritable distress. To be oneself, to assess oneself according to one's own weights and measures—that was contrary to the taste of the time. The inclination to do so would be perceived as madness, for being alone was bound up with every misery and every fear. At that time, "free will" was in closest proximity to bad conscience, and the more unfreely one acted, the more that herd instinct rather than personal sense expressed itself in one's action, the more moral one took oneself to be. Everything that damaged the herd, whether the individual had willed it or not, created pangs of conscience for the individual—and for his neighbor too, in fact for the entire herd!—In this respect we have reversed our attitude most of all.

118

Good will.—Is it virtuous when a cell transforms itself into the function of a stronger cell? It has no choice. And is it evil when the stronger cell assimilates the weaker? It has no choice either: it is necessary for it, since it strives for a profusion of replacements and wants to regenerate itself. Consequently, in good will, one has to distinguish the drive to appropriate and the drive to submit, and consider whether it is the stronger or the weaker that feels good will. Joy and desire go together in the stronger, who wants to turn something into a function; joy and wanting to be desired go together in the weaker, who would like to become a function.—Pity is essentially the first sort of feeling: a pleasant arousal of the drive to appropriate at the sight of the weaker. In this connection, however, we must consider the fact that "strong" and "weak" are relative concepts.

119

No altruism!—In many people I see an excessively forceful and pleasurable wish to be a function; they have the finest scent for all those positions where precisely *they* can be a function, and that is where they rush to. To this group belong those women who transform themselves into the very function which is weakly developed in some man, and thus become his wallet, or his politics, or his sociability. Such beings preserve themselves best when they fit themselves into a foreign organism; if they do not succeed in doing so, they become annoyed, irritable, and eat themselves up.

120

Health of the soul.—The beloved medical formula for morality (whose originator is Ariston of Chios[10]), "Virtue is the health of the soul," would at

10. A prominent Stoic philosopher in Athens around 250 B.C.E.

least, in order to be serviceable, have to be changed into: "Your virtue is the health of your soul." For there is no health in itself, and all attempts to define such a thing have failed lamentably. It all depends on your aim, your horizon, your strengths, your inclinations, your errors, and especially on the ideals and phantasms of your soul—this is what determines *what*, even for your *body*, health must mean. Hence there are countless healths of the body. And the more one allows the individual and the incomparable to raise its head again—the more one unlearns the dogma of "human equality"—the more our medical doctors will have to abandon the concept of a normal health, as well as a normal diet and the normal course of a sickness. And only then could it be time to reflect on the health and sickness of the *soul* and to find each person's special virtue in the health of the soul—which could certainly look in one person like the opposite of health in another. In the end, there would still remain open the great question of whether we could *do without* getting sick, even in the development of our virtue, and whether specifically our thirst for knowledge and self-knowledge does not require the sick soul as much as the healthy one—in short, whether the exclusive will to health is not a prejudice, a cowardice, and perhaps a piece of highly delicate barbarism and backwardness.

121

Life no argument.—We have arranged a world for ourselves in which we can live—by postulating bodies, lines, planes, causes and effects, motion and rest, form and content; without these articles of faith, nobody could stand to live now! But this still does not mean that they have been proved. Life is no argument. One of the conditions of life could be error.

122

Moral skepticism in Christianity.—Even Christianity has made a great contribution to enlightenment: it taught moral skepticism—in a very impressive and effective way, accusing, embittering, but with tireless patience and subtlety. It destroyed in every individual human being the belief in one's "virtues." It made those great virtuous individuals, of whom antiquity had no lack, disappear forever from the earth—those popular individuals who strode around, confident in their own perfection, with the dignity of a bullfighting hero. When we today, raised in this Christian school of skepticism, read the moral treatises of the ancients, such as those of Seneca or Epictetus, we feel an entertaining superiority, and can see so far into them and over them, as if a child were speaking in front of an old man, or a pretty, enthusiastic young woman in front of La Rochefoucauld.[11] We know better what virtue is!

In the end, however, we have applied this same skepticism to all *religious* conditions and processes, such as sin, repentance, grace, sanctification, and have let the worm dig in so well that now we also have the same feeling of subtle superiority and insight when we read all Christian books. We know religious feelings better too! And it is time to know them well and describe them well, for the pious people of the old faith are also dying out; let us at least preserve their image and their type for the sake of knowledge!

124

In the horizon of the infinite.—We have left the land behind and boarded the ship! We have burned our bridges—more than that, we have demolished the land behind us! Now, little ship, watch out! By your side lies the ocean; true, it does not always roar, and sometimes it lies there like silk and gold and daydreams of kindness. But the hours are coming when you will recognize that it is infinite, and that there is nothing more terrifying than infinity. Oh, the poor bird that felt itself free and now collides with the walls of this cage! Alas, when homesickness for the land comes over you, as if there had been more *freedom* there—and there is no longer any "land!"

125

The madman.—Haven't you heard of that madman who lit a lantern in the bright morning, ran to the marketplace, and shouted unceasingly: "I seek God! I seek God!"? Since many of those who did not believe in God happened to be standing around there, he was the cause of great laughter. "Did he get lost, then?" said one. "Has he lost his way like a child?" said another. "Or is he hiding? Is he scared of us? Did he go for a boat ride? Did he emigrate?" They all shouted and laughed together.

The madman sprang into their midst and transfixed them with his gaze. "Where has God gone?" he cried, "I'll tell you where! *We've killed him*—you and I! We are all his murderers! But how have we done this? How could we have drunk up the sea? Who gave us the sponge to erase the whole horizon? What were we doing when we unchained this Earth from its sun? Now where is it going? Where are we moving? Away from all suns? Aren't we falling constantly? Backwards, sideways, forwards, in every direction? Is there

---

11. The *Maxims* of La Rochefoucauld (1613–1680) cast a skeptical eye on all claims to virtuous altruism.

still an above and a below? Aren't we wandering as if through an endless nothing? Isn't empty space breathing upon us? Hasn't it gotten colder? Isn't night and more night continuously coming upon us? Don't lanterns have to be lit in the morning? Don't we yet hear the noise of the gravediggers who are burying God? Don't we yet smell the divine rot?—For gods rot too! God is dead! God remains dead! And we have killed him!

"How can we console ourselves, the most murderous of all murderers? The holiest and mightiest possession of the world up to now has bled to death under our knives—who can wash this blood off us? With what water could we purify ourselves? What feasts of atonement, what holy games will we have to invent? Isn't the greatness of this deed too great for us? Don't we have to become gods ourselves just to seem worthy of it? There was never a greater deed—and whoever is born after us belongs, on account of this deed, to a history higher than all history up to now!"

Here, the madman grew silent and looked at his listeners again. They, too, grew silent and stared at him, amazed. Finally he threw his lantern on the ground, so that it shattered into pieces and went out. "I come too early," he said then, "it is not the right time for me yet. This colossal event is still on its way and wandering—it has not yet reached human ears. Lightning and thunder need time, the light of the stars needs time, deeds need time, even after they've been done, to be seen and heard. This deed is still farther from them than the farthest stars—*even though they were the ones who did it!*" They say further that the madman made his way into various churches that same day, and there he intoned his *requiem aeternam deo* [eternal requiem for God]. Whenever he was led out and called to account, he answered only this: "What are these churches anymore, then, if they aren't the crypts and catacombs of God?"

270

What does your conscience say?—"You shall become who you are."

276

For the new year.[12]—Still I live, still I think; I must still live, for I must still think. *Sum, ergo cogito; cogito, ergo sum.*[13] On this day, all allow themselves to express their wish and their most beloved thought. So I too want to say what I wished for from myself today, and what thought first ran across my heart

12. This section is the first of the fourth book of *The Gay Science*, which is subtitled *Sanctus Januarius* (Saint Januarius, or holy January), and dated January 1882.

13. I am, therefore I think; I think, therefore I am. "I think, therefore I am" is the first principle of the philosophy of Descartes (*Discourse on Method*, Part 4).

this year—what thought shall be for me the ground, guarantee, and sweetness of all further life! I want to learn more and more to see as beautiful what is necessary in things—in this way I will be one of those who make things beautiful. *Amor fati* [love of fate]: let that be my love from now on! I do not want to wage any war against what is ugly. I do not want to accuse; I do not even want to accuse the accusers. Let *looking away* be my only negation! And all in all, to sum it up: some day I want to be only a Yes-sayer!

283

Preparatory human beings.—I welcome all the signs that a more virile, a more warlike age is upon us, an age that above all will return bravery to its place of honor! For this age shall prepare the way for a still higher age, and gather the strength that that age will someday need—an age that will bring heroism into knowledge and *wage wars* for the sake of thoughts and their consequences.

For now, this requires many preparatory, brave human beings, who certainly cannot arise from nothing—any more than from the sand and slime of today's civilization and big-city culture; human beings who understand how to be satisfied with constant, invisible activity—silent, solitary, and resolute; human beings who have an inner penchant for seeking in all things what is *to be overcome* in them; human beings to whom cheerfulness, patience, simplicity, and contempt for the great vanities belong as much as do magnanimity in victory and indulgence for the small vanities of all the defeated; human beings with a sharp and free judgment about all victors, and about the role played by chance in all victory and fame; human beings with their own holidays, their own workdays, their own periods of mourning, who are used to command and sure in commanding, and are no less prepared to obey when it is appropriate, equally proud in one and in the other case, equally serving their own interests; more endangered human beings, more fruitful human beings, happier human beings!

For, believe me, the secret to reaping the greatest fruitfulness and the greatest enjoyment from existence is *to live dangerously!* Build your cities by Vesuvius! Send your ships into unexplored seas! Live at war with your fellows and with yourselves! Be robbers and conquerors, as long as you cannot be rulers and possessors, you knowing ones! The time is nearly gone when it could be enough for you to live hidden in the woods like shy deer! At last knowledge will reach out its hand for what is due to it—it will want to *rule* and *possess*, and you will too, along with it!

289

To the ships!—Consider the effect that a total philosophical justification of one's way of living and thinking has on every individual: it acts like a warming, blessing, fertilizing sun that illuminates one especially. Consider how it makes one independent of praise and blame, self-sufficient, rich, generous in happiness and goodwill; how it incessantly transmutes what is evil into what is good, allows all one's forces to blossom and ripen, and does not let the small or great weeds of sorrow and sulkiness appear at all. When one considers all this, one finally calls out and demands: Oh, let many such new suns still be created! Even evil, unhappy, exceptional human beings shall have their own philosophy, their own good right, their own sunshine! There is no need to pity them—we must unlearn this arrogant caprice, no matter how long humanity has up to now learned and practiced precisely this. We do not have to set up any confessors, exorcists, or forgivers of sins for them! Rather, a new *justice* is what is needed! And a new battle cry! And new philosophers! The moral Earth is also round! The moral Earth also has its antipodes! The antipodes also have their right to existence! There is still another world to discover—and more than one! To the ships, you philosophers!

290

One thing is needful.—"Giving style" to one's character—a great and rare art! It is practiced by those who survey everything that their nature offers in the way of strengths and weaknesses, and then fit them all into an artistic plan, until each thing appears as art and reason, and even the weakness charms the eye. Here a great mass of second nature has been added, there a piece of first nature has been removed—in both cases, through long practice and daily work. Here the ugliness that resists removal has been hidden, there it has been reinterpreted into the sublime. Much that is vague and resists formation has been saved up and used for views from afar—it is meant to signal in the direction of the distant and immeasurable. Finally, when the work is complete, it becomes clear how it was the compulsion of a single taste that was ruling and forming, in things both great and small. Whether the taste was a good or a bad one means less than one thinks—it is enough that it is *one* taste!

  It will be the strong, domineering natures who, in such a compulsion, in such a constraint and completion under their own laws, will savor their most refined joy. The passion of their formidable wills is relieved by the contemplation of all stylized nature, all conquered nature in a position of service; if they have to build palaces and lay out gardens, it also goes against their grain to set nature free.—In contrast, it is the weak characters, lacking power over themselves, who *hate* the constraint of style; they feel that if this grievous compulsion were imposed on them, they would have to be *debased* by it; they become slaves as soon as they serve, they hate service. Such spirits, who can be spirits of the first rank, are always out to fashion or explain themselves and their surroundings as *free* nature—wild, arbitrary, fantastic, disordered, and surprising. And this is good for them to do, for only thus can they do themselves good!

For one thing is needful: that human beings *attain* satisfaction with themselves—be it through this or that poetry and art—for only then can one stand to look at human beings! Those who are dissatisfied with themselves are constantly ready to take revenge for this; the rest of us will be their victims, if only by always having to stand the ugly sight of them. For the sight of the ugly makes one bad and somber.

335

Hurray for physics!—How many people really understand how to observe? And among the few who do understand it—how many observe themselves? "One is always furthest from oneself"—all who try the reins know this, to their own discontent. And the saying, "Know yourself," in the mouth of a god and spoken to human beings, is virtually malicious.

But nothing better indicates that self-observation is hopeless than the way in which *almost everyone* speaks about the essence of a moral action—this quick, willing, convinced, talkative way, with its look, its smile, its likeable eagerness! One seems to want to say to you, "But my dear friend, that's exactly *my* specialty! You're asking the one who's *qualified* to answer; it so happens that there's nothing I'm wiser about that this. So: when a human being judges, '*that's what's right*', concludes, '*therefore it must happen!*' and then *does* what has thus been recognized as right and designated as necessary—that's when the essence of the action is *moral*!"

But, my friend, you are telling me about three actions there rather than one. Judging—for instance, "that's what's right"—is also an action; can't judgments already be made in both a moral and in an immoral way? *Why* do you take this, and precisely this, to be right?

"Because my conscience tells me so. The conscience never speaks immorally; in fact, it is what first determines what should be moral!"

But why do you *listen* to the voice of your conscience? And how much right do you have to consider such a judgment true and non-deceptive? As regards this *faith*—is there no conscience anymore? Don't you know anything about an intellectual conscience? A conscience behind your "conscience"? Your judgment "that's what's right" has a prehistory in your drives, inclinations, disinclinations, experiences and lack of experience. "*How* did this judgment arise?," you must ask, and still further, "*What* really drives me to lend an ear to it?" You can lend an ear to its commands like a soldier responding to the command of his officer. Or like a woman who loves the one who is commanding. Or like a flatterer and coward who is afraid of the commander. Or like a dummy who follows because he has nothing to say against doing so. In short, there are a hundred ways in which you can lend an ear to your conscience. But the fact that you listen to this and that judgment as the voice of conscience—that you perceive something as right, in other words—may be caused by the fact that you have never reflected on yourself, and are blindly accepting what has been designated as *right* to you since childhood. The cause may also be that what you call your duty has brought you bread and honors up to now—it counts as "right" for you because it seems to you to be *your* "condition of existence" (and that you have a *right* to existence appears irrefutable to you!). The *steadiness* of your moral judgment could still turn out to be a proof precisely of your personal misery or impersonality; your "moral strength" could have its source in your stubbornness—or in your inability to catch sight of new ideals! And, briefly put: if you had thought more subtly, observed better, and learned more, you would at all events no longer call this "duty" and "conscience" of yours duty and conscience. The insight into *how, in each case, moral judgments have arisen to begin with* would spoil these lofty words for you—just as other lofty words such as "sin," "salvation of the soul," and "redemption" have already been spoiled for you.

And don't talk to me now about the categorical imperative, my friend! This term tickles my ear and I have to laugh, despite your ever so earnest presence. It makes me think of old Kant, who, as a punishment for having *stolen away with* "the thing in itself"—another very laughable business!— had the "categorical imperative" steal upon him, and with it in his heart, *strayed back* to "God," "soul," "freedom," and "immortality," like a fox that strays back into his cage—and it was *his* strength and cleverness that had *broken open* this cage![14]—What? You admire the categorical imperative within you?[15] This "steadiness" of your so-called moral judgment? This "absoluteness" of the feeling, "all others must judge as I do in this case?"

14. Kant claims in the *Critique of Pure Reason* that we have access not to things as they are in themselves, but only to appearances. Nevertheless, he insists that things in themselves do exist. Our ideas of God, freedom, and an immortal soul are ideas of things in themselves, constructed by reason, that can never correspond to any object in our experience; hence, we can have no objective knowledge of these things. In the *Critique of Practical Reason*, however, Kant claims that morality demands that we "postulate," that is, have faith in, God, freedom, and immortality. Morality is based on the categorical imperative: "Act only according to a maxim such that you can at the same time will that it be a universal law."

15. "There are two things that fill the mind with ever new and ever growing admiration and wonder, the more often and more steadily we reflect on them: the starry heavens above me and the moral law within me."—*Critique of Practical Reason,* conclusion.

Admire instead your *selfishness* in this! And the blindness, pettiness, and un-
pretentiousness of your selfishness! For it is selfishness to perceive one's *own*
judgment as a universal law. And it is a blind, petty, and unpretentious
selfishness to boot, because it betrays the fact that you have not yet discovered yourself, have not yet created your own, ownmost ideal for yourself—for this could never be the ideal of another, not to mention of all, all!

All who still judge, "everyone would have to act this way in this case,"
have not yet progressed five steps in self-knowledge. Otherwise they would
know that identical actions neither exist nor can exist—that every action
that has been done, was done in a completely unique and irretrievable way,
and that the same will hold of every future action; that all prescriptions for
action relate only to the crass exterior (even the most interior and subtle prescriptions of all moralities up to now); that with these prescriptions, we may
well attain an appearance of sameness, *but only an appearance*; that *every* action, whether you look into it or look back at it, is and remains an impenetra-
ble thing; that our opinions about "good," "noble," "great," can never be
proved by our actions, because every action is unknowable; that certainly our
opinions, valuations, and tables of goods are among the most powerful gears
in the clockwork of our actions, but that in every particular case the law of
their mechanism is unprovable.

Let us *confine* ourselves, then, to purifying our opinions and valuations,
and to *creating our own new tables of goods*—but we no longer want to brood
over the "moral value of our actions!" Yes, my friends! As regards all the
moral blather of some people about others, it's time to feel sick. Sitting in
moral judgment should be contrary to our taste! Let's leave this blather and
this bad taste to those who have nothing else to do except drag the past a bit
farther through time, and who themselves are never the present—in other
words, the many, the majority! We, however, *want to become who we are*—the
new, the unique, the incomparable, those who give themselves the law, those
who create themselves! And for this, we must become the best learners and
discoverers of everything lawful and necessary in the world; we must be
physicists so that we can be *creators* in this sense—while up to now, all valuations and ideals were built on *ignorance* of physics or in *contradiction* to it.
And thus: hurray for physics! And a still bigger cheer for what *forces* us to
it—our honesty!

341

The heaviest weight.—What if one day or one night a demon slinked after
you into your loneliest loneliness and said to you: "This life, as you live it
now and as you have lived it, you will have to live once more and countless
times more. And there will be nothing new about it, but every pain and

every pleasure, and every thought and sigh, and everything unspeakably small and great in your life must come back to you, and all in the same series and sequence—and likewise this spider and this moonlight between the trees, and likewise this moment and I myself. The eternal hourglass of existence is turned over again and again—and you with it, you mote of dust!"

Wouldn't you throw yourself down and gnash your teeth and damn the demon who spoke this way? Or have you ever experienced a prodigious moment in which you would answer him: "You are a god and I have never heard anything more godlike!" If that thought took control of you, it would change you as you are, and maybe shatter you. The question in each and every thing, "Do you will this once more and countless times more?" would lie as the heaviest weight upon your acts! Or how benevolent would you have to become toward yourself and toward life in order to *long for nothing more ardently* than for this ultimate eternal sanction and seal?

342

Incipit tragoedia.[16]—When Zarathustra was thirty years old, he left his home and Lake Urmi, and went into the mountain. There he savored his spirit and his solitude, and did not grow tired of it for ten years. But finally his heart changed—and one morning he got up with the dawn, stood before the sun, and spoke to it thus: "You great star! What would your happiness be if you did not have those on whom you shed your light? For ten years you came up here to my cave; you would have been sated with your light and this path without me, my eagle, and my snake. But we waited for you on every morning, took your overflow from you, and blessed you for it. See! I am overfull of my wisdom, like the bee that has gathered too much honey; I need outstretched hands; I would like to give away and share, until the wise among human beings have once again grown glad for their foolishness, and the poor have once again grown glad for their riches. For this, I must descend into the depths—as you do in the evening, when you go behind the sea and still bring light to the underworld, you over-rich star! I must, like you, *go under*, as the human beings call it to whom I want to descend. So bless me then, you tranquil eye that can see even an all too great happiness without envy! Bless the cup that wants to run over, so that water may flow golden from it, and carry the reflection of your bliss everywhere! See! This cup wants to become empty again, and Zarathustra wants to become human again."— Thus Zarathustra began to go under.

16. "Now begins the tragedy." This section, the last one in the first edition of *The Gay Science*, is very similar to the opening of Nietzsche's next book, *Thus Spoke Zarathustra*.

343

What our cheerfulness means.—The greatest recent event—that "God is dead," that the belief in the Christian God has become unbelievable—already begins to cast its first shadows on Europe. At least for the few whose eye, the *suspicion* in whose eye is strong and keen enough for this spectacle, some sun seems to have gone down, some deep old trust seems to have turned into doubt. To them, our old world has to seem duskier, more distrustful, more alien, "older" from day to day. For the most part, however, we may assert that the event is far too great, too distant, too removed from most people's capacity to comprehend, for us even to say that the news of it has *arrived* yet—much less that many know yet *what* has really taken place here, and what must all collapse now, once this belief has been undermined, because it was built on it, leaning on it, grown into it—for instance, our entire European morality. This long profusion and procession of breakdown, destruction, decline, and upheaval that now stands before us—who today has yet guessed enough of this to have to serve as the teacher and harbinger of this tremendous logic of terror, the prophet of a gloom and an eclipse of the sun, the like of which has probably never yet happened on earth?

Even we born riddle-solvers who wait, as it were, on the mountaintops, stationed between today and tomorrow, and suspended in the contradiction between today and tomorrow, we firstborns and premature births of the coming century, into whose sight the shadows that must soon envelop Europe *should* really have already come—how is it that even we await the arrival of this gloom without truly being wrapped up in it, and above all, without care and fear for *ourselves*? Are we perhaps still too concerned with the *immediate consequences* of this event? After all, these immediate consequences, its consequences for *us*, are, contrary to what one might expect, not at all sad and gloomy, but rather like a new kind of light that is hard to describe, a new kind of happiness, alleviation, cheering, encouragement, and dawn. In fact, when we hear the news that the "old God is dead," we philosophers and "free spirits" feel as if we were struck by the rays of a new dawn; at this news, our heart overflows with thankfulness, wonder, presentiment, expectation. At last the horizon appears free to us again, even granted that it is not bright. At last our ships may set out again, set out towards every danger. Every daring act of the knower is allowed again. The sea, *our* sea lies open there again; maybe there was never before such an "open sea."

344

To what extent even we are still pious.—In science, convictions have no civil rights, it is said with good reason. Only when they make up their minds to descend to the modest position of a hypothesis, a provisional experimental standpoint, a regulative fiction, may they be allowed entry to the realm of knowledge, and even a certain value within this realm—with the restriction, nevertheless, that they must remain under police surveillance, under the police force of mistrust.

But doesn't that mean, considered more precisely, that conviction may gain entry to science only when it *stops* being conviction? Wouldn't the discipline of the scientific spirit begin by allowing itself no more convictions?

That is probably the case. What remains to be asked is simply whether *in order for this discipline to begin*, a conviction must not already be there—in fact, such a commanding and unconditional conviction that it sacrifices all other convictions to itself. One can see that even science rests upon a faith; there is no such thing as a science that is "free of presuppositions." The question of whether *truth* is needed must not only have been answered "yes" in advance, but must have been answered "yes" with such force that in this affirmation there is expressed the proposition, the faith, the conviction, "there is *nothing needed more* than truth, and in comparison to it, everything else has only secondary value."

This unconditional will to truth: what is it? Is it the will *not to let oneself be deceived*? Is it the will *not to deceive*? For the will to truth could also be interpreted in this latter way—provided that under the generalization "I will not deceive" one includes the individual case, "I will not deceive *myself*." But why not deceive? But why not let oneself be deceived?—Notice that the grounds for the former lie in a domain quite different from that of the grounds of the latter; one does not want to let oneself be deceived under the assumption that it is harmful, dangerous, disastrous to be deceived. In this sense, science would be a sort of extended prudence, caution, or utility, to which however one could easily object: Come now, is wanting not to let oneself be deceived really less harmful, less dangerous, less disastrous? What do you know in advance about the character of existence in order to be able to determine whether the greater advantage lies on the side of the unconditionally mistrustful, or the unconditionally trusting?

But in the case that both should be necessary, much trust *and* much mistrust, then from what could science derive the unconditional faith upon which it rests, its conviction that truth is more important than any other thing, even any other conviction? This very conviction could never have arisen if truth *and* untruth had both continually demonstrated that they are useful—as is the case. Thus, the faith in science, which after all indisputably exists, cannot have originated in such a calculation of utility, but rather *in spite of the fact* that the lack of utility and the dangerousness of the "will to truth," of "truth at any price," is continually being proved. "At any price": oh, we understand that well enough, once we have offered and slaughtered one faith after the other at this altar!

Consequently, "will to truth" does *not* mean, "I will not let myself be deceived," but rather—there is no option left—"I will not deceive, not even myself." *And with this, we have reached morality as a basis.* For let one just ask oneself seriously, "Why will you not deceive?" particularly if it should appear—and it does appear!—as if life were designed for appearance—I mean for error, deceit, dissimulation, delusion, self-delusion—and if in addition the great sort of life has always in fact shown itself to be on the side of the most unscrupulous *polytropoi.*[17] Such a resolution could perhaps be interpreted mildly as a quixotism, an enthusiastic bit of insanity. But it could also be something worse, namely, a destructive principle, hostile to life. "Will to truth"—that could be a concealed will to death.

In this manner, the question, "Why science?" leads back to the moral problem: *what is the purpose of morality at all* if life, nature, and history are "immoral?" There is no doubt that truthful people, in the extreme and ultimate sense required by the faith in science, *affirm with this faith another world* than that of life, nature, and history. And in so far as they affirm this "other world," mustn't they by the same token *deny* its counterpart, this world, *our* world?

But you will have grasped where I am headed—namely, that our faith in science still rests upon a *metaphysical faith*; that even we knowers of today, we godless ones and anti-metaphysicians, still take even *our* fire from the flame first lit by a faith thousands of years old, that faith of Christians which was also the faith of Plato, that God is truth, that truth is divine. But what if precisely this is becoming more and more unbelievable, if nothing is proving to be divine anymore, unless it be error, blindness, lies—what if God himself is proving to be our longest lie?

345

Morality as a problem.—A defect in personality takes its revenge everywhere; a weakened, thin, washed-out, self-denying, and self-disowning personality is no longer fit for any good thing—least of all for philosophy. "Selflessness" has no value in heaven or on earth; the great problems all require *great love*, and only strong, well-rounded, secure spirits are capable of such love, spirits solidly grounded in themselves. It makes the most substantial difference whether a thinker has a personal relation to his problems, so that he finds in them his destiny, his need, and also his best happiness, or whether his relation is "impersonal"—that is, he only knows how to touch and grasp his problems with the feelers of cold and curious thought. In the latter case,

impersonal approach to morality

---

17. Plural of *polytropos*, "of many devices" or "of many ways"—an adjective applied in Homer to the tricky, versatile, and experienced Odysseus.

nothing will come of it, that much can be promised. For the great problems, if they let themselves be grasped at all, do not let themselves be *held* by frogs and weaklings. That has eternally been their taste—a taste, by the way, that they share with all feisty little females.

Now, how is it that I have never yet met anyone, not even in books, who stood in this personal relation to morality, who was familiar with morality as a problem and as *his* personal need, torture, sensuality and passion? Evidently morality was no problem at all up to now. Rather, it was precisely what people could agree on after all the mistrust, antagonism, and contradiction—it was the sacred place of peace where thinkers rested even from themselves, breathed freely, and revived. I see no one who dared to offer a *critique* of moral value judgments. In this area I miss even the experiments of scientific curiosity, the meticulous experimental imagination of psychologists and historians, which easily heads off a problem and snatches it in its flight, without rightly knowing what it has snatched.

I have barely detected a few sketchy starts at developing a *history of the development* of these feelings and valuations (which is something different from a critique of them, and still different from the history of ethical systems). In a single case, I have done everything I could to encourage an inclination and gift for this sort of history—in vain, as it seems to me today.[18] There is little to these historians of morality (mostly Englishmen). Usually they themselves are still unsuspectingly under the command of a particular morality, and unwittingly serve as its shield-bearers and followers—obeying, say, that popular superstition of Christian Europe which is still so earnestly repeated, that the characteristic of moral action consists in selflessness, self-disowning, self-sacrifice, or in sympathy, in compassion.

The usual mistake they make in their presuppositions is that they assert some consensus of peoples, or at least of civilized nations, about certain principles of morality, and from this they infer that these principles are unconditionally binding for you and me as well. Or, conversely, once they have realized the truth that among different peoples, moral assessments are *necessarily* different, they draw the inference that *no* morality is binding—and both of these inferences show equally great childishness. The mistake of the subtler among them is that they discover and criticize the perhaps foolish opinions of a people about its morality, or of human beings about all human morality, and believe that with this they have criticized this morality itself. But the value of a command, "you shall," is fundamentally different from and independent of these sorts of opinions about it, and from the weeds of error with which it is perhaps overgrown—just as certainly as the value of a

18. An allusion to Paul Rée, who under Nietzsche's influence wrote *The Origin of Moral Perceptions* (1877) and *The Development of Conscience* (1885).

medication for a sick person is completely independent of whether the sick person thinks about medicine like a scientist or like an old woman. A morality could even have grown *from* an error—but even with this insight, the problem of its value would not have been touched at all.

Thus, no one up to now has tested the *value* of that most famous of all medicines, called morality. And the first element of this test would be, for once—*to put it into question*. Well then—this is precisely our job.

346

Our question mark.—But you don't understand this? Indeed, one will have trouble in understanding us. We are searching for words; maybe we are also searching for ears. But who are we anyway? If we simply wished to use some older expressions and call ourselves godless, or faithless, or even immoralists, we would think these expressions were still far from designating us. We are all three, in too late a stage for one to grasp—for *you* to grasp, my curious friends—how it feels to be in such a state. No! No more of the bitterness and passion of the one who has torn away, but who has to take faithlessness and out of it concoct yet another faith, an aim, a martyrdom! We have been boiled down in this insight and grown cold and hard in it: in the world, things just don't happen in a way that is godly—no, not even, by human standards, in a way that is rational, or merciful, or just. We know well that the world in which we live is ungodly, immoral, "inhuman"—we have interpreted it all too long falsely and dishonestly, but according to the wish and will of our reverence, that is, according to a *need*. For human beings are reverential animals! But they are also mistrustful ones. And that the world is *not* worth what we believed it was, is about the surest thing that our mistrust has finally grasped. So much mistrust, so much philosophy.

To be sure, we are careful not to say that the world is worth *less*. Today it would seem laughable to us if human beings wanted to take it upon themselves to invent values that should *exceed* the value of the actual world—that is exactly what we have retreated from, as from an exorbitant aberration of human vanity and unreason that long went unrecognized. It had its last expression in modern pessimism, and an older, stronger one in the teaching of the Buddha, but Christianity also contains it, in a form that is admittedly more dubious and ambiguous, yet no less seductive for all that. The whole attitude of "man *against* world," man as a "world-negating" principle, man as the measure of the value of things, as judge of worlds, who in the end lays existence itself upon the scales and finds it too light—the atrocious tactlessness of this attitude has dawned on us as such, and disgusts us; we laugh even when we find "man *and* world" put side by side, separated by the sublime arrogance of the little word "and!"

But wait—haven't we precisely by laughing gone just another step further in despising humanity? And thus also in pessimism, in despising the existence that can be known by *us*? Aren't we precisely thereby subject to the suspicion of an opposition: an opposition between the world in which we were at home until now with our reverences—for the sake of which we perhaps *endured* living—and another world, *which we ourselves are?* This relentless, underlying, and deepest suspicion about ourselves is gaining ever greater and worse power over us Europeans, and could easily confront the coming generations with the terrible either-or: "Either do away with your reverences or—*with yourselves!*" The latter would be nihilism. But wouldn't the former also be—nihilism?—This is *our* question mark.

347

Believers and their need for belief.—How much one needs *faith* in order to thrive, how much that is "solid" and that one doesn't want to be shaken because one is *supporting oneself on it*—this is a measure of the degree of one's strength (or, to speak more clearly, of one's weakness). Even today, as it seems to me, most people in old Europe have need of Christianity; this is why it still continues to find faith. For such are human beings: an article of faith can be refuted before them a thousand times; provided that they need it, they will still continue to consider it "true"—in accordance with that famous "proof of strength" of which the Bible speaks.[19] Some still have need of metaphysics. But some also need that impetuous *longing for certainty* which is discharging itself scientifically-positivistically among great masses of people, the longing that *wants* by all means to have something solid (while on account of the ardor of this longing, one is more negligent and careless about giving grounds for one's assurance). This too is still the longing for support, a prop, in short, that *instinct of weakness* which, it is true, does not create religions, metaphysical systems, and convictions of all sorts—but conserves them.

In fact, around all these positivistic systems there puffs the vapor of a certain pessimistic gloom, a touch of fatigue, fatalism, disappointment, fear of a new disappointment—or a show of anger, a bad mood, the anarchism of exasperation, and every sort of symptom and masquerade of the feeling of weakness. Even the intensity with which our brightest contemporaries lose themselves in pitiful nooks and crannies, for instance in fatherlandery (that's my term for what in France is called *chauvinisme* and in Germany is called "German"), or in narrow aesthetic theories of the same type as Parisian *naturalisme* (which emphasizes and lays bare only the part of nature that pro-

19. I Cor. 2:4.

duces both nausea and amazement—today one likes to call this part *la verité vraie* [true truth]), or in nihilism on the St. Petersburg model (that is, *belief in disbelief*, to the point of martyrdom for its sake)—all this always shows above all the *need* for faith, support, backbone, backing.

Faith is always most desired, most urgently necessary, where will is lacking, for the will, as the feeling of command, is the distinctive sign of self-assured authority and strength. In other words, the less one knows how to command, the more urgently one desires some commander, some strict commander—a god, prince, class, doctor, confessor, dogma, or party conscience. From this we should perhaps infer that the reason for the development of both the world religions, Buddhism and Christianity, and above all the reason for their sudden expansion, may be an immense *sickness of the will.* And so it truly was: both religions came across a longing for a "you shall" that had been absurdly overdeveloped by a sickness of the will and was reaching the point of desperation; both religions were teachers of fanaticism in times of debility of the will, and thus offered countless people a support, a new possibility of willing, an enjoyment in willing. For fanaticism is the only "strength of the will" to which even the weak and insecure can be brought, as a sort of hypnotism of the entire sensory and intellectual system by virtue of the over-rich feeding (hypertrophy) of a single point of view and feeling, which then dominates—Christians call it their *faith.*

When people reach the basic conviction that they *must* be commanded, they become "believers." In contrast, one could conceive of a pleasure and strength in self-determination, a *freedom* of the will in which a spirit takes its leave of every faith, every wish for certainty, practiced as it is in supporting itself on slender cords and possibilities, and dancing even by abysses. Such a spirit would be the *free spirit par excellence.*

348

On the origin of scholars.—In Europe the scholar grows in every sort of class and social circumstance, as a plant that needs no particular kind of soil; hence scholars belong, essentially and involuntarily, among the representatives of democratic thought. But their origins betray themselves. If one has trained one's eye to some extent to recognize in a scholarly book or a scientific treatise the intellectual *idiosyncrasy* of the scholar—every scholar has one—and to catch it red-handed, behind this idiosyncrasy one will nearly always catch sight of the "prehistory" of the scholar, the scholar's family, and in particular the family's occupations and trades. Wherever the feeling finds expression, "This has now been proved, I have finished," it is commonly the ancestors in the blood and instincts of the scholar who from the viewpoint of their own corner are approving the "finished job"; the belief in

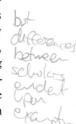

the proof is just a symptom of what has long been seen in a hard-working family as a "good job."

An example: the children of clerks and office scribes of every kind—whose primary task was always to put diverse material into order, to divide it into files, and in general to schematize—if they ever become scholars, show a predilection for taking a problem to have been virtually solved by the fact that they have schematized it. There are philosophers who at bottom are just schematizing brains—for them, the formal aspect of their father's trade has become the content. The talent for classifications, for tables of categories, betrays something; there is a price to be paid for being the child of one's parents.

The children of a courtroom lawyer will also have to be lawyers as scholars; they want, in the first place, to defend the rights of their cause, and in the second place, maybe, to be right.

The children of Protestant clergymen and schoolteachers can be recognized by the naive assurance with which, as scholars, they take their cause to have been already proved if only they have presented it from the heart and with warmth. For they are thoroughly accustomed to being *believed*—for their fathers, that was part of the "trade!"

Jews, in contrast, in accordance with the business circles and the past of their people, are least accustomed precisely to this—that they should be believed. Take a look in this connection at Jewish scholars: they all put great stock in logic, that is, in *forcing* assent through reasons; they know that they are bound to conquer with reasons, even where there is racial and class hostility against them, where people do not like to believe them. For nothing is more democratic than logic: it ignores personal looks, and takes even crooked noses to be straight. (By the way, Europe is more than a little indebted to the Jews precisely in regards to logical thinking and *neater* mental habits; this goes especially for the Germans, as a lamentably *déraisonnable* [unreasonable] race—even today one must always begin by giving them "a piece of one's mind."[20] Wherever Jews have gained influence, they have taught people to make finer distinctions, to draw consequences more precisely, to write more clearly and cleanly; their task was always to bring a people "to reason.")

349

The origin of scholars once again.—Wanting to preserve oneself expresses a situation of emergency, a constriction of the real, fundamental drive of life, which aims at *extending its power*, and in this willing, often enough puts self-

20. The German expression is "washing their heads."

preservation into question and sacrifices it. One should take it as symptomatic if particular philosophers, such as the consumptive Spinoza for example, saw the decisive point precisely in the so-called drive for self-preservation, had to see it there—for they were people in situations of emergency. The fact that our modern natural sciences have entangled themselves to such an extent in the Spinozistic dogma (finally and most crudely in Darwinism, with its unbelievably one-sided doctrine of the "struggle for existence") is probably a result of the ancestry of most natural scientists: in this respect they belong to the "people"; their ancestors were poor and humble folks who were all too familiar with the difficulty of surviving. There hovers over the whole of English Darwinism something like the stale air of English overpopulation, reeking of small people and their cramped needs. But as a natural scientist, one should emerge from one's human corner. And in nature what *rules* is not emergency situations, but overflow, superfluity, even to the point of absurdity. The struggle for existence is only an *exception*, a temporary restriction of the will to live; everywhere the struggle, both great and small, revolves around supremacy, around growth and expansion, around power, in accordance with the will to power, which is precisely the will of life.

353

On the origin of religions.—What the founders of religions have really invented is: first, setting up a particular way of life and everyday customs that operates as a *disciplina voluntatis* [discipline of the will] and at the same time eliminates boredom, and second, giving this very way of life an *interpretation* thanks to which it seems to be lit up by the highest value, so that now it becomes a good for which one struggles and under certain circumstances gives up one's life. Actually, of these two inventions, the second is the more essential; the first, the way of life, usually existed already, but side by side with other ways of life, and without any awareness of what sort of value it contained. The significance, the originality of founders of religions usually consists in the fact that they *see* a way of life, that they *pick it out*, that they *guess* for the first time what it can be used for, how it can be interpreted.

Jesus (or Paul), for instance, found before him the life of a small community in the Roman province, a modest, virtuous, oppressed life. He interpreted it, and interpolated into it the highest meaning and value—and thus endowed it with the courage to despise every other way of life, the quiet fanaticism of the Moravians,[21] the secret, subterranean self-confidence that grows and grows and is finally ready "to overcome the world" (that is,

21. A pietistic Christian brotherhood.

Rome, and the higher classes in the entire empire). Similarly, Buddha found before him, but spread throughout all the classes and social levels of his people, human beings of the type that, out of sluggishness, are good and kind (and above all, inoffensive)—that, also out of sluggishness, live abstinently and virtually without needs. He understood how such a type of human being would inevitably, with all its *vis inertiae* [force of inertia], have to roll into a faith that promises to *avoid* the recurrence of earthly troubles (that is, work, action in general); this "understanding" was his genius.

Proper to founders of religions is a psychological infallibility in knowing about a certain average type of souls who have not yet *recognized* that they belong together. The founders are the ones who bring them together; the founding of a religion thus always becomes an extended festival of recognition.

354

On the "genius of the species."—The problem of consciousness (or, more correctly, the problem of becoming conscious) first confronts us when we begin to comprehend to what extent we could dispense with it. And physiology and the history of animals are now bringing us to this beginning of comprehension (they have therefore needed two centuries to catch up with the forward-soaring suspicion of *Leibniz*).[22] For we could think, feel, will, remember—we could likewise "act" in every sense of the word—and nevertheless, none of this would have to "enter our consciousness" (as one says figuratively). All of life would be possible without seeing itself, as it were, in a mirror, and in fact, even in us now, by far the greatest part of this life still plays itself out without this mirroring—yes, even our thinking, feeling, willing life, as offensive as this may sound to an older philosopher. What is consciousness *for* in the first place, if on the whole it is *superfluous*?

Now if you want to hear my answer to this question, and the perhaps extravagant supposition it involves, it seems to me that the subtlety and

22. "*Leibniz's* incomparable insight [was] that consciousness is just an *accidens* [nonessential attribute] of perception and *not* its necessary and essential attribute—that, in other words, what we call consciousness constitutes merely a condition of our spiritual and psychic world (perhaps a sick condition) and *is far from constituting this world itself*": The Gay Science, §357. Cf. Leibniz, "Preface to the New Essays on the Understanding," in R. Ariew and D. Garber, eds., *Philosophical Essays* (Indianapolis and Cambridge: Hackett Publishing Co., 1989), 295: "there are a thousand indications that allow us to judge that at every moment there is an infinity of perceptions in us, but without apperception [consciousness] and without reflection—that is, changes in the soul itself, which we do not consciously perceive."

strength of consciousness are always related to the *capacity for communica-* *tion* of a human being (or an animal), and the capacity for communication, in turn, is related to the *need for communication*. This is not to be understood as if the particular individual who is a master of communicating his needs and making them understandable must also be most dependent on others for his needs. However, in regards to entire races and chains of generations, it does seem to me to be the case that wherever need, necessity, has long forced people to communicate, to understand each other promptly and accurately, there is finally an oversupply of this strength and art of communication, a capability, as it were, that has gradually built itself up and now is waiting for an heir to spend and squander it (so-called artists are these heirs, as are the orators, preachers, writers—all of them human beings who always come at the end of a long chain, "late-born" in every case in the best sense of the term, and as I said, *squanderers* according to their essence).

Provided that this observation is correct, I may go on to the supposition that *consciousness in general has developed only under the pressure of the need for communication*—that from the start, it was necessary, it was useful, only between one human being and another (especially between those commanding and those obeying), and furthermore, that it has developed only in relation to the degree of this usefulness. Consciousness is really just a connecting network between one human being and another. Only as such a network has it had to develop; a solitary and predatory human being would not have needed it. The very fact that our actions, thoughts, feelings, motions—or at least part of them—enter our consciousness is the consequence of a "must" that held sway for a terribly long time over human beings. As the most endangered animals, they *needed* help and protection, they needed their fellow humans; they had to express their necessities, to know how to make themselves understood—and for all this, they first required "consciousness," that is, "knowing" what they themselves lacked, "knowing" how they felt, "knowing" what they thought. For, once again: human beings, like every living creature, are thinking constantly but do not know it. The thinking that becomes *conscious* is only the smallest part of thought, and we say it is the most superficial, the worst part—for all this conscious thought *occurs in words, that is, in communicative signs*, and here the origin of consciousness reveals itself. Briefly put, the development of language and the development of consciousness (*not* reason, but merely reason's becoming conscious) go hand in hand. Add to this that language is not the only thing that serves as a bridge between one human being and another, but so do looks, squeezes, gestures. Our own becoming conscious of our sense impressions, the capacity to fix them and, as it were, to put them outside ourselves, increased to the degree that the necessity of conveying them to *others* by signs grew. Human beings who invent signs are also human beings who are becoming more and more sharply conscious of themselves; only as social animals did human beings learn to become conscious of themselves—they are still doing so, they are doing so more and more.

herd origin of consciousness

My thought is, as you see, that consciousness does not really belong to the individual existence of human beings, but rather to the social and herd nature in them; that, as a consequence, consciousness is subtly developed only in regards to social and herd usefulness, and that consequently each of us, despite the best will to understand oneself as individually as possible, "to know oneself," will always just bring to one's consciousness precisely what is not individual in one, what is "average"; that our very thinking constantly *follows majority rule*, so to speak, and is retranslated into the perspective of the herd due to the character of consciousness—due to the "genius of the species" that rules in it. All of our actions are at bottom incomparably personal, unique, boundlessly individual, there is no doubt. But as soon as we translate them into consciousness, *they no longer seem to be so.*

herd/species nature of consciousness

This is genuine phenomenalism and perspectivism as *I* understand it: the nature of *animal consciousness* entails that the world of which we can become conscious is only a world of surfaces and signs, a world shared in common, reduced to the common; that everything that becomes conscious *becomes*, by the same token, shallow, thin, relatively stupid, general, a sign, a signal of the herd; that all becoming-conscious is bound up with a great and radical perversion, falsification, superficialization, and generalization. Growing consciousness is finally a danger, and whoever lives among the most conscious Europeans knows that it is even a sickness. As you can guess, it is not the opposition of subject and object that concerns me here; this distinction I leave to the theorists of knowledge, who have remained caught in the traps of grammar (the metaphysics of the people). It is certainly not the opposition of "thing in itself" and appearance, for we are far from "knowing" enough to be able even to make this *distinction*. For we do not even have any organ at all for *knowing*, for "truth"; we "know" (or believe or imagine) exactly as much as may be *useful* in the interest of the human herd, the species. And even what is here called "usefulness" is in the end just another belief, a product of the imagination, and perhaps is precisely that most dangerous stupidity that will someday ruin us.

355

The origin of our concept of "knowledge."—I take this explanation from the street. I heard one of the ordinary people say, "He knew me right away." At this, I asked myself: What do the people understand by knowledge? What do they want when they want "knowledge?" Nothing but this: something

will to know

strange should be explained in terms of something *familiar*.[23] And we philosophers—have we really understood anything *more* by knowledge? What is familiar is what we are used to, so that we no longer wonder at it: the everyday, some rule in which we are stuck, each and every thing in which we feel at home. Now, isn't our need for knowledge just this need for the familiar, the will to discover in everything strange, unusual, questionable, something that no longer disturbs us? Isn't it the *instinct of fear* that calls on us to know? Isn't the rejoicing of the one who knows just the rejoicing of the restored feeling of security?

This philosopher here fancied that the world was "known" when he explained it in terms of the "idea"; ah, wasn't this because the "idea" was so familiar to him, because he was so used to it—because he was so much less afraid of the "idea"?—Oh, this self-satisfaction of the knowers! Just look at their principles and their solutions to the riddle of the world! When they once again find in things, under things, behind things, something that is unfortunately very familiar to us, such as our times tables, or our logic, or our willing and desiring, how happy they are right away! For "what is familiar is known": they all agree on this. Even the careful ones are of the opinion that at least what is familiar is *more easily knowable* than what is strange; for example, they make it a rule of method to begin with the "internal world," with the "facts of consciousness," because this is the world that is *more familiar to us*! Error of errors! The familiar is what we are used to—and what we are used to is what is hardest to "know," that is, to see as a problem, that is, to see as strange, as distant, as "outside us."

The great certitude of the natural sciences, as compared to psychology and the critique of the elements of consciousness—*unnatural* sciences, as one could almost say—rests precisely on the fact that the natural sciences take what is *strange* as their object, while it is almost something contradictory and nonsensical even to *want* to take what is not strange as one's object.

356

How things will get more and more "artistic" in Europe.—The need to make a living still forces upon nearly all male Europeans a *role*, their so-called profession—even today, in our time of transition, when so much is ceasing to force things upon us. Some retain the freedom, an apparent freedom, to choose this role themselves; most have it chosen for them. The result is strange enough: nearly all Europeans confuse themselves with their role when they reach a more advanced age. They themselves are the victims of

23. The German words *Erkenntnis* (knowledge), *erkannt* (known), and *bekannt* (familiar, well-known) are closely related.

their "good acting"; they themselves have forgotten to what extent chance, moods, and whims controlled them when their "profession" was decided—and how many other roles they perhaps *could* have played, for now it is too late! Viewed more deeply, the role has really *become* character; and art, nature.

There have been ages in which one believed with solid confidence, in fact with piety, that one was predestined for precisely this business, precisely this way of earning one's bread, and simply did not want to recognize the element of chance, role, arbitrariness. Classes, guilds, and hereditary trade privileges brought about, with the help of this belief, those enormous social hierarchies that characterize the Middle Ages and which one has to credit with one thing at least: durability (and duration is, on earth, a value of the highest rank!).

But there are opposite ages, the really democratic ages, when people turn more and more against this belief, and a certain cheeky belief and contrary point of view comes to the fore—that belief of the Athenians, which was first noticed in the age of Pericles, that belief of the Americans today, which increasingly wants to become the belief of the Europeans. In such ages, individuals are convinced that they can do practically anything, *can handle practically any role*; they all experiment with themselves, improvise, experiment again, take pleasure in experimenting; all nature ceases and becomes art. Once the Greeks had adopted this *role-faith*—an artist's faith, if you will—they underwent step by step, as is well known, an amazing transformation, which is not in every respect worthy of imitation: *they really became actors*. As actors, they worked their magic on the whole world and conquered it, finally including even the "conqueror of the world" (for the *Graeculus histrio*[24] defeated Rome, and *not* Greek culture, as innocents usually say).

But what I fear, what today we can already grasp with our hands if we feel like doing so, is that we modern human beings are already on the same path; in every case where human beings begin to discover to what extent they are playing a role and to what extent they *can* be actors, they *become* actors. With this, there emerges a new human flora and fauna, of a type which cannot develop in more stable and confined ages—or is left "beneath," beneath the ban and suspicion of dishonor. With this, there always emerge the most interesting and craziest ages of history, in which the "actors," *all* sorts of actors, are the real masters. By the same token, another class of human beings is put at an ever greater disadvantage, and is finally made impossible—above all, the great "architects"; constructive energy is paralyzed; the courage to make plans for the long run is discouraged; the organizational geniuses begin to be rare; who dares anymore to undertake works for whose completion one

24. Latin: "little Greek actor," with a contemptuous tone.

would have to *count on* millennia? For that basic faith is dying out on which one can count in that way, the faith on the basis of which one can make promises, anticipate the future in a plan, sacrifice the future to one's plan: namely, the faith that human beings have value, have meaning, only in so far as they are *stones in a great construction*—for which purpose they must first of all be *stable*, "stones," and above all not actors!

Briefly put—ah, it will still be kept silent long enough!—what from now on will no longer be constructed, no longer *can* be constructed, is a *society* in the old sense of the word; we are lacking everything to build this construction—above all, the material. *None of us is material for a society anymore*—there's a truth that is timely! It makes no difference to me that meanwhile the most short-sighted, perhaps most honest, and in any case the noisiest kind of human being that there is today, our friends the socialists, believe, hope for, dream, and above all, scream and scribble roughly the opposite—for one can already read their watchword for the future, "free society," on every table and wall. Free society! Yes, yes! But you know, gentlemen, don't you, what such a thing is built of? Wooden iron! The famous wooden iron! And this wooden iron isn't even wooden.[25]

370

What is romanticism?—It will perhaps be remembered, at least among my friends, that in the beginning I broke free of this modern world with some crude errors and overestimates, and in any case, as one who was full of hope.[26] I understood—who knows on the basis of which personal experiences?—the philosophical pessimism of the nineteenth century as if it were the symptom of a higher strength of thought, of extraordinary valor, of a more triumphant *fullness* of life than had typified the eighteenth century, the age of Hume, Kant, Condillac, and the sensualists. Thus, tragic knowledge appeared to me to be the real *luxury* of our culture, its most precious, noble, and dangerous kind of extravagance, but still, because of its exceeding richness, a luxury that our culture was *allowed*. Similarly, I reinterpreted German music for myself as the expression of a Dionysian power in the German soul; in it, I thought I heard the earthquake with which an ancient force, dammed up for ages, was finally venting itself—indifferent as to whether everything else called culture would thereby start to totter.

You see, at that time I misunderstood, as regards both philosophical pessimism and German music, what constitutes their real character: their *roman-*

25. "Wooden iron" is a proverbial German example of an oxymoron, such as "square circle."
26. Nietzsche is referring to *The Birth of Tragedy*.

ticism. What is romanticism? Every art, every philosophy, may be seen as a means of health and assistance in the service of growing, struggling life; they always presuppose suffering and sufferers. But there are two kinds of sufferers: on the one hand, those who suffer from the *over-fullness of life*, who want a Dionysian art, and thus a tragic view and insight into life, and on the other hand, those who suffer from the *impoverishment of life*, who seek calm, stillness, smooth seas, salvation from themselves through art and knowledge, or else intoxication, convulsions, numbing and insanity. To the double needs of the *latter* type there corresponds all romanticism in arts and knowledge; to them there corresponded (and corresponds) Schopenhauer just as much as Richard Wagner, to name the most famous and marked romantics whom at that time I *misunderstood*—*not* to their disadvantage, by the way, as one may concede to me in all fairness. Those who are richest in the fullness of life, the Dionysian god and human being, can permit themselves not only the sight of the terrible and questionable, but even the terrible deed, and the luxury of destruction, disintegration, negation. With them, what is evil, senseless, and ugly seems to be allowed, as it were, as a result of an overflow of engendering, impregnating forces that can create a bountiful orchard from any wasteland. In contrast, those who suffer the most and are poorest in life would most need mildness, peacefulness, kindness in thought and action, and if possible, a god that is really a god for the sick, a "savior." They would equally need logic, the conceptual intelligibility of existence—for logic calms one, makes one confident—and in short, a certain warm, fear-dispelling narrowness and enclosure within optimistic horizons.

Thus I gradually learned to comprehend Epicurus, the opposite of a Dionysian pessimist, and likewise the "Christian," who in fact is just a kind of Epicurean and, like the Epicurean, is essentially a romantic. My sight grew ever sharper for that most difficult and dangerous form of *backward inference* in which the most mistakes are made: the backward inference from the work to the author, from the deed to the doer, from the ideal to the one who finds it *necessary*, from every way of thinking and valuing to the *need* that is in command behind it.

With regard to all aesthetic values, I now make use of this main distinction: I ask in every individual case, "Is it hunger or overflow that has become creative here?" Another distinction would seem to recommend itself more to begin with—it is more obvious by far—namely, paying attention to whether the longing for fixation, eternalization, *being*, is the cause of the creation, or whether it is the longing for destruction, change, the new, the future, *becoming*. But both forms of longing, considered more deeply, still prove to be ambiguous, and in fact they can be interpreted in terms of the previously mentioned and, as it seems to me, preferable scheme. The longing for *destruction*, change, becoming can be the expression of the over-full force pregnant with the future (my term for this is, as is known, the word "Dionysian"), but it can also be the hatred of the misfits, the destitute, and the hapless, who destroy, *must* destroy, because what endures, in fact all endurance, all being itself, irritates and incites them—in order to understand this emotion, take a close look at our anarchists.

The will to *eternalize* likewise requires a twofold interpretation. It can, on the one hand, come from gratitude and love; an art with this origin will always be an art of apotheosis, perhaps dithyrambic with Rubens, or blissfully playful with Hafiz, clear and kindly with Goethe, and shedding a Homeric light and glory upon all things. But this can also be that tyrannic will of one who is suffering severely, is struggling and tortured, and would like to forge what is most personal, individual, narrow, and really idiosyncratic in this suffering into a binding law and compulsion; who takes revenge, as it were, on all things by imprinting, branding, and forcing upon them *his* image, the image of *his* torture. The latter is *romantic pessimism* in its most explicit form, be it Schopenhauerian philosophy of will, or Wagnerian music—romantic pessimism, the last *great* event in the destiny of our culture.

(That there *could* still be a quite different pessimism, a classical pessimism—this premonition and vision belongs to me, as inseparable from me, as my *proprium* and *ipsissimum* [my own and most proper possession]; it's just that the word "classical" offends my ears; it is overused by far and has become too blunt and unrecognizable. I call this pessimism of the future—for it is coming, I see it coming!—*Dionysian* pessimism.)

373

"Science" as a prejudice.—It follows from the laws of ranking that scholars, insofar as they belong to the intellectual middle class, are not allowed to get the truly *great* problems and question marks into their sight at all. Besides, their courage and their eyesight do not reach that far—above all, their need that makes them into researchers, their inner predilections and wishes that things were *such and such*, their fearing and hoping reach tranquility, reach satisfaction all too soon. For instance, that which makes the pedantic Englishman Herbert Spencer gush in the way he does and draw a line of hope, a horizon of desirability—that eventual reconciliation of "egoism and altruism" that he spins tales about—almost nauseates people like us. A humanity with such Spencerian perspectives as ultimate perspectives would seem to us to deserve contempt, to deserve annihilation! But the very fact *that* something has to be perceived by him as the highest hope, something that to others counts, and can only count, merely as a repulsive possibility, is a question mark which Spencer would not have been able to foresee.

The same goes for that faith with which so many materialistic natural scientists are now content, the faith in a world which is supposed to have its equivalent and its measure in human thought, in human value concepts—a "world of truth," which we would be able to get at, once and for all, with the help of our four-cornered little human reason. What? Do we really want to let existence be degraded like this for us into a calculating exercise and a pastime for stay-at-home mathematicians? Above all, one should not want to divest existence of its *ambiguous* character; this is demanded by *good* taste, gentlemen, the taste of reverence for everything that lies beyond your horizon! To think that the only justified interpretation of the world is the one in which *you* are justified, in which it is possible to continue researching and working scientifically in *your* sense (you really mean *mechanistically?*), an interpretation that allows counting, calculating, weighing, seeing, and grabbing, and nothing further—that is a piece of crassness and naiveté, if not a mental illness, an idiocy. Wouldn't it be quite likely, to the contrary, that precisely what is most superficial and external in existence—its most apparent aspect, its skin and its sensory side—would be what let itself be grasped first? Maybe the *only* thing that let itself be grasped? A "scientific" interpretation of the world, as you understand it, could consequently still be one of the *stupidest*, that is, poorest in meaning, of all possible interpretations of the world—let me say this into the ears and consciences of our friends the mechanists, who like to run around amidst philosophers today and are thoroughly convinced that mechanics is the doctrine of the first and last laws upon which, as upon a ground floor, all existence must be built. But an essentially mechanical world would be an essentially *meaningless* world! Suppose that one assessed the *value* of a piece of music according to how much of it could be counted, calculated, put into formulas; how absurd such a "scientific" assessment of music would be! What would one have comprehended, understood, known about it? Nothing, absolutely nothing of what is really "music" in it!

374

Our new "infinite."—How far the perspectival character of existence reaches, or even whether existence has any other character; whether an existence without interpretation, without "sense," becomes precisely "nonsense"; whether, on the other hand, all existence is not essentially an *interpreting* existence—this cannot be figured out, and rightfully so, even by the most diligent and painfully conscientious analysis and self-examination of the intellect, since in this analysis the human intellect cannot help seeing itself under its own perspectival forms, and *only* in them. We cannot see around our own corner. It is hopeless curiosity to want to know what other sorts of intellect and perspective there *could* be—for instance, whether any beings can perceive time backwards, or alternately forwards and backwards (which would entail a different direction of life, and a different concept of cause and effect).

But I think that today we are at least far from the laughable presumption of decreeing from our corner that one is *allowed* to have perspectives only from this corner. Rather, the world has once more become "infinite" for us—inasmuch as we cannot exclude the possibility that it *contains infinite interpretations.* Once again the great horror takes hold of us—but who would want directly to deify *this* monster of an unknown world in the old style again? And, as it were, to worship the *unknown* from now on as "the *Unknown One?*" Ah, there are too many *ungodly* possibilities of interpretation comprised in this unknown, too much devilry, stupidity, folly of interpretation—our own human, all too human interpretation itself, which we know. . . .

375

Why we seem to be Epicureans.—We are wary, we moderns, of all ultimate convictions; our mistrust lies in wait for the enchantments and trickeries of conscience that lie in every strong belief, in every unconditional Yes and No; how is this to be explained? Perhaps one may see in this, to a large extent, the caution of the "burned child," the disappointed idealist. But the other and better factor is the rejoicing curiosity of an erstwhile corner-dweller who has been brought by his corner to the point of despair, and now revels and delights in the opposite of the corner, in the unlimited, in the "free in itself." Thus there develops a nearly Epicurean craving for knowledge which does not want to let the questionable character of things get by it easily; likewise, an aversion to big moral words and moral attitudes, a taste that rejects all crass, foursquare oppositions, and is proudly aware of its practiced restraint. For *that* is what constitutes our pride, this easy tightening of the reins in our headlong urge for certainty, this self-control of the rider in his wildest riding. For now, as before, we have mad and fiery beasts beneath us, and if we hesitate, it is danger least of all that makes us hesitate.

377

We homeless ones.—Among today's Europeans there is no lack of those who have a right to call themselves homeless in a sense that distinguishes and honors them; let them in particular take my secret wisdom and *gaya scienza*[27] to heart! For their lot is hard, their hope uncertain; it is quite a trick to devise consolation for them—but what good does it do? We children of the future, how *could* we be at home in this day? We are adverse to all ideals with which one could still feel at home even in this breakable, broken time of transition. And as for the "realities" of this time, we do not believe that they will *endure*. The ice that today still supports us has already grown very thin; the thawing wind is blowing; we ourselves, we homeless ones, are something that breaks up ice and other all too thin "realities."

We "conserve" nothing, and do not want to go back to any past; we are certainly not "liberal," we do not work for "progress," we do not need to plug our ears against the sirens in the marketplace who sing about the future; their song of "equal rights," "free society," "no more masters and no servants" does not charm us! We simply do not take it to be desirable for the kingdom of justice and concord to be established on earth (because at all events it would be a kingdom of the deepest mediocrity and Chinese-ism); we delight in all who, like us, love danger, war, adventure, who do not allow themselves to compromise, to be caught, placated, gelded; we count ourselves among the conquerors; we reflect on the necessity of new orders, even of a new slavery—for every strengthening and elevation of the type "human being" also includes a new kind of enslavement.

Is it not true that with all this, we must hardly feel at home in an age which loves to claim the honor of being called the most humane, gentle, and righteous age that the sun has ever seen? It is bad enough that precisely when we hear these beautiful words, our second thoughts are that much uglier; that in all this, we see only the expression—and the masquerade—of profound weakening, exhaustion, old age, declining strength! What can it matter to us with what kind of tinsel the sick dress up their weakness? Let them display it as their *virtue*; there is no doubt, after all, that weakness makes one gentle, oh so gentle, so righteous, so inoffensive, so "humane!"

The "religion of pity" into which one would like to persuade us—oh, we know well enough the hysterical little males and females who today have need of precisely this religion as a veil and fancy dress! We are no humanitarians; we would never dare to allow ourselves to speak of our "love for humanity"—our type isn't enough of an actor for that! Or not Saint-Simonist[28] enough, not French enough. One must already be saddled with a *Gallic* oversupply of erotic excitability and love-struck impatience in order even to get close to humanity with one's lust, in all sincerity. . . . Humanity!

27. The medieval Provençal troubadours referred to the art of poetry as *la gaya scienza*, and from this expression Nietzsche took the title of this book; the title page of the second edition reads: *Die fröhliche Wissenschaft ("la gaya scienza")*.

28. Claude Henri de Saint-Simon (1760–1825), French utopian socialist.

Has there ever been a more revolting old woman among all old women? (Unless perhaps it were "truth"—a question for philosophers.) No, we do not love humanity. But on the other hand, we are not nearly "German" enough either, in the sense in which the word "German" is thrown around today, to advocate nationalism and racial hatred, to be able to take joy in the national mange of the heart and blood poisoning on account of which today in Europe one people is cutting itself off, setting itself off from another as if by a quarantine. For that, we are too unbiased, too malicious, too spoiled, and also too well taught, too well "traveled." We prefer by far to live on mountains, apart, "untimely," in past or coming centuries, just in order to spare ourselves the silent rage to which we know we would be condemned as the witnesses to a politics that is laying waste the German spirit by making it idle, and which is, furthermore, *petty* politics—is it not necessary for this politics, in order to prevent its own creation from collapsing again right away, to plant it between two deadly hatreds? Does it not *have to* will the eternalization of the European system of petty states?

We homeless ones, we are too multifarious and mixed in race and descent, as "modern men," and consequently feel little temptation to take part in that mendacious racial self-admiration and obscenity, which displays itself today in Germany as the sign of a German attitude, and which, in the people with a "historical sense," strikes one as doubly false and indecent. We are, in a word—and it shall be our word of honor!—*good Europeans*, the heirs of Europe, the rich, overendowed, but also over-richly obligated heirs of millennia of the European spirit. As such, we have also outgrown Christianity and are averse to it—precisely because we have grown *out* of it, because our ancestors were Christians who were unwavering in their Christian integrity, who willingly sacrificed life and property, station and fatherland for the sake of their faith. We—we do the same. But for what? For our unbelief? For every sort of unbelief? No, you know better than that, my friends! The hidden *Yes* in you is stronger than all the Nos and Maybes that are making you sick, along with your time. And when you must go to sea, you emigrants, what forces you to do so is also—a *faith*!

(382)

The great health.—We new, nameless, hardly intelligible, premature births of a yet unproven future—for a new end, we also need a new means, namely a new health, a stronger, shrewder, tougher, bolder, gladder health than any health has been up to now. Whoever has a soul that thirsts to have experienced the entire range of values and desirables up to now, and to have sailed around all the coasts of this ideal "Mediterranean"; whoever wants to know from the adventures of one's ownmost experience how it feels to be a con-

new health

queror and discoverer of the ideal, and likewise an artist, a saint, a lawmaker, a sage, a scholar, a devotee, a soothsayer, a divine loner in the old style—requires one thing above all for this, *the great health*—a health such as one does not simply have, but also constantly acquires and must acquire, because one is giving it up again and again, and must do so!

And now, after having been on our way like this for a long time, we Argonauts of the ideal, braver perhaps than is prudent, and having been shipwrecked often enough and brought to grief, but healthier, as I said, than one would like to let us be, dangerously healthy, healthy ever again—now it would seem to us as if, as a reward for this, we have a yet-undiscovered land before us, whose boundaries no one has yet discerned, a Beyond to all lands and corners of the ideal up to now, a world so over-rich in what is beautiful, strange, questionable, terrible and divine, that our curiosity as well as our thirst for possession is beside itself—alas, nothing will satisfy us anymore!

How could we, after such views and with such a burning hunger in our conscience and our science, still be content *with the human beings of the present*? This is too bad, but it is unavoidable that when we look at their worthiest goals and hopes it is hard for us to keep a straight face, and maybe we will just not look at them anymore. A different ideal runs ahead of us, an odd, seductive, perilous ideal which we would not like to persuade anyone to follow, because we do not so easily grant anyone *the right to do so*: the ideal of a spirit that plays naively, that is, not deliberately but from overflowing fullness and power, with all that up to now was called holy, good, untouchable, divine; for whom the highest thing in which the common people find their fair standard of value would just amount to danger, decline, and debasement, or at least, rest, blindness, and temporary self-forgetfulness; the ideal of a human and superhuman well-being and goodwill that will often enough appear *inhuman*, for instance when beside all earthly seriousness up to now, beside every sort of solemnity in gesture, word, sound, look, morality and task, it presents itself as their most personified, involuntary parody—but with which, nonetheless, perhaps *the great seriousness* first begins, the real question mark is first posed, the destiny of the soul takes a turn, the clock's hand moves, the tragedy *begins*. . . .

383

Epilogue.—But while in conclusion I am slowly, slowly painting this gloomy question mark, and am still inclined to call to my readers' minds the virtues of the proper reader—oh, what forgotten and unknown virtues!—it occurs to me that the most malicious, mirthful, goblin-like laughter is resounding all around me; the spirits of my book themselves fall upon me, pull me by the ears, and call me to order.

"We can't stand it anymore," they shout at me, "away, away with this raven-black music. Isn't there bright morning all around us? And green, soft ground and turf, the kingdom of the dance? Was there ever a better hour to be gay? Who will sing us a song, a morning song, so sunny, so light, so feathered that it *doesn't* scare away the blues [*Grillen*], but instead invites the crickets [*Grillen*] to sing along and dance along? And even simple, rustic bagpipes would be better than such cryptic sounds, such toad-croakings, voices from the grave and marmot whistles with which you have regaled us up to now in your wilderness, Mr. Hermit and Musician of the Future! No! Not such tones! Let's instead strike up more agreeable and joyful tones!"[29]

Is *that* how you'd like it, my impatient friends? All right! Who wouldn't gladly oblige you?[30] My bagpipes are already waiting, my throat as well; it may sound a little hoarse, but put up with it—we're in the mountains, you know! But at least what you're about to hear is new. And if you don't understand it, if you misunderstand the *singer*, what difference does it make? That's just "the singer's curse."[31] You will be able to hear his music and melody all the more clearly, and also *dance* to his pipes all the better. Do you *will* that?

---

29. The last line is a quotation from Schiller's "Ode to Joy," used by Beethoven in the Ninth Symphony.

30. This final section of the second edition of *The Gay Science* is followed by a collection of songs.

31. The title of a ballad by Ludwig Uhland.

Twilight of the Idols

Or, How to Philosophize with the Hammer

THE PROBLEM OF SOCRATES

1

The wisest sages of all times have come to the same judgment about life: *it is good for nothing*. Always and everywhere we have heard the same sound escape their mouths—a sound full of diffidence, full of melancholy, full of fatigue with life, full of hostility to life. Even Socrates said, as he died, "Living—that means being sick a long time. I owe a rooster to the savior Asclepius."[1] Even Socrates had had enough.

What does that *demonstrate*? What does that *indicate*? In the past one would have said (oh, one has said it, and loud enough, especially our pessimists!): "Here there must be something true in any case! The *consensus sapientium* [agreement of the wise] demonstrates the truth." Shall we still speak this way today? *May* we do so? "Here there must be some *sickness* in any case"—that's *our* answer; these wisest sages of all times, one should first take a close look at them! Were they perhaps, all of them, no longer steady on their legs? Worn out? Shaky? *Décadents*? Does wisdom perhaps appear on Earth as a scavenger bird, excited by the scent of rotting meat?

2

In my own case this disrespectful thought—that the great sages are *declining types*—first occurred to me precisely in regards to an instance where learned and unlearned prejudice most strongly opposes it. I recognized Socrates and Plato as symptoms of decay, as instruments of the Greek dissolution, as pseudo-Greek, as anti-Greek (*Birth of Tragedy*, 1872). That *consensus sapientium*—this I grasped better and better—demonstrates least of all that they were right about what they agreed on. Rather, it demonstrates that they

Selections from Nietzsche, *Twilight of the Idols*, translated by Richard Polt, © 1995, Hackett Publishing Co. Reprinted with permission.

1. Asclepius was the god of medicine. See Plato, *Phaedo* 118a.

themselves, these wisest ones, were somehow in *physiological* agreement, so that they took the same negative stance toward life—and *had* to take it.

Judgments, value judgments about life, for or against, can in the final analysis never be true; they have value only as symptoms, they come into consideration only as symptoms—in themselves, such judgments are stupidities. One absolutely must reach out and try to grasp this astounding *finesse, that the value of life cannot be assessed.* Not by the living, since they are parties to the dispute—in fact, they are the objects of contention, and not the judges; not by the dead, for another reason. Thus, when philosophers see a problem in the *value* of life, this even amounts to an objection to them, a question mark attached to their wisdom, an unwisdom.—What? And all these great sages—are we saying they were not only *décadents*, but they were not even wise to begin with? But here I come back to the problem of Socrates.

3

Socrates belonged by origin to the lowest folk; Socrates was rabble. One knows, one can still see for oneself, how ugly he was. But ugliness, which in itself is an objection, was among the Greeks virtually a refutation. Was Socrates a Greek at all? Ugliness is often enough the expression of a blocked development, a development *hampered* by interbreeding. Otherwise, it comes to light as a development in *decline.* Forensic anthropologists tell us that the typical criminal is ugly: *monstrum in fronte, monstrum in animo* [monster in the face, monster in the soul]. But the criminal is a *décadent.* Was Socrates a typical criminal?—At any rate this would not clash with that well-known judgment of a physiognomist which sounded so offensive to Socrates' friends. A visitor who knew about faces, when he passed through Athens, said to Socrates' face that he *was* a *monstrum*—that he contained all bad vices and cravings within him. And Socrates simply answered: "You know me, sir!"

4

Socrates' *décadence* is signaled not only by the confessed depravity and anarchy of his instincts, but also by the overdevelopment of the logical and that *arthritic nastiness* that characterizes him. And let us not forget those auditory hallucinations which have been interpreted in religious terms as "Socrates' *daimonion* [divine sign]." Everything about him is exaggerated, *buffo*, a caricature; everything is at the same time covert, subliminal, ulterior.—I am trying to grasp from what idiosyncrasy that Socratic equation—reason =

virtue = happiness—stems, the most bizarre equation that there is, and one which in particular has all the instincts of the older Hellenes against it.

5

With Socrates, Greek taste takes a turn in favor of dialectic. What is actually happening there? Primarily, a *noble* taste is thereby defeated; with dialectic, the rabble rises to the top. Before Socrates, dialectical manners were rejected in good society. They were taken to be bad manners, they were a compromising exposure. One warned the youth against them. And all such presentation of one's reasons was mistrusted. Respectable things, like respectable people, just don't carry their reasons around on their sleeves like that. It is improper to show your whole hand. Whatever has to get itself proved in advance is not worth much. Wherever authority is still considered good form, so that one does not "give reasons" but commands, the dialectician is a sort of clown. One laughs at him; one does not take him seriously. Socrates was the clown who *succeeded in making people take him seriously*; what actually happened there?

6

Dialectic is chosen only as a last resort. It is well-known that it creates mistrust, that it is not very convincing. Nothing can be wiped away more easily than a dialectician's effect; this is proven by the experience of every gathering where people speak. It can only be a *last resort* deployed by those who have no other weapons. One needs to get one's rights by *force*; otherwise, one makes no use of it. This is why the Jews were dialecticians. Reynard the Fox was one. What? And Socrates was one too?

7

Is Socrates' irony an expression of revolt? Of the rabble's *ressentiment*?[2] Does he, as one of the oppressed, relish his own ferocity in the knife-thrusts of the syllogism? Does he take *revenge* on the nobles whom he fascinates? As dialectician, one has a merciless instrument at hand; one can play the tyrant with it; one compromises by conquering. The dialectician lays on his opponent the burden of proving that he is not an idiot. He infuriates, and at the same time paralyzes. The dialectician *disempowers* the intellect of his opponent.—What? Is dialectic just a form of *revenge* in Socrates?

2. Resentful vengefulness (French). Nietzsche develops this concept at length in *On the Genealogy of Morals* (1887).

8

I have made it understandable how Socrates could be repulsive. Now it is all the more necessary to explain why he was *fascinating*.—The fact that he discovered a new kind of *agon* [contest], that in this contest he served as the first fencing master for the noble circles of Athens, is the first point. He fascinated by stimulating the combative drive of the Hellenes: he introduced a variant into the wrestling match between young men and youths. Socrates was also a great *erotic*.

9

But Socrates surmised even more. He saw *past* his noble Athenians; he grasped that *his* case, his idiosyncratic case, was already not exceptional. The same kind of degeneration was silently preparing itself everywhere; the old Athens was coming to an end. And Socrates understood that all the world had *need* of him—his means, his cure, his personal device for self-preservation. Everywhere, the instincts were in anarchy; everywhere, one was five steps away from excess; the *monstrum in animo* was the general threat. "The drives want to play the tyrant; a *counter-tyrant* who is stronger must be invented."

When that physiognomist had exposed to Socrates who he was, a cave of all bad cravings, the great ironist allowed himself another word that gives us the key to him. "That is true," he said, "but I became the master of them all." *How* did Socrates become master of *himself*? His case was at bottom only the extreme case, only the most striking example of what began at that time to be the general emergency: the fact that no one was master of himself any more, that the instincts were turning *against* each other. He was fascinating as this extreme case—his fearsome ugliness displayed him as such to every eye. He was even more fascinating, of course, as an answer, as a solution, as the semblance of a *cure* for this case.

10

When one finds it necessary to make a tyrant out of *reason*, as Socrates did, then there must be no small danger that something else should play the tyrant. Rationality was at that time surmised to be a *savior*; neither Socrates nor his "sick patients" were rational by free choice—it was de rigueur, it was their *final* means. The fanaticism with which all Greek speculation throws itself at rationality betrays a situation of emergency—they were in danger, they had to make *this* choice: either to be destroyed, or—to be *absurdly rational*.

The moralism of the Greek philosophers from Plato on is pathologically conditioned; likewise their assessment of dialectic. Reason = virtue = happiness simply means: one must imitate Socrates and produce a permanent *daylight* against the dark desires—the daylight of reason. One must be cunning, sharp, clear at all costs; every acquiescence to the instincts, to the unconscious, leads *downward*.

11

I have made it understandable how Socrates was fascinating: he appeared to be a doctor, a savior. Is it necessary to go on to point out the error which lay in his belief in "rationality at all costs?"—It is a self-deception on the part of philosophers and moralists to think that they can escape from *décadence* merely by making war against it. Such an escape is beyond their strength. What they choose as a means, as salvation, is itself just another expression of *décadence*—they *alter* its expression, they do not do away with it itself. Socrates was a misunderstanding; *the whole morality of betterment, that of Christianity included, was a misunderstanding*. The most glaring daylight, rationality at all costs, a life bright, cold, careful, aware, without instinct, in resistance to the instincts, was itself just a sickness, another sickness—and not at all a way back to "virtue," to "health," to happiness. To *have* to fight the instincts—that is the formula for *décadence*. As long as life *is ascending*, happiness is the same as instinct.

12

Did he himself still grasp that, this most cunning of all self-outwitters? Did he tell himself this in the end, in the *wisdom* of his courage in the face of death? Socrates *wanted* to die—not Athens, but *he* gave himself the poison cup, he forced Athens to give him the poison cup. "Socrates is no doctor," he said to himself softly, "death is the only doctor here . . . Socrates himself has just been sick for a long time. . . ."

"REASON" IN PHILOSOPHY

1

You ask me what is idiosyncratic about philosophers? . . . There is, for instance, their lack of a sense of history, their hatred for the very notion of becoming, their Egyptianism. They think they are *honoring* a thing if they de-historicize it, see it *sub specie aeterni*[3]—if they make a mummy out of it. Everything that philosophers have handled, for thousands of years now, has been a conceptual mummy; nothing real escaped their hands alive. They kill and stuff whatever they worship, these gentlemen who idolize concepts; they endanger the life of whatever they worship. In their view, death, change, and age, like procreation and growth, are objections—refutations, even. That which is, does not *become*; that which becomes, *is* not.

Now, they all believe, desperately even, in that which *is*. But since they fail to get it into their grasp, they look for the reason why it withholds itself from them. "There must be an illusion, a trick, at work that prevents us from perceiving that which *is*; where's the trickster?"—"We've got the trickster!" they cry happily, "it's sensation! These senses, *which are so immoral anyway*, trick us about the *true* world. The moral is: free yourself from the senses' trickery, from becoming, from history, from the lie; history is nothing but belief in the senses, belief in the lie. The moral is: say No to everything that lends credence to the senses, to all the rest of humanity; all that is merely 'the masses'. Be a philosopher, be a mummy, portray monotono-theism with a gravedigger's pantomime!—And above all, away with the *body*, this pathetic *idée fixe* [pet idea] of the senses, afflicted with every logical error there is, refuted, even impossible—although it has the nerve to behave as if it were real!" . . .

2

I set aside with great respect the name of *Heraclitus*. While the rest of the mass of philosophers were rejecting the testimony of their senses, because they displayed plurality and change, he rejected the testimony of the senses because they displayed things as if they had duration and unity. Heraclitus did not do justice to the senses either. They do not lie either in the way the Eleatics[4] thought, or in the way that he thought—they do not lie at all. What we *make* of their testimony is what first introduces the lie—for instance, the lie of unity, the lie of thinghood, of substance, of duration. . . . "Reason" is what causes us to falsify the testimony of the senses. Insofar as the senses display becoming, passing away, and change, they do not lie. But Heraclitus will always be in the right for saying that being is an empty fiction. The "apparent" world is the only world; the "true world" is merely *added to it by a lie*.

3. "From the perspective of the eternal"—an expression used by Spinoza.

4. Followers of Parmenides of Elea (ca. 475 B.C.E.), who asserted that that which is, is unchangeable, uniform and unitary.

3

And what fine tools of observation we have in our senses! This nose, for instance, of which no philosopher has yet spoken with admiration and gratitude, is in fact the most delicate instrument at our disposal; it can register minimal differences in motion which even the spectroscope fails to register. The extent to which we possess science today is precisely the extent to which we have decided to *accept* the testimony of the senses—and learned to sharpen them, arm them, and think them through to their end. The rest is a miscarriage and not-yet-science—that is, metaphysics, theology, psychology, epistemology. Or it is formal science, a theory of signs, such as logic and that applied logic, mathematics. In these formal sciences, reality makes no appearance at all, not even as a problem; nor is there any hint of the question of what value such a convention of signs has in the first place.

4

The *other* idiosyncrasy of philosophers, which is no less dangerous, consists in confusing what is first with what is last. They posit what comes at the end—unfortunately, for it should never come at all!—the "highest concepts," that is, the most universal and emptiest concepts, the final wisp of evaporating reality—these they posit at the beginning *as* the beginning. This, again, just expresses their way of honoring something: the higher is not *permitted* to grow out of the lower, is not *permitted* to have grown at all.

The moral is: everything that is of the first rank must be *causa sui* [cause of itself]. Origination from something else counts as an objection that casts doubt on the value of what has so originated. All the supreme values are of the first rank; all the highest concepts—that which *is*, the unconditional, the good, the true, the perfect—all this cannot have become, and *must* consequently be *causa sui*. But all this cannot be at odds with itself either, cannot contradict itself. That's where they get their stupendous concept "God." The last, the thinnest, the emptiest concept is posited as the first, as a cause in itself, as *ens realissimum* [the most real being]. To think that humanity has had to take seriously the mental distortions of sickly web-spinners!—And it has paid dearly for having done so!

5

Let us, finally, present the opposing way in which *we* (I politely say we) view the problem of error and illusion. It used to be that one took alteration, change, becoming in general as a proof of illusion, as a sign that something must be there, leading us astray. Today, in contrast, it is precisely to the extent that we are compelled by the prejudice of reason to posit unity, identity, duration, substance, cause, thinghood, being, that we see ourselves, as it were, entangled in error, *forced* into error—so sure are we, on the basis of a rigorous self-examination, that it is here that the error lies.

This case is just like the supposed motions of our great star. In that case, error has our eyes as its constant advocates, whereas in the first case, its advocate is our *language*. In its origin, language belongs to the time of the most rudimentary type of psychology; we encounter a crude set of fetishes when we pay attention to the basic presuppositions of the metaphysics of language—or, to put it plainly, *reason*. *Reason* sees actors and actions everywhere; it believes in the will as an absolute cause; it believes in the "I," in the I as a being, in the I as a substance, and *projects* its belief in the I-substance onto all things—that is how it first *creates* the concept "thing." Being is thought into things everywhere as a cause, is *imputed* to things; from the conception "I" there follows the derivative concept "being." At the beginning there stands the great and fatal error of thinking that the will is something that *acts*—that will is an *ability*. Today we know that it is merely a word.

Much, much later, in a world that was more enlightened by a thousandfold, philosophers were startled to become aware of their *certitude*, their subjective *certainty* in manipulating the categories of reason; they concluded that these categories could not come from experience—all experience stands in contradiction to them, after all. *So where did they come from?*—And in India, as in Greece, they made the same mistake: "We must already have been at home in a higher world"—instead of *in a far lower one*, which would have been the truth!—"we must have been divine, *since* we have reason!"

In fact, nothing up to now has been more naively persuasive than the error of being, as it was formulated by the Eleatics, for instance; after all, it has on its side every word, every sentence we speak! Even the opponents of the Eleatics fell prey to the seduction of their concept of being—among others, Democritus did so in inventing his *atom*. "Reason" in language: oh, what a tricky old woman she is! I'm afraid we're not rid of God because we still believe in grammar.

6

One will be thankful to me if I condense such an essential and new insight into four theses; I thus make it easier to understand, and I challenge you to argue against it.

First proposition. The grounds on which "this" world has been designated as apparent are, rather, grounds for its reality; *another* kind of reality is absolutely indemonstrable.

Second proposition. The distinguishing marks which one has given to the "true being" of things are the distinguishing marks of nonbeing, of *nothing.* The "true world" has been constructed by contradicting the actual world— this "true world" is in fact an apparent world, insofar as it is merely a *moral-optical* illusion.

Third proposition. It makes no sense whatsoever to tell fables about "another" world than this one, provided that the instinct to slander, trivialize, and look down upon life is not powerful in us; in that case, we *revenge* ourselves on life with the phantasmagorias of "another," "better" life.

Fourth proposition. To divide the world into a "true" and an "apparent" world, whether in the style of Christianity or in the style of Kant (a *sneaky* Christian to the end) is merely a sign of *décadence*—a symptom of *declining* life.—The fact that the artist prizes appearance over reality is no objection to this proposition. For "appearance" here means reality *once again*, but in the form of a selection, an emphasis, and a correction. Tragic artists are *not* pessimists—in fact, they say *Yes* to everything questionable and terrible itself; they are *Dionysian.*

HOW THE "TRUE WORLD" FINALLY BECAME A FICTION

History of an Error

1. The true world, attainable for those who are wise, devout, virtuous— they live in it, *they are it.*

    (Oldest form of the idea, relatively clever, simple, convincing. Paraphrase of the assertion, "I, Plato, *am* the truth.")

2. The true world, unattainable for now, but promised to those who are wise, devout, virtuous ("to the sinner who does penance").

    (Progress of the idea: it becomes more refined, more devious, more mystifying—*it becomes woman*, it becomes Christian.)

3. The true world, unattainable, unprovable, unpromisable, but a consolation, an obligation, an imperative, merely by virtue of being thought.

    (The old sun basically, but glimpsed through fog and skepticism; the idea become sublime, pallid, Nordic, Königsbergian.[5])

5. An allusion to Kant, who lived all his life in Königsberg. For Kant, it is impossible for us to know about "things in themselves"—including God, free will, and an immortal soul; however, rational morality obliges us to "postulate" such things.

4. The true world—unattainable? In any case, unattained. And if it is unattained, it is also *unknown*. Hence it is also not consoling, redeeming, obligating; to what could something unknown obligate us?

    (Grey dawn. First yawnings of reason. Rooster's crow of positivism.)

5. The "true world"—an idea that is useful for nothing anymore, no longer even obligating—an idea become useless, superfluous, *hence* a refuted idea; let us do away with it!

    (Bright day; breakfast; return of *bon sens* [good sense] and cheerfulness; Plato's blush; pandemonium of all free spirits.)

6. We have done away with the true world; what world is left over? The apparent one, maybe? . . . But no! *Along with the true world, we have also done away with the apparent!*

    (Midday; moment of the shortest shadow; end of the longest error; high point of humanity; INCIPIT ZARATHUSTRA [here begins Zarathustra].)

Heidegger

Martin Heidegger was born in 1889 in Messkirch, a small town on the edge of the Black Forest in Germany. His original intention was to enter the priesthood, and in 1909 he entered the Jesuit novitiate, though he withdrew two weeks later due to poor health. Heidegger claimed that his interest in the "question of Being" was first aroused when he was given Franz Brentano's *On the Manifold Meaning of Being in Aristotle* in 1907. His early development was also influenced by Kierkegaard's newly translated works, Wilhelm Dilthey's hermeneutics (theory of interpretation), and Edmund Husserl's phenomenology. Heidegger received his doctorate in philosophy at the University of Freiburg, where he also worked as an academic assistant to Husserl. In 1927, while at the University of Marburg, he published *Being and Time*, and the following year he was appointed to Husserl's chair at the University of Freiburg. Heidegger was appointed rector of the university in 1933, and he joined the National Socialist Party shortly thereafter. He resigned as rector a year later, but new evidence suggests that, though he became increasingly critical of the Nazis, he continued to support them until the end of the war. During the 1930s and early 1940s, Heidegger lectured extensively on the German poet, Hölderlin, and on Nietzsche. He was banned from teaching after the denazification hearings of 1945, but he was reinstated in 1950 and became emeritus professor at Freiburg in 1951. Some of his publications include "Letter on Humanism" (1947), in which he distanced himself from Sartre's existentialism, *Introduction to Metaphysics* (1935 lectures, first published in 1953), *On the Way to Language* (1959), and the two-volume work, *Nietzsche* (1961). He died in 1976.

1. The Question of Being

Heidegger begins his greatest work, *Being and Time* (1927), with a question as bizarre to our ears as any we have ever heard. The aim of this book, he says, is to answer the question, "What is the meaning of Being?" This, we are told, is the most basic question humans can ask, yet most of us will feel that nothing we have ever thought about or studied prepares us for this question. What does the word "Being" refer to? And what is it to ask about the *meaning* of Being?[1]

Because Heidegger's project is part of the ancient philosophical discipline called "metaphysics," we might try to make sense of this question by looking at Aristotle's *Metaphysics*, which begins with the words, "All human beings by nature reach out for understanding."[2] Here Aristotle is making a very straightforward observation about humans. His point is that we find ourselves thrown into the midst of a world where things often seem strange or confusing, and where we need to get a handle on what is going on around us if we are to be able to function. Because of this need to get clear on things, it is natural for humans to try to understand how things add up or what things are all about. If we define "metaphysics" as the attempt to make sense of what things *are* in the broadest sense of the word, then we can see why Aristotle thinks metaphysics is so deeply ingrained in human nature. Because we need to be able to deal with the things we find around us, we are constantly trying to understand what these things are, that is, to understand their "Being" as entities of particular types.

Like Aristotle, Heidegger holds that "the question of Being, the striving for an understanding of Being, is the basic determinant of [human] existence."[3] He believes we all already have some understanding of the Being of entities, and that we are all concerned with getting a better, clearer understanding of what things are in general. And because it is our nature to ask the "question of Being," the project of working out a "fundamental ontology"—that is, the attempt to formulate a basic overall account of the Being of entities in general—is merely a more rigorous version of what we are all doing all the time.

The point here is that everyone has some sense of what things are. This vague and unformulated grasp of things is something that is found in our skilled practices rather than in our explicit thoughts. For example, every

1. The German word *Sein* is translated as "Being" with a capital B in the English edition of *Being and Time*, but it is good to keep in mind that all nouns are capitalized in German, so the word translated as "Being" is really just the ordinary word for what it is to be: "being." For the purposes of this introduction, we will continue to use the capitalized form for "Being" (as well as Heidegger's word for human being, "Dasein"), but we will use lower case for all other words that are capitalized in the English translation.

2. This is Martha Nussbaum's translation in her book, *The Fragility of Goodness* (Cambridge: Cambridge University Press, 1986), 247.

3. Martin Heidegger, *The Metaphysical Foundations of Logic*, trans. Michael Heim (Bloomington: Indiana University Press, 1984), 16.

time you turn a doorknob to enter a room, you manifest your understanding of doorknobs, doors, rooms, and so on. Heidegger calls this prior sense of things our "pre-ontological understanding of Being," meaning that it is something we have before we begin to engage in explicit reflection about the Being of entities (the traditional area of metaphysics known as "ontology"). The pre-reflective "know-how" we have in everyday activities is generally tacit and not yet conceptualized. Though you know how to deal with door-knobs and doors, you probably would have a hard time putting this know-how into words. So even though we all have a background sense of things that guides and orients our ordinary dealings with the world, for the most part that understanding has not been articulated or conceptualized. To ask "the question of Being," then, is to try to conceptualize and clarify the grasp of things we already have in our day-to-day lives. And to ask about the *meaning* of Being is to ask about how things come to show up as *counting* or *mattering* in specific ways in relation to our lives (where the word "meaning" is used in the sense in which we say "This book meant a lot to me" or "That affair didn't mean a thing").

Of course, Heidegger is well aware that there have been a number of on-tological theories formulated over the centuries. At different times philoso-phers have suggested that Being is to be accounted for in terms of cosmic functions, God's creation, monads, unknowable things-in-themselves, mat-ter in causal interactions, and so on. But he feels that these theories, al-though disclosing and clarifying a great deal, have also tended to give us a somewhat distorted and narrow view of the nature of reality. There has been a pervasive tendency to think of reality as a collection of objects of various types that are just *there*, existing independent of us and our prac-tices. In Heidegger's jargon, traditional ontology has viewed the world as an aggregate of "present-at-hand" objects, as continuously existing things oc-cupying positions in space. This conception of Being as the enduring pres-ence of things is at the root of the different conceptions of *substance* that have been formulated throughout the history of philosophy. As Heidegger points out, when philosophers have asked about Being, they have tended to answer the question with some version of a substance ontology.

Heidegger thinks it is especially important to raise the question of Being once again, because he thinks that our understanding of ourselves and our world has come to be shaped by a way of thinking that is so all-pervasive and powerful that we have difficulty even questioning it today. The dominant understanding of reality in contemporary life is that which emerged with the rise of modern science, the pivotal event that has shaped our modern worldview in the West. The rise of modern science has led to what we might call an "objectified" view of reality. According to this objectified view, the universe is a vast aggregate of material objects in causal interactions. These material objects have such features as mass, space-time position, velocity, and other quantifiable properties—the so-called "primary qualities" identified by the scientists of the seventeenth and eighteenth centuries.

What is problematic, given this objectified outlook, is how we can make sense of the idea that these objects contain meanings or values in themselves. Indeed, many scientifically oriented thinkers have assumed that reality consists only of intrinsically meaningless and valueless objects. On such a view, it is natural to assume that values and meanings, if they exist at all, can exist only in our minds, not in objective reality itself. Thus, the objectified view of reality is correlated with a particular view of human beings. According to this view, we are objects among others in the causal order of nature. But we are also subjects or minds who can represent objects in our ideas, and who can develop attitudes and beliefs about those objects. On this "subjectified" view of the self, we are essentially conscious beings or subjects who form ideas about the external world and try to get a correct view of that world in order to function in it efficiently. Thus, it becomes important to clearly distinguish what is really out there in objective reality—the material objects that make up the universe—and what is purely subjective, a projection of our own feelings and desires onto things.

Now Heidegger is well aware that this objectified view of reality has been a tremendous cultural achievement that has opened innumerable doors to technological advance and improved living. It would be a mistake to think that Heidegger is anti-science in any way. But he also believes that the modern understanding of reality we inherit from the rise of modern science has generated a number of pressing problems for contemporary life, problems that are especially intractable because we seem to lack any basis for critically reflecting on the ontology that creates them.

First, the modern worldview tends to assume that in order to give a full account of reality, we need to draw a sharp distinction between subject and object—between what is within the minds of humans and what is out there in the material world. This subject-object model, as is well known, leads to difficult problems for the theory of knowledge. For if we have access to the world only through the mediation of our own ideas and interpretations, how can we ever really be sure that those ideas give us correct information about the way the world is in itself? Moreover, the subject-object model in its original form was tied up with a particular view about the ultimate constituents of reality: the mind-matter ontology that has come down to us in its modern form from Descartes. According to this ontology, there are two kinds of stuff in the universe: mental stuff (known directly through introspection) and physical stuff (known through sensory experience). It is interesting to note that a more general distinction between mind and matter tends to persist even when philosophers reject the idea that the mind is a distinct sort of substance. Even when they give up on the idea that there is some special sort of spiritual *stuff* called "mind," they still tend to assume that no account of human phenomena is complete unless it explains the physical side of action by what goes on in the mind. Thus, the distinction between mind and matter tends to be a standard fixture in our thinking even when we try to get rid of immaterial mental stuff.

The second problem that arises from the modern objectified worldview is a pervasive sense of a "loss of meaning" in life. The modern outlook tends to assume that values and meanings are purely subjective constructs, products of our needs and desires. But if this is the case, then it becomes difficult to see how there could be any solid basis for forming the notion of a genuinely "higher" or "better" way of life beyond just coping and doing what feels good. With no notion of a cosmic order that defines right and wrong, good and bad, we seem to have trouble identifying a stable basis for assessing our behavior and forming aspirations. In other words, we lack the resources for envisioning the kind of "better" life implied in Socrates' words, "What is important is not just to live, but to live well." The concern with confronting this wide-spread sense of a loss of meaning in modern life is one of the central aims of *Being and Time*.

Heidegger's teacher, Edmund Husserl, had explored the idea that the source of these modern problems was "naturalism," the view of reality given to us by modern natural science. But Heidegger rejects this explanation. In his view, the outlook of natural science is just a modern version of an age-old tendency to see the world from a point of view that gives us a distorted and concealed understanding of things. The real problem, he suggests, is not naturalism, but the tendency to focus on how things show up for us when we adopt a theoretical attitude toward the world. In his words, "It is not just naturalism, as [Husserl] thinks . . . but the general domination of the *theoretical* that really deforms the problematic."[4] The idea here is that when we adopt a detached, theoretical stance toward things—when we try to be dispassionate and disinterested in the way Plato and Descartes and most other traditional philosophers do—we are going to get something very much like the objectified view of modern science. Once again, Heidegger is not opposed to such a view of things; he does not think it is bad. But he does think that such a theoretical outlook is only one specialized outlook among others—one "regional" way of looking at things—with no privileged access to the truth about the way the world really is.

Heidegger's claim, then, is that the objectified outlook gives us a rather

4. Martin Heidegger, *Zur Bestimmung der Philosophie*, in the collected works of Heidegger (*Gesamtausgabe*) Vol. 56/57 (Frankfurt am Main: Klostermann, 1987), 87.

one-sided and distorted view of reality that is out of touch with the concrete, lived realities of everyday life. The dominance of this worldview in contemporary life reflects a deep-seated tendency toward "forgetfulness" or "concealment" in humans. To say that we are prone to forgetfulness is to say that we have a tendency to become so preoccupied with the way things show up for us in our world that we lose sight of the background conditions (what Heidegger calls "worldhood") that first make it possible to encounter anything at all. Heidegger suggests in such works as the *Introduction to Metaphysics* that the pre-Platonic Greeks had some insight into worldhood in their understanding of Being as *physis*, which he renders as "coming-into-presence" or "emerging-into-Being."[5] But we today have lost sight of this older way of understanding Being, with the result that we take our current outlook as self-evidently true and beyond criticism.

The only way to overcome this forgetfulness, Heidegger claims, is to try to recover a more basic understanding of the world and our place in it, a sense of things that is concealed by the objectified view of modernity. This is the aim of the question of the meaning of Being. It sets out to ask how entities in general come to show up for us as mattering in determinate ways—how they come to *mean* something to us in relation to our lives. In the course of dealing with this question, we will be led to recover or "retrieve" a forgotten sense of the background conditions that make any experience of reality whatsoever possible. Heidegger therefore sees the aim of "phenomenology" (Husserl's method of description) as looking for the "hidden ground and meaning" of what ordinarily shows up in the world (§7).

If we are to avoid slipping into the assumptions of the objectified view, however, we need to start out from a description of things as they appear not in detached reflection or theorizing, but as they show up in the midst of our ordinary lives as agents when we are dealing with the practical life-world. This is why Heidegger decides to start out from a "phenomenology of everydayness"—from a description of familiar contexts of activity prior to theory and abstract reflection. If it is true, as Heidegger suspects, that the theoretical attitude gives us a one-sided and misleading understanding of the world, then it will be necessary to work out our ordinary pre-reflective sense of things to get a sense of what gets covered over in theoretical reflection.

As we shall see, this phenomenology of everydayness raises fundamental questions about the dominant view of reality circulating in our contemporary world. The parts of *Being and Time* that seem to have the greatest sig-

5. Martin Heidegger, *An Introduction to Metaphysics*, trans. Ralph Manheim (New Haven: Yale University Press, 1980).

nificance for modern philosophy are Heidegger's attacks on the subject-object model and on mind-matter dualism. In criticizing this dualism, he does not try to show that the mental is reducible to matter, as many modern physicalists try to do. On the contrary, what he tries to show is that the whole assumption that we have to understand reality in terms of substances, *whether mental or material*, is suspect. In his account of being-in-the-world as a unified phenomenon, one of the most basic assumptions of modern ontology—the assumption that we need to make reference either to the mental or to the material in giving an account of reality—is called in question. Given the description of everydayness that emerges in *Being and Time*, such concepts as those of mind and matter, inner and outer, and subject and object come to appear as rather high-level abstractions with no essential or necessary role to play in making sense of the world as we normally encounter it. From the standpoint of Heidegger's new view of the Being of entities, the problems created by the modern worldview seem to dissolve. Whatever we may think of Heidegger's painfully difficult style of writing, we cannot fail to be struck by the fresh and original vision of the meaning of Being he works out through his descriptions of everydayness.

2. Human Being (Dasein) as Being-in-the-world

Heidegger tells us at the outset of *Being and Time* that his preliminary aim is to give an account of that entity that has some understanding of what it is to be, namely human being, or, as he calls it, *Dasein*, the ordinary German word for existence or "being-there." The first chapters of division one of the work begin with a detailed description of our everyday way of being as agents engaged in activities in practical contexts. The aim of this description is to characterize the world as we encounter it prior to the kinds of reflection and theorizing common to the theoretical attitude. By starting from Dasein as it is in concrete, particular contexts of activity, Heidegger hopes to arrive at a characterization of the Being of everyday life-worlds in general. Or, to put the same point in Heidegger's technical vocabulary, by starting out at the "ontic" and "existentiell" level (descriptions of actual life-situations) we are to arrive at "ontological" insights about entities generally and "existential" truths about humans as such. What comes out of this description is a picture of Dasein as *being-in-the-world*. The aim of this description, as we shall see, is to deflate both the subjectified view of the self as a mind, where this is understood as a sort of container in which mental activities occur, and the objectified view of worldly entities as brute, present-at-hand objects.

Heidegger's description of the world of everydayness is one of his most original contributions to philosophy.[6] As we have seen, Heidegger holds that we have a tendency to overlook or lose sight of the background that makes it possible for us to encounter entities in any specific way. In the detached stance of the theoretical attitude, entities seem to be just *there*; they show up as objects with properties that exist independent of us and our practices. Heidegger thinks that, to some extent at least, this forgetfulness or concealment is inevitable. Just as we can see what is illuminated by the light in a room only if the light itself remains unnoticed, so we can succeed in handling the entities that appear in the world only if the world itself remains unnoticed. But he believes that this background is always accessible to us, even though it tends to be overlooked for the most part. In this respect Heidegger seems quite close to Wittgenstein, who says, "The aspects of things that are most important for us are hidden because of their simplicity and familiarity. (One is unable to notice something—because it is always before one's eyes.)"[7]

In his description of our practical activities, Heidegger is trying to call our attention to features of the world that are so familiar and all-pervasive that they are hardly ever noticed. His basic claim is that "proximally and for the most part," that is, in most of our everyday affairs, we encounter the world around us as a context of *equipment* in which entities have the character of what he calls "readiness-to-hand." The everyday life world presents itself initially (but in a way that is generally unnoticed) as a holistic "context of significance" that is not reducible to mere present-at-hand things.

The plausibility of Heidegger's novel view depends on our getting a feel for his detailed descriptions of our everyday practical involvements. These descriptions try to catch a glimpse of the way things show up for us in our activities before we step back and start to explicitly scrutinize them—for example, when we are riding a bicycle or cooking a meal and everything is running smoothly. His own example is the sense of things a skilled craftsman has in the process of building something in a workshop.

Think of what it is like when you are working away at some activity you are quite familiar with. If you are building a bookcase and everything is going well, you usually do not have any explicit awareness of the hammer,

6. This has been especially true thanks to the writings of Hubert L. Dreyfus. See his *What Computers Still Can't Do* (Cambridge, Mass.: MIT Press, 1992) for his use of Heidegger in criticizing artificial intelligence and cognitive science programs. For Dreyfus's own detailed account of Heidegger's notions of worldhood, see his *Being-in-the-World: A Commentary on Heidegger's "Being and Time," Division I* (Cambridge, Mass.: MIT Press, 1991).

7. Ludwig Wittgenstein, *Philosophical Investigations*, trans. G.E.M. Anscombe (New York: Macmillan, 1958), §129.

nails, and boards you are dealing with. What shows up in such contexts is not a "hammer-thing" with properties, Heidegger says, but rather the smooth flow of *hammering* through which the shelves and frame of the bookcase begin to take shape. In fact, for the most part in our pre-reflective, skilled activities, the entire workshop is encountered as a totality of functional relations organized around our purposes. The hammer shows up *in* hammering, which is *in order to* fasten these boards together, which is *for* building a bookcase. All these relationships of "in doing which," "in order to," and "for which" are oriented around our own projects as agents in this context. The hammering and construction is *for the sake of* your being, say, a home craftsman or a tidy person. In this way, what you are doing with your life determines how equipment can present itself as *relevant* in this setting.

Our way of being in ordinary situations, according to Heidegger, is "concernful absorption." In such cases, we "lose ourselves" in the world of our current concerns, handling equipment "without noticing it explicitly" (§16). The equipment shows up in its familiar forms of "serviceability, conduciveness, usability, manipulability" thanks to the web of relations of "significance" opened by our purposes (§15). What is "given" in such ordinary situations, then, is a holistic web of means-ends relationships pointing toward the work to be accomplished. Heidegger says that "taken strictly, there 'is' no such thing as *an* equipment. To the Being of any equipment there always belongs a totality of equipment, in which it can *be* this equipment that it is" (§15). The web of functional relations defining this workshop—hammering in the nails, nailing the boards together, fitting together the completed sections, being a craftsman—is what makes it possible for anything to show up here at all. The way that things show up as "significant" or "relevant" determines the *Being* of those entities. And our *own* Being when we are engrossed in such activities is defined by our ways of being "out there" with the project, caught up in the flow of things. For the most part, we have no sense of ourselves as being minds distinct from objects. If there is any "mental" activity in such cases, it is what psychologists sometimes call "flow consciousness," where no distinction appears between what is "in here" in the mind and what is "out there" in the world.

When equipment is genuinely ready-to-hand in this way, things are normally unobtrusive and unnoticed. Heidegger says that the ready-to-hand must "withdraw" into its usability "in order to *be* ready-to-hand quite authentically" (§15). According to this story, we can begin to explicitly attend to items in the work context only when there is a *breakdown* in the smooth flow of our competent dealings with things—when the hammer head breaks off, for example, or when a nail bends. It is only when something goes wrong in this way that we begin to pay attention to what is in front of us. And it is this explicit attentiveness that first gives rise to the idea, so central to traditional philosophy, that what has been there "all along" has been mere present-at-hand things existing independent of us, invested by us with a use-value. In the breakdown, Heidegger says, "the ready-to-hand becomes deprived of its worldhood [the background of significance relations organized around our projects] so that just being-present-at-hand comes to the fore" (§16). And because the present-at-hand obtrudes and captures our explicit attention, we begin to think that what is most "basic" in the world is mere present-at-hand objects.

But it is important to see that the contextless objects taken as basic by the tradition can come to the fore only as a result of the breakdown of smoothly flowing contexts of activity, what Heidegger calls the "disworlding of the world." The notion that there are " 'at first' only things present-at-hand . . . in a space in general" is an "illusion," Heidegger says, because it conceals the more fundamental way of Being of entities as they show up in the practical life-world.[8] In other words, when we focus on the objects that have been stripped from the contexts of significance in which they first appear, we lose sight of the background of significance that makes it possible for anything to stand out as mattering or counting in some way in the first place, and this creates the "illusion" that all along there have really only been present-at-hand things.

Heidegger's claim is that entities encountered as ready-to-hand are more "primordial" than (or are ontologically prior to) what philosophers have traditionally focused on in their theories, the present-at-hand objects taken as most basic by the tradition. To say that the ready-to-hand is *more primordial* than the present-at-hand is to make two claims: (1) that our ability to encounter present-at-hand things is derivative from and parasitic on our prior ways of dealing with contexts of what is ready-to-hand, and (2) that there is no way to account for the ready-to-hand solely in terms of characteristics of what is present-at-hand. If this primordiality claim is right, then it follows that the view of reality we get from modern natural science—the assumption that the world at the most basic level consists of inherently meaningless objects that we humans come to endow with significance and value—does not reveal the most basic way of Being of entities. On the contrary, Heidegger wants to show that the world at the most basic level is initially and most fundamentally a meaning-filled context in which we carry out our practical lives. From this standpoint, the belief that what "really" exists is a vast aggregate of present-at-hand objects in causal interactions is an idea that arises only when we adopt the rather specialized stance of detached theoretical reflection.

8. Martin Heidegger, *Being and Time*, trans. John Macquarrie and Edward Robinson (New York: Harper & Row, 1962), 421.

Heidegger's description of contexts of equipment also aims to show that there is a reciprocal interdependence between the world of everyday activities and our own identity as agents doing things in those contexts. First, it is our own self-understanding as agents dealing with things in the world that determines the Being of the ready-to-hand we encounter around us in our projects. In other words, it is the concrete stands we take on our lives in our everyday activities that determine the *relevance* or *significance* things can have for us in relation to our projects. My understanding of myself as a college teacher, for example, carries with it a mastery of the practices of academic life in general, and in terms of that grasp of university life I encounter the blackboard and lectern in a classroom as having a specific role to play in relation to my teaching. When I enter a classroom, I orient myself behind the lectern and in front of the blackboard, while the students, given their mastery of their own roles in this context, seat themselves facing the front of the room. All of this typically occurs without much conscious reflection on our part. Yet in the process of our dealings with the classroom, the entities in this setting come to be articulated in a specific way. As Heidegger says, the particular involvement something has in relation to our undertakings "is *ontologically* definitive for the Being of such an entity" (§18). For the custodian cleaning the classroom at the end of the day, the Being of the lectern and blackboard will be construed very differently.

Our skillful comportment in the world Heidegger calls "understanding." His point here is that our own self-understanding in familiar roles (for example, my understanding of myself as a teacher) carries with it a set of skills in dealing with practical contexts (my competence in dealing with department offices and classrooms) that determine how ordinary settings can show up in relation to my projects (encountering a classroom as a site for lecturing). As we shall see, the understanding that articulates life-worlds is something that is *shared*. As we become participants in the public world, we come to master the ordinary practices in our culture, and these skills give us a handle on how to deal with the contexts of equipment we find around us. The general sense of things embodied in our skilled mastery, as we saw above, is called "pre-ontological understanding." Heidegger notes that the German word for *understanding* means "'being able to manage something', 'being a match for it', 'being competent to do something'" (§31). It is a tacit know-how embodied in our activities (comparable to the skilled auto mechanic's grasp of a carburetor in doing a tune up). This background mastery of specific forms of life and everyday settings provides the basis on which we are able to go to work addressing the tasks before us.

According to Heidegger's description of the world, our self-understanding as agents comes to be realized and made concrete in specific ways of handling things. Such ordinary ways of dealing with things as "preparing, putting to rights, repairing, improving, [and] rounding out" are called "interpretation" (the German word for interpretation, *Auslegung*, means literally "laying out"). Heidegger says that in interpretation we "take apart" what is grasped in understanding—the entire context of practical activity—and we *appropriate* it in some way through our ways of acting there. Interpretation is what lets entities present themselves *as* the sorts of things they are: the eraser shows up in erasing the blackboard, the lectern presents itself as holding notes, and so on. In Heidegger's way of putting it, this "*as*-structure of interpretation" lets the ready-to-hand stand out as counting or mattering in determinate ways, and these ways of mattering define the Being of what is ready-to-hand.

This account of the Being of equipment shows how our understanding defines the Being of what is ready-to-hand in the world. But Heidegger also points out that the equipmental contexts of the world define our *own Being* as agents handling things. My activity of speaking in a classroom can count as an academic lecture only because of its place within the overall world of academia with its classrooms, offices, libraries, and campus life in general. If I were suddenly lifted out of the classroom and somehow transported to the pitcher's mound at Yankee Stadium, my activity would no longer count as an academic lecture. What this shows is that the "worldhood" of the world provides the medium in which I can realize my identity *as* a person of a particular type. On campus I can *be* a college teacher or a student or a custodian, but not (or not normally) a ship's captain giving orders to the crew.

We now can see more clearly why Heidegger says that being-in-the-world is a "unified phenomenon." On the one hand, our own Being as agents of specific sorts lets entities of various types show up as the entities they are. On the other hand, the contexts of worldhood in which we find ourselves first let *us* show up as agents of specific types. In Heidegger's words, "Self and world belong together in the single entity, Dasein. Self and world are not two beings, like subject and object, . . . [rather] self and world are the basic determination of Dasein in the unity of the structure of being-in-the-world."[9]

With this description of the worldhood of the world, Heidegger hoped to resolve the traditional epistemological debate between realism and idealism. Realists are people who hold that there is a real world outside of and independent of our minds, and that we can come to know what this world is like. Idealists, as Heidegger uses this term, are people who believe that because we are always trapped within the veil of our own ideas, we can never know

9. This is the way Heidegger put it in his 1927 lectures, *The Basic Problems of Phenomenology*, trans. Albert Hofstadter (Bloomington: Indiana University Press, 1982), 297.

for sure whether there is in fact a real world existing independent of our minds, let alone what it is like.

Heidegger's way of dealing with the debate between realists and idealists is to show that it gets off the ground only if at the outset we presuppose a particular picture of our human predicament. According to this picture, we are essentially subjects forming mental representations (sensations, images, ideas) in our minds, and our task is to correctly represent objects in the world outside our minds. Given this picture of our initial situation, the question naturally arises, Do we ever really gain access to objects as they are in themselves "out there" in the world, or are we forever trapped within our own minds, cut off from any access to an external world?

Heidegger's account of being-in-the-world is supposed to undercut the picture of our human situation that gets this debate going in the first place. If our own being as agents is always such that we are already "out there" in the midst of the practical life-world, and if the world at the deepest level consists not of contextless present-at-hand objects but rather of ready-to-hand equipment bound up with what we are doing, then the idea that we are essentially cut off from the world by a veil of representations comes to appear as an illusion. The description of the world was supposed to show that the idea that we are at the most basic level minds or subjects set over against a world of objects can arise only as the result of a breakdown in our ordinary ways of being as agents. But if this is the case, then it is a mistake to assume that we are essentially minds only indirectly in touch with a world of objects. Thus, given this account of our situation, the subject-object model of traditional epistemology turns out to be derivative from a more "primordial" way of being as practical agents. And if this is the case, then the "problem of knowing the external world" turns out to be a pseudo-problem with no relevance for understanding our actual predicament in the world.

To help us get away from the traditional view of ourselves as minds essentially distinct from a world of material objects, Heidegger proposes that we think of Dasein not as a thing, but as a "clearing" or "lighting," in which both practical contexts and roles show up in determinate ways. Understood as a clearing, Heidegger says, "Dasein *is* its world existingly."[10] As there is no gap between ourselves and ready-to-hand entities on this view, it is possible to be a hard-headed "realist" about the practical life-world: we cannot make sense of the idea of the ready-to-hand not existing, because its existence is a condition for the possibility of our own existence as agents. At the same time, however, Heidegger's view lets us dispense with the traditional assumption that there is an "external world" of present-at-hand objects existing independent of us and our practices. What shows up for us as present-

10. Heidegger, *Being and Time*, 416.

at-hand, on this view, is the result of a specialized way of working over entities for particular purposes.

On Heidegger's view of our basic situation, science comes to be seen as derived from and parasitic on the background of everyday being-in-the-world. Heidegger develops what he calls an "existential conception of science" according to which science is a useful tool for redescribing the world for particular purposes, but does not necessarily give us any privileged information about "the way the world really is." Science emerges when communities of scientists create a "clearing" in terms of which entities can show up in particular ways, particular sorts of questions make sense, and procedures of confirmation count as appropriate. In terms of such clearings, certain claims about the world will count as true. But the truth of such claims should be understood as relative to the clearing that makes them possible. This is what Heidegger means when he says, "Before Newton's laws were discovered, they were not 'true'."[11] The point here is not that Newton created the regularities described by classical mechanics, but instead that the clearing of a world in which regularities can show up in certain ways was made possible by the cultural transformations brought to a head by Newton and others. Of course, given our world with its contemporary system of mathematical projection and "objective" procedures of confirmation, we can now retroactively regard the universe as having always obeyed Newton's laws. But, in Heidegger's view, the "truth" revealed by modern science is possible only against the background of the more primordial truth understood as the "clearing" opened by our shared, practical life-world.

3. The Structure of Human Agency

Although the aim of *Being and Time* is to clarify the Being of entities in general (rocks, chairs, stars, numbers, minds, and so on), only about one-third of the planned work was ever published, and that part deals primarily with the Being of humans, or Dasein. In trying to grasp human existence, Heidegger says, we must avoid falling into the rather specialized interpretations of things found in such "regional" sciences as biology, psychology, and epistemology. These theories tend to uncritically presuppose an objectified view of humans as substances or objects of a particular sort. It is precisely assumptions of this sort that are called into question by fundamental ontology.

In order to avoid slipping into traditional presuppositions about what humans are, Heidegger focuses on our being as *agents* doing things rather than on our ways of being when we are subjects engaged in self-reflection. To

11. Ibid., 269.

simplify Heidegger's complex account of human existence, we might present his view as a series of interrelated claims. The first claim is that humans are beings who *care* about what they are. What is characteristic of us is that we care about what our lives are amounting to, and because of that we care about our surroundings and what happens to us there. Heidegger formulates this by saying that Dasein is the entity whose being is *at stake* or *in question* for it. I care about whether my life makes sense, whether it adds up to something worthwhile, or whether it is really my own. And it is because my own life in the world is of concern to me that things in general *mean* something to me in the sense that they *count* or *matter* to me in some way in relation to my undertakings.

Second, because humans care about who and what they are, they have always taken some *stand* on their lives. In living out our lives, we have all seized on some set of roles, personality traits, lifestyles, and status relations in realizing our lives in the world. Each of us has taken some stand on his or her own existence, and it is through taking such a stand that we come to have an *understanding* of Being in Heidegger's special sense of this term. In the example we used before, my understanding of the ways of the academic world results from my having taken a stand on my own life by becoming a college teacher. For Heidegger, Dasein is the entity that understands what it is to be, and it has this understanding by virtue of its ways of being engaged in the stands it takes in the world.

The third claim is that humans just *are* the stands they take in living out their lives. Humans *are* what they *do*. This point follows from the awareness that there is no fixed human essence given to us in advance—no "Form of Humanity" or "proper function of humans" that determines what we are and ought to be. Instead, humans just are what they make of themselves in growing up within the context of a particular historical culture. We are "self-interpreting" or "self-constituting" beings in the sense that our Being (or identity) is something we *make* in the course of living out our active lives. In Heidegger's view, even our existence as "selves," far from being something directly given in the flow of everyday life, is simply one way of being among others. As he says, "the self is . . . 'only' a *way* of being" of Dasein.[12]

The fourth claim follows directly from this non-essentialist picture of humans. If we *are* what we make of ourselves in our lives, then what is definitive of our "Being" is not the continuing presence of a substance of some sort, whether that substance be thought of as mind or as physical substance. Instead, the self is an *event*—Heidegger calls it a "becoming" or a "happening"—that is defined by what one *does* throughout one's live. In other

12. Ibid., 153.

words, I *am* what I emerge-into-presence as being throughout the course of my life, "from birth to death." I am what I become in living out my life story as a whole.

The picture of a human's Being as determined by the totality of what she does throughout her life implies that the *self* is something that is discovered not through self-reflection or introspection, but rather through what she *does* as being-in-the-world. As Heidegger puts it, Dasein's worldly kind of being "goes so far that even one's *own* Dasein becomes something that it can itself proximally 'come across' only when it *looks away* from 'experiences' and the 'center of its actions', or does not as yet 'see' them at all. Dasein finds itself' proximally in *what* it does"(§26).

This conception of the being of the self as defined by concrete agency in the world leads to a way of understanding action that is quite different from traditional conceptions of human agency. We can see this by contrasting Heidegger's view of action with that of the standard view accepted by most philosophers today. On the standard view, action must be understood as physical movement that is caused by an inner impetus—by intentions or desires located in the agent's mind. Such a view assumes that the physical movement itself is secondary and derivative, not much different from the movement of a billiard ball around a pool table. If we want to understand the movement as *action*, then, we have to read backward from the outer physical movement to the inner mental cause that animates it—the agent's intentions or motives. The standard view therefore relies on a strong distinction between the mental and the physical, the inner and the outer.

In contrast to such standard conceptions of action, Heidegger puts forward what we might call an "expressivist" view of agency, a view in which the distinctions between mind and matter, inner and outer, generally have no real role to play.[13] On an expressivist view, what I actually do in the world is not regarded as something secondary or derivative, something that is to be understood only by tracing it back to mental events. Instead, what I do is seen as *defining* and *bringing to realization* the person I am. As Heidegger puts it, "being-a-self *is* . . . only in its process of realization."[14] It is what we *do* that shapes our Being as selves with motives and intentions, not the converse.

---

13. This use of the term "expressivist" should not be confused with the Romantic idea of expressing one's inner essential nature. For Heidegger, as we have seen, there is no inner essence we need to express (though, as we shall see, facts about the temporal *structure* of human existence have implications for what can count as an authentic life).

14. Heidegger, *Metaphysical Foundations of Logic*, 139.

We might try to clarify Heidegger's view of agency by thinking about how we normally encounter and understand a person's actions. When a friend touches me lightly on the arm in the course of an ordinary conversation, I encounter her gesture as typical of her being the warm and considerate person she is. The action is understood in terms of her personality traits of warmth and thoughtfulness. These traits themselves, however, are not usually thought of as "hidden," inner mental states *distinct from* the things this person does. On the contrary, her being the warm person she is, for the most part, is nothing other than this and the countless other things she does in relating to people on a day-to-day basis. What defines the Being of this person, then, just is her familiar ways of acting throughout her lifetime. For her, everything is out front—what you see is what you get. In Heidegger's language, we could say that her being as a warm and kind person is something that "comes-into-presence" or "emerges-into-being" in all that she does. The behavior is not just an external sign of something inner that is going on beneath the surface. Instead, her ways of being manifest in the world *define* her as a person of a particular sort. They *are* her Being, just as my consistently being on time for appointments *is* my being a punctual person.

It should be obvious that Heidegger is presenting a view that is radically opposed to some of the deepest assumptions of the modern outlook. We saw that modern thought tends to assume that recourse to the mental is always necessary if we are to understand human phenomena. Even when philosophers give up the idea of the mind as a spiritual substance and try to be hard-headed physicalists, they still tend to assume that recourse to the mental is necessary to explain how physical movements can count as action. In this sense, the assumption that the mental is crucial to explaining human phenomena is, in Wittgenstein's words, "like a pair of glasses on our nose through which we see whatever we look at. It never occurs to us to take them off."[15]

On Heidegger's view of action, in contrast, this requirement no longer seems so pressing. He holds that, seen from a purely phenomenological standpoint, there is simply no basis for assuming that there is anything in particular going on in our friend's mind when she does the nice things she does. Innumerable things—or nothing—might be "going through her mind" as she lightly touches my shoulder. Of course, if asked, one could always retroactively cook up some story about what must have been going on in her mind when she did the nice things she does. But the fact that we *can* concoct such after-the-fact stories does not prove that we are thereby dis-

---

15. Wittgenstein, *Philosophical Investigations*, §103.

covering truths about what actually occurred. As a rule, questions about "what is really going on in her mind" can arise and make sense only when there are breaks in the otherwise smooth flow of her behavior. Indeed, it seems that under normal conditions, questions about what is going on in someone's mind can arise only against a background of forms of life in which people for the most part just are what they do in the course of their familiar activities.

Heidegger's claim, then, is that the demand that we find a mental component behind every human action is a requirement based solely on the uncritical objectifying ontology of modernity. In saying this, he does not want to deny that mental events occur or that they are sometimes very important. Indeed, he even suggests that working out a "formal phenomenology of consciousness" might be a worthy sort of specialized inquiry (§25). But he does want to claim that our being as subjects with minds or fields of consciousness is only one specialized way of being for humans among others, and that it is derivative from and parasitic on a more primordial way of being as being-in-the-world. On the view Heidegger holds, what is mental gains its determinate character and significance from its place within the clearing opened by our everyday activities.

The fifth claim is that, understood as a life-happening, human existence has a distinctive temporal structure. There are two main temporal structures (or "existentialia") definitive of Dasein's existence as an unfolding life-course. The first of these existential structures is called "throwness." Dasein always finds itself "thrown" into a particular cultural setting, with certain choices it has already made and obligations it has undertaken. For example, it is part of what Heidegger calls my "facticity" that, as a parent, I find myself "stuck" with certain obligations given my past choices and my society's expectations. This throwness into specific situations and entanglements is encountered as a *task* that I must take up in some way or other. We are, Heidegger says, "delivered over to ourselves" as something we must be. Our facticity is revealed to us in particular moods that tune us in to the world in specific ways (the German word for mood also means "being in tune"). These moods color the ways the world shows up, and they determine how entities will show up as "mattering" for us. For example, the laid-back attitude of the 1960s presented situations and roles in a way quite different from the feverish acquisitiveness of the 1980s.

Throwness defines Dasein's Being as "already in" a world, and it makes up the temporal dimension of pastness or what Heidegger calls "having been." The second temporal structure of Dasein's temporal Being determines the element of "futurity," that is, the future-directedness of Dasein's life story. As agents, we are always already "ahead of ourselves" to the extent that each of us has taken a stand on our throwness and, through our actions, we are accomplishing something with our lives. To say that as an agent my Being is characterized by future-directedness is to say that each of my actions points toward a realization, and that in everything I do, I am moving toward a final realization of my identity. If as a parent I tend to be lax or negligent, it is part of my *Being* that I am a parent of that sort. If I don't change my ways, it will be correct to say of me "in the end" that I *am* an uncaring parent. Our directedness toward the future Heidegger calls "projection," and his claim is that it is my being as a "thrown projection" that constitutes my identity as an agent. Only because Dasein exists as "ahead-of-itself-as-already-in-a-world" can it be involved with things in the present.

Heidegger emphasizes that in this temporal structure of a human life-happening, the most basic dimension is the future. Because our Being—our identity as a totality—is something that remains outstanding and still impending so long as our lives are still under way, it seems right to say that we can only *be* something once our lives are completed. But because a person's Being *ends* when his or her life is completed, Heidegger does not want to say that we *are* something only when we are dead. Instead, he claims that what is definitive of our lives is best thought of as "being-*toward*-the-end" or "being-*toward*-death." Just as the events in a story gain their meaning from the contribution they make to the outcome of the story as a whole, its completion, so the events in one's life gain their meaning from their relation to the overarching projects that define one's life story as a totality, right up to the end. And that means that my actions in the present have to be understood in terms of what they *undertake* for the future, that is, in terms of the commitments I make (often without any awareness of it) as to what kind of person I am being "in the long run."

Our futurity as agents in the world lets our pasts become meaningful as resources for our current activities, and it also lets entities in the world stand out as significant in relation to our projects. Heidegger captures this idea by saying that our projection towards the future opens a leeway (*Spielraum*) or clearing, a field of intelligibility in which things can stand forth as counting for us in some determinate way or other. Through my project of being a parent, such things as schools and day-care centers stand out as relevant for me, whereas singles bars recede into the background. And it is because of the stands I take—my "understanding," in Heidegger's special sense of this word—that the familiar world shows up for me as significant in familiar ways. As I take over the task of preparing breakfast for my children, for example, the spatula presents itself as ready-to-hand in flipping eggs, which is *for* preparing breakfast, which is *for* raising healthy children. As a result, the world presents itself to me as an ordered totality of proximal and long-range goals, already laden with significance in relation to my practices and undertaking. In fact, it takes an effort to try to *disinvest* things of their ordinary meanings in order to see them as brute, decontextualized present-at-hand things with no place in the meaningful contexts in which I normally find myself. (Try looking at a spatula as if you were an alien from another planet who had no idea of its possible functions.)

The sixth claim about human existence is that the temporal unfolding of a life is always embedded in a wider communal context from which it draws its possibilities of self-interpretation and self-assessment. Just as the story of a character in a novel makes sense only in its interchange with the ongoing stories of the other characters, so my own life story makes sense only within the wider context of my family, community, and culture. For the most part, we are *participants* within a shared context that provides us with our sense of meaningful options in dealing with things. Thus, my understanding of who I am as a parent is made possible by the guidelines of norms and conventions laid out in the public world. Moreover, in my social context, I am a parent in relation to children, other parents, teachers, guidance counselors, and day-care providers, and it is in constant interchange with these co-participants in the world of child-rearing that I compose and revise my own life story in this role.

On Heidegger's view, then, it is by becoming initiated into the contexts of shared practices circulating in our public world that we pick up both our sense of how things count for our community and our grasp of what is at stake in living in the world. We can see how this is so by considering the way that people who grow up in America generally tend to be much more un-comfortable with nudity than some people in other parts of the world. Ob-viously, Americans attach a special significance to their bodies, a significance not shared by people elsewhere. Yet they are generally quite unaware that this is a cultural trait, and so they are initially shocked or amused when they encounter cultures that do not share their sense of modesty.

Or consider our immediate, pre-reflective response to cases of cruelty to animals or to small children. This is so deeply ingrained in us that it seems to be "natural," and we are appalled when we learn that other cultures do not always share our sensibilities. We feel that they have hardened their hearts or have lost some distinctively human capacity for compassion. Nev-ertheless, what to us feels like "nature" is in fact primarily "second nature," a product of our attunement into the practices and responses of a particular type of culture rather than a universally inevitable instinctual reaction.

These examples show how our shared sense of reality is something that is largely shaped by our enculturation into a public world. Heidegger does not see this tendency to fall into step with the crowd as something that is en-tirely negative. On the contrary, his claim is that our attunement to the so-cial practices of a culture is an enabling condition that first gives us an understanding of the world. Being the "they," therefore, is a *"primordial phe-nomenon that belongs to Dasein's positive constitution"* (§27). It is only because we are in sync with the regularized patterns of acting and reacting of a con-crete social world that we can come to be humans with a clearly defined identity and "fix" on things. I can be a parent in my community, for exam-ple, only because I am tuned in to the standardized ways of handling situa-tions involving children established by my society.

Because the meaningful life-world is shaped by the practices of the pub-lic, Heidegger says that the "they" itself "articulates the referential context of significance" of the world (§27). In other words, it is the practices of the social world in general that define how things can count and what sorts of self-interpreting activities will make sense for a people. As Heidegger puts it, "Dasein is originally being with others. . . . The different modes of fac-tical being-with-one-another constitute in each case . . . [the] disclosure of the world and . . . the unanimity of world-understanding."[16] And this means that the *content* we take over for our lives (our roles, careers, lifestyle enclaves, personality traits, and so on) are all taken over from the pool of possibilities circulating in the public. Without such conventions and pat-terns of acting, we would be not so much "free spirits" or "noble savages" as bundles of utterly diffuse raw capacities lacking any focus or content whatsoever.

4. Authenticity

One of the most influential ideas in *Being and Time* for existentialist thought has been the notion of authenticity spelled out in the second half of that work. If we want to understand Heidegger's notion of authenticity, we should be careful not to confuse it with popular notions of "getting in touch with your feelings" or "being true to your inner self." These notions suggest that being authentic is a matter of pulling back from the social world in order to concentrate on oneself as an individual. As we shall see, however, Heidegger's ideal of authenticity is a matter not so much of being in touch with oneself as of becoming more intensely engaged in the world of one's historical culture.

We can begin to get a sense of what authenticity is by recalling the de-scription of Dasein as a "thrown projection." According to this description, there are two equally basic structures determining our temporal being. The first of these, as we have seen, is thrownness. Dasein is always situated within a shared cultural context that defines its possibilities for self-understanding and action. For the most part, Dasein is engaged in everyday

16. Heidegger, *Basic Problems of Phenomenology*, 297.

practical occupations, and it undertakes these in accordance with the guidelines laid out by the "they." Heidegger describes our social embedded-ness in this way:

> As something factical, Dasein's projection of itself understandingly is in each case already at home in a world that has been discovered. From this world it takes its possibilities, and it does so first in accordance with the way things have been inter-preted by the they. This interpretation has already restricted the possible options of choice to what lies within the range of the familiar, the attainable, the respect-able—that which is fitting and proper.[17]

In other words, all our concrete possibilities of understanding and inter-pretation are drawn from the pool of interpretations opened by the public world in which we find ourselves. Seen in this way, our being as social agents is not some harsh imposition cast over a pregiven core of unique personal traits. On the contrary, it is only by taking over the concrete roles and possi-bilities circulating in our communal life-world that we can even *become* hu-man in the sense of being agents capable of making meaningful choices and understanding what is at stake in life. Only in terms of this backdrop of so-cial practices can we come to create the permutations of our culture's ways of being that make it possible for us to become distinctive, "unique" indi-viduals.

But Heidegger also suggests that this absorption in a social world can have a pernicious effect. In our everyday lives, there is a tendency to go with the flow, enacting socially approved roles and getting lost in the mundane chores and rituals approved of by the they. The result, Heidegger says, is a "dim-ming down of the possible as such," a leveling down of all possibilities to "what one does" in ordinary situations.[18] We tend to get lost in the latest fads and fancies, and we drift along with the crowd in the busy-ness of day-to-day existence. Life then becomes a mere sequence of episodes in which we try to take care of each new thing that comes along. As we struggle to handle the business of practical life, our existence becomes a series of means-ends strategies with no overarching unity or cohesiveness. We be-come so engrossed in what is in front of us at the moment that we are blind to the larger background that makes our actions possible.

Heidegger calls this kind of absorption in current concerns "making pres-ent," and he sees it as leading to the "forgetfulness"of everyday life. In his view, a certain kind of forgetfulness is unavoidable if we are to throw our-selves into what we do: "The self must forget itself," he says, "if, lost in the

17. Heidegger, *Being and Time*, 239.
18. Ibid.

world of equipment, it is to be able 'actually' to go to work and manipulate something."[19] What is insidious, however, is the way this first-order forgetting is compounded by a second-order forgetting in which one "not only forgets the forgotten but forgets the forgetting itself."[20] In other words, in our day-to-day activities we fail to see that our ordinary practical lives are possible only because we are blind to the background conditions that make our agency possible. Lacking any wider sense of what life is all about, we come to accept the current, socially accepted outlook as the ultimate truth about reality. And as the prevalent outlook comes to be taken as self-evidently true, we feel assured we are doing well so long as we play by the socially prescribed rules. The result is that we no longer see our own existence as *in question* or *at issue* for us. We end up being adrift on the seas of what is called "proper" by the they, and we assume that our lives make sense and are justified so long as we do what "one does." As a result of this forgetfulness, however, we not only lose track of our sense of what life is all about, we lose the ability to take a coherent, focused stand on our lives as a whole.

This absorption in the everyday social world is called "falling." Heidegger claims that such falling is not just an occasional slip or bit of carelessness. On the contrary, insofar as our involvements in the world make us the people we are, falling is an "existential" structure definitive of our Being. But falling is pernicious insofar as it aggravates our tendency toward forgetfulness. What we forget in falling is the second existential structure of our temporal being: our existence as an ongoing, future-directed "happening." In other words, our dispersal in everyday preoccupations makes us forget that our lives as "being-toward-the-end" are finite. We lose sight of the fact that our life stories will be completed at some point, and that each of our current actions is contributing to realizing our Being in its entirety.

What can shake us out of this complacent drifting through life is the mood of anxiety (*Angst*).[21] Heidegger calls anxiety a "ground mood" because it brings us face to face with a fundamental fact about the human situation, a fact we find so distressing we usually try our best to avoid confronting it. In anxiety, Heidegger says, the familiar world of equipment in which we find ourselves at home suddenly collapses into insignificance. The idea here seems to be that anxiety makes us see that the roles we play in everydayness are anonymous, "anyone" roles. In filling such roles, one's Being

19. Ibid., 405.

20. Heidegger, *Basic Problems of Phenomenology*, 290.

21. A complete account of Heidegger's concept of authenticity would include a discussion of his analyses of the phenomena of "conscience" and "guilt." For the purposes of this introduction, however, an examination of the concept of anxiety should be sufficient to sketch out the basis of authenticity.

is generally "replaceable" or "dispensable." In my everyday identity as a teacher, say, or as a left-fielder on the softball team, others can fill in for me if I am incapacitated in some way. But that means that our everyday social existence is not by itself sufficient to assure us that our lives are "our own" in a deep sense. *As* playing our normal public roles, we are not really *ourselves*.

When we see that our social roles are really anonymous, "anyone-roles," however, we also confront the fact that we alone are responsible for making something of our own lives. In anxiety, I encounter my own existence as a temporal unfolding or happening that it is up to me alone to define and make my own. Heidegger says that anxiety discloses our "ability to be" as "individualized, pure, and thrown" (§40). Anxiety is characterized by "uncanniness" to the extent that we are no longer "at home" in the familiar world (the German word for "uncanny," *unheimlich*, means literally "homeless"). As the world loses its familiarity and at-home-ness, we confront our own "naked Dasein" as something we have to take over as being-in-the-world.[22]

Anxiety reveals to us our "thrownness unto death." As Heidegger puts it, in anxiety, "Dasein finds itself *face to face* with the 'nothing' of the possible impossibility of its existence."[23] Anxiety can make us realize that our normal tendency to throw ourselves into publicly approved roles is actually a form of *fleeing* or *evasion*. The forgetfulness characteristic of everydayness turns out to be a motivated cover-up designed to conceal from us something we find threatening. What we are running away from in everydayness is the fact that we are finite beings whose lives will be completed. What this means will become clearer if we recall that death in Heidegger's sense refers not just to physical demise, but to the culmination or realization of a life story. Just as a story gains its meaning from where it is heading as a whole—its outcome or realization—so our own lives gain their meaning from where they are headed as a totality—their "being-*toward*-the-end." And just as each of the events in a story contributes to the overall meaning of that story—how things finally turn out—so, for our lives, each of our actions is contributing to the final configuration of meaning our lives will have "in the end."

In anxiety, we are brought to see that every one of our actions is contributing to realizing a content for our lives as a whole, and that our Being as representatives of the they cannot by itself give our lives the kind of integrity that would make them truly our own. Heidegger thinks that recognizing our finitude can bring about a transformation in our way of living. When we face up to our "being-toward-death," we are forced to confront the fact that

22. Heidegger, *Being and Time*, 394.
23. Ibid., 310.

it is up to us to make something of our lives as a whole. This recognition of our own responsibility for our lives can counteract the tendency toward forgetfulness and dispersal running through everydayness. Instead of merely drifting into public roles and losing ourselves in whatever tasks come along, we can begin to take over our own lives and make them our own in all that we do. We can become authentic in the sense of *owning up* to our lives. (Because the German word for authenticity, *Eigentlichkeit*, comes from the stem *eigen* meaning "own," it could be read as "owned-ness.")

To become authentic, we must first accept the fact that we are ultimately *responsible* for what our lives are adding up to. If you face up to your finitude and take responsibility for your own existence, Heidegger thinks, you will achieve a level of clear-sightedness and intensity that was lacking in inauthentic everydayness. If you grasp the fact that everything you do is contributing to defining your life in its entirety, you can be led to acknowledge the fact that you are responsible for taking hold of your existence and giving it a coherent shape of your own making.

This confrontation with finitude might not change the actual *content* of your life. In becoming authentic, Heidegger says, "the 'world' which is ready-to-hand does not become another one 'in its content,' nor does the circle of others get exchanged for a new one" (§60). There is no reason to think that you would necessarily have to change your career or lifestyle if you became authentic. But even though authenticity does not entail any change in *what* you do, it seems that it could transform the *way* you live. To be authentic is to seize on some set of roles you have drawn from the public world and to make them into your own through a resolute and clear-sighted stand on them.

In this respect, authenticity seems to involve a capacity for "self-focusing" that is lacking in everyday falling. "Once one has grasped the finitude of one's existence," Heidegger says, "one is snatched back from the endless multiplicity of possibilities which offer themselves as closest to one—those of comfortableness, shirking, and taking things lightly."[24] Facing up to one's own death, one becomes "free for [one's] ownmost possibilities, which are determined by the *end* and so are understood as finite" (§53). This suggests that in becoming authentic, one appropriates the possibilities one has taken over from the public, and organizes them into a coherent, unified project definitive of one's existence as a whole. Once anxiety makes us realize that we are "delivered over to ourselves" and that it is up to us alone to make something of our lives, we will "simplify" our lives, shaping the roles we have adopted into a form that gives them direction and focus.[25]

24. Ibid., 435.
25. Ibid.

Heidegger calls this more focused stance toward one's own life "resoluteness," and he says that such resoluteness involves "choosing to choose." As agents dealing with situations in the world, we have all already made choices for our lives. But, as we have seen, these choices usually take the form of dispersal and drifting into public possibilities, so that we have not really made them our own. To say that we should "choose to choose," then, is to say that we should embrace the choices we make, and that we should give structure to our lives by continuously reaffirming those choices in everything we do. Someone who is resolute about being an artist, for example, would accept the inevitable sacrifices involved in such a way of life, and would order her other activities around the project she has chosen as bedrock for her life. This would require constantly renewing her decision to be an artist in the specific choices she makes of friends and activities. How exactly this is to be worked out is something she alone will decide; there are no fixed rules that determine in advance how to be an artist in every possible situation. What is important here is *how* one takes over one's life, not *what* specific things one does.

If we think of living out our own lives as composing our own autobiographies, then authentic self-focusing might be thought of as a way of imparting a narrative continuity to our life stories. Seeing that our Being is *at issue* for us, we take over social roles with a lucid sense of what we are trying to accomplish for our lives overall, right up to the end. The aim here is to shape our actions into a cohesive story of our own making. For the resolute individual, life is no longer a disjointed series of means-ends strategies; instead, it comes to be organized around a coherent set of commitments that shape the past, present, and future into a unified flow. This resoluteness is not just a matter of pigheadedly clinging to a life-defining project come what may. Heidegger emphasizes the fact that the authentic individual is always "ready for anxiety," and that means being open to the fact that, since no role can guarantee a meaning for one's life, one must be constantly open to the possibility of "taking back" one's commitment if conditions make that unavoidable (§62).

Heidegger has often been criticized for formulating an ideal of authenticity that gives us no specific information on how we ought to act or what choices we should make. The concept of authenticity does not tell us that we should be, say, liberals rather than conservatives, or that we should act on the basis of love rather than sticking to the letter of the law. In fact, the picture of authenticity as a life characterized by continuity, cumulativeness, and purposiveness seems to be consistent with any number of concrete lifestyles, including many that we would see as profoundly immoral. A number of critics have taken this fact as showing that there is something pernicious or immoral about the Heideggerian conception of authenticity.

Now it is certainly true that this concept of authenticity does not entail any particular moral theory or position. But even though Heidegger does not intend to make any pronouncements about morality, a closer look at his concept of authenticity suggests that it might have some substantive things to say about what constitutes a good life.[26] First, Heidegger's description of an ideally coherent and focused way of living points to certain character traits an individual needs to have in order to be authentic. We might call these ideal traits "second-order values," because they are necessary for making coherent, meaningful first-order choices about what sort of person one wants to be (choosing to be, for instance, a utilitarian or a libertarian or a Christian in acting in the world). Authenticity is said to require such traits as resoluteness, clearsightedness, and a "sober understanding" of what is demanded in current situations. In order to achieve the kind of continuity and cohesiveness of an authentic life, Heidegger says, one must develop such traits as steadfastness, integrity, and openness to change. And authenticity is also said to require courage and a willingness to take a stand despite the uncertainties of life.

If all these traits are necessary to being authentic, however, then it seems that the concept of authenticity does have something to say about what it is to be a good person. A person who is authentic would be less likely to slip into the kinds of self-deception and dishonesty involved in hiding behind roles or thinking of one's actions as justified because they are "what one does." Moreover, Heidegger says that authentic individuals have a deep sense of their indebtedness to and belonging within the wider communal context from which all concrete possibilities of self-interpretation and self-evaluation arise. Such a sense of participation in a shared project, he thinks, points to an enhanced awareness of our obligations to our society as a whole. When we understand our involvement with others in the common enterprise of living in the world, Heidegger says, we will "become *authentically* bound together" into an authentic community.[27] Thus, it seems that the notion of authenticity does give us an image of a more engaged and morally committed way of life that goes beyond just drifting along and doing whatever feels good.

The second way that the ideal of authenticity can define higher ideals for us is found in Heidegger's concept of "historicity." The idea of historicity arises from the description of human existence as an unfolding life course or

26. For a detailed discussion of the significance of Heidegger's thought for ethics, see Charles Guignon, "Authenticity, Moral Values, and Psychotherapy," in Guignon, ed. *The Cambridge Companion to Heidegger* (Cambridge: Cambridge University Press, 1993), 215–39.

27. Heidegger, *Being and Time*, 159.

"happening" that is enmeshed in the wider drama of a community's history. According to Heidegger, the lucid awareness of one's complicity in the "co-happening" of one's community can lead to a way of existing he calls "authentic historicity," a mode of existence that brings about a transformed understanding of one's historical context. As authentic historicity, Heidegger says, one grasps the past of one's community as a "heritage" or "legacy," that is, as a "sending" that is filled with promise and potential. And this brings with it a sense of our future as a shared "destiny" with specific tasks we need to fulfill through cooperative action. An authentically historical person therefore tries to "retrieve" the possibilities laid out by the past in order to realize certain "monumental" possibilities that are definitive of his or her culture. An example of this would be the way Martin Luther King tried to recover an appreciation of the biblical ideals central to American culture in order to achieve equality for all humans. Heidegger holds that we need to have some notion of a shared historical purpose if we are to have any basis for criticizing and reforming the practices of the "today." Thus, he says that authenticity "becomes a way of painfully detaching oneself from the falling publicness of the today" so that one can work toward realizing the ideals definitive of one's historical culture.[28]

The concept of authenticity makes is possible for us to envision a better, more meaningful life beyond mere subsisting and having fun. In this respect it gives us an image of the kind of life Socrates had in mind when he said, "What is important is not just to live, but to live well." The idea of authenticity therefore points to an alternative to what Heidegger saw as the flattened out life of modernity. But this ideal of authenticity has nothing to do with the "pop psychology" idea of getting in touch with an inner, essential truth about one's own self. Instead, it is a matter of being more fully and lucidly engaged in the shared "co-happening" of one's historical community. Thus, in the kind of existentialist view we find in Heidegger, becoming an authentic individual is at the same time being a committed participant in the wider social and historical context. This is a crucial part of the ideal Heidegger has in mind when he says that in becoming authentic you can "become what you are" (§31).

---

28. Ibid., 449.

Being and Time

"For manifestly you have long been aware of what you mean when you use the expression '*being*'. We, however, who used to think we understood it, have now become perplexed" (Plato, *Sophist* 244a).

Do we in our time have an answer to the question of what we really mean by the word 'being'? Not at all. So it is fitting that we should raise anew *the question of the meaning of Being*.

meaning of being (es) Being?

INTRODUCTION

1. The Question of Being

§1. The Necessity for Explicitly Restating the Question of Being
This question has today been forgotten. Even though in our time we deem it progressive to give our approval to 'metaphysics' again, it is held that we have been exempted from the exertions of a newly rekindled "battle of the giants concerning being" (Plato). . . .

oblivion

§2. The Formal Structure of the Question of Being
The question of the meaning of Being must be *formulated*. If it is a fundamental question, or indeed *the* fundamental question, it must be made transparent, and in an appropriate way. . . .

Inquiry, as a kind of seeking, must be guided beforehand by what is sought. So the meaning of Being must already be available to us in some way. As we have intimated, we always conduct our activities in an understanding of Being. Out of this understanding arise both the explicit question of the meaning of Being and the tendency that leads us towards it conception. We do not *know* what 'Being' means. But even if we ask, "What *is* 'Being'?," we keep within an understanding of the 'is', though we are unable to fix conceptually what that 'is' signifies. We do not even know the horizon in terms of which that meaning is to be grasped and fixed. *But this vague average understanding of Being is still a Fact.*

However much this understanding of Being (an understanding which is

skip. §16, 18, 29, 31, 32

already available to us) may fluctuate and grow dim, and border on mere acquaintance with a word, its very indefiniteness is itself a positive phenomenon which needs to be clarified. An investigation of the meaning of Being cannot be expected to give this clarification at the outset. If we are to obtain the clue we need for Interpreting this average understanding of Being, we must first develop the concept of Being. In the light of this concept and the ways in which it may be explicitly understood, we can make out what this obscured or still unillumined understanding of Being means, and what kinds of obscuration—or hindrance to an explicit illumination—of the meaning of Being are possible and even inevitable.

Further, this vague average understanding of Being may be so infiltrated with traditional theories and opinions about Being that these remain hidden as sources of the way in which it is prevalently understood. What we seek when we inquire into Being is not something entirely unfamiliar, even if at first we cannot grasp it at all. . . .

§3. The Ontological Priority of the Question of Being

. . . Being is always the Being of an entity. The totality of entities can, in accordance with its various domains, become a field for laying bare and delimiting certain definite areas of subject-matter. These areas, on their part (for instance, history, Nature, space, life, Dasein, language, and the like), can serve as objects which corresponding scientific investigations may take as their respective themes. Scientific research accomplishes, roughly and naïvely, the demarcation and initial fixing of the areas of subject-matter. The basic structures of any such area have already been worked out after a fashion in our pre-scientific ways of experiencing and interpreting that domain of Being in which the area of subject-matter is itself confined. The 'basic concepts' which thus arise remain our proximal clues for disclosing this area concretely for the first time. And although research may always lean towards this positive approach, its real progress comes not so much from collecting results and storing them away in 'manuals' as from inquiring into the ways in which each particular area is basically constituted—an inquiry to which we have been driven mostly by reacting against just such an increase in information.

The real 'movement' of the sciences takes place when their basic concepts undergo a more or less radical revision which is transparent to itself. The level which a science has reached is determined by how far it is *capable* of a crisis in its basic concepts. In such immanent crises the very relationship between positively investigative inquiry and those things themselves that are under interrogation comes to a point where it begins to totter. Among the various disciplines everywhere today there are freshly awakened tendencies to put research on new foundations. . . .

Basic concepts determine the way in which we get an understanding beforehand of the area of subject-matter underlying all the objects a science takes as its theme, and all positive investigation is guided by this understanding. Only after the area itself has been explored beforehand in a corresponding manner do these concepts become genuinely demonstrated and 'grounded'. But since every such area is itself obtained from the domain of entities themselves, this preliminary research, from which the basic concepts are drawn, signifies nothing else than an interpretation of those entities with regard to their basic state of Being. . . .

But such an inquiry itself—ontology taken in the widest sense without favoring any particular ontological directions or tendencies—requires a further clue. Ontological inquiry is indeed more primordial, as over against the ontical inquiry of the positive sciences. But it remains itself naïve and opaque if in its researches into the Being of entities it fails to discuss the meaning of Being in general. And the ontological task of a genealogy of the different possible ways of Being (which is not to be constructed deductively) is precisely of such a sort as to require that we first come to an understanding of "what we really mean by this expression 'Being'."

The question of Being aims therefore at ascertaining the a priori conditions not only for the possibility of the sciences which examine entities as entities of such and such a type, and, in so doing, already operate with an understanding of Being, but also for the possibility of those ontologies themselves which are prior to the ontical sciences and which provide their foundations. *Basically, all ontology, no matter how rich and firmly compacted a system of categories it has at its disposal, remains blind and perverted from its ownmost aim, if it has not first adequately clarified the meaning of Being, and conceived this clarification as its fundamental task.*

§4. The Ontical Priority of the Question of Being

Science in general may be defined as the totality established through an interconnection of true propositions. This definition is not complete, nor does it reach the meaning of science. As ways in which man behaves, sciences have the manner of Being which this entity—man himself—possesses. This entity we denote by the term '*Dasein*'. Scientific research is not the only manner of Being which this entity can have, nor is it the one which lies closest. Moreover, Dasein itself has a special distinctiveness as compared with other entities, and it is worth our while to bring this to view in a provisional way. Here our discussion must anticipate later analyses, in which our results will be authentically exhibited for the first time.

Dasein is an entity which does not just occur among other entities. Rather it is ontically distinguished by the fact that, in its very Being, that Being is an *issue* for it. But in that case, this is a constitutive state of Dasein's Being, and this implies that Dasein, in its Being, has a relationship towards that Being—a relationship which itself is one of Being. And this means further that there is some way in which Dasein understands itself in its Being, and that to some degree it does so explicitly. It is peculiar to this entity that with and through its Being, this Being is disclosed to it. *Understanding of Being is itself a definite characteristic of Dasein's Being.* Dasein is ontically distinctive in that it *is* ontological.

Here "Being-ontological" is not yet tantamount to "developing an ontology." So if we should reserve the term "ontology" for that theoretical inquiry which is explicitly devoted to the meaning of entities, then what we have had in mind in speaking of Dasein's "Being-ontological" is to be designated as something "pre-ontological." It does not signify simply "being-ontical," however, but rather "being in such a way that one has an understanding of Being."

That kind of Being towards which Dasein can comport itself in one way or another, and always does comport itself somehow, we call '*existence*'. And because we cannot define Dasein's essence by citing a "what" of the kind that pertains to a subject-matter and because its essence lies rather in the fact that in each case it has its Being to be, and has it as its own, we have chosen to designate this entity as 'Dasein', a term which is purely an expression of its Being.

Dasein always understands itself in terms of its existence—in terms of a possibility of itself: to be itself or not itself. Dasein has either chosen these possibilities itself, or got itself into them, or grown up in them already. Only the particular Dasein decides its existence, whether it does so by taking hold or by neglecting. The question of existence never gets straightened out except through existing itself. The understanding of oneself which leads *along this way* we call '*existentiell*'. The question of existence is one of Dasein's ontical 'affairs'. This does not require that the ontological structure of existence should be theoretically transparent. The question about that structure aims at the analysis of what constitutes existence. The context of such structures we call '*existentiality*'. Its analytic has the character of an understanding which is not existentiell, but rather *existential.* The task of an existential analytic of Dasein has been delineated in advance, as regards both its possibility and its necessity, in Dasein's ontical constitution.

So far as existence is the determining character of Dasein, the ontological analytic of this entity always requires that existentiality be considered beforehand. By 'existentiality' we understand the state of Being that is constitutive for those entities that exist. But in the idea of such a constitutive state of Being, the idea of Being is already included. And thus even the possibility of carrying through the analytic of Dasein depends on working out beforehand the question about the meaning of Being in general.

Fundamental ontology they Dasein Analytic

Sciences are ways of Being in which Dasein comports itself towards entities which it need not be itself. But to Dasein, Being in a world is something that belongs essentially. Thus Dasein's understanding of Being pertains with equal primordiality both to an understanding of something like a 'world', and to the understanding of the Being of those entities which become accessible within the world. So whenever an ontology takes for its theme entities whose character of Being is other than that of Dasein, it has its own foundation and motivation in Dasein's own ontical structure, in which a pre-ontological understanding of Being is comprised as a definite characteristic.

Therefore *fundamental ontology,* from which alone all other ontologies can take their rise, must be sought in the *existential analytic of Dasein.*

Dasein accordingly takes priority over all other entities in several ways. The first priority is an *ontical* one: Dasein is an entity whose Being has the determinate character of existence. The second priority is an *ontological* one: Dasein is in itself 'ontological', because existence is thus determinative for it. But with equal primordiality Dasein also possesses—as constitutive for its understanding of existence—an understanding of the Being of all entities of a character other than its own. Dasein has therefore a third priority as providing the ontico-ontological condition for the possibility of any ontologies. Thus Dasein has turned out to be, more than any other entity, the one which must first be interrogated ontologically.

But the roots of the existential analytic, on its part, are ultimately *existentiell,* that is, *ontical.* Only if the inquiry of philosophical research is itself seized upon in an existentiell manner as a possibility of the Being of each existing Dasein, does it become at all possible to disclose the existentiality of existence and to undertake an adequately founded ontological problematic. But with this, the ontical priority of the question of being has also become plain. . . .

If to Interpret the meaning of Being becomes our task, Dasein is not only the primary entity to be interrogated; it is also that entity which already comports itself, in its Being, towards what we are asking about when we ask this question. But in that case the question of Being is nothing other than the radicalization of an essential tendency-of-Being which belongs to Dasein itself—the pre-ontological understanding of Being.

2. The Twofold Task in Working Out the Question of Being

§5. The Ontological Analytic of Dasein as Laying Bare the Horizon for an Interpretation of the Meaning of Being in General

In designating the tasks of 'formulating' the question of Being, we have shown not only that we must establish which entity is to serve as our primary object of interrogation, but also that the right way of access to this entity is one which we must explicitly make our own and hold secure. We have already discussed which entity takes over the principal role within the question of Being. But how are we, as it were, to set our sights towards this entity, Dasein, both as something accessible to us and as something to be understood and interpreted?

In demonstrating that Dasein is ontico-ontologically prior, we may have misled the reader into supposing that this entity must also be what is given as ontico-ontologically primary not only in the sense that it can itself be grasped 'immediately', but also in that the kind of Being which it possesses is presented just as 'immediately'. Ontically, of course, Dasein is not only close to us—even that which is closest: we *are* it, each of us, we ourselves. In spite of this, or rather for just this reason, it is ontologically that which is farthest. To be sure, its ownmost Being is such that it has an understanding of that Being, and already maintains itself in each case as if its Being has been interpreted in some manner. But we are certainly not saying that when Dasein's own Being is thus interpreted pre-ontologically in the way which lies closest, this interpretation can be taken over as an appropriate clue, as if this way of understanding Being is what must emerge when one's ownmost state of Being is considered as an ontological theme. The kind of Being which belongs to Dasein is rather such that, in understanding its own Being, it has a tendency to do so in terms of that entity towards which it comports itself proximally and in a way which is essentially constant—in terms of the 'world'. In Dasein itself, and therefore in its own understanding of Being, the way the world is understood is, as we shall show, reflected back ontologically upon the way in which Dasein itself gets interpreted.

Thus because Dasein is ontico-ontologically prior, its own specific state of Being (if we understand this in the sense of Dasein's "categorial structure") remains concealed from it. Dasein is ontically "closest" to itself and ontologically farthest; but pre-ontologically it is surely not a stranger. . . .

Thus an analytic of Dasein must remain our first requirement in the question of Being. But in that case the problem of obtaining and securing the kind of access which will lead to Dasein, becomes even more a burning one. . . . We must . . . choose such a way of access and such a kind of interpretation that this entity can show itself in itself and from itself. And this means that it is to be shown as it is *proximally and for the most part*—in its average *everydayness*. In this everydayness there are certain structures which we shall exhibit—not just any accidental structures, but essential ones which, in every kind of Being that factical Dasein may possess, persist as determinative for the character of its Being. . . .

"Destruction" of traditional ontology

We shall point to *temporality* as the meaning of the Being of that entity which we call 'Dasein'. If this is to be demonstrated, those structures of Dasein which we shall provisionally exhibit must be Interpreted over again as modes of temporality. In thus interpreting Dasein as temporality, however, we shall not give the answer to our leading question as to the meaning of Being in general. But the ground will have been prepared for obtaining such an answer.

De-structuring

§6. The Task of Destroying the History of Ontology

All research—and not least that which operates within the range of the central question of Being—is an ontical possibility of Dasein. Dasein's Being finds its meaning in temporality. But temporality is also the condition which makes historicality possible as a temporal kind of Being which Dasein itself possesses, regardless of whether or how Dasein is an entity "in time." Historicality, as a determinate character, is prior to what is called 'history' (world-historical historizing).

'Historicality' stands for the state of Being that is constitutive for Dasein's 'historizing' as such; only on the basis of such 'historizing' is anything like 'world-history' possible or can anything belong historically to world-history. In its factical Being, any Dasein is as it already was, and it is 'what' it already was. It *is* its past, whether explicitly or not. And this is so not only in that its past is, as it were, pushing itself along 'behind' it, and that Dasein possesses what is past as a property which is still present-at-hand and which sometimes has after-effects upon it: Dasein 'is' its past in the way of *its* own Being, which, to put it roughly, 'historizes' out of its future on each occasion. Whatever the way of being it may have at the time, and thus with whatever understanding Being it may possess, Dasein has grown up both into and in a traditional way of interpreting itself: in terms of this it understands itself proximally and, within a certain range, constantly. By this understanding, the possibilities of its Being are disclosed and regulated. Its own past—and this always means the past of its 'generation'—is not something which *follows along after* Dasein, but something which already goes ahead of it. . . .

The ownmost meaning of Being which belongs to the inquiry into Being as an historical inquiry, gives us the assignment of inquiring into the history of that inquiry itself, that is, of becoming historiological. In working out the question of Being, we must heed this assignment, so that by positively making the past our own, we may bring ourselves into full possession of the ownmost possibilities of such inquiry. . . .

When tradition . . . becomes master, it does so in such a way that what it 'transmits' is made so inaccessible, proximally and for the most part, that it rather becomes concealed. Tradition takes what has come down to us and delivers it over to self-evidence; it blocks our access to those primordial 'sources' from which the categories and concepts handed down to us have been in part quite genuinely drawn. Indeed it makes us forget that they have had such an origin, and makes us suppose that the necessity of going back to these sources is something which we need not even understand. Dasein has had its historicality so thoroughly uprooted by tradition that if confines its interest to the multiformity of possible types, directions, and standpoints of philosophical activity in the most exotic and alien of cultures; and by this very interest it seeks to veil the fact that it has no ground of its own to stand on. . . .

If the question of Being is to have its own history made transparent, then this hardened tradition must be loosened up, and the concealments which it has brought about must be dissolved. We understand this task as one in which by taking *the question of Being as our clue*, we are to *destroy* the traditional content of ancient ontology until we arrive at those primordial experiences in which we achieved our first ways of determining the nature of Being—the ways which have guided us ever since.

In thus demonstrating the origin of our basic ontological concepts by an investigation in which their 'birth certificate' is displayed, we have nothing to do with a vicious relativizing of ontological standpoints. But this destruction is just as far from having the *negative* sense of shaking off the ontological tradition. We must, on the contrary, stake out the positive possibilities of that tradition, and this always means keeping it within its *limits*; these in turn are given factically in the way the question is formulated at the time, and in the way the possible field for investigation is thus bounded off. On its negative side, this destruction does not relate itself towards the past; its criticism is aimed at 'today' and at the prevalent way of treating the history of ontology, whether it is headed towards doxography, towards intellectual history, or towards a history of problems. But to bury the past in nullity is not the purpose of this destruction; its aim is *positive*; its negative function remains unexpressed and indirect.

§7. The Phenomenological Method

. . . What is it that phenomenology is to 'let us see'? What is it that must be called a 'phenomenon' in a distinctive sense? What is it that by its very essence is *necessarily* the theme whenever we exhibit something *explicitly?* Manifestly, it is something that proximally and for the most part does *not* show itself at all: it is something that lies *hidden*, in contrast to that which proximally and for the most part does show itself; but at the same time it is something that belongs to what thus shows itself, and it belongs to it so essentially as to constitute its meaning and its ground.

Yet that which remains *hidden* in an egregious sense, or which relapses and gets *covered up* again, or which shows itself only '*in disguise*', is not just this entity or that, but rather the *Being* of entities, as our previous observations have shown. This Being can be covered up so extensively that it becomes forgotten and no question arises about it or about its meaning. Thus that which demands that it become a phenomenon, and which demands this in a distinctive sense and in terms of its ownmost content as a thing, is what phenomenology has taken into its grasp thematically as its object.

Phenomenology is our way of access to what is to be the theme of ontology, and it is our way of giving it demonstrative precision. *Only as phenomenology, is ontology possible.* In the phenomenological conception of "phenomenon" what one has in mind as that which shows itself is the Being of entities, its meaning, its modifications and derivatives. And this showing-itself is not just any showing-itself, nor is it some such thing as appearing. Least of all can the Being of entities ever be anything such that "behind it" stands something else "which does not appear."

"Behind" the phenomena of phenomenology there is essentially nothing else; on the other hand, what is to become a phenomenon can be hidden. And just because the phenomena are proximally and for the most part *not* given, there is need for phenomenology. Covered-up-ness is the counter-concept to 'phenomenon'. . . .

With regard to its subject-matter, phenomenology is the science of the Being of entities—ontology. In explaining the tasks of ontology we found it necessary that there should be a fundamental ontology taking as its theme that entity which is ontologico-ontically distinctive, Dasein, in order to confront the cardinal problem—the question of the meaning of Being in general. Our investigation itself will show that the meaning of phenomenological description as a method lies in *interpretation*. The *logos* of the phenomenology of Dasein has the character of a *hermeneuein*, through which the authentic meaning of Being, and also those basic structures of Being which Dasein itself possesses, are *made known* to Dasein's understanding of Being. The phenomenology of Dasein is a *hermeneutic* in the primordial signification of this word, where it designates this business of interpreting. . . .

DIVISION ONE: ANALYSIS OF DASEIN

Chapter 1. The Task of a Preparatory Analysis of Dasein

§9. The Theme of the Analytic of Dasein

We are ourselves the entities to be analyzed. The Being of any such entity is *in each case mine.* These entities, in their Being, comport themselves towards their Being. As entities with such Being, they are delivered over to their own Being. *Being* is that which is an issue for every such entity. This way of characterizing Dasein has a double consequence:

1. The "essence" of this entity lies in its "to be." Its Being-what-it-is (*essentia*) must, so far as we can speak of it at all, be conceived in terms of its Being (*existentia*). But here our ontological task is to show that when we choose to designate the Being of this entity as "existence," this term does not and cannot have the ontological signification of the traditional term "*existentia*"; ontologically, *existentia* is tantamount to *Being-present-at-hand*, a kind of Being which is essentially inappropriate to entities of Dasein's character. To avoid getting bewildered, we shall always use the Interpretative expression "*presence-at-hand*" for the term "*existentia*," while the term "existence," as a designation of Being, will be allotted solely to Dasein.

The "essence" of Dasein lies in its existence. Accordingly those characteristics which can be exhibited in this entity are not "properties" present-at-hand of some entity which "looks" so and so and is itself present-at-hand; they are in each case possible ways for it to be, and no more than that. All the Being-as-it-is which this entity possesses is primarily Being. So when we designate this entity with the term 'Dasein', we are expressing not its "what" (as if it were a table, house or tree) but its Being.

2. That Being which is an *issue* for this entity in its very Being, is in each case mine. Thus Dasein is never to be taken ontologically as an instance or special case of some genus of entities as things that are present-at-hand. To entities such as these, their Being is "a matter of indifference"; or more precisely, they 'are' such that their Being can be neither a matter of indifference to them, nor the opposite. Because Dasein has *in each case mineness*, one must always use a *personal* pronoun when one addresses it: "I am," "you are."

Furthermore, in each case Dasein is mine to be in one way or another. Dasein has always made some sort of decision as to the way in which it is in each case mine. That entity which in its Being has this very Being as an issue, comports itself towards its Being as its ownmost possibility. In each case Dasein *is* its possibility, and it "has" this possibility, but not just as a property, as something present-at-hand would. And because Dasein is in each case essentially its own possibility, it can, in its very Being, "choose" itself and win itself; it can also lose itself and never win itself; or only "seem" to do so. But only in so far as it is essentially something which can be *authentic*—that is, something of its own—can it have lost itself and not yet won itself. As modes of Being, *authenticity* and *inauthenticity* (these expressions have been chosen terminologically in a strict sense) are both grounded in the fact that any Dasein whatsoever is characterized by mineness. But the inauthenticity of Dasein does not signify any 'less' Being or

any 'lower' degree of Being. Rather it is the case that even in its fullest concretion Dasein can be characterized by inauthenticity—when busy, when
excited, when interested, when ready for enjoyment.

The two characteristics of Dasein which we have sketched—the priority
of '*existentia*' over *essentia*, and the fact that Dasein is in each case mine—
have already indicated that in the analytic of this entity we are facing a peculiar phenomenal domain. Dasein does not have the kind of Being which belongs to something merely present-at-hand within the world, nor does it
ever have it. So neither is it to be presented thematically as something we
come across in the same way as we come across what is present-at-hand. The
right way of presenting it is so far from self-evident that to determine what
form it shall take is itself an essential part of the ontological analytic of this
entity. Only by presenting this entity in the right way can we have any understanding of its Being. No matter how provisional our analysis may be, it
always requires the assurance that we have started correctly.

In determining itself as an entity, Dasein always does so in the light of a
possibility which it *is* itself and which, in its very Being, it somehow understands. This is the formal meaning of Dasein's existential constitution. But
this tells us that if we are to Interpret this entity *ontologically,* the problematic of its Being must be developed from the existentiality of its existence.
This cannot mean, however, that 'Dasein' is to be construed in terms of
some concrete possible idea of existence. At the outset of our analysis it is
particularly important that Dasein should not be Interpreted with the differentiated character of some definite way of existing, but that it should be
uncovered in the undifferentiated character which it has proximally and for
the most part. This undifferentiated character of Dasein's everydayness is
not nothing, but a positive phenomenal characteristic of this entity. Out of
this kind of Being—and back into it again—is all existing, such as it is. We
call this everyday undifferentiated character of Dasein '*averageness*'. . . .

Chapter 2. Being-in-the-World in General
as the Basic State of Dasein

*§12. A Preliminary Sketch of Being-in-the-World, in terms of an Orientation
towards Being-in as such*

In our preparatory discussions we have brought out some characteristics of
Being which will provide us with a steady light for our further investigation,
but which will at the same time become structurally concrete as that investigation continues. Dasein is an entity which, in its very Being, comports
itself understandingly towards that Being. In saying this, we are calling

attention to the formal concept of existence. Dasein exists. Furthermore, Dasein is an entity which in each case I myself am. Mineness belongs to any existent Dasein, and belongs to it as the condition which makes authenticity and inauthenticity possible. In each case Dasein exists in one or the other of these two modes, or else it is modally undifferentiated.

But these are both ways in which Dasein's Being takes on a definite character, and they must be seen and understood a priori as grounded upon the state of Being which we have called '*Being-in-the-world*'. An interpretation of this constitutive state is needed if we are to set up our analytic of Dasein correctly.

The compound expression 'Being-in-the-world' indicates in the very way we have coined it, that it stands for a *unitary* phenomenon. This primary datum must be seen as a whole. But while Being-in-the-world cannot be broken up into contents which may be pieced together, this does not prevent it from having several constitutive items in its structure. Indeed the phenomenal datum which our expression indicates is one which may, in fact, be looked at in three ways. If we study it, keeping the whole phenomenon firmly in mind beforehand, the following items may be brought out for emphasis:

First, the '*in-the-world*'. With regard to this there arises the task of inquiring into the ontological structure of the 'world' and defining the idea of *worldhood* as such.

Second, that *entity* which in every case has Being-in-the-world as the way in which it is. Here we are seeking that which one inquires into when one asks the question "Who?" By a phenomenological demonstration we shall determine who is in the mode of Dasein's average everydayness.

Third, *Being-in* as such. We must set forth the ontological Constitution of inhood itself. Emphasis upon any one of these constitutive items signifies that the others are emphasized along with it; this means that in any such case the whole phenomenon gets seen. . . .

Dasein's facticity is such that its Being-in-the-world has always dispersed itself or even split itself up into definite ways of Being-in. The multiplicity of these is indicated by the following examples: having to do with something, producing something, attending to something and looking after it, making use of something, giving something up and letting it go, undertaking, accomplishing, evincing, interrogating, considering, discussing, determining. . . . All these ways of Being-in have *concern* as their kind of Being—a kind of Being which we have yet to characterize in detail. Leaving undone, neglecting, renouncing, taking a rest—these too are ways of concern; but these are all *deficient* modes, in which the possibilities of concern are kept to a 'bare minimum'. . . .

Worldhood (+ The Ready-to-Hand)

Chapter 3. The Worldhood of the World

§14. *The Idea of the Worldhood of the World in General*

Being-in-the-world shall first be made visible with regard to that item of its structure which is the 'world' itself. . . .

The discussion of the word 'world', and our frequent use of it have made it apparent that it is used in several ways. By unravelling these we can get an indication of the different kinds of phenomena that are signified, and of the way in which they are interconnected.

1. 'World' is used as an ontical concept, and signifies the totality of those entities which can be present-at-hand within the world.

2. 'World' functions as an ontological term, and signifies the Being of those entities which we have just mentioned. And indeed 'world' can become a term for any realm which encompasses a multiplicity of entities: for instance, when one talks of the 'world' of a mathematician, 'world' signifies the realm of possible objects of mathematics.

3. 'World' can be understood in another ontical sense—not, however, as those entities which Dasein essentially is not and which can be encountered within-the-world, but rather as that '*wherein*' a factical Dasein as such can be said to 'live'. 'World' has here a pre-ontological existentiell signification. Here again there are different possibilities: "world" may stand for the 'public' we-world, or one's 'own' closest (domestic) environment.

4. Finally, "world" designates the ontologico-existential concept of *worldhood*. Worldhood itself may have as its modes whatever structural wholes any special 'worlds' may have at the time; but it embraces in itself the a priori character of worldhood in general. We shall reserve the expression "world" as a term for our third signification. If we should sometimes use it in the first of these senses, we shall mark this with single quotation marks. . . .

§15. *The Being of the Entities Encountered in the Environment*

The Being of those entities which we encounter as closest to us can be exhibited phenomenologically if we take as our clue our everyday Being-in-the-world, which we also call our '*dealings*' *in* the world and *with* entities within-the-world. Such dealings have already dispersed themselves into manifold ways of concern. The kind of dealing which is closest to us is, as we have shown, not a bare perceptual cognition, but rather that kind of concern which manipulates things and puts them to use; and this has its own kind of 'knowledge'. The phenomenological question applies in the first instance to the Being of those entities which we encounter in such concern.

To assure the kind of seeing which is here required, we must first make a remark about method.

In the disclosure and explication of Being, entities are in every case our preliminary and our accompanying theme; but our real theme is Being. In the domain of the present analysis, the entities we shall take as our preliminary theme are those which show themselves in our concern with the en-*Umwelt* vironment. Such entities are not thereby objects for knowing the 'world' theoretically; they are simply what gets used, what gets produced, and so forth. . . . An investigation of Being . . . brings to completion, autonomously and explicitly, that understanding of Being which belongs already to Dasein and which 'comes alive' in any of its dealings with entities. Those entities which serve phenomenologically as our preliminary theme—in this case, those which are used or which are to be found in the course of production—become accessible when we put ourselves into the position of concerning ourselves with them in some such way. Taken strictly, this talk about "putting ourselves into such a position" is misleading; for the kind of Being which belongs to such concernful dealings is not one into which we need to put ourselves first. This is the way in which everyday Dasein always *is*: when I open the door, for instance, I use the latch. The achieving of phenomenological access to the entities which we encounter, consists rather in thrusting aside our interpretative tendencies, which keep thrusting themselves upon us and running along with us, and which conceal not only the phenomenon of such 'concern', but even more those entities themselves *as* encountered of their own accord *in* our concern with them. These entangling errors become plain if in the course of our investigation we now ask which entities shall be taken as our preliminary theme and established as the pre-phenomenal basis for our study.

One may answer: "Things." But with this obvious answer we have perhaps already missed the pre-phenomenal basis we are seeking. For in addressing these entities as 'Things' (*res*), we have tacitly anticipated their ontological character. . . .

We shall call those entities which we encounter in concern '*equipment*'. In our dealings we come across equipment for writing, sewing, working, transportation, measurement. The kind of Being which equipment possesses must be exhibited. The clue for doing this lies in our first defining what makes an item of equipment—namely, its equipmentality.

Taken strictly, there 'is' no such thing as *an* equipment. To the Being of any equipment there always belongs a totality of equipment, in which it can be this equipment that it is. Equipment is essentially "something in-order-to. . . ." A totality of equipment is constituted by various ways of the "in-order-to," such as serviceability, conduciveness, usability, manipulability.

In the "in-order-to" as a structure there lies an *assignment* or *reference* of something to something. Only in the analyses which are to follow can the phenomenon which this term 'assignment' indicates be made visible in its ontological genesis. Provisionally, it is enough to take a look phenomenally at a manifold of such assignments. Equipment—in accordance with its equipmentality—always is *in terms of* its belonging to other equipment: ink-stand, pen, ink, paper, blotting pad, table, lamp, furniture, windows, doors, room. These 'Things' never show themselves proximally as they are for themselves, so as to add up to a sum of *realia* and fill up a room. What we encounter as closest to us (though not as something taken as a theme) is the room; and we encounter it not as something 'between four walls' in a geometrical spatial sense, but as equipment for residing. Out of this the 'arrangement' emerges, and it is in this that any 'individual' item of equipment shows itself. *Before* it does so, a totality of equipment has already been discovered.

Equipment can genuinely show itself only in dealings cut to its own measure (hammering with a hammer, for example); but in such dealings an entity of this kind is not *grasped* thematically as an occurring Thing, nor is the equipment-structure known as such even in the using. The hammering does not simply have knowledge about the hammer's character as equipment, but it has appropriated this equipment in a way which could not possibly be more suitable. In dealings such as this, where something is put to use, our concern subordinates itself to the "in-order-to" which is constitutive for the equipment we are employing at the time; the less we just stare at the hammer-Thing, and the more we seize hold of it and use it, the more primordial does our relationship to it become, and the more unveiledly is it encountered as that which it is—as equipment. The hammering itself uncovers the specific 'manipulability' of the hammer. The kind of Being which equipment possesses—in which it manifests itself in its own right—we call "*readiness-to-hand.*" Only because equipment has *this* "Being-in-itself" and does not merely occur, is it manipulable in the broadest sense and at our disposal. No matter how sharply we just *look* at the 'outward appearance' of Things in whatever form this takes, we cannot discover anything ready-to-hand. If we look at Things just 'theoretically', we can get along without understanding readiness-to-hand. But when we deal with them by using them and manipulating them, this activity is not a blind one; it has its own kind of sight, by which our manipulation is guided and from which it acquires its specific Thingly character. Dealings with equipment subordinate themselves to the manifold assignments of the "in-order-to." And the sight with which they thus accommodate themselves is *circumspection.*

The ready-to-hand is not grasped theoretically at all, nor is it itself the sort of thing that circumspection takes proximally as a circumspective theme. The peculiarity of what is proximally ready-to-hand is that, in its readiness-to-hand, it must, as it were, withdraw in order to be ready-to-hand quite authentically. That with which our everyday dealings proximally dwell is not the tools themselves. On the contrary, that with which we concern ourselves primarily is the work—that which is to be produced at the time; and this is accordingly ready-to-hand too. The work bears with it that referential totality within which the equipment is encountered.

The work to be produced, as the "*towards-which*" of such things as the hammer, the plane, and the needle, likewise has the kind of Being that belongs to equipment. The shoe which is to be produced is for wearing (footgear); the clock is manufactured for telling the time. The work which we chiefly encounter in our concernful dealings—the work that is to be found when one is "at work" on something—has a usability which belongs to it essentially; in this usability it lets us encounter already the "towards-which" for which *it* is usable. A work that someone has ordered is only by reason of its use and the assignment-context of entities which is discovered in using it.

But the work to be produced is not merely usable for something. The production itself is a using *of* something for something. In the work there is also a reference or assignment to 'materials': the work is dependent on leather, thread, needles, and the like. Leather, moreover is produced from hides. These are taken from animals, which someone else has raised. Animals also occur within the world without having been raised at all; and, in a way, these entities still produce themselves even when they have been raised. So in the environment certain entities become accessible which are always ready-to-hand, but which, in themselves, do not need to be produced. Hammer, tongs, and needle, refer in themselves to steel, iron, metal, mineral, wood, in that they consist of these. In equipment that is used, 'Nature' is discovered along with it by that use—the 'Nature' we find in natural products.

Here, however, "Nature" is not to be understood as that which is just present-at-hand, nor as the *power of Nature*. The wood is a forest of timber, the mountain a quarry of rock; the river is water-power, the wind is wind 'in the sails'. As the 'environment' is discovered, the 'Nature' thus discovered is encountered too. If its kind of Being as ready-to-hand is disregarded, this 'Nature' itself can be discovered and defined simply in its pure presence-at-hand. But when this happens, the Nature which 'stirs and strives', which assails us and enthralls us as landscape, remains hidden. The botanist's plants are not the flowers of the hedgerow; the "source" which the geographer establishes for a river is not the "springhead in the dale."

. . . Any work with which one concerns oneself is ready-to-hand not only in the domestic world of the workshop but also in the *public world*. Along with the public world, the *environing Nature* is discovered and is accessible to everyone. In roads, streets, bridges, buildings, our concern discovers Nature as having some definite direction. A covered railway platform takes account of bad weather; an installation for public lighting takes account of the darkness, or rather of specific changes in the presence or absence of daylight—the "position of the sun." . . .

The kind of Being which belongs to these entities is readiness-to-hand. But this characteristic is not to be understood as merely a way of taking them, as if we were talking such 'aspects' into the 'entities' which we proximally encounter, or as if some world-stuff which is proximally present-at-hand in itself were "given subjective coloring" in this way. Such an Interpretation would overlook the fact that in this case these entities would have to be understood and discovered beforehand as something purely present-at-hand, and must have priority and take the lead in the sequence of those dealings with the 'world' in which something is discovered and made one's own. But this already runs counter to the ontological meaning of cognition, which we have exhibited as a *founded* mode of Being-in-the-world. To lay bare what is just present-at-hand and no more, cognition must first penetrate *beyond* what is ready-to-hand in our concern. *Readiness-to-hand is the way in which entities as they are "in themselves" are defined ontologico-categorially.* . . .

§16. How the Worldly Character of the Environment Announces itself in Entities Within-the-world

. . . To the everydayness of Being-in-the-world there belong certain modes of concern. These permit the entities with which we concern ourselves to be encountered in such a way that the worldly character of what is within-the-world comes to the fore. When we concern ourselves with something, the entities which are most closely ready-to-hand may be met as something unusable, not properly adapted for the use we have decided upon. The tool turns out to be damaged, or the material unsuitable. In each of these cases *equipment* is here, ready-to-hand. We discover its unusability, however, not by looking at it and establishing its properties, but rather by the circumspection of the dealings in which we use it. When its unusability is thus discovered, equipment becomes conspicuous. This *conspicuousness* presents the ready-to-hand equipment as in a certain un-readiness-to-hand. But this implies that what cannot be used just lies there; it shows itself as an equipmental Thing which looks so and so, and which, in its readiness-to-hand as looking that way, has constantly been present-at-hand too. Pure presence-at-hand announces itself in such equipment, but only to withdraw to the readiness-to-hand of something with which one concerns oneself—that is to say, of the sort of thing we find when we put it back into repair. . . .

In our concernful dealings, however, we not only come up against unusable things *within* what is ready-to-hand already: we also find things which are missing—which not only are not 'handy' but are not 'to hand' at all. Again, to miss something in this way amounts to coming across something un-ready-to-hand. When we notice what is un-ready-to-hand, that which is ready-to-hand enters the mode of *obtrusiveness*. The more urgently we need what is missing, and the more authentically it is encountered in its un-readiness-to-hand, all the more obtrusive does that which is ready-to-hand become—so much so, indeed, that it seems to lose its character of readiness-to-hand. It reveals itself as something just present-at-hand and no more, which cannot be budged without the thing that is missing. The helpless way in which we stand before it is a deficient mode of concern, and as such it uncovers the Being-just-present-at-hand-and-no-more of something ready-to-hand.

In our dealings with the world of our concern, the un-ready-to-hand can be encountered not only in the sense of that which is unusable or simply missing, but as something un-ready-to-hand which is *not* missing at all and *not* unusable, but which "stands in the way" of our concern. That to which our concern refuses to turn, that for which it has "no time," is something *un*-ready-to-hand in the manner of what does not belong here, of what has not as yet been attended to. Anything which is un-ready-to-hand in this way is disturbing to us, and enables us to see the *obstinacy* of that with which we must concern ourselves in the first instance before we do anything else. With this obstinacy, the presence-at-hand of the ready-to-hand makes itself known in a new way as the Being of that which still lies before us and calls for our attending to it.

The modes of conspicuousness, obtrusiveness, and obstinacy all have the function of bringing to the fore the characteristic of presence-at-hand in what is ready-to-hand. But the ready-to-hand is not thereby just *observed* and stared at as something present-at-hand; the presence-at-hand which makes itself known is still bound up in the readiness-to-hand of equipment. Such equipment still does not veil itself in the guise of mere Things. It becomes 'equipment' in the sense of something which one would like to shove out of the way. But in such a Tendency to shove things aside, the ready-to-hand shows itself as still ready-to-hand in its unswerving presence-at-hand. . . .

Being-in-the-world, according to our Interpretation hitherto, amounts to a non-thematic circumspective absorption in references or assignments constitutive for the readiness-to-hand of a totality of equipment. Any concern is already as it is, because of some familiarity with the world. In this familiarity Dasein can lose itself in what it encounters within-the-world and be fascinated with it. What is it that Dasein is familiar with? Why can the worldly character of what is within-the-world be lit up? The presence-at-hand of entities is thrust to the fore by the possible breaks in that referential totality in which circumspection "operates"; how are we to get a closer understanding of this totality? . . .

§18. Involvement and Significance; the Worldhood of the World
The ready-to-hand is encountered within-the-world. The Being of this entity, readiness-to-hand, thus stands in some ontological relationship towards the world and towards worldhood. In anything ready-to-hand the world is always "there." Whenever we encounter anything, the world has already been previously discovered, though not thematically. But it can also be lit up in certain ways of dealing with our environment. The world is that in terms of which the ready-to-hand is ready-to-hand. How can the world let the ready-to-hand be encountered? Our analysis hitherto has shown that what we encounter within-the-world has, in its very Being, been freed for our concernful circumspection, for taking account. What does this previous freeing amount to, and how is this to be understood as an ontologically distinctive feature of the world?

. . . Anything ready-to-hand is, at the worst, appropriate for some purposes and inappropriate for others; and its "properties" are, as it were, still bound up in these ways in which it is appropriate or inappropriate, just as presence-at-hand, as a possible kind of Being for something ready-to-hand, is bound up in readiness-to-hand. Serviceability too, however, as a constitutive state of equipment (and serviceability is a reference), is not an appropriateness of some entity; it is rather the condition (so far as Being is in question) which makes it possible for the character of such an entity to be defined by its appropriatenesses. But what, then, is "reference" or "assignment" to mean? To say that the Being of the ready-to-hand has the structure of assignment or reference means that it has in itself the character of *having been assigned or referred.* An entity is discovered when it has been assigned or referred to something, and referred as that entity which it is. *With* any such entity there is an involvement which it has *in* something. The character of Being which belongs to the ready-to-hand is just such an *involvement.* If something has an involvement, this implies letting it be involved in something. The relationship of the "with . . . in . . . " shall be indicated by the term "assignment" or "reference."

When an entity within-the-world has already been proximally freed for its Being, that Being is its "involvement." With any such entity as entity, there is some involvement. The fact that it has such an involvement is *ontologically* definitive for the Being of such an entity, and is not an ontical assertion about it. That in which it is involved is the "towards-which" of serviceability, and the "for-which" of usability. With the "towards-which" of serviceability there can again be an involvement: *with* this thing, for instance, which is ready-to-hand, and which we accordingly call a "hammer," there is an involvement in hammering; with hammering, there is an involvement in making something fast; with making something fast, there is an involvement in protection against bad weather; and this protection "is" for the sake of providing shelter for Dasein—that is to say, for the sake of a possibility of Dasein's Being. Whenever something ready-to-hand has an involvement with it, *what* involvement this is, has in each case been outlined in advance in terms of the totality of such involvements. In a workshop, for example, the totality of involvements which is constitutive for the ready-to-hand in its readiness-to-hand, is "earlier" than any single item of equipment; so too for the farmstead with all its utensils and outlying lands. But the totality of involvements itself goes back ultimately to a "towards-which" in which there is *no* further involvement: this "towards-which" is not an entity with the kind of Being that belongs to what is ready-to-hand within a world; it is rather an entity whose Being is defined as Being-in-the-world, and to whose state of Being, worldhood itself belongs. This primary "towards-which" is not just another "towards-this" as something in which an involvement is possible. The primary "towards-which" is a "for-the-sake-of-which." . . .

In understanding a context of relations such as we have mentioned, Dasein has assigned itself to an "in-order-to," and it has done so in terms of a potentiality-for-Being for the sake of which it itself is—one which it may have seized upon either explicitly or tacitly, and which may be either authentic or inauthentic. This "in-order-to" prescribes a "towards-this" as a possible "in-which" for letting something be involved; and the structure of letting it be involved implies that this is an involvement which something *has*—an involvement which is *with* something. Dasein always assigns itself from a "for-the-sake-of-which" to the "with-which" of an involvement; that is to say, to the extent that it is, it always lets entities be encountered as ready-to-hand. *That wherein* Dasein understands itself beforehand in the mode of assigning itself is *that for which* it has let entities be encountered beforehand. *The "wherein" of an act of understanding which assigns or refers itself, is that for which one lets entities be encountered in the kind of Being that belongs to involvements; and this "wherein" is the phenomenon of the world.* And the structure of that to which Dasein assigns itself is what makes up the *worldhood* of the world. . . .

Chapter 4. Being-in-the-World as Being-With and Being-One's-Self. The "They"

Our analysis of the worldhood of the world has constantly been bringing the whole phenomenon of Being-in-the-world into view, although its constitutive items have not all stood out with the same phenomenal distinctness as the phenomenon of the world itself. We have Interpreted the world ontologically by going through what is ready-to-hand within-the-world; and this Interpretation has been put first, because Dasein, in its everydayness (with regard to which Dasein remains a constant theme for study), not only is in a world but comports itself towards that world with one predominant kind of Being. Proximally and for the most part Dasein is fascinated with its world. Dasein is thus absorbed in the world; the kind of Being which it thus possesses, and in general the Being-in which underlies it, are essential in determining the character of a phenomenon which we are now about to study. We shall approach this phenomenon by asking *who* it is that Dasein is in its everydayness. . . . By directing our researches towards the phenomenon which is to provide us with an answer to the question of the "who," we shall be led to certain structures of Dasein which are equiprimordial with Being-in-the-world; *Being-with* and *Dasein-with.* In this kind of Being is grounded the mode of everyday Being-one's-Self; the explication of this mode will enable us to see what we may call the 'subject' of everydayness—the "they. . . . "

§25. *An Approach to the Existential Question of the 'Who' of Dasein*
The answer to the question of who Dasein is, is one that was seemingly given in Section 9, where we indicated formally the basic characteristics of Dasein. Dasein is an entity which is in each case I myself; its Being is in each case mine. This definition *indicates* an *ontologically* constitutive state, but it does no more than indicate it. At the same time this tells us *ontically* (though in a rough and ready fashion) that in each case an "I"—not Others—is this entity. The question of the "who" answers itself in terms of the "I" itself, the 'subject', the 'Self'. . . .

The assertion that it is I who in each case Dasein is, is ontically obvious; but this must not mislead us into supposing that the route for an ontological Interpretation of what is 'given' in this way has thus been unmistakably prescribed. Indeed it remains questionable whether even the mere ontical content of the above assertion does proper justice to the stock of phenomena belonging to everyday Dasein. It could be that the "who" of everyday Dasein just is *not* the "I myself." . . .

The kind of "giving" we have [in the direct givenness of the "I"] . . . is the mere, formal, reflective awareness of the "I"; and perhaps what it gives is indeed evident. This insight even affords access to a phenomenological problematic in its own right, which has in principle the signification of providing a framework as a "formal phenomenology of consciousness." . . .

But if the Self is conceived 'only' as a way of Being of this entity, this seems tantamount to volatilizing the real 'core' of Dasein. Any apprehensiveness however which one may have about this gets its nourishment from the perverse assumption that the entity in question has at bottom the kind of Being which belongs to something present-at-hand, even if one is far from attributing to it the solidity of an occurrent corporeal Thing. Yet man's *'substance'* is not spirit as a synthesis of soul and body; it is rather *existence*.

§26. The Dasein-with of Others and Everyday Being-with

The answer to the question of the "who" of everyday Dasein is to be obtained by analyzing that kind of Being in which Dasein maintains itself proximally and for the most part. Our investigation takes its orientation from Being-in-the-world—that basic state of Dasein by which every mode of its Being gets co-determined. If we are correct in saying that by the foregoing explication of the world, the remaining structural items of Being-in-the-world have become visible, then this must also have prepared us, in a way, for answering the question of the "who."

In our 'description' of that environment which is closest to us—the work-world of the craftsman, for example,—the outcome was that along with the equipment to be found when one is at work, those Others for whom the "work" is destined are "encountered too." If this is ready-to-hand, then there lies in the kind of Being which belongs to it (that is, in its involvement) an essential assignment or reference to possible wearers, for instance, for whom it should be "cut to the figure." Similarly, when material is put to use, we encounter its producer or "supplier" as one who "serves" well or badly. When, for example, we walk along the edge of a field but "outside it," the field shows itself as belonging to such-and-such a person, and decently kept up by him; the book we have used was bought at So-and-so's shop and given by such-and-such a person, and so forth. The boat anchored at the shore is assigned in its Being-in-itself to an acquaintance who undertakes voyages with it; but even if it is a "boat which is strange to us," it still is indicative of Others. The Others who are thus "encountered" in a ready-to-hand, environmental context of equipment, are not somehow added on in thought to some Thing which is proximally just present-at-hand; such "Things" are encountered from out of the world in which they are ready-to-hand for Others—a world which is always mine too in advance. . . .

By "Others" we do not mean everyone else but me—those over against whom the "I" stands out. They are rather those from whom, for the most part, one does *not* distinguish oneself—those among whom one is too. This Being-there-too with them does not have the ontological character of a Being-present-at-hand-along-'with' them within a world. This 'with' is something of the character of Dasein; the 'too' means a sameness of Being as circumspectively concernful Being-in-the-world. 'With' and 'too' are to be understood *existentially*, not categorically. By reason of this *with-like*

Being-in-the-world, the world is always the one that I share with Others. The world of Dasein is a *with-world*. Being-in is *Being-with* Others. Their Being-in-themselves within-the-world is *Dasein-with*. . . .

. . . We must hold fast to the phenomenal facts of the case which we have pointed out, namely, that Others are encountered *environmentally*. This elemental worldly kind of encountering, which belongs to Dasein and is closest to it, goes so far that even one's *own* Dasein becomes something that it can itself proximally "come across" only when it *looks away* from 'Experiences' and the "center of its actions," or does not as yet "see" them at all. Dasein finds "itself" proximally in *what* it does, uses, expects, avoids—in those things environmentally ready-to-hand with which it is proximally *concerned*. . . .

Being-with is such that the disclosedness of the Dasein-with of Others belongs to it; this means that because Dasein's Being is Being-with, its understanding of Being already implies the understanding of Others. This understanding, like any understanding, is not an acquaintance derived from knowledge about them, but a primordially existential kind of Being, which, more than anything else, makes such knowledge and acquaintance possible. Knowing oneself is grounded in Being-with, which understands primordially. It operates proximally in accordance with the king of Being which is closest to us—Being-in-the-world as Being-with; and it does so by an acquaintance with that which Dasein, along with the Others, comes across in its environmental circumspection and concerns itself with—an acquaintance in which Dasein understands. Solicitous concern is understood in terms of what we are concerned with, and along with our understanding of it. Thus in concernful solicitude the Other is proximally disclosed. . . .

One's own Dasein, like the Dasein-with of Others, is encountered proximally and for the most part in terms of the with-world with which we are environmentally concerned. When Dasein is absorbed in the world of its concern—that is, at the same time, in its Being-with towards Others—it is not itself. *Who* is it, then, who has taken over Being as everyday Being-with-one-another?

§27. Everyday Being-one's-Self and the "They" — *Das Man — The One*
The *ontologically* relevant result of our analysis of Being-with is the insight that the "subject character" of one's own Dasein and that of Others is to be defined existentially—that is, in terms of certain ways in which one may be. In that with which we concern ourselves environmentally the Others are encountered as what they are; they *are* what they do.

In one's concern with what one has taken hold of, whether with, for, or against, the Others, there is constant care as to the way one differs from them, whether that difference is merely one that is to be evened out, whether one's own Dasein has lagged behind the Others and wants to catch up in relationship to them, or whether one's Dasein already has some priority over them and sets out to keep them suppressed. The care about this distance between them is disturbing to Being-with-one-another, though this disturbance is one that is hidden from it. If we may express this existentially, such Being-with-one-another has the character of *distantiality*. The more inconspicuous this kind of Being is to everyday Dasein itself, all the more stubbornly and primordially does it work itself out.

But this distantiality which belongs to Being-with, is such that Dasein, as everyday Being-with-one-another, stands in *subjection* to Others. It itself *is not*; its Being has been taken away by the Others. Dasein's everyday possibilities of Being are for the Others to dispose of as they please. These Others, moreover, are not *definite* Others. On the contrary, any Other can represent them. What is decisive is just that inconspicuous domination by Others which has already been taken over unawares from Dasein as Being-with. One belongs to the Others oneself and enhances their power. "The Others" whom one thus designates in order to cover up the fact of one's belonging to them essentially oneself, are those who proximally and for the most part "*are there*" in everyday Being-with-one-another. The "who" is not this one, not that one, not oneself, not some people, and not the sum of them all. The 'who' is the neuter, *the "they."* das Man

We have shown earlier how in the environment which lies closest to us, the public "environment" already is ready-to-hand and is also a matter of concern. In utilizing public means of transport and in making use of information services such as the newspaper, every Other is like the next. This Being-with-one-another dissolves one's own Dasein completely into the kind of Being of "the Others," in such a way, indeed, that the Others, as distinguishable and explicit, vanish more and more. In this inconspicuousness and unascertainability, the real dictatorship of the "they" is unfolded. We take pleasure and enjoy ourselves as *they* take pleasure; we read, see, and judge about literature and art as *they* see and judge; likewise we shrink back from the "great mass" as *they* shrink back; we find "shocking" what *they* find shocking. The "they," which is nothing definite, and which all are, though not as the sum, prescribes the kind of Being of everydayness.

The "they" has its own ways in which to be. That tendency of Being-with which we have called "distantiality" is grounded in the fact that Being-with-one-another concerns itself as such with *averageness*, which is an existential characteristic of the "they." The "they," in its Being, essentially makes an issue of this. Thus the "they" maintains itself factically in the averageness of that which belongs to it, of that which it regards as valid and that which it does not, and of that to which it grants success and that to which it denies it. In this averageness with which it prescribes what can and

may be ventured, it keeps watch over everything exceptional that thrusts itself to the fore. Every kind of priority gets noiselessly suppressed. Over-
night, everything that is primordial gets glossed over as something that has
long been well known. Everything gained by a struggle becomes just something to be manipulated. Every secret loses its force. This care of averageness reveals in turn an essential tendency of Dasein which we call the "leveling down" of all possibilities of Being.

Distantiality, averageness, and leveling down, as ways of Being for the
"they," constitute what we know as "publicness." Publicness proximally
controls every way in which the world and Dasein get interpreted, and it is
always right—not because there is some distinctive and primary
relationship-of-Being in which it is related to 'Things'. . . . By publicness
everything gets obscured, and what has thus been covered up gets passed off
as something familiar and accessible to everyone. . . .

Thus the particular Dasein in its everydayness is *disburdened* by the
"they." Not only that; by thus disburdening it of its Being, the "they" accommodates Dasein if Dasein has any tendency to take things easily and
make them easy. And because the "they" constantly accommodates the particular Dasein by disburdening it of its Being, the "they" retains and enhances its stubborn dominion.

Everyone is the other, and no one is himself. The 'they', which supplies
the answer to the question of the 'who' of everyday Dasein, is the 'nobody' to
whom every Dasein has already surrendered itself in Being-among-one-
another. . . .

*The "they" is an existentiale; and as a primordial phenomenon, it belongs to
Dasein's positive constitution.* It itself has, in turn, various possibilities of becoming concrete as something characteristic of Dasein. The extent to which
its dominion becomes compelling and explicit may change in the course of
history.

The Self of everyday Dasein is the *they-self,* which we distinguish from
the *authentic Self*—that is, from the Self which has been taken hold of in its
own way. As they-self, the particular Dasein has been *dispersed into* the
'they', and must first find itself. This dispersal characterizes the 'subject' of
that kind of Being which we know as concernful absorption in the world we
encounter as closest to us. If Dasein is familiar with itself as they-self, this
means at the same time that the "they" itself prescribes that way of interpreting the world and Being-in-the-world which lies closest. Dasein is for
the sake of the "they" in an everyday manner, and the "they" itself Articulates the referential context of significance. When entities are encountered,
Dasein's world frees them for a totality of involvements with which the
"they" is familiar, and within the limits which have been established with
the "they's" averageness. *Proximally,* factical Dasein is in the with-world,

which is discovered in an average way. *Proximally,* it is not 'I', in the sense of my own Self, that "am," but rather the Others, whose way is that of the 'they'. In terms of the 'they', and as the 'they', I am "given" proximally to 'myself'. Proximally Dasein is 'they', and for the most part it remains so. If Dasein discovers the world in its own way and brings it close, if it discloses to itself its own authentic Being, then this discovery of the "world" and this disclosure of Dasein are always accomplished as a clearing-away of concealments and obscurities, as a breaking up of the disguises with which Dasein bars its own way. . . .

From the kind of Being which belongs to the 'they'—the kind which is closest—everyday Dasein draws its pre-ontological way of interpreting its Being. In the first instance ontological Interpretation follows the tendency to interpret it this way: it understands Dasein in terms of the world and comes across it as an entity within-the-world. But that is not all: even that meaning of Being on the basis of which these "subject" entities get understood, is one which that ontology of Dasein which is 'closest' to us lets itself present in terms of the "world." But because the phenomenon of the world itself gets passed over in this absorption in the world, its place gets taken by what is present-at-hand within-the-world, namely, Things. The Being of those entities which *are there with us,* gets conceived as presence-at-hand. Thus by exhibiting the positive phenomenon of the closest everyday Being-in-the-world, we have made it possible to get an insight into the reason why an ontological Interpretation of this state of Being has been missing. *This very state of Being, in its everyday kind of Being, is what proximally misses itself and covers itself up.*

If the Being of everyday Being-with-one-another is already different in principle from pure presence-at-hand—in spite of the fact that it is seemingly close to it ontologically—still less can the Being of the authentic Self be conceived as presence-at-hand. *Authentic Being-one's-Self* does not rest upon an exceptional condition of the subject, a condition that has been detached from the "they"; *it is rather an existentiell modification of the "they"—of the "they" as an essential existentiale.* . . .

Chapter 5. Being-in as Such

§28. *The Task of a Thematic Analysis of Being-in*
The entity which is essentially constituted by Being-in-the-world *is* itself in every case its "there." According to the familiar signification of the word, the "there" points to a "here" and a "yonder." The "here" of an "I-here" is always understood in relation to a "yonder" ready-to-hand, in the sense of a Being towards this "yonder"—a Being which is de-severant, directional,

and concernful. Dasein's existential spatiality, which thus determines its "location," is itself grounded in Being-in-the-world. The "yonder" belongs definitely to something encountered within-the-*world*. "Here" and "yonder" are possible only in a "there"—that is to say, only if there is an entity which has made a disclosure of spatiality as the Being of the "there." This entity carries in its ownmost Being the character of not being closed off. In the expression "there" we have in view this essential disclosedness. By reason of this disclosedness, this entity (Dasein), together with the Being-there of the world, is "there" for itself.

When we talk in an ontically figurative way of the *lumen naturale* in man, we have in mind nothing other than the existential-ontological structure of this entity, that it *is* in such a way as to be its "there." To say that it is "il-luminated" means that *as* Being-in-the-world it is cleared in itself, not through any other entity, but in such a way that it *is* itself the clearing. Only for an entity which is existentially cleared in this way does that which is present-at-hand become accessible in the light or hidden in the dark. By its very nature, Dasein brings its "there" along with it. If it lacks its "there," it is not factically the entity which is essentially Dasein; indeed, it is not this entity at all. *Dasein is its disclosedness.*

§29. Being there as State-of-mind

What we indicate *ontologically* by the term "state-of-mind" is *ontically* the most familiar and everyday sort of thing; our mood, our Being-attuned. Prior to all psychology of moods, a field which in any case still lies fallow, it is necessary to see this phenomenon as a fundamental *existentiale*, and to outline its structure. . . .

In having a mood, Dasein is always disclosed moodwise as that entity to which it has been delivered over in its Being; and in this way it has been delivered over to the Being which, in existing, it has to be. "To be dis-closed" does not mean "to be known as this sort of thing." And even in the most indifferent and inoffensive everydayness the Being of Dasein can burst forth as a naked "that it is and has to be." The pure 'that it is' shows itself, but the "whence" and the "whither" remain in darkness. . . .

This characteristic of Dasein's Being—this "that it is"—is veiled in its "whence" and "whither," yet disclosed in itself all the more unveiledly; we call it the "*thrownness*" of this entity into its "there"; indeed, it is thrown in such a way that, as Being-in-the-world, it is the "there." The expression "thrownness" is meant to suggest the *facticity of its being delivered over.* The "that it is and has to be" which is disclosed in Dasein's state-of-mind is not the same "that-it-is" which expresses ontologico-categorially the factuality belonging to presence-at-hand. This factuality becomes accessible only if we ascertain it by looking at it. The "that-it-is" which is disclosed in Dasein's state-of-mind must rather be conceived as an existential attribute of the entity which has Being-in-the-world as its way of Being. *Facticity is not the factuality of the factum brutum of something present-at-hand, but a characteristic of Dasein's Being—one which has been taken up into existence, even if proximally it has been thrust aside.* The "that-it-is" of facticity never becomes something that we can come across by beholding it. . . .

A mood assails us. It comes neither from "outside" nor from "inside," but arises out of Being-in-the-world, as a way of such Being. But with the negative distinction between state-of-mind and the reflective apprehending of something "within," we have thus reached a positive insight into their character as disclosure. *The mood has already disclosed, in every case, Being-in-the-world as a whole, and makes it possible first of all to direct oneself towards something.* Having a mood is not related to the psychical in the first instance, and is not itself an inner condition which then reaches forth in an enigmatical way and puts its mark on Things and persons. It is in this that the *second* essential characteristic of states-of-mind shows itself. We have seen that the world, Dasein-with, and existence are *equiprimordially disclosed*; and state-of-mind is a basic existential species of their disclosedness, because this disclosedness itself is essentially Being-in-the-world.

Besides these two essential characteristics of states-of-mind which have been explained—the disclosing of throwness and the current disclosing of Being-in-the-world as a whole—we have to notice a *third*, which contributes above all towards a more penetrating understanding of the worldhood of the world. As we have said earlier, the world which has already been disclosed beforehand permits what is within-the-world to be encountered. This prior disclosedness of the world belongs to Being-in and is partly constituted by one's state-of-mind. Letting something be encountered is primarily *circumspective*; it is not just sensing something, or staring at it. It implies circumspective concern, and has the character of becoming affected in some way; we can see this more precisely from the standpoint of state-of-mind. But to be affected by the unserviceable, resistant, or threatening character of that which is ready-to-hand, becomes ontologically possible only in so far as Being-in as such has been determined existentially beforehand in such a manner that what it encounters within-the-world can *"matter"* to it in this way. The fact that this sort of thing can "matter" to it is grounded in one's state-of-mind; and as a state-of-mind it has already disclosed the world—as something by which it can be threatened, for instance. Only something which is in the state-of-mind of fearing (or fearlessness) can discover that what is environmentally ready-to-hand is threatening. Dasein's openness to the world is constituted existentially by the attunement of a state-of-mind. . . .

§31. *Being-there as Understanding*

State-of-mind is *one* of the existential structures in which the Being of the "there" maintains itself. Equiprimordial with it in constituting this Being is *understanding*. A state-of-mind always has its understanding, even if it merely keeps it suppressed. Understanding always has its mood. . . .

When we are talking ontically we sometimes use the expression "understanding something" with the signification of "being able to manage something," "being a match for it," "being competent to do something." In understanding, as an *existentiale*, that which we have such competence over is not a "what," but Being as existing. The kind of Being which Dasein has, as potentiality-for-Being, lies existentially in understanding. Dasein is not something present-at-hand which possesses its competence for something by way of an extra; it is primarily Being-possible. Dasein is in every case what it can be, and in the way in which it is its possibility. The Being-possible which is essential for Dasein, pertains to the ways of its solicitude for Others and of its concern with the "world," as we have characterized them; and in all these, and always, it pertains to Dasein's potentiality-for-Being towards itself, for the sake of itself. The Being-possible which Dasein is existentially in every case, is to be sharply distinguished both from empty logical possibility and from the contingency of something present-at-hand, so far as with the present-at-hand this or that can "come to pass." As a modal category of presence-at-hand, possibility signifies what is *not yet* actual and what is *not at any time* necessary. It characterizes the *merely* possible. Ontologically it is on a lower level than actuality and necessity. On the other hand, possibility as an *existentiale* is the most primordial and ultimate positive way in which Dasein is characterized ontologically. As with existentiality in general, we can, in the first instance, only prepare for the problem of possibility. The phenomenal basis for seeing it at all is provided by the understanding as a disclosive potentiality-for-Being.

Possibility, as an *existentiale*, does not signify a free-floating potentiality-for-Being in the sense of the 'liberty of indifference' (*libertas indifferentiae*). In every case Dasein, as essentially having a state-of-mind, has already got itself into definite possibilities. As the potentiality-for-Being which is *is*, it has let such possibilities pass by; it is constantly waiving the possibilities of its Being, or else it seizes upon them and makes mistakes. But this means that Dasein is Being-possible which has been delivered over to itself— *thrown possibility* through and through. Dasein is the possibility of Being-free *for* its ownmost potentiality-for-Being. Its Being-possible is transparent to itself in different possible ways and degrees. . . .

Why does the understanding—whatever may be the essential dimensions of that which can be disclosed in it—always press forward into possibilities?

It is because the understanding has in itself the existential structure which we call "*projection.*" With equal primordiality the understanding projects Dasein's Being both upon its "for-the-sake-of-which" and upon significance, as the worldhood of its current world. The character of understanding as projection is constitutive for Being-in-the-world with regard to the disclosedness of its existentially constitutive state-of-Being by which the factical potentiality-for-Being gets its leeway. And as thrown, Dasein is thrown into the kind of Being which we call "projecting." Projecting has nothing to do with comporting oneself towards a plan that has been thought out, and in accordance with which Dasein arranges its Being. On the contrary, any Dasein has, as Dasein, already projected itself; and as long as it is, it is projecting. As long as it is, Dasein always has understood itself and always will understand itself in terms of possibilities. Furthermore, the character of understanding as projection is such that the understanding does not grasp thematically that upon which it projects—that is to say, possibilities. Grasping it in such a manner would take away from what is projected its very character as a possibility, and would reduce it to the given contents which we have in mind; whereas projection, in throwing, throws before itself the possibility as possibility, and lets it *be* as such. As projecting, understanding is the kind of Being of Dasein in which it *is* its possibilities.

Because of the kind of Being which is constituted by the *existentiale* of projection, Dasein is constantly "more" than it factually is, supposing that one might want to make an inventory of it as something-at-hand and list the contents of its Being, and supposing that one were able to do so. But Dasein is never more than it factically is, for to its facticity its potentiality-for-Being belongs essentially. Yet as Being-possible, moreover, Dasein is never anything less; that is to say, it *is* existentially that which, in its potentiality-for-Being, it is *not yet.* Only because the Being of the "there" receives its Constitution through understanding and through the character of understanding as projection, only because it *is* what it becomes (or alternatively, does not become), can it say to itself "Become what you are," and say this with understanding. . . .

§32. *Understanding and Interpretation*
As understanding, Dasein projects its Being upon possibilities. This *Being-towards-possibilities* which understands is itself a potentiality-for-Being, and it is so because of the way these possibilities, as disclosed, exert their counter-thrust upon Dasein. The projecting of the understanding has its own possibility—that of developing itself. This development of the understanding we call "interpretation." In it the understanding appropriates understandingly that which is understood by it. In interpretation, understanding does not become something different. It becomes itself. Such

interpretation is grounded existentially in understanding; the latter does not arise from the former. Nor is interpretation the acquiring of information about what is understood; it is rather the working-out of possibilities projecting in understanding. In accordance with the trend of these preparatory analyses of everyday Dasein, we shall pursue the phenomenon of interpretation in understanding the world—that is, in inauthentic understanding, and indeed in the mode of its genuineness.

In terms of the significance which is disclosed in understanding the world, concernful Being-alongside the ready-to-hand gives itself to understand whatever involvement that which is encountered can have. To say that "circumspection discovers" means that the "world" which has already been understood comes to be interpreted. The ready-to-hand comes *explicitly* into the sight which understands. All preparing, putting to rights, repairing, improving, rounding-out, are accomplished in the following way: we take apart in its "in-order-to" that which is circumspectively ready-to-hand, and we concern ourselves with it in accordance with what becomes visible through this process. That which has been circumspectively taken apart with regard to its "in-order-to," and taken apart as such—that which is *explicitly* understood—has the structure of *something as something*. The circumspective question as to what this particular thing that is ready-to-hand may be, receives the circumspectively interpretative answer that it is for such and such a purpose. If we tell what it is for, we are not simply designating something; but that which is designated is understood *as* that *as* which we are to take the thing in question. That which is disclosed in understanding—that which is understood—is already accessible in such a way that its "as which" can be made to stand out explicitly. The "as" makes up the structure of the explicitness of something that is understood. It constitutes the interpretation. In dealing with what is environmentally ready-to-hand by interpreting it circumspectively, we "see" it *as* a table, a door, a carriage, or a bridge; but what we have thus interpreted need not necessarily be also taken apart by making an assertion which definitely characterizes it. Any mere prepredicative seeing of the ready-to-hand is, in itself, something which already understands and interprets. . . .

But if we never perceive equipment that is ready-to-hand without already understanding and interpreting it, and if such perception lets us circumspectively encounter something as something, does this not mean that in the first instance we have experienced something purely present-at-hand, and then taken it *as* a door, *as* a house? This would be a misunderstanding of the specific way in which interpretation functions as disclosure. In interpreting, we do not, so to speak, throw a "signification" over some naked thing which is present-at-hand, we do not stick a value on it; but when something within-the-world is encountered as such, the thing in question already has an involvement which is disclosed in our understanding of the world, and this involvement is one which gets laid out by the interpretation. . . .

§38. *Falling and Thrownness*

Idle talk, curiosity and ambiguity characterize the way in which, in an everyday manner, Dasein is its "there"—the disclosedness of Being-in-the-world. As definite existential characteristics, these are not present-at-hand in Dasein, but help to make up its Being. In these, and in the way they are interconnected in their Being, there is revealed a basic kind of Being which belongs to everydayness; we call this the "*falling*" of Dasein.

This term does not express any negative evaluation, but is used to signify that Dasein is proximally and for the most part *alongside* the "world" of its concern. This "absorption in . . . " has mostly the character of Being-lost in the publicness of the "they." Dasein has, in the first instance, fallen away from itself as an authentic potentiality for Being its Self, and has fallen into the "world." "Fallenness" into the "world" means an absorption in Being-with-one-another, in so far as the latter is guided by idle talk, curiosity, and ambiguity. Through the Interpretation of falling, what we have called the "inauthenticity" of Dasein may now be defined more precisely. On no account, however, do the terms "inauthentic" and "non-authentic" signify "really not," as if in this mode of Being, Dasein were altogether to lose its Being. "Inauthenticity" does not mean anything like Being-no-longer-in-the-world, but amounts rather to a quite distinctive kind of Being-in-the-world—the kind which is completely fascinated by the "world" and by the Dasein-with of Others in the 'they'. Not-Being-its-self functions as a *positive* possibility of that entity which, in its essential concern, is absorbed in a world. This kind of *not-Being* has to be conceived as that kind of Being which is closest to Dasein and in which Dasein maintains itself for the most part. . . .

Dasein, tranquillized, and "understanding" everything, . . . drifts along towards an alienation in which its ownmost potentiality-for-Being is hidden from it. Falling Being-in-the-world is not only tempting and tranquillizing; it is at the same time *alienating.*

Yet this alienation cannot mean that Dasein gets factically torn away from itself. On the contrary, this alienation drives it into a kind of Being which borders on the most exaggerated "self-dissection," tempting itself with all possibilities of explanation, so that the very "characterologies" and "typologies" which it has brought about are themselves already becoming something that cannot be surveyed at a glance. This alienation *closes off* from Dasein its authenticity and possibility, even if only the possibility of genuinely foundering. It does not, however, surrender Dasein to an entity which Dasein itself is not, but forces it into its inauthenticity—into a possi-

Anxiety

ble kind of Being *of itself.* The alienation of falling—at once tempting and tranquillizing—leads by its own movement, to Dasein's getting *entangled* in itself.

The phenomena we have pointed out—temptation, tranquillizing, alienation and self-entangling (entanglement)—characterize the specific kind of Being which belongs to falling. This 'movement' of Dasein in its own Being, we call its *"downward plunge"* Dasein plunges out of itself into itself, into the groundlessness and nullity of inauthentic everydayness. But this plunge remains hidden from Dasein by the way things have been publicly interpreted, so much so, indeed, that it gets interpreted as a way of "ascending" and "living concretely."

This downward plunge into and within the groundlessness of the inauthentic Being of the 'they', has a kind of motion which constantly tears the understanding away from the projecting of authentic possibilities, and into the tranquillized supposition that it possesses everything, or that everything is within its reach. Since the understanding is thus constantly torn away from authenticity and into the "they" (though always with a sham of authenticity), the movement of falling is characterized by *turbulence.* . . .

In falling, nothing other than our potentiality-for-Being-in-world is the issue, even if in the mode of inauthenticity. Dasein *can* fall only *because* Being-in-the-world understandingly with a state-of-mind is an issue for it. On the other hand, *authentic* existence is not something which floats above falling everydayness; existentially, it is only a modified way in which such everydayness is seized upon.

The phenomenon of falling does not give us something like a "night view" of Dasein, a property which occurs ontically and may serve to round out the innocuous aspects of this entity. Falling reveals an *essential* ontological structure of Dasein itself. . . .

Chapter 6. Care as the Being of Dasein

§40. The Basic State-of-mind Befindlichkeit *of Anxiety as a Distinctive Way in which Dasein is Disclosed*

Since our aim is to proceed towards the Being of the totality of the structural whole, we shall take as our point of departure the concrete analyses of falling which we have just carried through. Dasein's absorption in the 'they' and its absorption in the 'world' of its concern, make manifest something like a *fleeing* of Dasein in the face of itself—of itself as an authentic potentiality-for-Being-its-Self. This phenomenon of Dasein's fleeing *in the face of itself* and in the face of its authenticity, seems at least a suitable phenomenal basis for the following investigation. But to bring itself face to face with itself, is precisely what Dasein does *not* do when it thus flees. It turns *away from* itself in accordance with its ownmost inertia of falling. In investigating such phenomena, however, we must be careful not to confuse ontico-existentiell characterization with ontologico-existential Interpretation nor may we overlook the positive phenomenal bases provided for this Interpretation by such a characterization.

From an existentiell point of view, the authenticity of Being-one's-Self has of course been closed off and thrust aside in falling; but to be thus closed off is merely the *privation* of a disclosedness which manifests itself phenomenally in the fact that Dasein's fleeing is a fleeing *in the face of itself.* That in the face of which Dasein flees, is precisely what Dasein comes up "behind." Only to the extent that Dasein has been brought before itself in an ontologically essential manner through whatever disclosedness belongs to it, *can* it flee *in the face of* that in the face of which it flees. . . .

That in the face of which one has anxiety is Being-in-the-world as such. What is the difference phenomenally between that in the face of which anxiety is anxious and that in the face of which fear is afraid? That in the face of which one has anxiety is not an entity within-the-world. Thus it is essentially incapable of having an involvement. This threatening does not have the character of a definite detrimentality which reaches what is threatened, and which reaches it with definite regard to a special factical potentiality-for-Being. That in the face of which one is anxious is completely indefinite. Not only does this indefiniteness leave factically undecided which entity within-the-world is threatening us, but it also tells us that entities within-the-world are not 'relevant' at all. Nothing which is ready-to-hand or present-at-hand within the world functions as that in the face of which anxiety is anxious. Here the totality of involvements of the ready-to-hand and the present-at-hand discovered within-the-world, is, as such, of no consequence; it collapses into itself; the world has the character of completely lacking significance. In anxiety one does not encounter this thing or that thing which, as something threatening, must have an involvement. . . .

In that in the face of which one has anxiety, the "It is nothing and nowhere" becomes manifest. The obstinacy of the "nothing and nowhere within-the-world" means as a phenomenon that *the world as such is that in the face of which one has anxiety.* The utter insignificance which makes itself known in the "nothing and nowhere," does not signify that the world is absent, but tells us that entities within-the-world are of so little importance in themselves that on the basis of this *insignificance* of what is within-the-world, the world in its worldhood is all that still obtrudes itself.

What oppresses us is not this or that, nor is it the summation of everything present-at-hand; it is rather the *possibility* of the ready-to-hand in general; that is to say, it is the world itself. When anxiety has subsided, then in our everyday way of talking we are accustomed to say that "it was really nothing." . . . If the "nothing"—that is, the world as such—exhibits itself as that in the face of which one has anxiety, this means that *Being-in-the-world itself is that in the face of which anxiety is anxious.*

Being-anxious discloses, primordially and directly, the world as world. It is not the case, say, that the world first gets thought of by deliberating about it, just by itself, without regard for the entities within-the-world, and that, in the face of this world, anxiety then arises; what is rather the case is that the *world as world* is disclosed first and foremost by anxiety, as a mode of state-of-mind. . . .

Anxiety is not only anxiety in the face of something, but, as a state-of-mind, it is also *anxiety about* something. That which anxiety is profoundly anxious about is not a *definite* kind of Being for Dasein or a *definite* possibility for it. Indeed the threat itself is indefinite, and therefore cannot penetrate threateningly to this or that factically concrete potentiality-for-Being. That which anxiety is anxious about is Being-in-the world itself. In anxiety what is environmentally ready-to-hand sinks away, and so, in general, do entities within-the-world. The "world" can offer nothing more, and neither can the Dasein-with of Others. Anxiety thus takes away from Dasein the possibility of understanding itself, as it falls, in terms of the "world" and the way things have been publicly interpreted. Anxiety throws Dasein back upon that which it is anxious about—its authentic potentiality-for-Being-in-the-world. Anxiety individualizes Dasein for its ownmost Being-in-the-world, which as something that understands, projects itself essentially upon possibilities. Therefore, with that which it is anxious about, anxiety discloses Dasein *as Being-possible,* and indeed as the only kind of thing which it can be of its own accord as something individualized in individualization.

Anxiety makes manifest in Dasein its *Being towards* its ownmost potentiality-for-Being—that is, its *Being-free for* the freedom of choosing itself and taking hold of itself. Anxiety brings Dasein face to face with its *Being-free for (propensio in . . .)* the authenticity of its Being, and for this authenticity as a possibility which it always is. But at the same time, this is the Being to which Dasein as Being-in-the-world has been delivered over.

That *about which* anxiety is anxious reveals itself as that *in the face of which* it is anxious—namely, Being-in-the-world. The selfsameness of that in the face of which and that about which one has anxiety, extends even to anxiousness itself. For, as a state-of-mind, anxiousness is a basic kind of Being-in-the-world. *Here the disclosure and the disclosed are existentially selfsame in such a way that in the latter the world has been disclosed as world, and Being-in has been disclosed as a potentiality-for-Being which is individualized, pure, and thrown; this makes it plain that with the phenomenon of anxiety a distinctive state-of-mind has become a theme for Interpretation.* Anxiety individu-

alizes Dasein and thus discloses it as "*solus ipse.*" But this existential "solip-
sism" is so far from the displacement of putting an isolated subject-Thing
into the innocuous emptiness of a worldless occurring, that in an extreme
sense what it does is precisely to bring Dasein face to face with its world as
world, and thus bring it face to face with itself as Being-in-the-world.

Again everyday discourse and the everyday interpretation of Dasein furnish our most unbiased evidence that anxiety as a basic state-of-mind is disclosive in the manner we have shown. As we have said earlier, a state-of-
mind makes manifest "how one is." In anxiety one feels "*uncanny.*" Here the
peculiar indefiniteness of that which Dasein finds itself alongside in anxiety,
comes proximally to expression: the "nothing and nowhere." But here "uncanniness" also means "not-being-at-home. . . ." Unheimlich

§41. Dasein's Being as Care

Dasein is an entity for which, in its Being, that Being is an issue. The phrase
"is an issue" has been made plain in the state-of-Being of understanding—
of understanding as self-projective Being towards its ownmost potentiality-
for-Being. This potentiality is that for the sake of which any Dasein is as it
is. In each case Dasein has already compared itself, in its Being, with a possibility of itself. Being-free *for* one's ownmost potentiality-for-Being, and
therewith for the possibility of authenticity and inauthenticity, is shown,
with a primordial, elemental concreteness, in anxiety. But ontologically,
Being towards one's ownmost potentiality-for-Being means that in each case
Dasein is already *ahead* of itself in its Being. Dasein is always "beyond itself" not as a way of behaving towards other entities which it is *not*, but as
Being towards the potentiality-for-Being which it is itself. This structure of
Being, which belongs to the essential 'is an issue', we shall denote as Da-
sein's "*Being-ahead-of-itself.* . . ."

The formally existential totality of Dasein's ontological structural whole
must therefore be grasped in the following structure: the Being of Dasein
means ahead-of-itself-Being-already-in-(the world) as Being-alongside (entities encountered within-the-world). This Being fills in the signification of
the term 'care'. . . .

DIVISION TWO: DASEIN AND TEMPORALITY

Chapter 1. Dasein's Possibility of Being-a-whole, and Being-toward-death

§47. The Possibility of Experiencing the Death of Others

. . . Proximally and for the most part everyday Dasein understands itself in
terms of that with *which* it is customarily concerned. "One is" what one

Dying — Death (ownmost possibility) — over actuality (non-relational not to be outstripped)

does. In relation to this sort of Being (the everyday manner in which we join with one another in absorption in the 'world' of our concern) representability is not only quite possible but is even constitutive for our being with one another. *Here* one Dasein can and must, within certain limits, "*be*" another Dasein.

However, this possibility of representing breaks down completely if the issue is one of representing that possibility-of-Being which makes up Dasein's coming to an end, and which, as such, gives to it its wholeness. *No one can take the Other's dying away from him.* Of course someone can "go to his death for another." But that always means to sacrifice oneself for the Other "*in some definite affair.*" Such "dying for" can never signify that the Other has thus had his death taken away in even the slightest degree. Dying is something that every Dasein itself must take upon itself at the time. By its very essence, death is in every case mine, in so far as it "is" at all. And indeed death signifies a peculiar possibility-of-Being in which the very Being of one's own Dasein is an issue. In dying, it is shown that mineness and existence are ontologically constitutive for death. Dying is not an event; it is a phenomenon to be understood existentially; and it is to be understood in a distinctive sense which must be still more closely delimited.

But if "ending," as dying, is constitutive for Dasein's totality, then the Being of this wholeness itself must be conceived as an existential phenomenon of a Dasein which is in each case one's own. In "ending," and in Dasein's Being-a-whole, for which such ending is constitutive, there is, by its very essence, no representing. These are the facts of the case existentially; one fails to recognize this when one interposes the expedient of making the dying of Others a substitute theme for the analysis of totality. . . .

§50. Preliminary Sketch of the Existential-ontological Structure of Death
. . . Death is a possibility-of-Being which Dasein itself has to take over in every case. With death, Dasein stands before itself in its ownmost potentiality-for-Being. This is a possibility in which the issue is nothing less than Dasein's Being-in-the-world. Its death is the possibility of no-longer being-able-to-be-there. If Dasein stands before itself as this possibility, it has been *fully* assigned to its ownmost potentiality-for-Being. When it stands before itself in this way, all its relations to any other Dasein have been undone. This ownmost nonrelational possibility is at the same time the uttermost one.

As potentiality-for-Being, Dasein cannot outstrip the possibility of death. Death is the possibility of the absolute impossibility of Dasein. Thus death reveals itself as that *possibility which is one's ownmost, which is nonrelational, and which is not to be outstripped.* As such, death is something *distinctively* impending. Its existential possibility is based on the fact that Dasein is essentially disclosed to itself, and disclosed, indeed, as ahead-of-itself. This item in the structure of care has its most primordial concretion in Being-towards-death. As a phenomenon, Being-towards-the-end becomes plainer as Being towards that distinctive possibility of Dasein which we have characterized. . . .

§51. Being-towards-death and the Everydayness of Dasein

. . . The analysis of the phrase "one dies" reveals unambiguously the kind of Being which belongs to everyday Being-towards-death. In such a way of talking, death is understood as an indefinite something which, above all, must duly arrive from somewhere or other, but which is proximally *not yet present-at-hand* for oneself, and is therefore no threat. The expression "one dies" spreads abroad the opinion that what gets reached, as it were, by death, is the "they." In Dasein's public way of interpreting, it is said that 'one dies', because everyone else and oneself can talk himself into saying that "in no case is it I myself," for this "one" is *the "nobody."* "Dying" is levelled off to an occurrence which reaches Dasein, to be sure, but belongs to nobody in particular. If idle talk is always ambiguous, so is this manner of talking about death. Dying, which is essentially mine in such a way that no one can be my representative, is perverted into an event of public occurrence which the "they" encounters. In the way of talking which we have characterized, death is spoken of as a "case" which is constantly occurring. Death gets passed off as always something "actual"; its character as a possibility gets concealed, and so are the other two items that belong to it—the fact that it is non-relational and that it is not to be outstripped. By such ambiguity, Dasein puts itself in the position of losing itself in the "they" as regards a distinctive potentiality-for-Being which belongs to Dasein's ownmost Self. The "they" gives its approval, and aggravates the *temptation* to cover up from oneself one's ownmost Being-towards-death. This evasive concealment in the face of death dominates everydayness so stubbornly that, in Being with one another, the "neighbors" often still keep talking the "dying person" into the belief that he will escape death and soon return to the tranquillized everydayness of the world of his concern. Such "solicitude" is meant to "console" him. It insists upon bringing him back into Dasein, while in addition it helps him to keep his ownmost non-relational possibility-of-Being completely concealed. In this manner the "they" provides *a constant tranquillization about death*. At bottom, however, this is a tranquillization not only for him who is "dying" but just as much for those who "console" him. And even in the case of a demise, the public is still not to have its own tranquillity upset by such an event, or be disturbed in the carefreeness with which it concerns itself. Indeed the dying of Others is seen

not ownmost

not as possibility

often enough as a social inconvenience, if not even a downright tactlessness, against which the public is to be guarded.

But along with this tranquillization, which forces Dasein away from its death, the "they" at the same time puts itself in the right and makes itself respectable by tacitly regulating the way in which *one* has to comport oneself towards death. It is already a matter of public acceptance that "thinking about death" is a cowardly fear, a sign of insecurity on the part of Dasein, and a somber way of fleeing from the world. *The "they" does not permit us the courage for anxiety in the face of death.* The dominance of the manner in which things have been publicly interpreted by the "they," has already decided what state-of-mind is to determine our attitude towards death. In anxiety in the face of death, Dasein is brought face to face with itself as delivered over to that possibility which is not to be outstripped. The "they" concerns itself with transforming this anxiety into fear in the face of an oncoming event. In addition, the anxiety which has been made ambiguous as fear, is passed off as a weakness with which no self-assured Dasein may have any acquaintance. What is "fitting" according to the unuttered decree of the "they," is indifferent tranquillity as to the "fact" that one dies. The cultivation of such a "superior" indifference *alienates* Dasein from its ownmost nonrelational potentiality-for-Being.

But the temptation, tranquillization, and alienation are distinguishing marks of the kind of Being called *"falling."* As falling, everyday Being-towards-death is a constant *fleeing in the face of death.* Being-*towards*-the-end has the mode of *evasion in the face of it*—giving new explanations for it, understanding it inauthentically, and concealing it. Factically one's own Dasein is always dying already; that is to say, it is in a Being-towards-its-end. And it hides this Fact from itself by recoining "death" as just a "case of death" in Others—an everyday occurrence which, if need be, gives us the assurance still more plainly that 'oneself' is still 'living'. But in thus falling and fleeing *in the face of death,* Dasein's everydayness attests that the very "they" itself already has the definite character of *Being-towards-death,* even when it is not explicitly engaged in "thinking about death." *Even in average everydayness, this ownmost potentiality-for-Being, which is nonrelational and not to be outstripped, is constantly an issue for Dasein. This is the case when its concern is merely in the mode of an untroubled indifference* towards *the uttermost possibility of existent.* . . .

§53. Existential Projection of an Authentic Being-towards-death

. . . Being towards this possibility, as Being-towards-death, is so to comport ourselves towards *death* that in this Being, and for it, death reveals itself *as a possibility.* Our terminology for such Being towards this possibility is *"anticipation"* of this possibility. . . .

The more unveiledly this possibility gets understood, the more purely does the understanding penetrate into it *as the possibility of the impossibility of any existence of all.* Death, as possibility, gives Dasein nothing to be "actualized," nothing which Dasein, as actual, could itself *be.* It is the possibility of the impossibility of every way of comporting oneself towards anything, of every way of existing. In the anticipation of this possibility it becomes "greater and greater"; that is to say, the possibility reveals itself to be such that it knows no measure at all, no more or less, but signifies the possibility of the measureless impossibility of existence. In accordance with its essence, this possibility offers no support for becoming intent on something, "picturing" to oneself the actuality which is possible, and so forgetting its possibility. Being-towards-death, as anticipation of possibility, is what first *makes* this possibility *possible,* and sets it free as possibility.

Being-towards-death is the anticipation of a potentiality-for-Being of that entity whose kind of Being is anticipation itself. In the anticipatory revealing of this potentiality-for-Being, Dasein discloses itself to itself as regards its uttermost possibility. But to project itself on its ownmost potentiality-for-Being means to be able to understand itself in the Being of the entity so revealed—namely, to exist. Anticipation turns out to be the possibility of understanding one's *ownmost* and uttermost potentiality-for-Being—that is to say, the possibility of *authentic existence.* The ontological constitution of such existence must be made visible by setting forth the concrete structure of anticipation of death. How are we to delimit this structure phenomenally? Manifestly, we must do so by determining those characteristics which must belong to an anticipatory disclosure so that it can become the pure understanding of that ownmost possibility which is non-relational and not to be outstripped—which is certain and, as such, indefinite. It must be noted that understanding does not primarily mean just gazing at a meaning, but rather understanding oneself in that potentiality-for-Being which reveals itself in projection.

Death is Dasein's *ownmost* possibility. Being towards this possibility discloses to Dasein its *ownmost* potentiality-for-Being, in which its very Being is the issue. Here it can become manifest to Dasein that in this distinctive possibility of its own self, it has been wrenched away from the 'they'. This means that in anticipation any Dasein can have wrenched itself away from the 'they' already. But when one understands that this is something which Dasein 'can' have done, this only reveals its factical lostness in the everydayness of the they-self.

The ownmost possibility is *nonrelational.* Anticipation allows Dasein to understand that that potentiality-for-being in which its ownmost Being is an issue, must be taken over by Dasein alone. Death does not just "belong" to one's own Dasein in an undifferentiated way; death *lays claim* to it as an *indi-*

vidual Dasein. The non-relational character of death, as understood in anticipation, individualizes Dasein down to itself. This individualizing is a way in
which the 'there' is disclosed for existence. It makes manifest that all Being-
alongside the things with which we concern ourselves, and all Being-with
Others, will fail us when our ownmost potentiality-for-Being is the issue.
Dasein can be *authentically itself* only if it makes this possible for itself of its
own accord. . . .

The ownmost, non-relational possibility is *not to be outstripped.* Being towards this possibility enables Dasein to understand that giving itself up im-
pends for it as the uttermost possibility of its existence. Anticipation, however, unlike inauthentic Being-towards-death, does not evade the fact that
death is not to be outstripped; instead, anticipation frees itself *for* accepting
this. When, by anticipation, one becomes free *for* one's own death, one is liberated from one's lostness in those possibilities which may accidentally
thrust themselves upon one; and one is liberated in such a way that for the
first time one can authentically understand and choose among the factical
possibilities lying ahead of that possibility which is not to be outstripped.
Anticipation discloses to existence that its uttermost possibility lies in giving
itself up, and thus it shatters all one's tenaciousness to whatever existence
one has reached. In anticipation, Dasein guards itself against falling back behind itself, or behind the potentiality-for-Being which it has understood. It
guards itself against "becoming too old for its victories" (Nietzsche). It is
free for its ownmost possibilities, which are determined by the *end* and so are
understood as *finite.* . . .

We may now summarize our characterization of authentic Being-
towards-death as we have projected it existentially: *anticipation reveals to Dasein its lostness in the they-self, and brings it face to face with the possibility of
being itself,* primarily unsupported by concernful solicitude, but of being itself,
rather in an *impassioned* freedom towards death—*a freedom which has been released from the Illusions of the 'they', and which is factical, certain of itself, and
anxious.* . . .

Chapter 2. Authenticity and Resoluteness

§60. The Existential Structure of this Authentic Potentiality for-Being
In resoluteness we have now arrived at that truth of Dasein which is most
primordial because it is *authentic.* Whenever a "there" is disclosed, its whole
Being-in-the-world—that is to say, the world, Being-in, and the Self which,
as an 'I am', this entity is—is disclosed with equal primordiality. Whenever
the world is disclosed, entities within-the-world have been discovered already. The discoveredness of the ready-to-hand and the present-at-hand is

based on the disclosedness of the world, for if the current totality of involvements is to be freed, this requires that significance be understood beforehand. In understanding significance, concernful Dasein submits itself
circumspectively to what it encounters as ready-to-hand. Any discovering of
a totality of involvements goes back to a "for-the-sake-of-which"; and on
the understanding of such a "for-the-sake-of-which" is based in turn the
understanding of significance as the disclosedness of the current world. In
seeking shelter, sustenance, livelihood, we do so "for the sake of" constant
possibilities of Dasein which are very close to it; upon these the entity for
which its own Being is an issue, has already projected itself. Thrown into its
"there," every Dasein has been factically submitted to a definite "world"—
its "world." At the same time those factical projections which are closest to
it, have been guided by its concernful *lostness* in the "they." To this lostness,
one's own Dasein can appeal, and this appeal can be understood in the way
of resoluteness. But in that case this *authentic* disclosedness modifies with
equal primordiality both the way in which the "world" is discovered (and
this is founded upon that disclosedness) and the way in which the Dasein-
with of Others is disclosed. The "world" which is ready-to-hand does not
become another one "in its content," nor does the circle of Others get exchanged for a new one; but both one's Being towards the ready-to-hand understandingly and concernfully, and one's solicitous Being with Others, are
now given a definite character in terms of their ownmost potentiality-for-
Being-their-Selves.

Resoluteness, as *authentic Being-one's-Self,* does not detach Dasein from
its world, nor does it isolate it so that it becomes a free-floating "I." And
how should it, when resoluteness as authentic disclosedness, is *authentically*
nothing else than *Being-in-the-world*? Resoluteness brings the Self right into
its current concernful Being-alongside what is ready-to-hand, and pushes it
into solicitous Being with Others.

In the light of the "for-the-sake-of-which" of one's self-chosen
potentiality-for-Being, resolute Dasein frees itself for its world. Dasein's
resoluteness towards itself is what first makes it possible to let the Others
who are with it 'be' in their ownmost potentiality-for-Being, and to co-
disclose this potentiality in the solicitude which leaps forth and liberates.
When Dasein is resolute, it can become the "conscience" of Others. Only by
authentically Being-their-Selves in resoluteness can people authentically be
with one another—not by ambiguous and jealous stipulations and talkative
fraternizing in the 'they' and in what 'they' want to undertake.

Resoluteness, by its ontological essence, is always the resoluteness of some
factical Dasein at a particular time. The essence of Dasein as an entity is its
existence. Resoluteness "exists" only as a resolution which understandingly
projects itself. But on what basis does Dasein disclose itself in resoluteness?

On what is it to resolve? *Only* the resolution itself can give the answer. One would completely misunderstand the phenomenon of resoluteness if one should want to suppose that this consists simply in taking up possibilities which have been proposed and recommended, and seizing hold of them. *The resolution is precisely the disclosive projection and determination of what is factically possible at the time.* To resoluteness, the *indefiniteness* characteristic of every potentiality-for-Being into which Dasein has been factically thrown, is something that necessarily *belongs.* Only in a resolution is resoluteness sure of itself. The *existentiell indefiniteness* of resoluteness never makes itself definite except in a resolution; yet it has, all the same, its *existential definiteness.*

What one resolves upon in resoluteness has been prescribed ontologically in the existentiality of Dasein in general as a potentiality-for-Being in the manner of concernful solicitude. As care, however, Dasein has been Determined by facticity and falling. Disclosed in its "there," it maintains itself both in truth and in untruth with equal primordiality. This "really" holds in particular for resoluteness as authentic truth. Resoluteness appropriates untruth authentically. Dasein is already in irresoluteness and soon, perhaps, will be in it again. The term "irresoluteness" merely expresses that phenomenon which we have Interpreted as a Being-surrendered to the way in which things have been prevalently interpreted by the "they." Dasein, as a they-self, gets "lived" by the common-sense ambiguity of that publicness in which nobody resolves upon anything but which has always made its decision. "Resoluteness" signifies letting oneself be summoned out of one's lostness in the "they." The irresoluteness of the "they" remains dominant notwithstanding, but it cannot impugn resolute existence. In the counter-concept to irresoluteness, as resoluteness as existentially understood, we do not have in mind any ontico–psychical characteristic in the sense of Being-burdened with inhibitions. Even resolutions remain dependent upon the "they" and its world. The understanding of this is one of the things that a resolution discloses, inasmuch as resoluteness is what first gives authentic transparency to Dasein. In resoluteness the issue for Dasein is its ownmost potentiality-for-Being, which, as something thrown, can project itself only upon definite factical possibilities. Resolution does not withdraw itself from "actuality," but discovers first what is factically possible; and it does so by seizing upon it in whatever way is possible for it as its ownmost potentiality-for-Being in the 'they'. . . .

Chapter 3. Temporality as the Ontological Meaning of Care

§62. Anticipatory Resoluteness and Existentiell Authenticity

. . . The phenomenon of resoluteness has brought us before the primordial *truth* of existence. As resolute, Dasein is revealed to itself in its current factical potentiality-for-Being, and in such a way that Dasein itself *is* this revealing and Being-revealed. To any truth, there belongs a corresponding holding-for-true. The explicit appropriating of what has been disclosed or discovered is *Being*-certain. The primordial truth of existence demands an equiprimordial Being-certain, in which one maintains oneself in what resoluteness discloses. It *gives* itself the current factical Situation, and *brings* itself into that Situation. The Situation cannot be calculated in advance or presented like something present-at-hand which is waiting for someone to grasp it. It merely gets disclosed in a free resolving which has not been determined beforehand but is open to the possibility of such determination. *What, then, does the certainty which belongs to such resoluteness signify?* Such certainty must maintain itself in what is disclosed by the resolution. But this means that it simply cannot *become rigid* as regards the Situation, but must understand that the resolution, in accordance with its own meaning as a disclosure, must be *held open* and free for the current factical possibility. The certainty of the resolution signifies that one *holds oneself free for* the possibility of *taking it back*—a possibility which is factically necessary. However, such holding-for-true in resoluteness (as the truth of existence) by no means lets us fall back into irresoluteness. On the contrary, this holding-for-true, as a resolute holding-oneself-free for taking back, is *authentic resoluteness which resolves to keep repeating itself.* . . .

Anticipatory resoluteness is not a way of escape, fabricated for the "overcoming" of death; it is rather that understanding which follows the call of conscience and which frees for death the possibility of acquiring *power* over Dasein's *existence* and of basically dispersing all fugitive Self-concealments. Nor does wanting-to-have-a-conscience, which has been made determinate as Being-towards-death, signify a kind of seclusion in which one flees the world; rather, it brings one without Illusions into the resoluteness of "taking action." Neither does anticipatory resoluteness stem from 'idealistic' exactions soaring above existence and its possibilities; it springs from a sober understanding of what are factically the basic possibilities for Dasein. Along with the sober anxiety which brings us face to face with our individualized potentiality-for-Being, there goes an unshakable joy in this possibility. In it Dasein becomes free from the entertaining "incidentals" with which busy curiosity keeps providing itself—primarily from the events of the world. . .

F

Ppe

Past

Vorlaufen
(Anticipation)

Augenblick
(moment of vision)

Wiederholen
(Repetition)

I

Erwarten
(waiting)

Gegenwärtigen
(making-present)

Vergessenheit
(Forgetting)

Sartre

Jean-Paul Sartre was born in Paris on June 21, 1905. His father died when he was only one, and he was brought up by his mother and grandparents. He graduated from the prestigious École Normale Supérieure in 1929, and for years he taught philosophy at various *lycées* (roughly equivalent to American high schools). It was also in 1929 that he met Simone de Beauvoir, his constant companion and co-worker until his death. During a period of study in Berlin in 1933–34, Sartre discovered phenomenology and wrote his early works, *Nausea* and *The Transcendence of the Ego*. His *Sketch for a Theory of the Emotions* appeared in 1939, followed by *The Psychology of the Imagination* in 1940, and *Being and Nothingness* in 1943. The 1940s also saw the publication of such literary works as *The Wall, The Flies, No Exit,* and *The Age of Reason*. Sartre was imprisoned by the Germans in 1940 (during which time he taught Heidegger to his fellow prisoners), and was active in the Resistance during the war. In 1945, he began editing *Les Temps modernes*, the most important journal for French intellectuals until the 1960s. The same year he delivered his lecture, "The Humanism of Existentialism" (published in 1946), inaugurating the vogue of existentialism. Throughout the 1950s and 1960s Sartre was involved in a number of political movements. He was generally a staunch supporter of communism, though he criticized Stalinism and attacked the Communist Party for not supporting the student uprising of May 1968. In the 1960s Sartre sat with Bertrand Russell on a committee to judge American politicians as war criminals for U.S. involvement in the Vietnam War. Among his many important later works are *Saint Genet* (1952), *Critique of Dialectical Reason* (1960), *The Words* (1963), and *The Idiot of the Family* (three volumes, 1971–72). Sartre did most of his writing in cafés because, he said, the noise and activity helped him concentrate. In 1964 he refused to accept the Nobel Prize for literature as a protest against the way such prizes transform writers into institutions. When he died on April 15, 1980, tens of thousands of people accompanied his coffin to its final resting place.

1. What is Existentialism?

Of the writers whose works appear in this volume, Sartre is the only one who explicitly characterized himself as an existentialist. It is Sartre, in fact, who lays out what is widely accepted as the defining idea in existentialism.

Existence precedes essence

This is the idea that, for humans, *existence precedes essence*: that what we are, and what gives our lives significance, is not pre-established for us, but is something for which we ourselves are responsible. The meaning of this idea is worked out in "The Humanism of Existentialism," where Sartre contrasts existentialism with the traditional view that, for humans, essence precedes existence.

Let us begin by exploring the terminology used to state these ideas. In the Aristotelian scheme, a description of the essence of a thing answers the question: "What kind of a thing is it?" And thus, a thing's essence is made up of the characteristics it has that make it the kind of thing it is—characteristics that cannot be removed without the thing ceasing to be the kind of thing it is. For example, the Aristotelian idea that humans are essentially rational animals implies that in order to be a human, an entity has to be a organism with a certain degree of biological structure and has to have the potential for rational reflection, and if these characteristics were removed from an entity, it would cease to be human.

Sartre thinks that there do exist entities for which their essence precedes their existence. Tools are one example. A tool like a hammer has an essence: it is a tool designed for a particular purpose, driving in nails, and that purpose defines its nature as the particular tool it is. To say that this essence precedes the existence of any particular hammer means that for a thing to exist as a hammer at all, it *must* have this essence—it must be a tool designed for driving in nails. If something doesn't have this essence, if it isn't a tool designed for driving in nails, then it cannot exist as a hammer.

For human beings, by contrast, existence precedes essence. This means, first of all, that there are no characteristics whatsoever that we must have in order for us to exist as human beings. Sartre's view is illuminated by a contrast to the religious belief that God creates human beings as having an essence. In this picture, God has endowed us with certain characteristics that make up our true nature as human beings, for example, the characteristic of having the purpose to glorify God. Now Sartre suggests that this sort of "essentialism" is untenable once we realize the force of Nietzsche's claim that God is dead. He thinks that if there is no "absolute" lying above or beyond the world, if there is no transcendent First Cause or Rational Principle governing the universe, then it becomes difficult to see how there could be a pre-established set of characteristics that determines our true nature and proper function on earth. And this leads to Sartre's radical rejection of essentialism: his claim that, for human beings, existence precedes essence. "If God does not exist," he says, "there is at least one being in whom existence precedes essence, and . . . this being is man, or, as Heidegger says, human reality." Sartre thinks that humans initially just exist: they show up on the scene; they just appear one day in the midst of beings, with no fixed characteristics or plan determining what they are or what they ought to be. And thus, there is no Form of Humanity or proper function of humans, no genetic code or neurophysiology that fixes our identity in one specific set of traits or accomplishments rather than others. Sartre expresses this idea dramatically by saying that humans find themselves "forlorn" in a world that is not of their choosing; they are "abandoned" in the midst of beings, with no pregiven nature or identity that gives purpose to their lives.

Once we exist, however, it is up to each one of us to create an essence for ourselves through our actions. Specifically, we create an essence for ourselves through our "projects," life-defining plans that we freely choose. In Sartre's view we do not create a single essence for human beings as a whole in this way, but rather by deciding on projects each individual creates an essence just for him or herself. It is therefore up to each one of us to shape his or her own individual identity and defining traits by choosing projects. And thus, each human being is a self-making or self-constituting being: we are what we make of ourselves throughout our lives.

In "The Humanism of Existentialism" Sartre says of a human being that "at first he is nothing, . . . only afterward will he be something, and he himself will have made what he will be." Because we enter the world with no determinate characteristics that make us one kind of thing rather than another, we are initially nothing in particular. If I have a small frame by nature, or if I come from a bad part of town, those traits by themselves do not determine that I have to be, say, a coward or a loser. For I always have the ability to take a particular stand on my traits and transform them through my actions. Even if I am short and thin, I can stand up to bigger kids and refuse to be pushed around. I can learn martial arts and become stronger through exercise. If I have come from a poor family, I can make an effort to learn the social graces needed to be at ease in high society. Or, to take Sartre's example, no one can simply be a coward (as, say, a glass simply is brittle). "There is no such thing as a cowardly constitution." If a person is a coward, it is because he has made himself a coward by backing down or running away when faced by threatening situations—"he has made himself a coward by his acts."

Sartre's point, then, is that I always have the ability to rise above my condition and transform it through my actions. This is what he means when he says, "Man is nothing else but what he makes of himself." My essence or identity as a human is not something forced upon me; it is something I make in my actions. And so: "Man . . . exists only to the extent that he fulfills himself; he is therefore nothing else than the ensemble of his acts, nothing else than his life."

The idea that existence precedes essence can be clarified in terms of Sartre's conception of humans as combining both "facticity" and "transcendence." Sartre holds that humans can be understood as having two aspects or dimensions of their being. On the one hand, humans are *factical* beings to the extent that they just exist in the world (like cauliflowers and lecterns). They are embodied beings with specific traits, and they find themselves already engaged in situations and in social contexts where they must deal with other people. Our facticity includes particular sexual desires and bodily needs that are just there, as things we have to make something of. At the level of facticity, humans are not much different from other animals: they have bodies, immediate needs, and desires and cravings that push them to do certain sorts of things.

In Sartre's view, however, humans are different from animals in an important respect. For human consciousness at its deepest level always goes beyond the level of mere facticity. This "going beyond" Sartre calls *transcendence*. Humans transcend their facticity to the extent that they are never simply trapped by their drives and desires, never forced to act in certain ways. In Sartre's view, nothing in our facticity can be thought of as absolutely fixed and determined, for our facticity always presents itself to us as already endowed with a meaning that is constituted by the projects we freely choose. As Sartre says, I can never directly apprehend my facticity (as if it were the brute factual nature of a thing), for my past and my present situation always show up for me through a web of meanings that are determined by my transcendence. Thus, if I see my size as meaning that I will never be able to stand up for myself, or if I see my disadvantaged background as meaning that I can never accomplish much in life, then these are my choices. I am choosing to see my facticity in these ways, for I could just as well choose to see my physical condition and background in different terms (for example, as the assets I need to be a jockey or as equipping me to be a social worker). If I instead go around feeling like a victim of circumstances and fate, or feeling depressed because my facticity is holding me down, then that is my choice, and I am responsible for it.

The idea that human existence is characterized by transcendence explains why Sartre says that "if existence really does precede essence, [then] man is responsible for what he is. Thus, existentialism's first move is to make every man aware of what he is and to make the full responsibility of his existence rest on him." We will return to this crucial Sartrean idea of responsibility later. For now, it is enough to see that the being or essence of a human is made up by the projects the person chooses throughout his or her life. Sartre sums this up at the end of "The Humanism of Existentialism" by saying that "a man is nothing else than a series of undertakings, . . . he is the sum, the organization, the ensemble of the relationships [or involvements] which make up those undertakings."

Subjectivity — stating point

In the same essay Sartre also says that existentialism means that the "subjectivity of the individual is . . . our point of departure." As he is well aware, this comment is potentially misleading, for it opens existentialism to charges that it is "subjectivistic" in the sense of emphasizing emotions and denigrating rationality. But Sartre has a different notion of subjectivity in mind here. In saying that subjectivity is the starting point, he means that, because there are no transcendent truths that are given to us to serve as foundations for our inquiries, existentialism must begin with the concrete, existing individual and that individual's own sense of self and world. The bedrock for description and theory must be "the absolute truth of consciousness becoming aware of itself." Though Sartre connects this idea to Descartes's "I think, therefore I exist," it would be a mistake to think that he is buying into the whole framework of Cartesian philosophy. On the contrary, what he has in mind here is something much closer to the methodological starting point of Edmund Husserl's phenomenology. His point is that any attempt to work out an ontology (an account of the Being of beings) must start from a description of the way our own lives and the world present themselves to us in the course of our actual, pre-theoretical experience. Our aim must be to avoid introducing uncritical ontological assumptions taken from various specialized disciplines (for example, from physics or psychology), and instead build up our account of reality in terms of what Husserl called "the things themselves." Like Heidegger before him, Sartre believed that it is only on the basis of such a bedrock account of life as it is actually experienced that we will have a way of evaluating the various views of reality presented by religion, science, and so-called common sense.

2. Being, Consciousness, and Nothingness

In *Being and Nothingness*, Sartre develops a metaphysical view that supports and explains the basic existentialist picture we have just outlined. Like Heidegger in *Being and Time*, Sartre aims to answer the question, "What is Being?" And like both Husserl and Heidegger, he maintains that in answering this question we should avoid presupposing the duality of subject and object, and should instead start out by characterizing being-in-the-world as a totality. In an earlier work, *Transcendence of the Ego* (1936), Sartre argues that an accurate description of what presents itself in ordinary experience does not reveal a self or ego understood as a conscious subject. For example, in my experience of chasing a bus, what is revealed is a "bus-to-be-caught," not a conscious subject who is chasing a bus. Anyone who has attained some skill at a sport like skiing is familiar with this kind of experience. When you are skiing down a slope, you are "out there" with the turns and moguls, at one with the skis, the poles, and the trails. There is no consciousness of a self who is doing the skiing. In fact, as soon as you become self-conscious, you usually lose your ability to handle the slopes.

Sartre's conception of human existence borrows two fundamental ideas from Husserl's phenomenology. First, Sartre adopts Husserl's view that the defining characteristic of consciousness is "intentionality." To say that consciousness is intentional is to say that whenever one is conscious, one is conscious *of something*. Consciousness always points beyond itself toward something—it is always directed toward some object. Thus, when I feel fear, the fear is of, say, this bee buzzing around my head, and when I have a desire, it is a desire for a pizza or for world peace.

Second, Sartre takes from Husserl the idea that consciousness is always a meaning-giving activity. My conscious acts do not just passively represent some object in the world. On the contrary, in consciously intending any object, I simultaneously endow that object with a meaning. Even ordinary perception involves more than simply receiving sense impressions and registering them in my awareness. For when I perceive something, I always perceive it as such and such—I see the pizza as delicious when I am hungry, or I see the bee as capable of stinging me. This *perceiving as* involves activity on my part. Even when we do our best to be detached, objective observers, we do not just passively receive sense data. For what we call "objectivity" is just one special way of conferring meaning on what we encounter (in the case of objective observation, we endow things with a special meaning, such as "item that exists independent of my consciousness"). In Sartre's words, human being is the "being which is compelled to decide the meaning of being—within it and everywhere outside it."

Of course, most of us are not at all aware that we are endowing the world with meaning in our experience. Most of us assume that we are just seeing things the way they are (for example, the threatening bee or the tasty pizza). So, to make his story plausible, Sartre has to do two things. First, he has to give an account of being that displays the crucial role of human consciousness in constituting what shows up for us as reality. And, second, he has to explain why we normally do not consider ourselves accountable for the meaning of things in our experience—why we are disinclined to believe that we are partly responsible for the way we experience things.

Turning to the first of these tasks, the best way to understand Sartre's view of human meaning-giving activity is by looking at Sartre's view of being as it is "in-itself," independent of any human consciousness. For Sartre, being-in-itself is just undifferentiated stuff, and in this respect it is similar to the unformed matter of Aristotle or the prime matter of St. Thomas Aquinas. It is also a "plenum," filling everything and extending everywhere. Further, he says that there is no "non-being" or "not" within

Being-in-itself

the totality of being-in-itself. And because there is no "not" in being-in-itself, it does not admit of any distinctions, such as the distinctions between red and non-red or dog and non-dog. (In various respects, this view of being-in-itself recalls the ancient Greek philosopher Parmenides' description of being.) Sartre evocatively characterizes being-in-itself as a bloated overflow, a superabundance; it is, he says, *de trop*, superfluous. It fills everything and, like porridge, is sticky, slimy, viscous, constantly oozing into every nook and cranny. It is because hot cereal is a primal symbol of being-in-itself that all children naturally feel disgusted when they first encounter oatmeal.

For Sartre, one effect of being-in-itself is that it is nauseating. Since it sucks everything into itself, it seems to suck your very being out of you. In his early novel *Nausea*, Sartre describes a character named Roquentin who for a moment is able to experience the being-in-itself of the roots of a chestnut tree under his park bench.

> All of a sudden, there it was, clear as day: existence [i.e., pure being-in-itself] had suddenly unveiled itself. It had lost the harmless look of an abstract category: it was the very paste of things, this root was kneaded into existence. Or rather the root, the park gates, the bench, the sparse grass, all that had vanished: the diversity of things, their individuality, were only an appearance, a veneer. This veneer had melted, leaving soft, monstrous masses, all in disorder—naked, in a frightful, obscene nakedness.[1]

Sartre's point here is that since diversity and order imply a "not" (this thing, not that one; this way, not that way), and since there is no "not" in being-in-itself, it contains neither diversity nor order. When Roquentin experiences pure being, then, he experiences an amorphous massiveness without any differentiation or organization. And because this plenum obliterates all differences and fills all holes, sucking everything into it, Roquentin experiences this as nausea. Being is suffocating; its sucks your breath out; it empties your stomach: "I understood that I had found the key to Existence," he says, "the key to my Nauseas."[2]

If there are no differentiations within being-in-itself, then how does differentiation arise? For Sartre, the answer to this question is found in the fact that in addition to being-in-itself, there are conscious beings (ourselves), beings who care about their own existence and who, given this concern, make distinctions in their dealings with the world. Determinate reality arises with the appearance of consciousness into the totality of what is.

1. Jean-Paul Sartre, *Nausea*, trans. Lloyd Alexander (Norfolk, Conn.: New Directions, 1959), 127.
2. Ibid., 129.

Nothingness originates in Consciousness

Sartre introduces his discussion of the role of human consciousness in shaping the world by first looking at the nature of questions as such. He points out that to ask a question, such as the ontological question asked in *Being and Nothingness*, is to step back and adopt a detached attitude of interrogation toward being-in-itself (§1).[3] Sartre notes that this attitude of questioning is not our original relationship to being-in-itself. On the contrary, in our everyday activities we are not at all detached, but are instead absorbed in doing things in a pre-reflective way. In an everyday activity like counting cigarettes, to take Sartre's example, what I am conscious of is the cigarettes, and I have only a tacit, background sense of my activity of counting.[4] Sartre calls this nonfocal, unexplicit background awareness of what one is doing the "pre-reflective *cogito*," and he claims that this is our normal condition as being-in-the-world. For him our questioning is a rather specialized, reflective mode of consciousness that is first made possible by modifying our ordinary, pre-reflective way of being-in-the-world.

Nevertheless, questioning shows us something about what human consciousness introduces into the world. Sartre says that in the act of questioning, I open up a space in which the "not" can arise in the midst of being. First, questioning presupposes an expectation of a certain sort: to ask how it stands with things is to be open to the answer that it is not such and such. "The reply will be a 'yes' or a 'no'. . . . There exists then for the questioner the permanent objective possibility of a negative reply." Second, the question, "What is X?" assumes the possibility of arriving at a determinate answer of the form, "It is so and so." But to say it is so and so is to say it is not something else, which means once again that the act of questioning introduces a "not" into being. The very fact that questioning can open a range of possibilities, including the possibility of a "this, not that," serves as a clue to the fact that it is human consciousness that is the source of the "not" or "nothingness" in our experience.

In Sartre's view, then, if there were no such thing as consciousness, there would be no distinctions or differentiations within the realm of being. Taking over from Spinoza and Hegel the basic principle that "all determination is negation," Sartre claims that determinate reality with its differentiations and distinctions is possible only because one thing is distinguished from another, and this means that there must be negations within being.[5] And it is consciousness that introduces determinations into reality by introducing negations. For example, the very existence of males is dependent on con-

3. Section numbers refer to selections below from Jean-Paul Sartre, *Being and Nothingness*, trans. Hazel Barnes (New York: Philosophical Library, 1956).

4. Ibid., lii–liii.

5. Ibid., 14–15.

scious beings thinking of males as not being female. Human consciousness cuts up the world in accord with its concerns and projects, and this activity of cutting up is the metaphysical foundation of the existence of distinctions. Sartre describes the process whereby distinctions come to be as "a limiting cutting into being by a being, which, . . . already is a process of nihilation." For there to be distinctions in the realm of being-in-itself, then, there has to be a conscious being that takes things as such-and-such and takes other things as not being such-and-such.

Sartre's claim that distinctions require consciousness is opposed to the scientific realist position, according to which the fact that the world is carved into natural kinds such as *electron* and *proton* is independent of consciousness. Even if there were no conscious beings, in this view, the world would still really be cut up into electrons and non-electrons. Hence, there are distinctions in being without consciousness. For Sartre, by contrast, distinctions are *made*, not *found*. They are our creations, not our discoveries. They are produced by our introducing nothingness into the realm of being-in-itself.

Furthermore, Sartre claims that the existence of nothingness can be grounded phenomenologically: nothingness is something we encounter in the world. His most famous example of how this is so is his story about arriving in a café and looking for his friend, Pierre, who is supposed to meet him there (§2). He looks around the café and sees that Pierre is not there. Sartre claims that the café by itself, independent of anyone's consciousness, exhibits no non-being or absence: "its patrons, its tables, its booths, its mirrors, its light, its smoky atmosphere, and the sounds of its voices, rattling saucers, and the footsteps that fill it—the café is a fullness of being." Nevertheless if one is a consciousness seeking something in the café, one can apprehend an absence or non-being in the café, in this case, the absence of Pierre.

In order to clarify the experience of perceiving an absence, Sartre makes use of the figure-ground distinction central to Gestalt psychology. According to this distinction, a figure can emerge into the foreground in order to be perceived only against a background that determines how that figure can appear. Thus, the appearance of a figure is possible only against a background that recedes into something peripheral or nonfocal in relation to the figure. That is why there can be familiar sorts of figure-ground reversals like the vase that flips into two people kissing and then back into a vase again. Using this figure-ground distinction, Sartre describes the experience of looking for Pierre in this way: as he looks around the room, the being-in-itself of the café retreats to the margins of consciousness where it functions as the ground upon which the figure of Pierre is expected to appear. In this experience, everything in the café keeps receding into the background, while the

Consciousness is a Nothingness (handwritten)

absence of Pierre keeps flickering against that backdrop. From a phenomenological standpoint, then, one directly apprehends a certain lack or "not," the absence of Pierre, which Sartre calls a "flickering of nothingness."

Another example of how a "not" or "negativity" can appear in the heart of being is found in experience of destruction (§2). According to Sartre, without consciousness there could be no such thing as destruction. Being-in-itself can contain no destruction. Earthquakes and storms "do not destroy," he says, "or at least they do not destroy directly; they merely modify the distribution of masses of being. There is no less after the storm than before." A storm can knock down a field of wheat and tear apart a house. But all this is, at most, a redistribution of matter within the totality of being. In Sartre's view, it is only if there is a consciousness who cares about these events (a farmer, for example) that this rearrangement or displacement of matter can count as "destruction." Similarly, the biological functions of cattle can be terminated by a flood. But only if there is some conscious being who makes a project of caring for the cattle could those biological transformations count as the destruction of a herd. Thus, only when being-in-itself is apprehended by a consciousness is room made for the possibility of destruction in reality. So again, it is consciousness that first makes possible negation within being-in-itself.

What is it about consciousness that makes it possible for it to introduce nothingness into the world? Sartre's answer is that consciousness at its very core is itself a nothingness. On this view, consciousness is not an object or thing, but is instead a nothing. The "upsurge" of consciousness in the midst of beings is what introduces a lack or a gap into the heart of being. Consciousness opens a fissure or absence by virtue of which the "not" is first introduced into the world.

We can understand why he argues this way if we recall that consciousness for Sartre has a dual structure. On the one hand, humans are factical beings that are just there among other beings in the world. We have bodies with distinctive characteristics, we have made decisions in the past that we must live with now, we are involved with other people who tend to see us as objects, and so on. Sartre calls this dimension of facticity in humans their being as "in-itself" (*en soi*), and he sees it as correlated with the past—what we have been up until the present moment. On the other hand, as we have seen, humans are beings who can transcend their being as mere facticity. Sartre tries to capture this dimension of transcendence by saying that, for humans, their own being is in question for them. That is, humans have an ability to see their own lives as mattering or as being at stake for them in some determinate sense. And because our being is in question for us in this way, our facticity is always encountered not as something fixed and unchangeable, but as presenting a task or undertaking that we must accomplish in living out our lives. We have to make something of our facticity, and we do so by endowing our lives with a meaning that is defined by the projects we choose for our lives. To be human, then, is not just to be in–itself, but also "for–itself" (*pour soi*). To the extent that we are always taking some stand on our own existences and making something of our lives in what we do, our being is something that is *for* us.

To return to our earlier example, if I am short and frail by nature, I can never encounter those features of my stature as they are in themselves. That is so because such things can never be purely neutral to me. In my society, there is a temptation to think of such traits as limitations or shortcomings, and I might have fallen into step with this public interpretation in such a way that I see my size as a handicap. Or I might have seen through the stereotypes of my society so that I see my stature as something to be proud of. In any event, because I always encounter my facticity in terms of some interpretation or other, I always transcend my being as in–itself. And for Sartre that in turn means that there is always a gap or leeway—a "nothingness"—between my being as in–itself and my being as for–itself. In his words, "The Being by which Nothingness arrives in the world is a being such that in its Being, the Nothingness of its Being is in question." It is precisely this fissure within consciousness that first makes possible the kinds of self-detachment found in questioning, doubting, abstaining from belief, and other forms of reflective consciousness.

3. Freedom

The most central concept in Sartre's account of human beings is freedom. In Sartre's view, nothingness first arises only because human existence is characterized by a particular kind of freedom. As we have seen, human consciousness embodies a gap between facticity and transcendence, between the in–itself and the for–itself. This gap implies that, as for–itself, humans are not ever the same as they are in–itself, and they are always more than they are in–itself. For us, there can never be a perfect coincidence of the in–itself and the for–itself. Or, as Sartre puts it, "human reality, in its most immediate being, in the intrastructure of the pre-reflective *cogito*, must be what it is not and not be what it is" (§5).

The noncoincidence found within the self is possible, Sartre contends, only because human existence is characterized by freedom. Sartre tries to clarify this conception of freedom through a description of "anguish." He begins by distinguishing anguish from fear (§3). Both fear and anguish are manifest in the experience of vertigo or dizziness one feels at high altitudes. Suppose I am on a narrow path that runs along a high cliff where there is no guard-rail. In a such a situation I will, first of all, feel fear that I might be caused to fall over by objects or events that are beyond my control, like slipping on a stone or having the earth crumble under my feet. Sartre says, "a situation provokes fear if there is a possibility of my life being changed from without." My fear is directed toward something outside of me in the world, and in my fear I experience myself as a thing among other things in the world, as something passive to which things might happen.

In response I will react with circumspection: "I will pay attention to the stones in the road; I will keep myself as far as possible from the edge of the path." This reaction involves projecting a number of possibilities for future conduct. Sartre notes that these possibilities do not appear to me as determined, either by causes outside me or by causes within me, for otherwise they would appear not as genuine possibilities, but instead as things that are simply "about-to-happen." In particular, I do not apprehend myself as psychologically determined to choose one of these possibilities. Although I am conscious of having motives for acting in particular ways given my horror of the precipice, "I am conscious of that horror as not determinant in relation to my possible conduct." Instead, actions other than those suggested by my fear present themselves to me as real possibilities, including even such extreme actions as throwing myself over the cliff.

And here anguish comes into play. The fact that one can feel a fear of heights even when one is relatively safe is due not to fear, but to anguish. Anguish results from the awareness that I have several possibilities of action available to me, none of which is determined in advance, and that I can choose any one of them. This means that I might go on protecting myself from danger, or that I might hurl myself over the precipice. My anguish, then, is my experience of myself as a being which is capable of freely choosing from among an array of possibilities. In anguish, I encounter my own life as not determined by forces beyond my control, but instead as something I must choose. Thus, anguish is not directed toward some object outside me in the world, but rather toward my own self as a for-itself capable of choosing from a range of open possibilities. As Sartre puts it, "fear is fear of beings in the world whereas anguish is anguish before myself."

At the close of his discussion of anguish, Sartre draws some conclusions about human existence. On the one hand, the experience of anguish shows that "I am indeed already there in the future; it is for the sake of that being which I will be there at the turning of the path that I now exert all my strength." Because I am concerned about the being that I will be in the future, I exist as a projection into the realm of future possibilities. In this sense, "I am the self which I will be." But on the other hand, it is also true that "I am not the self which I will be." This is so not just because time separates me from my future being, but because my present being is not the foundation of my future being. Since I stand out into an open range of possibilities, none of which is determined in advance, it seems that nothing actual in the present can determine where I am going in the future. Thus, "a nothingness has slipped into the heart of this relation" within myself (§3). As capable of taking a stand on my facticity, I am, as transcendence, always more than I am as facticity, and that means, according to Sartre, that I can never be completely determined by my facticity.

Sartre's notion of ontological freedom has the radical consequence that we can always transform our situation through our free choice of projects. It is because of this freedom that Sartre says in "The Humanism of Existentialism" that we are "condemned to be free." Each of us "carries the weight of the whole world on his shoulders; he is responsible for the world and for himself as a way of being."

To illustrate this notion of our responsibility, he discusses the experience of finding oneself in a situation where a war has broken out (§8). Surely, we might say, a war is something that just happens to us. If, independent of anything I decide, my country goes to war and I am inducted into the army, there would seem to be an intuitive sense in which I am not responsible for the war. But Sartre claims that nevertheless there is a also sense in which I am responsible for the war:

> If I am mobilized in a war, this war is my war; it is in my image and I deserve it. I deserve it first because I could always get out of it by suicide or by desertion; these ultimate possibles are those which must always be present for us when there is a question of envisaging a situation. For lack of getting out of it, I have chosen it. . . . But in addition the war is mine because by the sole fact that it arises in a situation which I cause to be and that I can discover it there only by engaging myself for or against it, I can no longer distinguish at present the choice which I make of myself from the choice which I make of the war. To live this war is to choose myself through my choice of myself. (§8)

The point here is that by taking a concrete stand—by choosing to engage myself in the world in some determinate way or other—I simultaneously confer a meaning on the worldly context in which I find myself. If I choose to encounter the war as a terrible force befalling me from outside myself, then that interpretation of the war is my choice, and I am responsible for it. This is so because there are always other ways of interpreting the war available to me: I could see it as a chance to develop my character, for example, or as a noble crusade to stamp out a tyrant.

Moreover, there is always the "ultimate possible" in every situation—the possibility of committing suicide and putting an end to both my own engagement and the world as I encounter it. So if I decide to go on living, I have chosen to be engaged in the world, and in doing that I have chosen an

attitude that makes the world show up in a specific way. In that choice, however, I have chosen the war as meaning such and such to me, and I am therefore responsible for that war. (When Sartre says that at present I cannot
"distinguish" the choice I make of myself from the choice I make of the war,
he means that there is no way for me to drive in a wedge between the war as
it really is and the war as it is encountered as a result of the choices I make.)

To show the extent of our responsibility for the world as we encounter it,
Sartre goes so far as to say that "I choose being born." This does not mean,
of course, that I chose my parents or that I caused them to have me. It
means, rather, that I am responsible for what the fact of my birth means to
me, that is, for how it counts in my life. If I go around complaining about
being born too late or whining about my unhappy childhood, then that is
my decision. I am choosing to let my birth have a negative meaning for me. I
could always change my interpretation if I wished to. As Sartre says, the
"fact of my birth never appears as a brute fact but always across a projective
reconstruction of my for-itself." It is the way I project the meaning of my
birth that determines what the event of my birth means to me. And because
I always encounter events in the world as endowed with a meaning through
the choices I make, there is no way to make sense of the idea that I could
come face to face with my birth as it is in itself.

"Facticity is everywhere," Sartre says "but [it is] inapprehensible; I never
encounter anything except my responsibility" (§8). In other words, even
though our condition is characterized by facticity, we can never gain access
to that facticity as it is in itself, but only as it shows up in a specific way as a
result of the choices we make. What we deal with in life is not raw facts, but
opportunities for creating specific meanings through our choices. As Sartre
says, "every event in the world can be revealed to me only as an opportunity." And because even other people "are themselves only opportunities
and chances, the responsibility of the for-itself extends to the entire world as
a peopled-world." To be human, then, is to be "a being which is compelled
to decide the meaning of being—within it and everywhere outside of it"
(§8). The only thing we are not free about is whether or not we are free.

One might question whether our consciousness of freedom has the dramatic consequences for the structure of the self Sartre thinks it does. My
future may indeed appear to me as an array of possibilities among which I
may freely select. But this does not entail that I am *really* free. It may be that
given all the causal factors that precede any particular situation of choice, I
do not have the power to choose otherwise than how I in fact choose. And if
this is so, consciousness of freedom is an illusion. This could reveal a problem for Sartre's phenomenological project. If, in the last analysis, his account of freedom and human existence is simply a matter of how things appear to us, and it may not really be true, then perhaps we should undertake

an investigation other than the phenomenological one to decide how relevant the consciousness of freedom is to the meaning and structure of our lives.

4. Bad Faith and Authenticity

Sartre believes that the structure of human existence as a combination of facticity and freedom results in a pervasive tendency toward *bad faith* (§§4– 6). Bad faith occurs when a conscious being denies her freedom to choose from among a range of possibilities, or when she denies an aspect of her facticity, for instance, that there are certain choices that she has made in the past, or that these choices make up a certain pattern. Sartre believes that these are cases of a certain kind of *self-deception*, the kind in which the subject is conscious that she is free and at the same time denies it to herself, or is conscious that her past actions have a certain character and simultaneously denies it to herself.

In order to explore the notion of bad faith, Sartre develops a number of vivid examples. One of these is of a waiter in a café:

> His movement is quick and forward, a little too precise, a little too rapid. He comes toward the patrons with a step a little too quick. He bends forward a little too eagerly; his voice, his eyes express an interest a little too solicitous for the order of the customer. Finally there he returns, trying to imitate in his walk the inflexible stiffness of some kind of automaton while carrying his tray with the recklessness of a tight-rope-walker by putting it in a perpetually unstable, perpetually broken equilibrium which he perpetually reestablishes by a light movement of the arm and hand. All his behavior seems to us a game. He applies himself to chaining his movements as if they were mechanisms, the one regulating the other; his gestures and his voice seem to be mechanisms; he gives himself the quickness and pitiless rapidity of things. He is playing, he is amusing himself. But what is he playing? We need not watch long before we can explain it: he is playing *at being* a waiter in a café. (§5)

Sartre analyzes this waiter as giving in to a societal demand for someone occupied in a trade to *be* nothing other than someone who has a certain occupation: "a grocer who dreams is offensive to the buyer, because such a grocer is not wholly a grocer. Society demands that he limit himself to his function as a grocer." But it is false that the waiter *is* a waiter, in the sense that "this inkwell *is* an inkwell, or the glass is a glass" (§5). The waiter is someone whose choices for future possibilities are open to him; he is not a thing that is restricted to certain functions, the way an inkwell is. And thus, when the waiter thinks that he *is* a waiter, he is deceiving himself. As a conscious and free being, he is not a being-*in*-itself, but rather transcendence, a being-*for*-itself.

Nonetheless, in Sartre's view, there is a sense in which the waiter *is* a waiter, for otherwise he could just as well be called a diplomat or a reporter. He is not, however, a waiter in the mode of being-in-itself, but "in the mode of *being what I am not*" (§5). Though being a waiter is a role he plays, it is *his* role, and if he is to avoid bad faith, he must acknowledge that it is and not deny it.

For Sartre, there are two sorts of bad faith. In one kind of bad faith, a person denies (some aspect of) her being-for-itself, her freedom, and in the second, a person denies (some aspect of) her being-in-itself. Sartre thinks that bad faith is a pervasive feature of human beings, and further, that it is very difficult to avoid because of the structure of consciousness. He considers one sort of attempt to avoid bad faith, the pursuit of *sincerity*, a quality he characterizes as trying "to be what one is" (§5). Sartre argues that any attempt to achieve sincerity will itself result in bad faith. He develops his case with the example of a homosexual who refuses to acknowledge that he is a homosexual. The homosexual's friend, the champion of sincerity, becomes irritated at this refusal, and wants him to "be what he is," to declare that he is a homosexual. In Sartre's view, there is truth in the homosexual's refusal, for no person is a homosexual in the way that a table is a table. No person is a homosexual as being-in-itself. And thus, the homosexual would be right if he denied being a homosexual in the sense of "I am not what I am" (§5). He might declare to himself, "To the extent that a pattern of conduct is defined as the conduct of a *paederast* and to the extent that I have adopted this conduct, I am a *paederast*. But to the extent that human reality can not be finally defined by patterns of conduct, I am not one." But this is not how Sartre's homosexual is thinking: "he understands 'not being' in the sense of 'not being-in-itself.' He lays claim to 'not being a *paederast*' in the sense in which this table *is not* an inkwell. He is in bad faith." This man maintains that he is not a homosexual even as being-in-itself—insofar as he is constituted by past choices and actions. And in this respect the homosexual deceives himself.

But would he also be in bad faith were he to become sincere? His friend is asking, Sartre explains, that the homosexual acknowledge that he *is* a homosexual, because admitting some aspect of what you really are lets you disown it as something merely in-itself. The friend wants the homosexual "to be what he is in order no longer to be what he is." But if the homosexual were to undertake this psychological maneuver, Sartre claims, he would be in bad faith. He would then be agreeing that he is a homosexual in the sense that an inkwell is an inkwell. He would be affirming that he is a homosexual in the sense of being-in-itself, yet at the same time he would be aware that this view of himself is false.

In Sartre's view, no one can ever simply *be anything*. This is because being something in particular (for example being a student or a woman) is always a matter of *assuming* a particular identity and *sustaining* its existence. But insofar as our own identity is something we make, it is not something we really are. There is always a gap or a *not* between ourselves as for-itself and what we are as in-itself, and of this we are always in some sense aware. Thus sincerity—trying to be what you are—always results in bad faith.

In Sartre's view, bad faith is extremely difficult to avoid due to certain structural features of human ontology. We are a combination of being-for-itself, whose nature it is to strive perpetually to complete itself, and being-in-itself, which does not strive because it is already complete. As being-for-itself, we attempt to achieve the completeness of being-in-itself, while at the same time not forfeiting our being-for-itself, for that would eliminate our character as conscious and free. In short, we want to achieve *completed being-for-itself*, or as Sartre describes it, to become "in-and-for-itself." We wish to realize "the ideal of a consciousness that would be the foundation of its own being-in-itself by virtue of the pure consciousness it would have of itself" (§9). Sartre calls our desire to realize this ideal "the desire to be God." But we cannot achieve this ideal, because as being-for-itself we can never be completed. In consequence, as a combination of being-in-itself and being-for-itself, we are perpetually unstable or "metastable" constructions: we are constantly flipping back and forth between regarding ourselves solely as being-in-itself and solely as being-for-itself (§5). Because we aim at completeness, we tend to regard ourselves as being-in-itself and deny our being-for-itself, and because we aim to affirm our freedom we tend to regard ourselves as being-for-itself and deny our being-in-itself. The pervasiveness of bad faith is therefore grounded in our being metastable constructions of this sort.

In *Being and Nothingness*, Sartre does not talk about how one can avoid bad faith and be authentic. We might, however, imagine a criminal saying, "To the extent that a pattern of conduct is defined as the conduct of an evil person and to the extent that I have adopted this conduct, I am an evil person. But to the extent that human reality can not be finally defined by patterns of conduct, I am not an evil person. Though it is true that I am evil, it is also true that I am not identical to that evil person I have been, for I always have the ability to change" (§5). No deception about his own nature and capacities is manifested in this attitude. According to Simone de Beauvoir in *The Ethics of Ambiguity*, authenticity involves, first of all, a lucid awareness of the structural ambiguity in a person between being-in-itself and being-for-itself.[6] The authentic person is lucidly aware of her past actions and what they add up to, but at the same time does not view these past actions as determining what she will be, for she clearly sees herself as being able to freely choose from among the possibilities that open up for her. In addition,

6. Simone de Beauvoir, *The Ethics of Ambiguity*, trans. Bernard Frechtman (New York: Citadel, 1970), 77–78, 156–59.

according to Beauvoir, the authentic person *assumes* her freedom as opposed
to fleeing it, and she does this by being *actively engaged* in her projects in the
world, and also in rejecting all forms of oppression.

5. The Other and the Question of Ethics

Sartre has been criticized for developing a view of human existence that
seems to undermine ethics. Like Nietzsche before him, Sartre believes that
if God is dead and there are no transcendental bases for value judgments,
then values can only be human creations. But if this is the case, then values
seem to lack any higher justification or grounding. In "The Humanism of
Existentialism," he says that "if God does not exist, we find no values or
commands to turn to which legitimize our conduct." For Sartre, all values
are products of individual choices, and, furthermore, any criteria by which
we might evaluate values are also products of our choices. "So, in the bright
realm of values," he concludes, "we have no excuse behind us, nor justification before us. We are alone, with no excuses." A similar point is made in
Being and Nothingness where Sartre says, "my freedom is the unique foundation of values, [and so] nothing, absolutely nothing, justifies me in adopting
this or that particular value, this or that particular scale of values."[7] From
this standpoint, it seems that if someone were to decide in favor of racist or
genocidal values, there would be no way to criticize such a choice. And thus
it would seem difficult to secure ethical standards to which we could legit-
imately hold in our attempt to live together in this world.

Moreover, Sartre's account of human relations in *Being and Nothingness*
makes it hard to see how one central component of a moral point of view,
genuine respect for others, could arise. We can get a sense of why this is so if
we look at the description of human relations in that work. Sartre claims that
my awareness of my own self is dependent on others: I can only become
aware of my self through what he calls the "look" of another person. To
support this claim, he considers a case in which someone is peering through
a keyhole (§7). If I am secretly watching someone in this way, I am aware of
the scene I am watching, but I do not yet have any awareness of my own self.
Suppose now that I hear footsteps coming down the hall and I become aware
that someone is looking at me. When this happens, I will suddenly become
aware of myself: "I see myself because somebody sees me." Now also for the
first time I can feel something like shame. As Sartre points out, a feeling like
shame is not just an inner state I can discover through introspection or

---

7. Sartre, *Being and Nothingness*, 38. This passage, and the issue it raises, is discussed
by Richard Bernstein in *Praxis and Action* (Philadelphia: University of Pennsylvania
Press, 1971), 146–48.

inward-turning. My "inner" experience of shame is something I can discover only through the look of another person, for shame necessarily involves seeing myself as another sees me.

With his "look," the other views me in a way that is quite different from the sense I had of myself before I noticed him. The other views me as an object, that is, as a being that lacks transcendence and freedom and is driven merely by basic drives and needs—in this case, as a voyeur or peeping Tom. In the eyes of the other, I just am a voyeur, as a rock just is a rock. By looking at me as "in-itself" in this way, the other seems to deprive me of my being as a "for-itself."

And further, the objectifying look of the other makes it possible for me to become aware of an aspect of myself that was not explicit earlier: my being-in-itself. Seeing myself through the other's eyes, I begin to regard myself as an object. I internalize his perception of me, and begin to think of myself as a subhuman thing driven by basic animal motivations. Moreover, I can see myself in this way only because the other presents himself as being-for-itself, that is, as a conscious and free subject who is capable of interpreting and evaluating what he sees. In this respect, he presents himself as superior to me, and I feel dehumanized by his look. My response will be to try to prove that I am more than he sees me as, and this means that I will treat him as an object whose look carries no special weight.

Sartre believes that this type of conflict extends throughout human relationships.[8] Human relationships are characterized by a struggle for self-assertion that will never result in stable and tranquil co-existence. In attempting to assert his transcendence, the other will objectify me. I will then resist the other's objectification of me by trying to make him recognize me as a free and creative subject capable of transcendence. But in this process, I objectify him. In response, he will resist my attempts at domination, and will try to assert himself as the truly free and creative subject, but he will thereby objectify me again.

This struggle for self-assertion has been vividly described by Simone de Beauvoir in *The Second Sex*.[9] There she claims that what motivates people is not just a desire for happiness, but a desire or need to realize one's transcendence: "Every individual concerned to justify his existence feels that his existence involves an undefined need to transcend himself, to engage in freely chosen projects." In fact, a person's very being as a subject is defined by

8. Sartre, *Being and Nothingness*, 361–430. See also Piotr Hoffman, *The Human Self and the Life and Death Struggle*, (Gainesville, Tampa: University Presses of Florida, 1983).

9. Simone de Beauvoir, *The Second Sex*, trans. H. M. Parshley (New York: Alfred A. Knopf, 1957). All quotes are from pp. xxviii–xxix.

"exploits or projects that serve as a mode of transcendence; he achieves liberty only through a continual reaching out toward other liberties." Ultimately, merely feeling good or being contented will not be fulfilling. It can be experienced as a loss of humanity: "Every time transcendence falls back into immanence [being a thing among others in the world], stagnation, there is a degradation of existence into the *'en-soi'*—the brutish life of subjection to given conditions—and of liberty into constraint and contingence."

But the project of self-affirmation—of realizing and manifesting one's own being as "for-itself"—generally takes the form of lording it over another person, whom one treats as an inferior being, as mere "in-itself." Historically, this has been evident in the way men have treated women:

> Now, what peculiarly signalizes the situation of women is that she—a free and autonomous being like all human creatures—nevertheless finds herself living in a world where men compel her to assume the status of Other. They propose to stabilize her as object and to doom her to immanence since her transcendence is to be overshadowed and forever transcended by another ego which is [treated as] essential and sovereign. The drama of woman lies in this conflict between the fundamental aspirations of every subject (ego)—who always regards the self as essential—and the compulsions of a situation in which she is [treated as] the inessential.

Thus, the oppression of women has been motivated by a deeper dynamic according to which one subject tries to demonstrate its sovereignty and superiority by objectifying another.

It is perhaps because of this rather pessimistic view of human relations that Sartre tried, three years after the publication of *Being and Nothingness*, to present a basis for ethics in his essay, "The Humanism of Existentialism." This essay takes on a Kantian turn to the extent that it emphasizes a kind of universalizability—choosing to govern our actions by reasons and principles that we can and would want others to choose to govern their actions by as well. This seems to be what motivates such passages as the following:

> When we say that man chooses his own self, we mean that every one of us does likewise; but we also mean by that that in making this choice he also chooses all men. In fact, in creating the man that we want to be, there is not a single one of our acts which does not at the same time create an image of man as we think he ought to be. . . . We always choose the good, and nothing can be good for us without being good for all.

The tangle of problems this passage creates might explain why Sartre later repudiated his "Humanism" essay. Even granting for the moment the claim that we always choose what we perceive as being good for ourselves (a questionable bit of moral psychology), what reason could he have for saying that anything I regard as good for myself I should also regard as good for everyone? Yet he claims, for example, that "if I want to marry, I am involving all humanity in monogamy and not merely myself. . . . In choosing myself, I choose man." Given Sartre's picture of the individual self as the source of all values, however, it is not at all clear why I should have any regard for the good of others, or why others are necessarily implicated in the value-choices I make.

Both Sartre and Beauvoir at times hoped to formulate an ethics according to which acknowledging one's own freedom would lead to a commitment to acknowledging the freedom of all humanity. In "The Humanism of Existentialism" Sartre says,

> Of course, freedom as the definition of man does not depend on others, but as soon as there is involvement, I am obliged to want others to have freedom at the same time that I want my own freedom. I can take freedom as my goal only if I take that of others as a goal as well. Consequently, when, in all honesty, I've recognized that man is a being in whom existence precedes essence, that he is a free being who, in various circumstances, can only want his freedom, I have at the same time recognized that I can want only the freedom of others.

A passage like this gives us a sense of Sartre's heartfelt moral commitments. Here he presents us with a picture of an ideal state of affairs: a society characterized by a universally shared commitment to the freedom of all people. Nevertheless, it is hard to see the connections Sartre is making in this passage. If all people are already free (as a matter of ontological fact), then why would they also *want* to be free? And if I am "a being which is compelled to decide the meaning of being," then why must I care about the condition of others?

Sartre spent years attempting to formulate an ethics, and the verdict is not yet in on whether his efforts were a success.[10] But whatever we think of the possibility of developing an existentialist ethics, we have to be struck by the insights in Sartre's and Beauvoir's characterization of human relations as involving a struggle for self-affirmation and self-realization. Seen from their standpoint, the Romantic assumption that people tend to be good and loving by nature seems highly questionable. And we cannot fail to be struck by their account of authenticity and of the fundamental place of freedom in human life. In its emphasis on responsibility and our ability to take charge of our lives, Sartre's thought still addresses the most critical issues in the search for meaning and fulfillment in human existence.

10. Sartre's *Cahiers pour une morale* (*Notebooks for an Ethics*) was published in 1983.

The Humanism of Existentialism

1946

I should like on this occasion to defend existentialism against some charges which have been brought against it.

First, it has been charged with inviting people to remain in a kind of desperate quietism because, since no solutions are possible, we should have to consider action in this world as quite impossible. We should then end up in a philosophy of contemplation; and since contemplation is a luxury, we come in the end to a bourgeois philosophy. The communists in particular have made these charges.

On the other hand, we have been charged with dwelling on human degradation, with pointing up everywhere the sordid, shady, and slimy, and neglecting the gracious and beautiful, the bright side of human nature; for example, according to Mlle. Mercier, a Catholic critic, with forgetting the smile of the child. Both sides charge us with having ignored human solidarity, with considering man as an isolated being. The communists say that the main reason for this is that we take pure subjectivity, the *Cartesian I think*, as our starting point; in other words, the moment in which man becomes fully aware of what it means to him to be an isolated being; as a result, we are unable to return to a state of solidarity with the men who are not ourselves, a state which we can never reach in the *cogito*.

From the Christian standpoint, we are charged with denying the reality and seriousness of human undertakings, since, if we reject God's commandments and the eternal verities, there no longer remains anything but pure caprice, with everyone permitted to do as he pleases and incapable, from his own point of view, of condemning the points of view and acts of others.

I shall try today to answer these different charges. Many people are going to be surprised at what is said here about humanism. We shall try to see in what sense it is to be understood. In any case, what can be said from the very beginning is that by existentialism we mean a doctrine which makes human life possible and, in addition, declares that every truth and every action implies a human setting and a human subjectivity.

As is generally known, the basic charge against us is that we put the

From *Existentialism and Human Emotion* by Jean-Paul Sartre, translated by Bernard Frechtman, © 1957 by Philosophical Library. Reprinted with permission.

268

emphasis on the dark side of human life. Someone recently told me of a lady who, when she let slip a vulgar word in a moment of irritation, excused herself by saying, "I guess I'm becoming an existentialist." Consequently, existentialism is regarded as something ugly; that is why we are said to be naturalists; and if we are, it is rather surprising that in this day and age we cause so much more alarm and scandal than does naturalism, properly so called. The kind of person who can take in his stride such a novel as Zola's *The Earth* is disgusted as soon as he starts reading an existentialist novel; the kind of person who is resigned to the wisdom of the ages—which is pretty sad—finds us even sadder. Yet, what can be more disillusioning than saying "true charity begins at home" or "a scoundrel will always return evil for good?"

We know the commonplace remarks made when this subject comes up, remarks which always add up to the same thing: we shouldn't struggle against the powers-that-be; we shouldn't resist authority; we shouldn't try to rise above our station; any action which doesn't conform to authority is romantic; any effort not based on past experience is doomed to failure; experience shows that man's bent is always toward trouble, that there must be a strong hand to hold him in check, if not, there will be anarchy. There are still people who go on mumbling these melancholy old saws, the people who say, "It's only human!" whenever a more or less repugnant act is pointed out to them, the people who glut themselves on *chansons réalistes*; these are the people who accuse existentialism of being too gloomy, and to such an extent that I wonder whether they are complaining about it, not for its pessimism, but much rather its optimism. Can it be that what really scares them in the doctrine I shall try to present here is that it leaves to man a possibility of choice? To answer this question, we must re-examine it on a strictly philosophical plane. What is meant by the term *existentialism*?

Most people who use the word would be rather embarrassed if they had to explain it, since, now that the word is all the rage, even the work of a musician or painter is being called existentialist. A gossip columnist in *Clartés* signs himself *The Existentialist*, so that by this time the word has been so stretched and has taken on so broad a meaning, that it no longer means anything at all. It seems that for want of an advance-guard doctrine analogous to surrealism, the kind of people who are eager for scandal and flurry turn to this philosophy which in other respects does not at all serve their purposes in this sphere.

Actually, it is the least scandalous, the most austere of doctrines. It is intended strictly for specialists and philosophers. Yet it can be defined easily. What complicates matters is that there are two kinds of existentialist; first, those who are Christian, among whom I would include Jaspers and Gabriel Marcel, both Catholic; and on the other hand the atheistic existentialists,

existentialism:
humans
exist
before
essence.

subjectivity
starting
point

vs: objective

vs. thing
essence
before
existence

among whom I class Heidegger, and then the French existentialists and my-self. What they have in common is that they think that existence precedes essence, or, if you prefer, that subjectivity must be the starting point.

Just what does that mean? Let us consider some object that is manufac-tured, for example, a book or a paper-cutter: here is an object which has been made by an artisan whose inspiration came from a concept. He referred to the concept of what a paper-cutter is and likewise to a known method of production, which is part of the concept, something which is, by and large, a routine. Thus, the paper-cutter is at once an object produced in a certain way and, on the other hand, one having a specific use; and one cannot postu-late a man who produces a paper-cutter but does not know what it is used for. Therefore, let us say that, for the paper-cutter, essence—that is, the en-semble of both the production routines and the properties which enable it to be both produced and defined—precedes existence. Thus, the presence of the paper-cutter or book in front of me is determined. Therefore, we have here a technical view of the world whereby it can be said that production precedes existence.

theistic
concep.
of
human
essence
before
existence

When we conceive God as the Creator, He is generally thought of as a superior sort of artisan. Whatever doctrine we may be considering, whether one like that of Descartes or that of Leibniz, we always grant that will more or less follows understanding or, at the very least, accompanies it, and that when God creates He knows exactly what He is creating. Thus, the concept of man in the mind of God is comparable to the concept of paper-cutter in the mind of the manufacturer, and, following certain techniques and a con-ception, God produces man, just as the artisan, following a definition and a technique, makes a paper-cutter. Thus, the individual man is the realization of a certain concept in the divine intelligence.

Atheist
concept
of
human
too

In the eighteenth century, the atheism of the *philosophes* discarded the idea of God, but not so much for the notion that essence precedes existence. To a certain extent, this idea is found everywhere; we find it in Diderot, in Voltaire, and even in Kant. Man has a human nature; this human nature, which is the concept of the human, is found in all men, which means that each man is a particular example of a universal concept, man. In Kant, the result of this universality is that the wild-man, the natural man, as well as the bourgeois, are circumscribed by the same definition and have the same basic qualities. Thus, here too the essence of man precedes the historical ex-istence that we find in nature.

Atheistic
existentialism

no God
no pred...

Atheistic existentialism, which I represent, is more coherent. It states that if God does not exist, there is at least one being in whom existence precedes essence, a being who exists before he can be defined by any concept, and that this being is man, or, as Heidegger says, human reality. What is meant here by saying that existence precedes essence? It means that, first of all, man ex-

Responsibility

ists, turns up, appears on the scene, and, only afterwards, defines himself. If
man, as the existentialist conceives him, is indefinable, it is because at first he
is nothing. Only afterward will he be something, and he himself will have
made what he will be. Thus, there is no human nature, since there is no God
to conceive it. Not only is man what he conceives himself to be, but he is
also only what he wills himself to be after this thrust toward existence.

Man is nothing else but what he makes of himself. Such is the first principle of existentialism. It is also what is called subjectivity, the name we are
labeled with when charges are brought against us. But what do we mean by
this, if not that man has a greater dignity than a stone or table? For we mean
that man first exists, that is, that man first of all is the being who hurls himself toward a future and who is conscious of imagining himself as being in
the future. Man is at the start a plan which is aware of itself, rather than a
patch of moss, a piece of garbage, or a cauliflower; nothing exists prior to
this plan; there is nothing in heaven; man will be what he will have planned
to be. Not what he will want to be. Because by the word "will" we generally
mean a conscious decision, which is subsequent to what we have already
made of ourselves. I may want to belong to a political party, write a book, get
married; but all that is only a manifestation of an earlier, more spontaneous
choice that is called "will." But if existence really does precede essence, man
is responsible for what he is. Thus, existentialism's first move is to make
every man aware of what he is and to make the full responsibility of his existence rest on him. And when we say that a man is responsible for himself, we
do not only mean that he is responsible for his own individuality, but that he
is responsible for all men.

The word subjectivism has two meanings, and our opponents play on the
two. Subjectivism means, on the one hand, that an individual chooses and
makes himself; and, on the other, that it is impossible for man to transcend
human subjectivity. The second of these is the essential meaning of existentialism. When we say that man chooses his own self, we mean that every one
of us does likewise; but we also mean by that that in making this choice he
also chooses all men. In fact, in creating the man that we want to be, there is
not a single one of our acts which does not at the same time create an image
of man as we think he ought to be. To choose to be this or that is to affirm at
the same time the value of what we choose, because we can never choose
evil. We always choose the good, and nothing can be good for us without
being good for all.

If, on the other hand, existence precedes essence, and if we grant that we
exist and fashion our image at one and the same time, the image is valid for
everybody and for our whole age. Thus, our responsibility is much greater
than we might have supposed, because it involves all mankind. If I am a
workingman and choose to join a Christian trade-union rather than be a

(handwritten: Anguish)

communist, and if by being a member I want to show that the best thing for man is resignation, that the kingdom of man is not of this world, I am not only involving my own case—I want to be resigned for everyone. As a result, my action has involved all humanity. To take a more individual matter, if I want to marry, to have children; even if this marriage depends solely on my own circumstances or passion or wish, I am involving all humanity in monogamy and not merely myself. Therefore, I am responsible for myself and for everyone else. I am creating a certain image of man of my own choosing. In choosing myself, I choose man.

This helps us understand what the actual content is of such rather grandiloquent words as anguish, forlornness, despair. As you will see, it's all quite simple.

First, what is meant by anguish? The existentialists say at once that man is anguish. What that means is this: the man who involves himself and who realizes that he is not only the person he chooses to be, but also a lawmaker who is, at the same time, choosing all mankind as well as himself, cannot help escape the feeling of his total and deep responsibility. Of course, there are many people who are not anxious; but we claim that they are hiding their anxiety, that they are fleeing from it. Certainly, many people believe that when they do something, they themselves are the only ones involved, and when someone says to them, "What if everyone acted that way?" they shrug their shoulders and answer, "Everyone doesn't act that way." But really, one should always ask himself, "What would happen if everybody looked at things that way?" There is no escaping this disturbing thought except by a kind of double-dealing. A man who lies and makes excuses for himself by saying "not everybody does that," is someone with an uneasy conscience, because the act of lying implies that a universal value is conferred upon the lie.

Anguish is evident even when it conceals itself. This is the anguish that Kierkegaard called the anguish of Abraham. You know the story: an angel has ordered Abraham to sacrifice his son; if it really were an angel who has come and said, "You are Abraham, you shall sacrifice your son," everything would be all right. But everyone might first wonder, "Is it really an angel, and am I really Abraham? What proof do I have?"

There was a madwoman who had hallucinations; someone used to speak to her on the telephone and give her orders. Her doctor asked her, "Who is it who talks to you?" She answered, "He says it's God." What proof did she really have that it was God? If an angel comes to me, what proof is there that it's an angel? And if I hear voices, what proof is there that they come from heaven and not from hell, or from the subconscious, or a pathological condition? What proves that they are addressed to me? What proof is there that I have been appointed to impose my choice and my conception of man on humanity? I'll never find any proof or sign to convince me of that. If a voice addresses me, it is always for me to decide that this is the angel's voice; if I consider that such an act is a good one, it is I who will choose to say that it is good rather than bad.

Now, I'm not being singled out as an Abraham, and yet at every moment I'm obliged to perform exemplary acts. For every man, everything happens as if all mankind had its eyes fixed on him and were guiding itself by what he does. And every man ought to say to himself, "Am I really the kind of man who has the right to act in such a way that humanity might guide itself by my actions?" And if he does not say that to himself, he is masking his anguish.

There is no question here of the kind of anguish which would lead to quietism, to inaction. It is a matter of a simple sort of anguish that anybody who has had responsibilities is familiar with. For example, when a military officer takes the responsibility for an attack and sends a certain number of men to death, he chooses to do so, and in the main he alone makes the choice. Doubtless, orders come from above, but they are too broad; he interprets them, and on this interpretation depend the lives of ten or fourteen or twenty men. In making a decision he cannot help having a certain anguish. All leaders know this anguish. That doesn't keep them from acting; on the contrary, it is the very condition of their action. For it implies that they envisage a number of possibilities, and when they choose one, they realize that it has value only because it is chosen. We shall see that this kind of anguish, which is the kind that existentialism describes, is explained, in addition, by a direct responsibility to the other men whom it involves. It is not a curtain separating us from action, but is part of action itself.

When we speak of forlornness, a term Heidegger was fond of, we mean only that God does not exist and that we have to face all the consequences of this. The existentialist is strongly opposed to a certain kind of secular ethics which would like to abolish God with the least possible expense. About 1880, some French teachers tried to set up a secular ethics which went something like this: God is a useless and costly hypothesis; we are discarding it; but, meanwhile, in order for there to be an ethics, a society, a civilization, it is essential that certain values be taken seriously and that they be considered as having an a priori existence. It must be obligatory, a priori, to be honest, not to lie, not to beat your wife, to have children, etc., etc. So we're going to try a little device which will make it possible to show that values exist all the same, inscribed in a heaven of ideas, though otherwise God does not exist. In other words—and this, I believe, is the tendency of everything called reformism in France—nothing will be changed if God does not exist.

We shall find ourselves with the same norms of honesty, progress, and humanism, and we shall have made of God an outdated hypothesis which will peacefully die off by itself.

no God
no absolute values
no a priori Good

The existentialist, on the contrary, thinks it very distressing that God does not exist, because all possibility of finding values in a heaven of ideas disappears along with Him; there can no longer be an a priori Good, since there is no infinite and perfect consciousness to think it. Nowhere is it written that the Good exists, that we must be honest, that we must not lie; because the fact is we are on a plane where there are only men. Dostoyevsky said, "If God didn't exist, everything would be possible." That is the very starting point of existentialism. Indeed, everything is permissible if God does not exist, and as a result man is forlorn, because neither within him nor without does he find anything to cling to. He can't start making excuses for himself.

all possible
permissible

no excuses

If existence really does precede essence, there is no explaining things away by reference to a fixed and given human nature. In other words, there is no determinism, man is free, man is freedom. On the other hand, if God does not exist, we find no values or commands to turn to which legitimize our conduct. So, in the bright realm of values, we have no excuse behind us, nor justification before us. We are alone, with no excuses.

no justification in terms of fixed human nature
no determinism
just freedom

That is the idea I shall try to convey when I say that man is condemned to be free. Condemned, because he did not create himself, yet, in other respects is free; because, once thrown into the world, he is responsible for everything he does. The existentialist does not believe in the power of passion. He will never agree that a sweeping passion is a ravaging torrent which fatally leads a man to certain acts and is therefore an excuse. He thinks that man is responsible for his passion.

condemned to be free

The existentialist does not think that man is going to help himself by finding in the world some omen by which to orient himself. Because he thinks that man will interpret the omen to suit himself. Therefore, he thinks that man, with no support and no aid, is condemned every moment to invent man. Ponge, in a very fine article, has said, "Man is the future of man." That's exactly it. But if it is taken to mean that this future is recorded in heaven, that God sees it, then it is false, because it would really no longer be a future. If it is taken to mean that, whatever a man may be, there is a future to be forged, a virgin future before him, then this remark is sound. But then we are forlorn.

to invent man

To give you an example which will enable you to understand forlornness better, I shall cite the case of one of my students who came to see me under the following circumstances: his father was on bad terms with his mother, and, moreover, was inclined to be a collaborationist; his older brother had been killed in the German offensive of 1940, and the young man, with

(Forlornness in ethical issues ...)

somewhat immature but generous feelings, wanted to avenge him. His mother lived alone with him, very much upset by the half-treason of her husband and the death of her older son; the boy was her only consolation.

The boy was faced with the choice of leaving for England and joining the Free French Forces—that is, leaving his mother behind—or remaining with his mother and helping her to carry on. He was fully aware that the woman lived only for him and that his going-off—perhaps his death—would plunge her into despair. He was also aware that every act that he did for his mother's sake was a sure thing, in the sense that it was helping her to carry on, whereas every effort he made toward going off and fighting was an uncertain move which might run aground and prove completely useless; for example, on his way to England he might, while passing through Spain, he detained indefinitely in a Spanish camp; he might reach England or Algiers and be stuck in an office at a desk job. As a result, he was faced with two very different kinds of action: one, concrete, immediate, but concerning only one individual; the other concerned an incomparably vaster group, a national collectivity, but for that very reason was dubious, and might be interrupted en route. And, at the same time, he was wavering between two kinds of ethics. On the one hand, an ethics of sympathy, of personal devotion; on the other, a broader ethics, but one whose efficacy was more dubious. He had to choose between the two.

Who could help him choose? Christian doctrine? No. Christian doctrine says, "Be charitable, love your neighbor, take the more rugged path, etc., etc." But which is the more rugged path? Whom should he love as a brother? The fighting man or his mother? Which does the greater good, the vague act of fighting in a group, or the concrete one of helping a particular human being to go on living? Who can decide a priori? Nobody. No book of ethics can tell him. The Kantian ethics says, "Never treat any person as a means, but as an end." Very well, if I stay with my mother, I'll treat her as an end and not as a means; but by virtue of this very fact, I'm running the risk of treating the people around me who are fighting, as means; and, conversely, if I go to join those who are fighting, I'll be treating them as an end, and, by doing that, I run the risk of treating my mother as a means.

If values are vague, and if they are always too broad for the concrete and specific case that we are considering, the only thing left for us is to trust our instincts. That's what this young man tried to do; and when I saw him, he said, "In the end, feeling is what counts. I ought to choose whichever pushes me in one direction. If I feel that I love my mother enough to sacrifice everything else for her—my desire for vengeance, for action, for adventure—then I'll stay with her. If, on the contrary, I feel that my love for my mother isn't enough, I'll leave."

But how is the value of a feeling determined? What gives his feeling for his mother value? Precisely the fact that he remained with her. I may say that I like so-and-so well enough to sacrifice a certain amount of money for him, but I may say so only if I've done it. I may say "I love my mother well enough to remain with her" if I have remained with her. The only way to determine the value of this affection is, precisely, to perform an act which confirms and defines it. But, since I require this affection to justify my act, I find myself caught in a vicious circle.

On the other hand, Gide has well said that a mock feeling and a true feeling are almost indistinguishable; to decide that I love my mother and will remain with her, or to remain with her by putting on an act, amount somewhat to the same thing. In other words, the feeling is formed by the acts one performs; so, I cannot refer to it in order to act upon it. Which means that I can neither seek within myself the true condition which will impel me to act, nor apply to a system of ethics for concepts which will permit me to act. You will say, "At least, he did go to a teacher for advice." But if you seek advice from a priest, for example, you have chosen this priest; you already knew, more or less, just about what advice he was going to give you. In other words, choosing your adviser is involving yourself. The proof of this is that if you are a Christian, you will say, "Consult a priest." But some priests are collaborating, some are just marking time, some are resisting. Which to choose? If the young man chooses a priest who is resisting or collaborating, he has already decided on the kind of advice he's going to get. Therefore, in coming to see me he knew the answer I was going to give him, and I had only one answer to give: "You're free, choose, that is, invent." No general ethics can show you what is to be done; there are no omens in the world. The Catholics will reply, "But there are." Granted—but, in any case, I myself choose the meaning they have.

When I was a prisoner, I knew a rather remarkable young man who was a Jesuit. He had entered the Jesuit order in the following way: he had had a number of very bad breaks; in childhood, his father died, leaving him in poverty, and he was a scholarship student at a religious institution where he was constantly made to feel that he was being kept out of charity; then, he failed to get any of the honors and distinctions that children like; later on, at about eighteen, he bungled a love affair; finally, at twenty-two, he failed in military training, a childish enough matter, but it was the last straw.

This young fellow might well have felt that he had botched everything. It was a sign of something, but of what? He might have taken refuge in bitterness or despair. But he very wisely looked upon all this as a sign that he was not made for secular triumphs, and that only the triumphs of religion, holiness, and faith were open to him. He saw the hand of God in all this, and so he entered the order. Who can help seeing that he alone decided what the sign meant?

Some other interpretation might have been drawn from this series of set-backs; for example, that he might have done better to turn carpenter or revolutionist. Therefore, he is fully responsible for the interpretation. Forlornness implies that we ourselves choose our being. Forlornness and anguish go together.

As for despair, the term has a very simple meaning. It means that we shall confine ourselves to reckoning only with what depends upon our will, or on the ensemble of probabilities which make our action possible. When we want something, we always have to reckon with probabilities. I may be counting on the arrival of a friend. The friend is coming by rail or street-car; this supposes that the train will arrive on schedule, or that the street-car will not jump the track. I am left in the realm of possibility; but possibilities are to be reckoned with only to the point where my action comports with the ensemble of these possibilities, and no further. The moment the possibilities I am considering are not rigorously involved by my action, I ought to disengage myself from them, because no God, no scheme, can adapt the world and its possibilities to my will. When Descartes said, "Conquer yourself rather than the world," he meant essentially the same thing.

The Marxists to whom I have spoken reply, "You can rely on the support of others in your action, which obviously has certain limits because you're not going to live forever. That means: rely on both what others are doing elsewhere to help you, in China, in Russia, and what they will do later on, after your death, to carry on the action and lead it to its fulfillment, which will be the revolution. You even *have* to rely upon that, otherwise you're immoral." I reply at once that I will always rely on fellow-fighters insofar as these comrades are involved with me in a common struggle, in the unity of a party or a group in which I can more or less make my weight felt; that is, one whose ranks I am in as a fighter and whose movements I am aware of at every moment. In such a situation, relying on the unity and will of the party is exactly like counting on the fact that the train will arrive on time or that the car won't jump the track. But, given that man is free and that there is no human nature for me to depend on, I cannot count on men whom I do not know by relying on human goodness or man's concern for the good of society. I don't know what will become of the Russian revolution; I may make an example of it to the extent that at the present time it is apparent that the proletariat plays a part in Russia that it plays in no other nation. But I can't swear that this will inevitably lead to a triumph of the proletariat. I've got to limit myself to what I see.

Given that men are free and that tomorrow they will freely decide what man will be, I cannot be sure that, after my death, fellow-fighters will carry on my work to bring it to its maximum perfection. Tomorrow, after my death, some men may decide to set up Fascism, and the others may be

Ethics of Action (not quietism)

cowardly and muddled enough to let them do it. Fascism will then be the human reality, so much the worse for us.

Actually, things will be as man will have decided they are to be. Does that mean that I should abandon myself to quietism? No. First, I should involve myself; then, act on the old saw, "Nothing ventured, nothing gained." Nor does it mean that I shouldn't belong to a party, but rather that I shall have no illusions and shall do what I can. For example, suppose I ask myself, "Will socialization, as such, ever come about?" I know nothing about it. All I know is that I'm going to do everything in my power to bring it about. Beyond that, I can't count on anything. Quietism is the attitude of people who say, "Let others do what I can't do." The doctrine I am presenting is the very opposite of quietism, since it declares, "There is no reality except in action." Moreover, it goes further, since it adds, "Man is nothing else than his plan; he exists only to the extent that he fulfills himself; he is therefore nothing else than the ensemble of his acts, nothing else than his life."

According to this, we can understand why our doctrine horrifies certain people. Because often the only way they can bear their wretchedness is to think, "Circumstances have been against me. What I've been and done doesn't show my true worth. To be sure, I've had no great love, no great friendship, but that's because I haven't met a man or woman who was worthy. The books I've written haven't been very good because I haven't had the proper leisure. I haven't had children to devote myself to because I didn't find a man with whom I could have spent my life. So there remains within me, unused and quite viable, a host of propensities, inclinations, possibilities, that one wouldn't guess from the mere series of things I've done." Now, for the existentialist there is really no love other than one which manifests itself in a person's being in love. There is no genius other than one which is expressed in works of art; the genius of Proust is the sum of Proust's works; the genius of Racine is his series of tragedies. Outside of that, there is nothing. Why say that Racine could have written another tragedy, when he didn't write it? A man is involved in life, leaves his impress on it, and outside of that there is nothing. To be sure, this may seem a harsh thought to someone whose life hasn't been a success. But, on the other hand, it prompts people to understand that reality alone is what counts, that dreams, expectations, and hopes warrant no more than to define a man as a disappointed dream, as miscarried hopes, as vain expectations. In other words, to define him negatively and not positively. However, when we say, "You are nothing else than your life," that does not imply that the artist will be judged solely on the basis of his works of art; a thousand other things will contribute toward summing him up. What we mean is that a man is nothing else than a series of undertakings, that he is the sum, the organization, the ensemble of the relationships which make up these undertakings.

Tough Optimism, not Pessimism [handwritten annotation at top of page]

When all is said and done, what we are accused of, at bottom, is not our pessimism, but an optimistic toughness. If people throw up to us our works of fiction in which we write about people who are soft, weak, cowardly, and sometimes even downright bad, it's not because these people are soft, weak, cowardly, or bad; because if we were to say, as Zola did, that they are that way because of heredity, the workings of environment, society, because of biological or psychological determinism, people would be reassured. They would say, "Well, that's what we're like, no one can do anything about it." But when the existentialist writes about a coward, he says that this coward is responsible for his cowardice. He's not like that because he has a cowardly heart or lung or brain; he's not like that on account of his physiological make-up; but he's like that because he has made himself a coward by his acts. There's no such thing as a cowardly constitution; there are nervous constitutions; there is poor blood, as the common people say, or strong constitutions. But the man whose blood is poor is not a coward on that account, for what makes cowardice is the act of renouncing or yielding. A constitution is not an act; the coward is defined on the basis of the acts he performs. People feel, in a vague sort of way, that this coward we're talking about is guilty of being a coward, and the thought frightens them. What people would like is that a coward or a hero be born that way.

One of the complaints most frequently made about *The Ways of Freedom** can be summed up as follows: "After all, these people are so spineless, how are you going to make heroes out of them?" This objection almost makes me laugh, for it assumes that people are born heroes. That's what people really want to think. If you're born cowardly, you may set your mind perfectly at rest; there's nothing you can do about it; you'll be cowardly all your life, whatever you may do. If you're born a hero, you may set your mind just as much at rest; you'll be a hero all your life; you'll drink like a hero and eat like a hero. What the existentialist says is that the coward makes himself cowardly, that the hero makes himself heroic. There's always a possibility for the coward not to be cowardly any more and for the hero to stop being heroic. What counts is total involvement; some one particular action or set of circumstances is not total involvement.

Thus, I think we have answered a number of the charges concerning existentialism. You see that it cannot be taken for a philosophy of quietism, since it defines man in terms of action; nor for a pessimistic description of man—there is no doctrine more optimistic, since man's destiny is within himself; nor for an attempt to discourage man from acting, since it tells him

[right margin handwritten annotations: *not quietism / man = action / not pessimism / man holds future in hands*]

* *Les Chemins de la Liberté*, M. Sartre's projected trilogy of novels, two of which, *L'Age de Raison* (*The Age of Reason*) and *Le Sursis* (*The Reprieve*) have already appeared. Translator's note.

that the only hope is in his acting and that action is the only thing that enables a man to live. Consequently, we are dealing here with an ethics of action and involvement.

Nevertheless, on the basis of a few notions like these, we are still charged with immuring man in his private subjectivity. There again we're very much misunderstood. Subjectivity of the individual is indeed our point of departure, and this for strictly philosophic reasons. Not because we are bourgeois, but because we want a doctrine based on truth and not a lot of fine theories, full of hope but with no real basis. There can be no other truth to take off from than this: *I think; therefore, I exist.* There we have the absolute truth of consciousness becoming aware of itself. Every theory which takes man out of the moment in which he becomes aware of himself is, at its very beginning, a theory which confounds truth, for outside the Cartesian *cogito*, all views are only probable, and a doctrine of probability which is not bound to a truth dissolves into thin air. In order to describe the probable, you must have a firm hold on the true. Therefore, before there can be any truth whatsoever, there must be an absolute truth; and this one is simple and easily arrived at; it's on everyone's doorstep; it's a matter of grasping it directly.

Secondly, this theory is the only one which gives man dignity, the only one which does not reduce him to an object. The effect of all materialism is to treat all men, including the one philosophizing, as objects, that is, as an ensemble of determined reactions in no way distinguished from the ensemble of qualities and phenomena which constitute a table or a chair or a stone. We definitely wish to establish the human realm as an ensemble of values distinct from the material realm. But the subjectivity that we have thus arrived at, and which we have claimed to be truth, is not a strictly individual subjectivity, for we have demonstrated that one discovers in the *cogito* not only himself, but others as well.

The philosophies of Descartes and Kant to the contrary, through the *I think* we reach our own self in the presence of others, and the others are just as real to us as our own self. Thus, the man who becomes aware of himself through the *cogito* also perceives all others, and he perceives them as the condition of his own existence. He realizes that he cannot be anything (in the sense that we say that someone is witty or nasty or jealous) unless others recognize it as such. In order to get any truth about myself, I must have contact with another person. The other is indispensable to my own existence, as well as to my knowledge about myself. This being so, in discovering my inner being I discover the other person at the same time, like a freedom placed in front of me which thinks and wills only for or against me. Hence, let us at once announce the discovery of a world which we shall call intersubjectivity; this is the world in which man decides what he is and what others are.

Besides, if it is impossible to find in every man some universal essence which would be human nature, yet there does exist a universal human condition. It's not by chance that today's thinkers speak more readily of man's condition than of his nature. By condition they mean, more or less definitely, the a priori limits which outline man's fundamental situation in the universe. Historical situations vary; a man may be born a slave in a pagan society or a feudal lord or a proletarian. What does not vary is the necessity for him to exist in the world, to be at work there, to be there in the midst of other people, and to be mortal there. The limits are neither subjective nor objective, or, rather, they have an objective and a subjective side. Objective because they are to be found everywhere and are recognizable everywhere; subjective because they are *lived* and are nothing if man does not live them, that is, freely determine his existence with reference to them. And though the configurations may differ, at least none of them are completely strange to me, because they all appear as attempts either to pass beyond these limits or recede from them or deny them or adapt to them. Consequently, every configuration, however individual it may be, has a universal value.

Every configuration, even the Chinese, the Indian, or the Negro, can be understood by a Westerner. "Can be understood" means that by virtue of a situation that he can imagine, a European of 1945 can, in like manner, push himself to his limits and reconstitute within himself the configuration of the Chinese, the Indian, or the African. Every configuration has universality in the sense that every configuration can be understood by every man. This does not at all mean that this configuration defines man forever, but that it can be met with again. There is always a way to understand the idiot, the child, the savage, the foreigner, provided one has the necessary information.

In this sense we may say that there is a universality of man; but it is not given, it is perpetually being made. I build the universal in choosing myself; I build it in understanding the configuration of every other man, whatever age he might have lived in. This absoluteness of choice does not do away with the relativeness of each epoch. At heart, what existentialism shows is the connection between the absolute character of free involvement, by virtue of which every man realizes himself in realizing a type of mankind, an involvement always comprehensible in any age whatsoever and by any person whosoever, and the relativeness of the cultural ensemble which may result from such a choice; it must be stressed that the relativity of Cartesianism and the absolute character of Cartesian involvement go together. In this sense, you may, if you like, say that each of us performs an absolute act in breathing, eating, sleeping, or behaving in any way whatever. There is no difference between being free, like a configuration, like an existence which chooses its essence, and being absolute. There is no difference between being an absolute temporarily localized, that is, localized in history, and being universally comprehensible.

This does not entirely settle the objection to subjectivism. In fact, the objection still takes several forms. First, there is the following: we are told,

Objections 'No limits ⎰ᵃ anarchy
⎱ᵇ no judgmet of others possible
ᶜ all arbitrary

282   *Sartre*

"So you're able to do anything, no matter what!" This is expressed in various ways. First we are accused of anarchy; then they say, "You're unable to pass judgment on others, because there's no reason to prefer one configuration to another"; finally they tell us, "Everything is arbitrary in this choosing of yours. You take something from one pocket and pretend you're putting it into the other."

limits / must choose

These three objections aren't very serious. Take the first objection. ① "You're able to do anything, no matter what" is not to the point. In one sense choice is possible, but what is not possible is not to choose. I can always choose, but I ought to know that if I do not choose, I am still choosing. Though this may seem purely formal, it is highly important for keeping fantasy and caprice within bounds. If it is true that in facing a situation, for example, one in which, as a person capable of having sexual relations, of having children, I am obliged to choose an attitude, and if I in any way assume responsibility for a choice which, in involving myself, also involves all mankind, this has nothing to do with caprice, even if no a priori value determines my choice.

no ② anarchy

If anybody thinks that he recognizes here Gide's theory of the arbitrary act, he fails to see the enormous difference between this doctrine and Gide's. Gide does not know what a situation is. He acts out of pure caprice. For us, on the contrary, man is in an organized situation in which he himself is involved. Through his choice, he involves all mankind, and he cannot avoid making a choice; either he will remain chaste, or he will marry without having children, or he will marry and have children; anyhow, whatever he may do, it is impossible for him not to take full responsibility for the way he handles this problem. Doubtless, he chooses without referring to preestablished values, but it is unfair to accuse him of caprice. Instead, let us say that moral choice is to be compared to the making of a work of art. And before going any further, let it be said at once that we are not dealing here with an aesthetic ethics, because our opponents are so dishonest that they even accuse us of that. The example I've chosen is a comparison only.

Having said that, may I ask whether anyone has ever accused an artist who has painted a picture of not having drawn his inspiration from rules set up a priori? Has anyone ever asked, "What painting ought he to make?" It is clearly understood that there is no definite painting to be made, that the artist is engaged in the making of his painting, and that the painting to be made is precisely the painting he will have made. It is clearly understood that there are no a priori aesthetic values, but that there are values which appear subsequently in the coherence of the painting, in the correspondence between what the artist intended and the result. Nobody can tell what the painting of tomorrow will be like. Painting can be judged only after it has once been made. What connection does that have with ethics? We are in the same creative situation. We never say that a work of art is arbitrary. When we speak of a canvas of Picasso, we never say that it is arbitrary; we understand quite well that he was making himself what he is at the very time he was painting, that the ensemble of his work is embodied in his life.

The same holds on the ethical plane. What art and ethics have in common is that we have creation and invention in both cases. We cannot decide a priori what there is to be done. I think that I pointed that out quite sufficiently when I mentioned the case of the student who came to see me, and who might have applied to all the ethical systems, Kantian or otherwise, without getting any sort of guidance. He was obliged to devise his law himself. Never let it be said by us that this man—who, taking affection, individual action, and kind-heartedness toward a specific person as his ethical first principle, chooses to remain with his mother, or who, preferring to make a sacrifice, chooses to go to England—has made an arbitrary choice. Man makes himself. He isn't ready made at the start. In choosing his ethics, he makes himself, and force of circumstances is such that he cannot abstain from choosing one. We define man only in relationship to involvement. It is therefore absurd to charge us with arbitrariness of choice.

In the second place, it is said that we are unable to pass judgment on others. In a way this is true, and in another way, false. It is true in this sense, that, whenever a man sanely and sincerely involves himself and chooses his configuration, it is impossible for him to prefer another configuration, regardless of what his own may be in other respects. It is true in this sense, that we do not believe in progress. Progress is betterment. Man is always the same. The situation confronting him varies. Choice always remains a choice in a situation. The problem has not changed since the time one could choose between those for and those against slavery, for example, at the time of the Civil War, and the present time, when one can side with the Maquis Resistance Party, or with the Communists.

But, nevertheless, one can still pass judgment, for, as I have said, one makes a choice in relationship to others. First, one can judge (and this is perhaps not a judgment of value, but a logical judgment) that certain choices are based on error and others on truth. If we have defined man's situation as a free choice, with no excuses and no recourse, every man who takes refuge behind the excuse of his passions, every man who sets up a determinism, is a dishonest man.

The objection may be raised, "But why mayn't he choose himself dishonestly?" I reply that I am not obliged to pass moral judgment on him, but that I do define his dishonesty as an error. One cannot help considering the truth of the matter. Dishonesty is obviously a falsehood because it belies the complete freedom of involvement. On the same grounds, I maintain that there is also dishonesty if I choose to state that certain values exist prior to me; it is self-contradictory for me to want them and at the same state that they are imposed on me. Suppose someone says to me, "What if I want to be dishonest?" I'll answer, "There's no reason for you not to be, but I'm saying that that's what you are, and that the strictly coherent attitude is that of honesty."

Besides, I can bring moral judgment to bear. When I declare that freedom in every concrete circumstance can have no other aim than to want itself, if man has once become aware that in his forlornness he imposes values, he can no longer want but one thing, and that is freedom, as the basis of all values. That doesn't mean that he wants it in the abstract. It means simply that the ultimate meaning of the acts of honest men is the quest for freedom as such. A man who belongs to a communist or revolutionary union wants concrete goals; these goals imply an abstract desire for freedom; but this freedom is wanted in something concrete. We want freedom for freedom's sake and in every particular circumstance. And in wanting freedom we discover that it depends entirely on the freedom of others, and that the freedom of others depends on ours. Of course, freedom as the definition of man does not depend on others, but as soon as there is involvement, I am obliged to want others to have freedom at the same time that I want my own freedom. I can take freedom as my goal only if I take that of others as a goal as well. Consequently, when, in all honesty, I've recognized that man is a being in whom existence precedes essence, that he is a free being who, in various circumstances, can want only his freedom, I have at the same time recognized that I can want only the freedom of others.

Therefore, in the name of this will for freedom, which freedom itself implies, I may pass judgment on those who seek to hide from themselves the complete arbitrariness and the complete freedom of their existence. Those who hide their complete freedom from themselves out of a spirit of seriousness or by means of deterministic excuses, I shall call cowards; those who try to show that their existence was necessary, when it is the very contingency of man's appearance on earth, I shall call stinkers. But cowards or stinkers can be judged only from a strictly unbiased point of view.

Therefore though the content of ethics is variable, a certain form of it is universal. Kant says that freedom desires both itself and the freedom of others. Granted. But he believes that the formal and the universal are enough to constitute an ethics. We, on the other hand, think that principles which are too abstract run aground in trying to decide action. Once again, take the case of the student. In the name of what, in the name of what great moral maxim do you think he could have decided, in perfect peace of mind, to abandon his mother or to stay with her? There is no way of judging. The content is always concrete and thereby unforeseeable; there is always the element of invention. The one thing that counts is knowing whether the inventing that has been done, has been done in the name of freedom.

For example, let us look at the following two cases. You will see to what extent they correspond, yet differ. Take *The Mill on the Floss*. We find a certain young girl, Maggie Tulliver, who is an embodiment of the value of passion and who is aware of it. She is in love with a young man, Stephen, who is engaged to an insignificant young girl. This Maggie Tulliver, instead of heedlessly preferring her own happiness, chooses, in the name of human solidarity, to sacrifice herself and give up the man she loves. On the other hand, Sanseverina, in *The Charterhouse of Parma*, believing that passion is man's true value, would say that a great love deserves sacrifices; that it is to be preferred to the banality of the conjugal love that would tie Stephen to the young ninny he had to marry. She would choose to sacrifice the girl and fulfill her happiness; and, as Stendhal shows, she is even ready to sacrifice herself for the sake of passion, if this life demands it. Here we are in the presence of two strictly opposed moralities. I claim that they are much the same thing; in both cases what has been set up as the goal is freedom.

You can imagine two highly similar attitudes: one girl prefers to renounce her love out of resignation; another prefers to disregard the prior attachment of the man she loves out of sexual desire. On the surface these two actions resemble those we've just described. However, they are completely different. Sanseverina's attitude is much nearer that of Maggie Tulliver, one of heedless rapacity.

Thus, you see that the second charge is true and, at the same time, false. One may choose anything if it is on the grounds of free involvement.

The third objection is the following: "You take something from one pocket and put it into the other. That is, fundamentally, values aren't serious, since you choose them." My answer to this is that I'm quite vexed that that's the way it is; but if I've discarded God the Father, there has to be someone to invent values. You've got to take things as they are. Moreover, to say that we invent values means nothing else but this: life has no meaning a priori. Before you come alive, life is nothing; it's up to you to give it a meaning, and value is nothing else but the meaning that you choose. In that way, you see, there is a possibility of creating a human community.

I've been reproached for asking whether existentialism is humanistic. It's been said, "But you said in *Nausea* that the humanists were all wrong. You made fun of a certain kind of humanist. Why come back to it now?" Actually, the word humanism has two very different meanings. By humanism one can mean a theory which takes man as an end and as a higher value. Humanism in this sense can be found in Cocteau's tale *Around the World in Eighty Hours* when a character, because he is flying over some mountains in an airplane, declares, "Man is simply amazing." That means that I, who did not build the airplanes, shall personally benefit from these particular inventions, and that I, as man, shall personally consider myself responsible for, and honored by, acts of a few particular men. This would imply that we ascribe a value to man on the basis of the highest deeds of certain men. This humanism is absurd, because only the dog or the horse would be able to make such an over-all judgment about man, which they are careful not to do, at least to my knowledge.

But it cannot be granted that a man may make a judgment about man. Existentialism spares him from any such judgment. The existentialist will never consider man as an end because he is always in the making. Nor should we believe that there is a mankind to which we might set up a cult in the manner of Auguste Comte. The cult of mankind ends in the self-enclosed humanism of Comte, and, let it be said, of fascism. This kind of humanism we can do without.

But there is another meaning of humanism. Fundamentally it is this: man is constantly outside of himself; in projecting himself, in losing himself outside of himself, he makes for man's existing; and, on the other hand, it is by pursuing transcendent goals that he is able to exist; man, being this state of passing-beyond, and seizing upon things only as they bear upon this passing-beyond, is at the heart, at the center of this passing-beyond. There is no universe other than a human universe, the universe of human subjectivity. This connection between transcendency, as a constituent element of man—not in the sense that God is transcendent, but in the sense of passing beyond—and subjectivity, in the sense that man is not closed in on himself but is always present in a human universe, is what we call existentialism humanism. Humanism, because we remind man that there is no law-maker other than himself, and that in his forlornness he will decide by himself; because we point out that man will fulfill himself as man, not in turning toward himself, but in seeking outside of himself a goal which is just this liberation, just this particular fulfillment.

From these few reflections it is evident that nothing is more unjust than the objections that have been raised against us. Existentialism is nothing else than an attempt to draw all the consequences of a coherent atheistic position. It isn't trying to plunge man into despair at all. But if one calls every attitude of unbelief despair, like the Christians, then the word is not being used in its original sense. Existentialism isn't so atheistic that it wears itself out showing that God doesn't exist. Rather, it declares that even if God did exist, that would change nothing. There you've got our point of view. Not that we believe that God exists, but we think that the problem of His existence is not the issue. In this sense existentialism is optimistic, a doctrine of action, and it is plain dishonesty for Christians to make no distinction between their own despair and ours and then to call us despairing.

Being and Nothingness 1943

1. THE ORIGIN OF NEGATION: THE QUESTION

Our inquiry has led us to the heart of being. But we have been brought to an impasse since we have not been able to establish the connection between the two regions of being which we have discovered. No doubt this is because we have chosen an unfortunate approach. Descartes found himself faced with an analogous problem when he had to deal with the relation between soul and body. He planned then to look for the solution on that level where the union of thinking substance and extended substance was actually effected—that is, in the imagination. His advice is valuable. To be sure, our concern is not that of Descartes and we do not conceive of imagination as he did. But what we can retain is the reminder that it is not profitable first to separate the two terms of a relation in order to try to join them together again later. The relation is a synthesis. Consequently the *results* of analysis cannot be covered over again by the *moments* of this synthesis.

M. Laporte says that an abstraction is made when something not capable of existing in isolation is thought of as in an isolated state. The concrete by contrast is a totality which can exist by itself alone. Husserl is of the same opinion; for him *red* is an abstraction because color cannot exist without form. On the other hand, a spatial-temporal *thing,* with all its determinations, is an example of the concrete. From this point of view, consciousness is an abstraction since it conceals within itself an ontological source in the region of the in-itself, and conversely the phenomenon is likewise an abstraction since it must "appear" to consciousness. The concrete can be only the synthetic totality of which consciousness, like the phenomenon, constitutes only moments. The concrete is man within the world in that specific union of man with the world which Heidegger, for example, calls "being-in-the-world." We deliberately begin with the abstract if we question "experience" as Kant does, inquiring into the conditions of its possibility—or if we effect a phenomenological reduction like Husserl, who would reduce the world to the state of the noema-correlate of consciousness. But we will no more succeed in restoring the concrete by the summation or organization of the elements which we have abstracted from it than Spinoza can reach substance by the infinite summation of its modes.

The relation of the regions of being is an original emergence and is a part of the very structure of these beings. But we discovered this in our first observations. It is enough now to open our eyes and question ingenuously this

287

totality which is man-in-the-world. It is by the description of this totality that we shall be able to reply to these two questions: (1) What is the synthetic relation which we call being-in-the-world? (2) What must man and the world be in order for a relation between them to be possible? In truth, the two questions are interdependent, and we cannot hope to reply to them separately. But each type of human conduct, being the conduct of man in the world, can release for us simultaneously man, the world, and the relation which unites them, only on condition that we envisage these forms of conduct as realities objectively apprehensible and not as subjective affects which disclose themselves only in the face of reflection.

We shall not limit ourselves to the study of a single pattern of conduct. We shall try on the contrary to describe several and proceeding from one kind of conduct to another, attempt to penetrate into the profound meaning of the relation "man-world." But first of all we should choose a single pattern which can serve us as a guiding thread in our inquiry.

Now this very inquiry furnishes us with the desired conduct; this man that *I am*—if I apprehend him such as he is at this moment in the world, I establish that he stands before being in an attitude of interrogation. At the very moment when I ask, "Is there any conduct with can reveal to me the relation of man with the world?" I pose a question. This question I can consider objectively, for it matters little whether the questioner is myself or the reader who reads my work and who is questioning along with me. But on the other hand, the question is not simply the objective totality of the words printed on this page; it is indifferent to the symbols which express it. In a word, it is a human attitude filled with meaning. What does this attitude reveal to us?

In every question we stand before a being which we are questioning. Every question presupposes a being who questions and a being which is questioned. This is not the original relation of man to being-in-itself, but rather it stands within the limitations of this relation and takes it for granted. On the other hand, this being which we question, we question *about* something. That *about which* I question the being participates in the transcendence of being. I question being about its ways of being or about its being. From this point of view the question is a kind of expectation; I expect a reply from the being questioned. That is, on the basis of a pre-interrogative familiarity with being, I expect from this being a revelation of its being or of its way of being. The reply will be a "yes" or a "no." It is the existence of these two equally objective and contradictory possibilities which on principle distinguishes the question from affirmation or negation. There are questions which on the surface do not permit a negative reply— like, for example, the one which we put earlier, "What does this attitude re-

Triple non-being in question

veal to us?" But actually we see that it is always possible with questions of this type to reply, "Nothing" or "Nobody" or "Never." Thus at the moment when I ask, "Is there any conduct which can reveal to me the relation of man with the world?" I admit *on principle* the possibility of a negative reply such as, "No, such a conduct does not exist." This means that we admit to being faced with the transcendent fact of the non-existence of such conduct.

One will perhaps be tempted not to believe in the objective existence of a non-being; one will say that in this case the fact simply refers me to my subjectivity; I would learn from the transcendent being that the conduct sought is a pure fiction. But in the first place, to call this conduct a pure fiction is to disguise the negation without removing it. "To be pure fiction" is equivalent here to "to be only a fiction." Consequently to destroy the reality of the negation is to cause the reality of the reply to disappear. This reply, in fact, is the very being which gives it to me; that is, reveals the negation to me. There exists then for the questioner the permanent objective possibility of a negative reply. In relation to this possibility the questioner by the very fact that he is questioning, posits himself as in a state of indetermination; he *does not know* whether the reply will be affirmative or negative. Thus the question is a bridge set up between two non-beings: the non-being of knowing in man, the possibility of non-being of being in transcendent being. Finally the question implies the existence of a truth. By the very question the questioner affirms that he expects an objective reply, such that we can say of it, "It is thus and not otherwise." In a word the truth, as differentiated from being, introduces a third non-being as determining the question—the non-being of limitation. This triple non-being conditions every question and in particular the metaphysical question, which is *our* question.

We set out upon our pursuit of being, and it seemed to us that the series of our questions had led us to the heart of being. But behold, at the moment when we thought we were arriving at the goal, a glance cast on the question itself has revealed to us suddenly that we are encompassed with nothingness. The permanent possibility of non-being, outside us and within, conditions our questions about being. Furthermore it is non-being which is going to limit the reply. What being *will be* must of necessity arise on the basis of what *it is not.* Whatever being is, it will allow this formulation: "Being is *that* and outside of that, *nothing.*"

Thus a new component of the real has just appeared to us—non-being. Our problem is thereby complicated, for we may no longer limit our inquiry to the relations of the human being to being in-itself, but must include also the relations of being with non-being and the relations of human non-being with transcendent-being. But let us consider further.

2. NEGATIONS

Someone will object that being-in-itself cannot furnish negative replies. Did not we ourselves say that it was beyond affirmation as beyond negation? Furthermore ordinary experience reduced to itself does not seem to disclose any non-being to us. I think that there are fifteen hundred francs in my wallet, and I find only thirteen hundred; that does not mean, someone will tell us, that experience had discovered for me the non-being of fifteen hundred francs but simply that I have counted thirteen hundred-franc notes. Negation proper (we are told) is unthinkable; it could appear only on the level of an act of judgment by which I should establish a comparison between the result anticipated and the result obtained. Thus negation would be simply a quality of judgment and the expectation of the questioner would be an expectation of the judgment-response. As for Nothingness, this would derive its origin from negative judgments; it would be a concept establishing the transcendent unity of all these judgments, a propositional function of the type, "X is not."

We see where this theory is leading; its proponents would make us conclude that being-in-itself is full positivity and does not contain in itself any negation. This negative judgment, on the other hand, by virtue of being a subjective act, is strictly identified with the affirmative judgment. They cannot see that Kant, for example, has distinguished in its internal texture the negative act of judgment from the affirmative act. In each case a synthesis of concepts is operative; that synthesis, which is a concrete and full event of psychic life, is operative here merely in the manner of the copula "is" and there in the manner of the copula "is not." In the same way the manual operation of sorting out (separation) and the manual operation of assembling (union) are two objective conducts which possess the same reality of fact. Thus negation would be "at the end" of the act of judgment without, however, being "in" being. It is like an unreal encompassed by two full realities neither of which claims it; being-it-itself, if questioned about negation, refers to judgment, since being is only what it is—and judgment, a *wholly* psychic positivity, refers to being since judgment formulates a negation which concerns being and which consequently is transcendent. Negation, the result of concrete psychic operations, is supported in existence by these very operations and is incapable of existing by itself; it has the existence of a noema-correlate; its *esse* resides exactly in its *percipi*. Nothingness, the conceptual unity of negative judgments, cannot have the slightest trace of reality, save that which the Stoics confer on their "lecton." Can we accept this concept?

The question can be put in these terms: Is negation as the structure of the judicative proposition at the origin of nothingness? Or on the contrary is nothingness as the structure of the real, the origin and foundation of nega-tion? Thus the problem of being had referred us first to that of the question as a human attitude, and the problem of the question now refers us to that of the being of negation.

It is evident that non-being always appears within the limits of a human expectation. It is because I expect to find fifteen hundred francs that I find *only* thirteen hundred. It is because a physicist *expects* a certain verification of his hypothesis that nature can tell him no. It would be in vain to deny that negation appears on the original basis of a relation of man to the world. The world does not disclose its non-beings to one who has not first posited them as possibilities. But is this to say that these non-beings are to be reduced to pure subjectivity? Does this mean to say that we ought to give them the importance and the type of existence of the Stoic "lecton," of Husserl's noema? We think not.

First it is not true that negation is only a quality of judgment. The question is formulated by an interrogative judgment, but it is not itself a judgment; it is a pre-judicative attitude. I can question by a look, by a gesture. In posing a question I stand facing being in a certain way and this relation to being is a relation of being; the judgment is only one optional expression of it. At the same time it is not necessarily a person whom the questioner questions about being; this conception of the question by making of it an inter-subjective phenomenon, detaches it from the being to which it adheres and leaves it in the air as pure modality of dialogue. On the contrary, we must consider the question in dialogue to be only a particular species of the genus "question;" the being in question is not necessarily a thinking being. If my car breaks down, it is the *carburetor*, the *spark plugs, etc.*, that I question. If my watch stops, I can question the watchmaker about the cause of the stopping, but it is the various mechanisms of the watch that the watchmaker will in turn question. What I expect from the carburetor, what the watchmaker expects from the works of the watch, is not a judgment; it is a disclosure of being on the basis of which we can make a judgment. And if I *expect* a disclosure of being, I am prepared at the same time for the eventuality of a disclosure of a non-being. If I question the carburetor, it is because I consider it possible that "there is nothing there" in the carburetor. Thus my question by its nature envelops a certain pre-judicative comprehension of non-being; it is in itself a relation of being with non-being, on the basis of the original transcendence; that is, in a relation of being with being.

Moreover if the proper nature of the question is obscured by the fact that questions are frequently put by one man to other men, it should be pointed out here that there are numerous non-judicative conducts which present this immediate comprehension of non-being on the basis of being—in its original purity. If, for example, we consider *destruction*, we must recognize that it is an *activity* which doubtless could utilize judgment as an instrument but which cannot be defined as uniquely or even primarily judicative. "Destruction" presents the same structure as "the question." In a sense, certainly, man is the only being by whom a destruction can be accomplished. A geological plication, a storm do not destroy—or at least they do not destroy *directly*; they merely modify the distribution of masses of beings. There is no *less* after the storm than before. There is *something else*. Even this expression is improper, for to posit otherness there must be a witness who can retain the past in some manner and compare it to the present in the form of *no longer*. In the absence of this witness, there is being before as after the storm—that is all. If a cyclone can bring about the death of certain living beings, this death will be destruction only if it is experienced as such. In order for destruction to exist, there must be first a relation of man to being—*i.e.*, a transcendence; and within the limits of this relation, it is necessary that man apprehend one being as destructible. This supposes a limiting cutting into being by a being, which, as we saw in connection with truth, is already a process of nihilation. The being under consideration is *that* and outside of that *nothing*. The gunner who has been assigned an objective carefully points his gun in a certain direction *excluding* all others. But even this would still be nothing unless the being of the gunner's objective is revealed as *fragile*. And what is fragility if not a certain probability of non-being for a given being under determined circumstances. A being is fragile if it carries in its being a definite possibility of non-being. But once again it is through man that fragility comes into being, for the individualizing limitation which we mentioned earlier is the condition of fragility; *one* being is fragile and not *all* being, for the latter is beyond all possible destruction. Thus the relation of individualizing limitation which man enters into with *one* being on the original basis of his relation to being causes fragility to enter into this being as the appearance of a permanent possibility of non-being. But this is not all. In order for destructibility to exist, man must determine himself in the face of this possibility of non-being, either positively or negatively; he must either take the necessary measures to realize it (destruction proper) or, by a negation of non-being, to maintain it always on the level of a simple possibility (by preventive measures). Thus it is man who renders cities destructible, precisely because he posits them as fragile and as precious and because he adopts a system of protective measures with regard to them. It is because of this ensemble of measures that an earthquake or a volcanic eruption can *destroy* these cities or these human constructions. The original meaning and aim of war are contained in the smallest building of man. It is necessary then to recognize that destruction is an essentially human thing and that *it is* man who destroys his cities through the agency of earthquakes or directly, who destroys his ships through the agency of cyclones or directly. But at the same time it is necessary to acknowledge that destruction supposes a prejudicative comprehension of nothingness as such and a conduct *in the face of nothingness.* In addition destruction although coming into being through man, is an *objective fact* and not a thought. Fragility has been impressed upon the very being of this vase, and its destruction would be an irreversible absolute event which I could only verify. There is a transphenomenality of non-being as of being. The examination of "destruction" leads us then to the same results as the examination of "the question."

But if we wish to decide with certainty, we need only to consider an example of a negative judgment and to task ourselves whether it causes non-being to appear at the heart of being or merely limits itself to determining a prior revelation. I have an appointment with Pierre at four o'clock. I arrive at the café a quarter of an hour late. Pierre is always punctual. Will he have waited for me? I look at the room, the patrons, and I say, "He is not here." Is there an intuition of Pierre's absence, or does negation indeed enter in only with judgment? At first sight it seems absurd to speak here of intuition since to be exact there could not be an intuition of *nothing* and since the absence of Pierre is this nothing. Popular consciousness, however, bears witness to this intuition. Do we not say, for example, "I suddenly saw that he was not there." Is this just a matter of misplacing the negation? Let us look a little closer.

It is certain that the café by itself with its patrons, its tables, its booths, its mirrors, its light, its smoky atmosphere, and the sounds of voices, rattling saucers, and footsteps which fill it—the café is a fullness of being. And all the intuitions of detail which I can have are filled by these odors, these sounds, these colors, all phenomena which have a transphenomenal being. Similarly Pierre's actual presence in a place which I do not know is also a plenitude of being. We seem to have found fullness everywhere. But we must observe that in perception there is always the construction of a figure on a ground. No one object, no group of objects is especially designed to be organized as specifically either ground or figure; all depends on the direction of my attention. When I enter this café to search for Pierre, there is formed a synthetic organization of all the objects in the café, on the ground of which Pierre is given as about to appear. This organization of the café as the ground is an original nihilation. Each element of the setting, a person, a table, a chair, attempts to isolate itself, to lift itself upon the ground constituted by the totality of the other objects, only to fall back once more into the undifferentiation of this ground; it melts into the ground. For the ground is that which is seen only in addition, that which is the object of a purely marginal attention. Thus the original nihilation of all the figures which appear and are swallowed up in the total neutrality of a *ground* is the necessary condition for the appearance of the principle figure, which is here the person of Pierre. This nihilation is given to my intuition; I am witness to the successive disappearance of all the objects which I look at—in particular of the faces, which detain me for an instant (Could this be Pierre?) and which as quickly decompose precisely because they "are not" the face of Pierre. Nevertheless if I should finally discover Pierre, my intuition would be filled by a solid element, I should be suddenly arrested by his face and the whole café would organize itself around him as a discrete presence.

But now Pierre is not here. This does not mean that I discover his absence in some precise spot in the establishment. In fact Pierre is absent from the *whole* café; his absence fixes the café in its evanescence; the café remains *ground*; it persists in offering itself as an undifferentiated totality to my only marginal attention; it slips into the background; it pursues its nihilation. Only it makes itself ground for a determined figure; it carries the figure everywhere in front of it, presents the figure everywhere to me. This figure which slips constantly between my look and the solid, real objects of the café is precisely a perpetual disappearance; it is Pierre raising himself as nothingness on the ground of the nihilation of the café. So that what is offered to intuition is a flickering of nothingness; it is the nothingness of the ground, the nihilation of which summons and demands the appearance of the figure, and it is the figure—the nothingness which slips as a *nothing* to the surface of the ground. It serves as foundation for the judgment—"Pierre is not here." It is in fact the intuitive apprehension of a double nihilation. To be sure, Pierre's absence supposes an original relation between me and this café: there is an infinity of people who are without any relation with this café for want of a real expectation which establishes their absence. But, to be exact, I myself expected to see Pierre, and my expectation has caused the absence of Pierre *to happen* as a real event concerning this café. It is an objective fact at present that I have *discovered* this absence, and it presents itself as a synthetic relation between Pierre and the setting in which I am looking for him. Pierre absent haunts this café and is the condition of its self-nihilating organization as ground. By contrast, judgments which I can make subsequently to amuse myself, such as, "Wellington is not in this café, Paul Valéry is no longer here, *etc.*"—these have a purely abstract meaning; they are pure applications of the principle of negation without real or efficacious foundation, and they never succeed in establishing a *real* relation between the cafe and Wellington or Valéry. Here the relation "is not" is merely *thought*. This example is sufficient to show that non-being does not come to things by a negative judgment; it is the negative judgment, on the contrary, which is conditioned and supported by non-being.

How could it be otherwise? How could we even conceive of the negative form of judgment if all is plenitude of being and positivity? We believed for a moment that the negation could arise from the comparison instituted between the result anticipated and the result obtained. But let us look at that comparison. Here is an original judgment, a concrete, positive psychic act which establishes a fact: "There are 1300 francs in my wallet." Then there is another which is something else, no longer it but an establishing of fact and an affirmation: "I expected to find 1500 francs." There we have real and objective facts, psychic, and positive events, affirmative judgments. Where are we to place negation? Are we to believe that it is a pure and simple application of a category? And do we wish to hold that the mind in itself possesses the *not* as a form of sorting out and separation? But in this case we remove even the slightest suspicion of negativity from the negation. If we admit that the category of the "not" which exists *in fact* in the mind and is a positive and concrete process to brace and systematize our knowledge, if we admit first that it is suddenly released by the presence in us of certain affirmative judgments and then that it comes suddenly to mark with its seal certain thoughts which result from these judgments—by these considerations we will have carefully stripped negation of all negative function. For negation is a refusal of existence. By means of it a being (or a way of being) is posited, then thrown back to nothingness. If negation is a category, if it is only a sort of plug set indifferently on certain judgments, then how will we explain the fact that it can nihilate a being, cause it suddenly to arise, and then appoint it to be thrown back to non-being? If prior judgments establish fact, like those which we have taken for examples, negation must be like a free discovery, it must tear us away from this wall of positivity which encircles us. Negation is an abrupt break in continuity which cannot in any case *result* from prior affirmations; it is an original and irreducible event. Here we are in the realm of consciousness. Consciousness moreover cannot produce a negation except in the form of consciousness of negation. No category can "inhabit" consciousness and reside there in the manner of a thing. The *not*, as an abrupt intuitive discovery, appears as consciousness (of being), consciousness of the *not*. In a word, if being is everywhere, it is not only Nothingness which, as Bergson maintains, is inconceivable; for negation will never be derived from being. The necessary condition for our saying *not* is that non-being be a perpetual presence in us and outside of us, that nothingness haunt being.

But where does nothingness come from? If it is the original condition of the questioning attitude and more generally of all philosophical or scientific inquiry, what is the original relation of the human being to nothingness? What is the original nihilating conduct? . . .

3. THE ORIGIN OF NOTHINGNESS

It would be well at this point to cast a glance backward and to measure the
road already covered. We raised first the question of being. Then examining
this very question conceived as a type of human conduct, we questioned this
in turn. We next had to recognize that no question could be asked, in particular not that of being, if negation did not exist. But this negation itself
when inspected more closely referred us back to Nothingness as its origin
and foundation. In order for negation to exist in the world and in order that
we may consequently raise questions concerning Being, it is necessary that
in some way Nothingness be given. We perceived then that Nothingness can
be conceived neither *outside of* being, nor as a complementary, abstract notion, nor as an infinite milieu where being is suspended. Nothingness must
be given at the heart of Being, in order for us to be able to apprehend that
particular type of realities which we have called *négatités*. But this intra-
mundane Nothingness cannot be produced by Being-in-itself; the notion of
Being as full positivity does not contain Nothingness as one of its structures. We cannot even say that Being excludes it. Being lacks all relation
with it. Hence the question which is put to us now with a particular
urgency: if Nothingness can be conceived neither outside of Being, nor in
terms of Being, and if on the other hand, since it is non-being, it cannot
derive from itself the necessary force to "nihilate itself," *where does Nothingness come from?*

If we wish to pursue the problem further, we must first recognize that we
cannot grant to nothingness the property of "nihilating itself." For although the expression "to nihilate itself" is thought of as removing from
nothingness the last semblance of being, we must recognize that only *Being*
can nihilate itself; however it comes about, in order to nihilate itself, it must
be. But Nothingness *is not*. If we can speak of it, it is only because it possesses an appearance of being, a borrowed being, as we have noted above.
Nothingness is not, Nothingness "is made-to-be,"[1] Nothingness does not
nihilate itself; Nothingness "is nihilated." It follows therefore that there
must exist a Being (this cannot be the In-itself) of which the property is to
nihilate Nothingness, to support it in its being, to sustain it perpetually in
its very existence, *a being by which nothingness comes to things*. But how can

1. The French is *est été*, which literally means "is been," an expression as meaningless in ordinary French as in English. Maurice Natanson suggests "is-was." (*A Critique of Jean-Paul Sartre's Ontology*. University of Nebraska Studies. March 1951.
p. 59.) I prefer "is made-to-be" because Sartre seems to be using *être* as a transitive
verb, here in the passive voice, thus suggesting that nothingness has been subjected
to an act involving being. Other passages containing this expression will, I believe,
bear out this interpretation. Tr.

this Being be related to Nothingness so that through it Nothingness comes to things? We must observe first that the being postulated cannot be passive in relation to Nothingness, cannot receive it; Nothingness could not *come* to this being except through another Being—which would be an infinite regress. But on the other hand, the Being by which Nothingness comes to the world cannot *produce* Nothingness while remaining indifferent to that production—like the Stoic cause which produces its effect without being itself changed. It would be inconceivable that a Being which is full positivity should maintain and create outside itself a Nothingness or transcendent being, for there would be nothing in Being by which Being could surpass itself toward Non-Being. The Being by which Nothingness arrives in the world must nihilate Nothingness in its Being, and even so it still runs the risk of establishing Nothingness as a transcendent in the very heart of immanence unless it nihilates Nothingness in its being *in connection with its own being*. The Being by which Nothingness arrives in the world is a being such that in its Being, the Nothingness of its Being is in question. *The being by which Nothingness comes to the world must be its own Nothingness.* By this we must understand not a nihilating act, which would require in turn a foundation in Being, but an ontological characteristic of the Being required. It remains to learn in what delicate, exquisite region of Being we shall encounter that Being which is its own Nothingness.

We shall be helped in our inquiry by a more complete examination of the conduct which served us as a point of departure. We must return to the question. We have seen, it may be recalled, that every question in essence posits the possibility of a negative reply. In a question we question a being about its being or its way of being. This way of being or this being is veiled; there always remains the possibility that it may unveil itself as a Nothingness. But from the very fact that we presume that an Existent can always be revealed as *nothing*, every question supposes that we realize a nihilating withdrawal in relation to the given, which becomes a simple *presentation*, fluctuating between being and Nothingness.

It is essential therefore that the questioner have the permanent possibility of dissociating himself from the causal series which constitutes being and which can produce only being. If we admitted that the question is determined in the questioner by universal determinism, the question would thereby become unintelligible and even inconceivable. A real cause, in fact, produces a real effect and the caused being is wholly engaged by the cause in positivity; to the extent that its being depends on the cause, it cannot have within itself the tiniest germ of nothingness. Thus in so far as the questioner must be able to effect in relation to the questioned a kind of nihilating withdrawal, he is not subject to the causal order of the world; he detaches himself from Being. This means that by a double movement of nihilation, he nihilates the thing questioned in relation to himself by placing it in a *neutral* state, between being and non-being—and that he nihilates himself in relation to the thing questioned by wrenching himself from being in order to be able to bring out of himself the possibility of a non-being. Thus in posing a question, a certain negative element is introduced into the world. We see nothingness making the world irridescent, casting a shimmer over things. But at the same time the question emanates from a questioner who in order to motivate himself in his being as one who questions, disengages himself from being. This disengagement is then by definition a human process. Man presents himself at least in this instance as a being who causes Nothingness to arise in the world, inasmuch as he himself is affected with non-being to this end.

These remarks may serve as a guiding thread as we examine the *négatités* of which we spoke earlier. There is no doubt at all that these are transcendent realities; distance, for example, is imposed on us as something which we have to take into account, which must be cleared with effort. However these realities are of a very peculiar nature; they all indicate immediately an essential relation of human reality to the world. They derive their origin from an act, an expectation, or a project of the human being; they all indicate an aspect of being as it appears to the human being who is engaged in the world. The relations of man in the world, which the *négatités* indicate, have nothing in common with the relations *à posteriori* which are brought out by empirical activity. We are no longer dealing with those relations *of instrumentality* by which, according to Heidegger, objects in the world disclose themselves to "human reality." Every *négatité* appears rather as one of the essential conditions of this relation of instrumentality. In order for the totality of being to order itself around us as instruments, in order for it to parcel itself into differentiated complexes which refer one to another and which can *be used*, it is necessary that negation rise up not as a thing among other things but as the rubric of a category which presides over the arrangement and the redistribution of great masses of being in things. Thus the rise of man in the midst of the being which "invests" him causes a world to be discovered. But the essential and primordial moment of this rise is the negation. Thus we have reached the first goal of this study. Man is the being through whom nothingness comes to the world. But this question immediately provokes another: What must man be in his being in order that through him nothingness may come to being?

Being can generate only being and if man is inclosed in this process of generation, only being will come out of him. If we are to assume that man is able to question this process—*i.e.*, to make it the object of interrogation—he must be able to hold it up to view as a totality. He must be able to put himself *outside of* being and by the same stroke weaken the structure of the being of being. Yet it is not given to "human reality" to annihilate even provisionally the mass of being which it posits before itself. Man's *relation* with being is that he can modify it. For man to put a particular existent out of circuit is to put himself out of circuit in relation to that existent. In this case he is not subject to it; he is out of reach; it cannot act on him, for he has retired *beyond a nothingness.* Descartes following the Stoics has given a name to this possibility which human reality has to secrete a nothingness which isolates it—it is *freedom.* But freedom here is only a name. If we wish to penetrate further into the question, we must not be content with this reply and we ought to ask now, What is human freedom if through it nothingness comes into the world?

It is not yet possible to deal with the problem of freedom in all its fullness. In fact the steps which we have completed up to now show clearly that freedom is not a faculty of the human soul to be envisaged and described in isolation. What we have been trying to define is the being of man in so far as he conditions the appearance of nothingness, and this being has appeared to us as freedom. Thus freedom as the requisite condition for the nihilation of nothingness is not a *property* which belongs among others to the essence of the human being. We have already noticed furthermore that with man the relation of existence to essence is not comparable to what it is for the things of the world. Human freedom precedes essence in man and makes it possible; the essence of the human being is suspended in his freedom. What we call freedom is impossible to distinguish from the *being* of "human reality." Man does not exist *first* in order to be free *subsequently*; there is no difference between the being of man and his *being-free.* This is not the time to make a frontal attack on a question which can be treated exhaustively only in the light of a rigorous elucidation of the human being. Here we are dealing with freedom in connection with the problem of nothingness and only to the extent that it conditions the appearance of nothingness.

What first appears evident is that human reality can detach itself from the world—in questioning, in systematic doubt, in skeptical doubt, in the ἐποχή, *etc.*—only if by nature it has the possibility of self-detachment. This was seen by Descartes, who is establishing doubt on freedom when he claims for us the possibility of suspending our judgments. Alain's position is similar. It is also in this sense that Hegel asserts the freedom of the mind to the degree that mind is mediation—i.e., the Negative. Furthermore it is one of the trends of contemporary philosophy to see in human consciousness a sort of escape from the self; such is the meaning of the transcendence of Heidegger. The intentionality of Husserl and of Brentano has also to a large extent the characteristic of a detachment from self. But we are not yet in a position to consider freedom as an inner structure of consciousness. We lack for the moment both instruments and technique to permit us to succeed in that enterprise. What interests us at present is a temporal operation since questioning is, like doubt, a kind of behavior; it assumes that the human being reposes first in the depths of being and then detaches himself from it by a nihilating withdrawal. Thus we are envisaging the condition of the nihilation as a relation to the self in the heart of a temporal process. We wish simply to show that by identifying consciousness with a causal sequence indefinitely continued, one transmutes it into a plenitude of being and thereby causes it to return into the unlimited totality of being—as is well illustrated by the futility of the efforts to dissociate psychological determinism from universal determinism and to constitute it as a separate series.

The room of someone absent, the books of which he turned the pages, the objects which he touched are in themselves only *books, objects; i.e.,* full actualities. The very traces which he has left can be deciphered as traces of him only within a situation where he has been already posited as absent. The dog-eared book with the well-read pages is not by itself a book of which Pierre has turned the pages, of which he no longer turns the pages. If we consider it as the present, transcendent motivation of my perception or even as the synthetic flux, regulated by my sensible impressions, then it is merely a volume with turned down, worn pages; it can refer only to itself or to present objects, to the lamp which illuminates it, to the table which holds it. It would be useless to invoke an association by contiguity as Plato does in the *Phaedo,* where he makes the image of the absent one appear on the margin of the perception of the lyre or of the cithara which he has touched. This image, if we consider it in itself and in the spirit of classical theories, is a definite plenitude; it is a concrete and positive psychic fact. Consequently we must of necessity pass on it a doubly negative judgment: subjectively, to signify that the image *is not* a perception; objectively, to deny that the Pierre of whom I form the image *is here* at this moment.

This is the famous problem of the characteristics of the true image, which has concerned so many psychologists from Taine to Spaier. Association, we see, does not solve the problem; it pushes it back to the level of reflection. But in every way it demands a negation; that is, at the very least, a nihilating withdrawal of consciousness in relation to the image apprehended as subjective phenomenon, in order to posit it precisely as being only a subjective phenomenon.

Now I have attempted to show elsewhere[2] that if we posit the image *first* as a renascent perception, it is radically impossible to distinguish it *subsequently* from actual perceptions. The image must enclose in its very structure a nihilating thesis. It constitutes itself qua image while positing its object as existing *elsewhere* or *not existing.* It carries within it a double negation;

2. *L'imagination.* Alcan, 1936.

first it is the nihilation of the world (since the world is not offering the imagined object as an actual object of perception), secondly the nihilation of the object of the image (it is posited as not actual), and finally by the same stroke it is the nihilation of itself (since it is not a concrete, full psychic process.) In explaining how I apprehend the absence of Pierre in the room, it would be useless to invoke those famous "empty intentions" of Husserl, which are in great part constitutive of perception. Among the various perceptive intentions, indeed, there are relations of *motivation* (but motivation is not causation), and among these intentions, some are full (*i.e.*, filled with what they aim at) and others empty. But precisely because the matter which should fill the empty intentions *does not exist,* it cannot be this which motivates them in their structure. And since the other intentions are full, neither can they motivate the empty intentions inasmuch as the latter are empty. Moreover these intentions are of psychic nature and it would be an error to envisage them in the mode of things; that is, as recipients which would first be given, which according to circumstances could be emptied or filled, and which would be by nature indifferent to their state of being empty or filled. It seems that Husserl has not always escaped the materialist illusion. To be empty an intention must be conscious of itself as empty and precisely as empty of the exact matter at which it aims. An empty intention constitutes itself as empty to the exact extent that it posits its matter as non-existing or absent. In short an empty intention is a consciousness of negation which transcends itself toward an object which it posits as absent or non-existent.

Thus whatever may be the explanation which we give of it, Pierre's absence, in order to be established or realized, requires a negative moment by which consciousness in the absence of all prior determination, constitutes itself as negation. If in terms of my perceptions of the room, I conceive of the former inhabitant who is no longer in the room, I am of necessity forced to produce an act of thought which no prior state can determine nor motivate, in short to effect in myself a break with being. And in so far as I continually use *négatités* to isolate and determine existents—i.e., to think them—the succession of my "states of consciousness" is a perpetual separation of effect from cause, since every nihilating process must derive its source only from itself. Inasmuch as my present state would be a prolongation of my prior state, every opening by which negation could slip through would be completely blocked. Every psychic process of nihilation implies then a cleavage between the immediate psychic past and the present. This cleavage is precisely nothingness. At least, someone will say, there remains the possibility of successive implication between the nihilating processes. My establishment of Pierre's absence could still be determinant for my regret at not seeing him; you have not excluded the possibility of a determinism of nihilations. But aside from the fact that the original nihilation of the series must necessarily be disconnected from the prior positive processes, what can be the meaning of a motivation of nothingness by nothingness? A being indeed can *nihilate itself* perpetually, but to the extent that it nihilates itself, it foregoes being the origin of another phenomenon, even of a second nihilation.

It remains to explain what this separation is, this disengaging of consciousness which conditions every negation. If we consider the prior consciousness envisaged as motivation, we see suddenly and evidently that *nothing* has just slipped in between that state and the present state. There has been no break in continuity within the flux of the temporal development, for that would force us to return to the inadmissible concept of the infinite divisibility of time and of the temporal point or instant as the limit of the division. Neither has there been an abrupt interpolation of an opaque element to separate prior from subsequent in the way that a knife blade cuts a piece of fruit in two. Nor is there a *weakening* of the motivating force of the prior consciousness; it remains what it is, it does not lose anything of its urgency. What separates prior from subsequent is exactly *nothing*. This nothing is absolutely impassable, just because it is nothing; for in every obstacle to be cleared there is something positive which gives itself as about to be cleared. The prior consciousness is always *there* (though with the modification of "pastness"). It constantly maintains a relation of interpretation with the present consciousness, but on the basis of this existential relation it is put out of the game, out of the circuit, between parentheses—exactly as in the eyes of one practicing the phenomenological ἐποχή, the world both is within him and outside of him.

Thus the condition on which human reality can deny all or part of the world is that human reality carry nothingness within itself as the *nothing* which separates its present from all its past. But this is still not all, for the *nothing* envisaged would not yet have the sense of nothingness; a suspension of being which would remain unnamed, which would not be consciousness of suspending being would come from outside consciousness and by reintroducing opacity into the heart of this absolute lucidity, would have the effect of cutting it in two. Furthermore this nothing would by no means be negative. Nothingness, as we have seen above, is the ground of the negation because it conceals the negation within itself, because it is the negation as being. It is necessary then that conscious being constitute itself in relation to its past as separated from this past by a nothingness. It must necessarily be conscious of this cleavage in being, but not as a phenomenon which it experiences, rather as a structure of consciousness which it is. Freedom is the human being putting his past out of play by secreting his own nothingness. Let us understand indeed that this original necessity of being its own nothingness does not belong to consciousness intermittently and on the occasion of particular negations. This does not happen just at a particular moment in psychic life when negative or interrogative attitudes appear; consciousness continually experiences itself as the nihilation of its past being.

But someone doubtless will believe that he can use against us here an objection which we have frequently raised ourselves: if the nihilating consciousness exists only as consciousness of nihilation, we ought to be able to define and describe a constant mode of consciousness, present *qua* consciousness, which would be consciousness of nihilation. Does this consciousness exist? Behold a new question has been raised here: if freedom is the being of consciousness, consciousness ought to exist as consciousness of freedom. What form does this consciousness of freedom assume? In freedom the human being *is* his own past (as also his own future) in the form of nihilation. If our analysis has not led us astray, there ought to exist for the human being, in so far as he is conscious of being, a certain mode of standing opposite his past and his future, as being both this past and this future and as not being them. We shall be able to furnish an immediate reply to this question; it is in anguish that man gets the consciousness of his freedom, or if you prefer, anguish is the mode of being of freedom as consciousness of being; it is in anguish that freedom is, in its being, in question for itself.

Kierkegaard describing anguish in the face of what one lacks characterizes it as anguish in the face of freedom. But Heidegger, whom we know to have been greatly influenced by Kierkegaard,[3] considers anguish instead as the apprehension of nothingness. These two descriptions of anguish do not appear to us contradictory; on the contrary the one implies the other.

First we must acknowledge that Kierkegaard is right; anguish is distinguished from fear in that fear is fear of beings in the world whereas anguish is anguish before myself. Vertigo is anguish to the extent that I am afraid not of falling over the precipice, but of throwing myself over. A situation provokes fear if there is a possibility of my life being changed from without; my being provokes anguish to the extent that I distrust myself and my own reactions in that situation. The artillery preparation which precedes the attack can provoke fear in the soldier who undergoes the bombardment, but anguish is born in him when he tries to foresee the conduct with which he will face the bombardment, when he asks himself if he is going to be able to "hold up." Similarly the recruit who reports for active duty at the beginning of the war can in some instances be afraid of death, but more often he is "afraid of being afraid"; that is, he is filled with anguish before himself. Most of the time dangerous or threatening situations present themselves in facets; they will be apprehended through a feeling of fear or of anguish according to whether we envisage the situation as acting on the man or the

3. J. Wahl: *Etudes Kierkegaardiennes*, Kierkegaard et Heidegger.

man as acting on the situation. The man who has just received a hard blow—for example, losing a great part of his wealth in a crash—can have the fear of threatening poverty. He will experience anguish a moment later when nervously wringing his hands (a symbolic reaction to the action which is imposed but which remains still wholly undetermined), he exclaims to himself: "What am I going to do? But what am I going to do?" In this sense fear and anguish are exclusive of one another since fear is unreflective apprehension of the self; the one is born in the destruction of the other. The normal process in the case which I have just cited is a constant transition from the one to the other. But there exist also situations where anguish appears pure; that is, without ever being preceded or followed by fear. If, for example, I have been raised to a new dignity and charged with a delicate and flattering mission, I can feel anguish at the thought that I will not be capable perhaps of fulfilling it, and yet I will not have the least fear in the world of the consequences of my possible failure.

What is the meaning of anguish in the various examples which I have just given? Let us take up again the example of vertigo. Vertigo announces itself through fear; I am on a narrow path—without a guard-rail—which goes along a precipice. The precipice presents itself to me as *to be avoided*; it represents a danger of death. At the same time I conceive of a certain number of causes, originating in universal determinism, which can transform that threat of death into reality; I can slip on a stone and fall into the abyss; the crumbling earth of the path can give way under my steps. Through these various anticipations, I am given to myself as a thing; I am passive in relation to these possibilities; they come to me from without; in so far as I am also an object in the world, subject to gravitation, they are *my* possibilities. At this moment *fear* appears, which in terms of the situation is the apprehension of myself as a destructible transcendent in the midst of transcendents, as an object which does not contain in itself the origin of its future disappearance. My reaction will be of the reflective order; I will pay attention to the stones in the road; I will keep myself as far as possible from the edge of the path. I realize myself as pushing away the threatening situation with all my strength, and I project before myself a certain number of future conducts destined to keep the threats of the world at a distance from me. These conducts are *my* possibilities. I escape fear by the very fact that I am placing myself on a plane where *my own* possibilities are substituted for the transcendent probabilities where human action had no place.

But these conducts, precisely because they are *my* possibilities, do not appear to me as determined by foreign causes. Not only is it not strictly certain that they will be effective; in particular it is not strictly certain that they will be adopted, for they do not have existence sufficient in itself. We could say, varying the expression of Berkeley, that their "being is a sustained-being" and that their "possibility of being is only an ought-to-be-sustained."[4] Due to this fact their possibility has as a necessary condition the possibility of negative conduct (*not* to pay attention to the stones in the road, to run, to think of something else) and the possibility of the opposite conduct (to throw myself over the precipice). The possibility which I make *my* concrete possibility can appear as my possibility only by raising itself on the basis of the totality of the logical possibilities which the situation allows. But these rejected possibles in turn have no other being than their "sustained-being"; it is I who sustain them in being, and inversely, their present non-being is an "ought-not-to-be-sustained." No external cause will remove them. I alone am the permanent source of their non-being, I engage myself in them; in order to cause *my* possibility to appear, I posit the other possibilities so as to nihilate them. This would not produce anguish if I could apprehend myself in my relations with these possibles as a cause producing its effects. In this case the effect defined as my possibility would *be strictly* determined. But then it would cease to be *possible*; it would become simply "about-to-happen." If then I wished to avoid anguish and vertigo, it would be enough if I were to consider the motives (instinct of self-preservation, prior fear, etc.), which make me reject the situation envisaged, as *determining* my prior activity in the same way that the presence at a determined point of one given mass determines the courses followed by other masses; it would be necessary, in other words, that I apprehend in myself a strict psychological determinism. But I am in anguish precisely because any conduct on my part is only *possible*, and this means that while constituting a totality of motives *for* pushing away that situation, I at the same moment apprehend these motives as not sufficiently effective. At the very moment when I apprehend my being as *horror* of the precipice, I am conscious of that horror as *not determinant* in relation to my possible conduct. In one sense that horror calls for prudent conduct, and it is in itself a pre-outline of that conduct: in another sense, it posits the final developments of that conduct only as possible, precisely because I do not apprehend it as the *cause* of these final developments but as need, appeal, *etc.*

Now as we have seen, consciousness of being is the being of consciousness. There is no question here of a contemplation which I could make after the event, of an horror already constituted; it is the very being of horror to appear to itself as "not being the cause" of the conduct it calls for. In short, to avoid fear, which reveals to me a transcendent future strictly determined, I take refuge in reflection, but the latter has only an undetermined future to offer. This means that in establishing a certain conduct as a possibility and precisely because it is *my* possibility, I am aware that *nothing* can compel me

---

4. We shall return to possibilities in the second part of this work.

to adopt that conduct. Yet I am indeed already there in the future; it is for the sake of that being which I will be there at the turning of the path that I now exert all my strength, and in this sense there is already a relation between my future being and my present being. But a nothingness has slipped into the heart of this relation; I *am* not the self which I will be. First I am not that self because time separates me from it. Secondly, I am not that self because what I am is not the foundation of what I will be. Finally I am not that self because no actual existent can determine strictly what I am going to be. Yet as I am already what I will be (otherwise I would not be interested in any one being more than another), *I am the self which I will be, in the mode of not being it.* It is through my horror that I am carried toward the future, and the horror nihilates itself in that it constitutes the future as possible. Anguish is precisely my consciousness of being my own future, in the mode of not-being. To be exact, the nihilation of horror as a *motive*, which has the effect of reinforcing horror as a *state*, has as its positive counterpart the appearance of other forms of conduct (in particular that which consists in throwing myself over the precipice) as *my* possible *possibilities*. If *nothing* compels me to save my life, *nothing* prevents me from precipitating myself into the abyss. The decisive conduct will emanate from a self which I am not yet. Thus the self which I am depends on the self which I am not yet to the exact extent that the self which I am not yet does not depend on the self which I am. Vertigo appears as the apprehension of this dependence. I approach the precipice, and my scrutiny is searching for myself in my very depths. In terms of this moment, I play with my possibilities. My eyes, running over the abyss from top to bottom, imitate the possible fall and realize it symbolically; at the same time suicide, from the fact that it becomes a *possibility* possible for *me*, now causes to appear possible motives for adopting it (suicide would cause anguish to cease). Fortunately these motives in their turn, from the sole fact that they are motives of a possibility, present themselves as ineffective, as non-determinant; they can no more *produce* the suicide than my horror of the fall can *determine me* to avoid it. It is this counter-anguish which generally puts an end to anguish by transmuting it into indecision. Indecision in its turn, calls for decision. I abruptly put myself at a distance from the edge of the precipice and resume my way. . . .

4. BAD FAITH AND FALSEHOOD

The human being is not only the being by whom *négatités* are disclosed in the world; he is also the one who can take negative attitudes with respect to himself. In our Introduction we defined consciousness as "a being such that in its being, its being is in question in so far as this being implies a being other than itself." But now that we have examined the meaning of "the question," we can at present also write the formula thus: "Consciousness is a being, the nature of which is to be conscious of the nothingness of its being." In a prohibition or a veto, for example, the human being denies a future transcendence. But this negation is not explicative. My consciousness is not restricted to *envisioning* a *négatité*. It constitutes itself in its own flesh as the nihilation of a possibility which another human reality projects as *its* possibility. For that reason it must arise in the world as a *Not*; it is as a Not that the slave first apprehends the master, or that the prisoner who is trying to escape sees the guard who is watching him. There are even men (*e.g.,* caretakers, overseers, gaolers,) whose social reality is uniquely that of the Not, who will live and die, having forever been only a Not upon the earth. Others so as to make the Not a part of their very subjectivity, establish their human personality as a perpetual negation. This is the meaning and function of what Scheler calls "the man of resentment"—in reality, the Not. But there exist more subtle behaviors, the description of which will lead us further into the inwardness of consciousness. Irony is one of these. In irony a man annihilates what he posits within one and the same act; he leads us to believe in order not to be believed; he affirms to deny and denies to affirm; he creates a positive object but it has no being other than its nothingness. Thus attitudes of negation toward the self permit us to raise a new question: What are we to say is the being of man who has the possibility of denying himself? But it is out of the question to discuss the attitude of "self-negation" in its universality. The kinds of behavior which can be ranked under this heading are too diverse; we risk retaining only the abstract form of them. It is best to choose and to examine one determined attitude which is essential to human reality and which is such that consciousness instead of directing its negation outward turns it toward itself. This attitude, it seems to me, is *bad faith* (*mauvaise foi*).

Frequently this is identified with falsehood. We say indifferently of a person that he shows signs of bad faith or that he lies to himself. We shall willingly grant that bad faith is a lie to oneself, on condition that we distinguish the lie to oneself from lying in general. Lying is a negative attitude, we will agree to that. But this negation does not bear on consciousness itself; it aims only at the transcendent. The essence of the lie implies in fact that the liar actually is in complete possession of the truth which he is hiding. A man does not lie about what he is ignorant of; he does not lie when he spreads an error of which he himself is the dupe; he does not lie when he is mistaken. The ideal description of the liar would be a cynical consciousness, affirming truth within himself, denying it in his *words,* and denying that negation as such. Now this doubly negative attitude rests on the transcendent; the fact expressed is transcendent since it does not exist, and the original negation rests on a *truth*; that is, on a particular type of transcendence.

As for the inner negation which I effect correlatively with the affirmation for myself of the truth, this rests on *words*; that is, on an event in the world. Furthermore the inner disposition of the liar is positive; it could be the object of an affirmative judgment. The liar intends to deceive and he does not seek to hide this intention from himself nor to disguise the translucency of consciousness; on the contrary, he has recourse to it when there is a question of deciding secondary behavior. It explicitly exercises a regulatory control over all attitudes. As for his flaunted intention of telling the truth ("I'd never want to deceive you! This is true! I swear it!")—all this, of course, is the object of an inner negation, but also it is not recognized by the liar as *his* intention. It is played, imitated, it is the intention of the character which he plays in the eyes of his questioner, but this character, precisely because he does *not exist*, is a transcendent. Thus the lie does not put into the play the inner structure of present consciousness; all the negations which constitute it bear on objects which by this fact are removed from consciousness. The lie then does not require special ontological foundation, and the explanations which the existence of negation in general requires are valid without change in the case of deceit. Of course we have described the ideal lie; doubtless it happens often enough that the liar is more or less the victim of his lie, that he half persuades himself of it. But these common, popular forms of the lie are also degenerate aspects of it; they represent intermediaries between falsehood and bad faith. The lie is a behavior of transcendence.

The lie is also a normal phenomenon of what Heidegger calls the "*Mitsein*."[5] It presupposes my existence, the existence of the Other, my existence *for* the Other, and the existence of the Other *for* me. Thus there is no difficulty in holding that the liar must make the project of the lie in entire clarity and that he must possess a complete comprehension of the lie and of the truth which he is altering. It is sufficient that an over-all opacity hide his intentions from the *Other*; it is sufficient that the Other can take the lie for truth. By the lie consciousness affirms that it exists by nature as *hidden from the Other*; it utilizes for its own profit the ontological duality of myself and myself in the eyes of the Other.

The situation cannot be the same for bad faith if this, as we have said, is indeed a lie to oneself. To be sure, the one who practices bad faith is hiding a displeasing truth or presenting as truth a pleasing untruth. Bad faith then has in appearance the structure of falsehood. Only what changes everything is the fact that in bad faith it is from myself that I am hiding the truth. Thus the duality of the deceiver and the deceived does not exist here. Bad faith on the contrary implies in essence the unity of a *single* consciousness. This does not mean that it cannot be conditioned by the *Mit-sein* like all other phenomena of human reality, but the *Mit-sein* can call forth bad faith only by

5. A "being-with" others in the world. Tr.

presenting itself as a *situation* which bad faith permits surpassing; bad faith does not come from outside to human reality. One does not undergo his bad faith; one is not infected with it; it is not a *state*. But consciousness affects itself with bad faith. There must be an original intention and a project of bad faith; this project implies a comprehension of bad faith as such and a pre-reflective apprehension (of) consciousness as affecting itself with bad faith. It follows first that the one to whom the lie is told and the one who lies are one and the same person, which means that I must know in my capacity as deceiver the truth which is hidden from me in my capacity as the one deceived. Better yet I must know the truth very exactly *in order* to conceal it more carefully—and this not at two different moments, which at a pinch would allow us to re-establish a semblance of duality—but in the unitary structure of a single project. How then can the lie subsist if the duality which conditions it is suppressed?

To this difficulty is added another which is derived from the total translucency of consciousness. That which affects itself with bad faith must be conscious (of) its bad faith since the being of consciousness is consciousness of being. It appears then that I must be in good faith, at least to the extent that I am conscious of my bad faith. But then this whole psychic system is annihilated. We must agree in fact that if I deliberately and cynically attempt to lie to myself, I fail completely in this undertaking; the lie falls back and collapses beneath my look; it is ruined *from behind* by the very consciousness of lying to myself which pitilessly constitutes itself well within my project as its very condition. We have here an *evanescent* phenomenon which exists only in and through its own differentiation. To be sure, these phenomena are frequent and we shall see that there is in fact an "evanescence" of bad faith, which, it is evident, vacillates continually between good faith and cynicism: Even though the existence of bad faith is very precarious, and though it belongs to the kind of psychic structures which we might call "metastable,"[6] it presents nonetheless an autonomous and durable form. It can even be the normal aspect of life for a very great number of people. A person can *live* in bad faith, which does not mean that he does not have abrupt awakenings to cynicism or to good faith, but which implies a constant and particular style of life. Our embarrassment then appears extreme since we can neither reject nor comprehend bad faith. . . .

5. PATTERNS OF BAD FAITH

If we wish to get out of this difficulty, we should examine more closely the patterns of bad faith and attempt a description of them. This description will permit us perhaps to fix more exactly the conditions for the possibility

6. Sartre's own word, meaning subject to sudden changes or transitions. Tr.

ex
of
woman
in
bad
faith

of bad faith; that is, to reply to the question we raised at the outset: "What must be the being of man if he is to be capable of bad faith?"

Take the example of a woman who has consented to go out with a particular man for the first time. She knows very well the intentions which the man who is speaking to her cherishes regarding her. She knows also that it will be necessary sooner or later for her to make a decision. But she does not want to realize the urgency; she concerns herself only with what is respectful and discreet in the attitude of her companion. She does not apprehend this conduct as an attempt to achieve what we call "the first approach;" that is, she does not want to see possibilities of temporal development which his conduct presents. She restricts this behavior to what is in the present; she does not wish to read in the phrases which he addresses to her anything other than their explicit meaning. If he says to her, "I find you so attractive!" she disarms this phrase of its sexual background; she attaches to the conversation and to the behavior of the speaker, the immediate meanings, which she imagines as objective qualities. The man who is speaking to her appears to her sincere and respectful as the table is round or square, as the wall coloring is blue or gray. The qualities thus attached to the person she is listening to are in this way fixed in a permanence like that of things, which is no other than the projection of the strict present of the qualities into the temporal flux. This is because she does not quite know what she wants. She is profoundly aware of the desire which she inspires, but the desire cruel and naked would humiliate and horrify her. Yet she would find no charm in a respect which would be only respect. In order to satisfy her, there must be a feeling which is addressed wholly to her *personality*—i.e., to her full freedom—and which would be a recognition of her freedom. But at the same time this feeling must be wholly desire; that is, it must address itself to her body as object. This time then she refuses to apprehend the desire for what it is; she does not even give it a name; she recognizes it only to the extent that it transcends itself toward admiration, esteem, respect and that it is wholly absorbed in the more refined forms which it produces, to the extent of no longer figuring anymore as a sort of warmth and density. But then suppose he takes her hand. This act of her companion risks changing the situation by calling for an immediate decision. To leave the hand there is to consent in herself to flirt, to engage herself. To withdraw it is to break the troubled and unstable harmony which gives the hour its charm. The aim is to postpone the moment of decision as long as possible. We know what happens next; the young woman leaves her hand there, but she *does not notice* that she is leaving it. She does not notice because it happens by chance that she is at this moment all intellect. She draws her companion up to the most lofty regions of sentimental speculation; she speaks of Life, of her life, she shows herself in her essential aspect—a personality, a consciousness. And during this time the divorce of the body from the soul is accomplished; the hand rests inert between the warm hands of her companion—neither consenting nor resisting—a thing.

We shall say that this woman is in bad faith. But we see immediately that she uses various procedures in order to maintain herself in this bad faith. She has disarmed the actions of her companion by reducing them to being only what they are; that is, to existing in the mode of the in-itself. But she permits herself to enjoy his desire, to the extent that she will apprehend it as not being what it is, will recognize its transcendence. Finally while sensing profoundly the presence of her own body—to the degree of being disturbed perhaps—she realizes herself as *not being* her own body, and she contemplates it as though from above as a passive object to which events can *happen* but which can neither provoke them nor avoid them because all its possibilities are outside of it. What unity do we find in these various aspects of bad faith? It is a certain art of forming contradictory concepts which unite in themselves both an idea and the negation of that idea. The basic concept which is thus engendered, utilizes the double property of the human being, who is at once a *facticity* and a *transcendence*. These two aspects of human reality are and ought to be capable of a valid coordination. But bad faith does not wish either to coordinate them nor to surmount them in a synthesis. Bad faith seeks to affirm their identity while preserving their differences. It must affirm facticity as *being* transcendence and transcendence as *being* facticity, in such a way that at the instant when a person apprehends the one, he can find himself abruptly faced with the other.

We can find the prototype of formulae of bad faith in certain famous expressions which have been rightly conceived to produce their whole effect in a spirit of bad faith. Take for example the title of a work by Jacques Chardonne, *Love Is Much More than Love*.[7] We see here how unity is established between *present* love in its facticity—"the contact of two skins," sensuality, egoism, Proust's mechanism of jealousy, Adler's battle of the *sexes*, etc.—and love as transcendence—Mauriac's "river of fire," the longing for the infinite, Plato's *eros*, Lawrence's deep cosmic intuition, etc. Here we leave facticity to find ourselves suddenly beyond the present and the factual condition of man, beyond the psychological, in the heart of metaphysics. On the other hand, the title of a play by Sarment, *I Am Too Great for Myself*,[8] which also presents characters in bad faith, throws us first into full transcendence in order suddenly to imprison us within the narrow limits of our factual essence. We will discover this structure again in the famous sentence: "He has become what he was" or in its no less famous opposite: "Eternity at last

7. *L'amour, c'est beaucoup plus que l'amour.*

8. *Je suis trop grand pour moi.*

changes each man into himself."[9] It is well understood that these various formulae have only the appearance of bad faith; they have been conceived in this paradoxical form explicitly to shock the mind and discountenance it by an enigma. But it is precisely this appearance which is of concern to us. What counts here is that the formulae do not constitute new, solidly structured ideas; on the contrary, they are formed so as to remain in perpetual disintegration and so that we may slide at any time from naturalistic present to transcendence and vice versa.

We can see the use which bad faith can make of these judgments which all aim at establishing that I am not what I am. If I were only what I *am*, I could, for example, seriously consider an adverse criticism which someone makes of me, question myself scrupulously, and perhaps be compelled to recognize the truth in it. But thanks to transcendence, I am not subject to all that I am. I do not even have to discuss the justice of the reproach. As Suzanne says to Figaro, "To prove that I am right would be to recognize that I can be wrong." I am on a plane where no reproach can touch me since what I really am is my transcendence. I flee from myself, I escape myself, I leave my tattered garment in the hands of the fault-finder. But the ambiguity necessary for bad faith comes from the fact that I affirm here that I *am* my transcendence in the mode of being of a thing. It is only thus, in fact, that I can feel that I escape all reproaches. It is in the sense that our young woman purifies the desire of anything humiliating by being willing to consider it only as pure transcendence, which she avoids even naming. But inversely "I Am Too Great for Myself," while showing our transcendence changed into facticity, is the source of an infinity of excuses for our failures or our weaknesses. Similarly the young coquette maintains transcendence to the extent that the respect, the esteem manifested by the actions of her admirer are already on the plane of the transcendent. But she arrests this transcendence, she glues it down with all the facticity of the present; respect is nothing other than respect, it is an arrested surpassing which no longer surpasses itself toward anything.

But although this *metastable* concept of "transcendence-facticity" is one of the most basic instruments of bad faith, it is not the only one of its kind. We can equally well use another kind of duplicity derived from human reality which we will express roughly by saying that its being-for-itself implies complementarily a being-for-others. Upon any one of my conducts it is always possible to converge two looks, mine and that of the Other. The conduct will not present exactly the same structure in each case. But as we shall see later, as each look perceives it, there is between these two aspects of my

9. *Il est devenu ce qu'il était.*
   Tel qu'en lui-même enfin l'éternité le change.

being, no difference between appearance and being—as if I were to my self the truth of myself and as if the Other possessed only a deformed image of me. The equal dignity of being possessed by my being-for-others and by my being-for-myself permits a perpetually disintegrating synthesis and a perpetual game of escape from the for-itself to the for-others and from the for-others to the for-itself. We have seen also the use which our young lady made of our being-in-the-midst-of-the-world—i.e., of our inert presence as a passive object among other objects—in order to relieve herself suddenly from the functions of her being-in-the-world—that is, from the being which causes there to be a world by projecting itself beyond the world toward its own possibilities. Let us note finally the confusing syntheses which play on the nihilating ambiguity of these temporal ekstases, affirming at once that I am what I have been (the man who deliberately *arrests himself* at one period in his life and refuses to take into consideration the later changes) and that I am not what I have been (the man who in the face of reproaches or rancor dissociates himself from his past by insisting on his freedom and on his perpetual re-creation). In all these concepts, which have only a transitive role in the reasoning and which are eliminated from the conclusion, (like hypochondriacs in the calculations of physicians), we find again the same structure. We have to deal with human reality as a being which is what it is not and which is not what it is.

But what exactly is necessary in order for these concepts of disintegration to be able to receive even a pretence of existence, in order for them to be able to appear for an instant to consciousness, even in a process of evanescence? A quick examination of the idea of sincerity, the antithesis of bad faith, will be very instructive in this connection. Actually sincerity presents itself as a demand and consequently is not a *state*. Now what is the ideal to be attained in this case? It is necessary that a man be *for himself* only what he *is*. But is this not precisely the definition of the in-itself—or if you prefer—the principle of identity? To posit as an ideal the being of things, is this not to assert by the same stroke that this being does not belong to human reality and that the principle of identity, far from being a universal axiom universally applied, is only a synthetic principle enjoying a merely regional universality? Thus in order that the concepts of bad faith can put us under illusion at least for an instant, in order that the candor of "pure hearts" (*cf.* Gide, Kessel) can have validity for human reality as an ideal, the principle of identity must not represent a constitutive principle of human reality and human reality must not be necessarily what it is but must be able to be what it is not. What does this mean?

If man is what he is, bad faith is for ever impossible and candor ceases to be his ideal and becomes instead his being. But is man what he is? And more generally, how can he *be* what he is when he exists as consciousness of being?

If candor or sincerity is a universal value, it is evident that the maxim "one must be what one is" does not serve solely as a regulating principle for judgments and concepts by which I express what I am. It posits not merely an ideal of knowing but an ideal of *being*; it proposes for us an absolute equivalence of being with itself as a prototype of being. In this sense it is necessary that *we make ourselves* what we are. But what are we then if we have the constant obligation to make ourselves what we are, if our mode of being is having the obligation to be what we are?

Let us consider this waiter in the café. His movement is quick and forward, a little too precise, a little too rapid. He comes toward the patrons with a step a little too quick. He bends forward a little too eagerly; his voice, his eyes express an interest a little too solicitous for the order of the customer. Finally there he returns, trying to imitate in his walk the inflexible stiffness of some kind of automaton while carrying his tray with the recklessness of a tight-rope-walker by putting it in a perpetually unstable, perpetually broken equilibrium which he perpetually reestablishes by a light movement of the arm and hand. All his behavior seems to us a game. He applies himself to chaining his movements as if they were mechanisms, the one regulating the other; his gestures and even his voice seem to be mechanisms; he gives himself the quickness and pitiless rapidity of things. He is playing, he is amusing himself. But what is he playing? We need not watch long before we can explain it: he is playing *at being* a waiter in a café. There is nothing there to surprise us. The game is a kind of marking out and investigation. The child plays with his body in order to explore it, to take inventory of it; the waiter in the café plays with his condition in order to *realize* it. This obligation is not different from that which is imposed on all tradesmen. Their condition is wholly one of ceremony. The public demands of them that they realize it as a ceremony; there is the dance of the grocer, of the tailor, of the auctioneer, by which they endeavour to persuade their clientele that they are nothing but a grocer, an auctioneer, a tailor. A grocer who dreams is offensive to the buyer, because such a grocer is not wholly a grocer. Society demands that he limit himself to his function as a grocer, just as the soldier at attention makes himself into a soldier-thing with a direct regard which does not see at all, which is no longer meant to see, since it is the rule and not the interest of the moment which determines the point he must fix his eyes on (the sight "fixed at ten paces"). There are indeed many precautions to imprison a man in what he is, as if we lived in perpetual fear that he might escape from it, that he might break away and suddenly elude his condition.

In a parallel situation, from within, the waiter in the café cannot be immediately a café waiter in the sense that this inkwell *is* an inkwell, or the glass is a glass. It is by no means that he cannot form reflective judgments or concepts concerning his condition. He knows well what it "means:" the obligation of getting up at five o'clock, of sweeping the floor of the shop before the restaurant opens, of starting the coffee pot going, *etc.* He knows the rights which it allows: the right to the tips, the right to belong to a union, etc. But all these concepts, all these judgments refer to the transcendent. It is a matter of abstract possibilities, of rights and duties conferred on a "person possessing rights." And it is precisely this person *who I have to be* (if I am the waiter in question) and who I am not. It is not that I do not wish to be this person or that I want this person to be different. But rather there is no common measure between his being and mine. It is a "representation" for others and for myself, which means that I can be he only in *representation*. But if I represent myself as him, I am not he; I am separated from him as the object from the subject, separated *by nothing*, but this nothing isolates me from him. I cannot be he, I can only play *at being* him; that is, imagine to myself that I am he. And thereby I affect him with nothingness. In vain do I fulfill the functions of a café waiter. I can be he only in the neutralized mode, as the actor is Hamlet, by mechanically making the *typical gestures* of my state and by aiming at myself as an imaginary café waiter through those gestures taken as an "analogue."[10] What I attempt to realize is a being-in-itself of the café waiter, as if it were not just in my power to confer their value and their urgency upon my duties and the rights of my position, as if it were not my free choice to get up each morning at five o'clock or to remain in bed, even though it meant getting fired. As if from the very fact that I sustain this role in existence I did not transcend it on every side, as if I did not constitute myself as one *beyond* my condition. Yet there is no doubt that I *am* in a sense a café waiter—otherwise could I not just as well call myself a diplomat or a reporter? But if I am one, this cannot be in the mode of being in-itself. I am a waiter in the mode of *being what I am not.*

Furthermore we are dealing with more than mere social positions; I am never any one of my attitudes, any one of my actions. The good speaker is the one who *plays* at speaking, because he cannot *be speaking.* The attentive pupil who wishes to *be* attentive, his eyes riveted on the teacher, his ears open wide, so exhausts himself in playing the attentive role that he ends up by no longer hearing anything. Perpetually absent to my body, to my acts, I am despite myself that "divine absence" of which Valéry speaks. I cannot say either that I *am* here or that I *am* not here, in the sense that we say "that box of matches *is* on the table;" this would be to confuse my "being-in-the-world" with a "being-in the midst of the world." Nor that I *am* standing,

---

10. Cf. *L'Imaginaire.* Conclusion.

nor that I *am* seated; this would be to confuse my body with the idiosyncratic totality of which it is only one of the structures. On all sides I escape being and yet—I am.

But take a mode of being which concerns only myself: I am sad. One might think that surely I am the sadness in the mode of being what I am. What is the sadness, however, if not the intentional unity which comes to reassemble and animate the totality of my conduct? It is the meaning of this dull look with which I view the world, of my bowed shoulders, of my lowered head, of the listlessness in my whole body. But at the very moment when I adopt each of these attitudes, do I not know that I shall not be able to hold on to it? Let a stranger suddenly appear and I will lift up my head, I will assume a lively cheerfulness. What will remain of my sadness except that I obligingly promise it an appointment for later after the departure of the visitor? Moreover is not this sadness itself a *conduct*? Is it not consciousness which affects itself with sadness as a magical recourse against a situation too urgent?[11] And in this case even, should we not say that being sad means first to make oneself sad? That may be, someone will say, but after all doesn't giving oneself the being of sadness mean to *receive* this being? It makes no difference from where I receive it. The fact is that a consciousness which affects itself with sadness *is* sad precisely for this reason. But it is difficult to comprehend the nature of consciousness; the being-sad is not a ready-made being which I give to myself as I can give this book to my friend. I do not possess the property or *affecting myself with being.* If I make myself sad, I must continue to make myself sad from beginning to end. I cannot treat my sadness as an impulse finally achieved and put it on file without recreating it, nor can I carry it in the manner of an inert body which continues its movement after the initial shock. There is no inertia in consciousness. If I make myself sad, it is because I *am* not sad—the being of the sadness escapes me by and in the very act by which I affect myself with it. The being-in-itself of sadness perpetually haunts my consciousness (of) being sad, but it is as a value which I cannot realize; it stands as a regulative meaning of my sadness, not as its constitutive modality.

Someone may say that my consciousness at least *is,* whatever may be the object or the state of which it makes itself consciousness. But how do we distinguish my consciousness (of) being sad from sadness? Is it not all one? It is true in a way that my consciousness *is,* if one means by this that for another it is a part of the totality of being on which judgments can be brought to bear. But it should be noted, as Husserl clearly understood, that my consciousness appears originally to the Other as an absence. It is the ob-

11. *Esquisse d'une théorie des émotions.* Hermann Paul. In English. *The Emotions. Outline of a Theory.* Philosophical Library. 1948.

ject always present as the *meaning* of all my attitudes and all my conduct—and always absent, for it gives itself to the intuition of another as a perpetual question—still better, as a perpetual freedom. When Pierre looks at me, I know of course that he is looking at me. His eyes, things in the world, are fixed on my body, a thing in the world—that is the objective fact of which I can say: it *is*. But it is also a fact *in the world*. The meaning of this look is not a fact in the world, and this is what makes me uncomfortable. Although I make smiles, promises, threats, nothing can get hold of the approbation, the free judgment which I seek; I know that it is always beyond. I sense it in my very attitude, which is no longer like that of the worker toward the things he uses as instruments. My reactions, to the extent that I project myself toward the Other, are no longer for myself but are rather mere *presentations*; they await being constituted as graceful or uncouth, sincere or insincere, *etc.*, by an apprehension which is always beyond my efforts to provoke, an apprehension which will be provoked by my efforts only if of itself it lends them force (that is, only in so far as it causes itself to be provoked from the outside), *which is its own mediator with the transcendent.* Thus the objective fact of the being-in-itself of the consciousness of the Other is posited in order to disappear in negativity and in freedom: consciousness of the Other is at not-being; its being-in-itself "here and now" is not-to-be.

Consciousness of the Other is what it is not.

Furthermore the being of my own consciousness does not appear to me as the consciousne of the Other. It *is* because it makes itself, since its being is consciousness of being. But this means that making sustains being; consciousness has to be its own being, it is never sustained by being; it sustains being in the heart of subjectivity, which means once again that it is inhabited by being but that it is not being: *consciousness is not what it is.*

Under these conditions what can be the significance of the ideal of sincerity except as a task impossible to achieve, of which the very meaning is in contradiction with the structure of my consciousness. To be sincere, we said, is to be what one is. That supposes that I am not originally what I am. But here naturally Kant's "You ought, therefore you can" is implicitly understood. I can *become* sincere; this is what my duty and my effort to achieve sincerity imply. But we definitely establish that the original structure of "not being what one is" renders impossible in advance all movement toward being in itself or "being what one is." And this impossibility is not hidden from consciousness; on the contrary, it is the very stuff of consciousness; it is the embarrasing constraint which we constantly experience; it is our very incapacity to recognize ourselves, to constitute ourselves as being what we are. It is this necessity which means that, as soon as we posit ourselves as a certain being, by a legitimate judgment, based on inner experience or correctly deduced from a priori or empirical premises, then by that very positing we surpass this being—and that not toward another being but toward emptiness, toward *nothing.*

How then can we blame another for not being sincere or rejoice in our own sincerity since this sincerity appears to us at the same time to be impossible? How can we in conversation, in confession, in introspection, even attempt sincerity since the effort will by its very nature be doomed to failure and since at the very time when we announce it we have a prejudicative comprehension of its futility? In introspection I try to determine exactly what I am, to make up my mind to be my true self without delay—even though it means consequently to set about searching for ways to change myself. But what does this mean if not that I am constituting myself as a thing? Shall I determine the ensemble of purposes and motivations which have pushed me to do this or that action? But this is already to postulate a causal determinism which constitutes the flow of my states of consciousness as a succession of physical states. Shall I uncover in myself "drives," even though it be to affirm them in shame? But is this not deliberately to forget that these drives are realized with my consent, that they are not forces of nature but that I lend them their efficacy by a perpetually renewed decision concerning their value. Shall I pass judgment on my character, on my nature? Is this not to veil from myself at that moment what I know only too well, that I thus judge a past to which by definition my present is not subject? The proof of this is that the same man who in sincerity posits that he is what in actuality he was, is indignant at the reproach of another and tries to disarm it by asserting that he can no longer be what he was. We are readily astonished and upset when the penalties of the court affect a man who in his new freedom *is no longer* the guilty person he was. But at the same time we require of this man that he recognize himself as *being* this guilty one. What then is sincerity except precisely a phenomenon of bad faith? Have we not shown indeed that in bad faith human reality is constituted as a being which is what it is not and which is not what it is?.

Let us take an example: A homosexual frequently has an intolerable feeling of guilt, and his whole existence is determined in relation to this feeling. One will readily foresee that he is in bad faith. In fact it frequently happens that this man, while recognizing his homosexual inclination, while avowing each and every particular misdeed which he has committed, refuses with all his strength to consider himself "*a paederast.*" His case is always "different," peculiar; there enters into it something of a game, of chance, of bad luck; the mistakes are all in the past; they are explained by a certain conception of the beautiful which women cannot satisfy; we should see in them the results of a restless search, rather than the manifestations of a deeply rooted tendency, etc., etc. Here is assuredly a man in bad faith who borders on the comic since, acknowledging all the facts which are imputed to him, he refuses to draw from them the conclusion which they impose. His friend, who is his most severe critic, becomes irritated with this duplicity. The critic asks only one thing—and perhaps then he will show himself indulgent: that the guilty one recognize himself as guilty, that the homosexual declare frankly—whether humbly or boastfully means little—"I am a paederast." We ask here: Who is in bad faith? The homosexual or the champion of sincerity?

The homosexual recognizes his faults, but he struggles with all his strength against the crushing view that his mistakes constitute for him a *destiny*. He does not wish to let himself be considered as a thing. He has an obscure but strong feeling that a homosexual is not a homosexual as this table is a table or as this red-haired man is red-haired. It seems to him that he has escaped from each mistake as soon as he has posited it and recognized it; he even feels that the psychic duration by itself cleanses him from each misdeed, constitutes for him an undetermined future, causes him to be born anew. Is he wrong? Does he not recognize in himself the peculiar, irreducible character of human reality? His attitude includes then an undeniable comprehension of truth. But at the same time he needs this perpetual rebirth, this constant escape in order to live; he must constantly put himself beyond reach in order to avoid the terrible judgment of collectivity. Thus he plays on the word *being*. He would be right actually if he understood the phrase, "I am not a paederast" in the sense of "I am not what I am." That is, if he declared to himself, "To the extent that a pattern of conduct is defined as the conduct of a paederast and to the extent that I have adopted this conduct, I am a paederast. But to the extent that human reality cannot be finally defined by patterns of conduct, I am not one." But instead he slides surreptitiously towards a different connotation of the word "being." He understands "not being" in the sense of "not-being-in-itself." He lays claim to "not being a paederast" in the sense in which this table *is not* an inkwell. He is in bad faith.

But the champion of sincerity is not ignorant of the transcendence of human reality, and he knows how at need to appeal to it for his own advantage. He makes use of it even and brings it up in the present argument. Does he not wish, first in the name of sincerity, then of freedom, that the homosexual reflect on himself and acknowledge himself as an homosexual? Does he not let the other understand that such a confession will win indulgence for him? What does this mean if not that the man who will acknowledge himself as a homosexual will no longer be *the same* as the homosexual whom he acknowledges being and that he will escape into the region of freedom and of good will? The critic asks the man then to be what he is in order no longer to be what he is. It is the profound meaning of the saying, "A sin confessed is half pardoned." The critic demands of the guilty one that he constitute himself as a thing, precisely in order no longer to treat him as a thing. And this contradiction is constitutive of the demand of sincerity. Who cannot see how offensive to the Other and how reassuring for me is a statement such as, "He's just a paederast," which removes a disturbing freedom from a trait and which aims at henceforth constituting all the acts of the Other as consequences following strictly from his essence. That is actually what the critic is demanding of his victim—that he constitute himself as a thing, that he should entrust his freedom to his friend as a fief, in order that the friend should return it to him subsequently—like a suzerain to his vassal. The champion of sincerity is in bad faith to the degree that in order to reassure himself, he pretends to judge, to the extent that he demands that freedom as freedom constitute itself as a thing. We have here only one episode in that battle to the death of consciousness which Hegel calls "the relation of the master and the slave." A person appeals to another and demands that in the name of his nature as consciousness he should radically destroy himself as consciousness, but while making this appeal he leads the other to hope for a rebirth beyond this destruction.

Very well, someone will say, but our man is abusing sincerity, playing one side against the other. We should not look for sincerity in the relation of the *Mit-sein* but rather where it is pure—in the relations of a person with himself. But who cannot see that objective sincerity is constituted in the same way? Who cannot see that the sincere man constitutes himself as a thing in order to escape the condition of a thing by the same act of sincerity? The man who confesses that he is evil has exchanged his disturbing "freedom-for-evil" for an inanimate character of evil; he *is* evil, he clings to himself, he is what he is. But by the same stroke, he escapes from that *thing*, since it is he who contemplates it, since it depends on him to maintain it under his glance or to let it collapse in an infinity of particular acts. He derives a *merit* from his sincerity, and the deserving man is not the evil man as he is evil but as he is beyond his evilness. At the same time the evil is disarmed since it is nothing, save on the plane of determinism, and since in confessing it, I posit my freedom in respect to it; my future is virgin; everything is allowed to me.

Thus the essential structure of sincerity does not differ from that of bad faith since the sincere man constitutes himself as what he is *in order not to be it.* This explains the truth recognized by all that one can fall into bad faith through being sincere. As Valéry pointed out, this is the case with Stendhal. Total, constant sincerity as a constant effort to adhere to oneself is by nature a constant effort to dissociate oneself from oneself. A person frees himself from himself by the very act by which he makes himself an object for himself. To draw up a perpetual inventory of what one is means constantly to redeny oneself and to take refuge in a sphere where one is no longer anything but a pure, free regard. The goal of bad faith, as we said, is to put oneself out of reach: it is an escape. Now we see that we must use the same terms to define sincerity. What does this mean?

In the final analysis the goal of sincerity and the goal of bad faith are not so different. To be sure, there is a sincerity which bears on the past and which does not concern us here; I am sincere if I confess *having had* this pleasure or that intention. We shall see that if this sincerity is possible, it is because in his fall into the past, the being of man is constituted as a being-in-itself. But here our concern is only with the sincerity which aims at itself in present immanence. What is its goal? To bring me to confess to myself what I am in order that I may finally coincide with my being; in a word, to cause myself to be, in the mode of the in-itself, what I am in the mode of "not being what I am." Its assumption is that fundamentally I am already, in the mode of the in-itself, what I have to be. Thus we find at the base of sincerity a continual game of mirror and reflection, a perpetual passage from the being which is what it is, to the being which is not what it is and inversely from the being which is not what it is to the being which is what it is. And what is the goal of bad faith? To cause me to be what I am, in the mode of "not being what one is," or not to be what I am in the mode of "being what one is." We find here the same game of mirrors. In fact in order for me to have an intention of sincerity, I must at the outset simultaneously be and not be what I am. Sincerity does not assign to me a mode of being or a particular quality, but in relation to that quality it aims at making me pass from one mode of being to another mode of being. This second mode of being, the ideal of sincerity, I am prevented by nature from attaining; and at the very moment when I struggle to attain it, I have a vague prejudicative comprehension that I shall not attain it. But all the same, in order for me to be able to conceive an intention in bad faith, I must have such a nature that within my being I escape from my being. If I were sad or cowardly in the way in which this inkwell is an inkwell, the possibility of bad faith could not even be conceived. Not only should I be unable to escape from by being; I could not even imagine that I could escape from it. But if bad faith is possible by virtue of a simple project, it is because so far as my being is concerned, there is no difference between being and non-being if I am cut off from my project.

Bad faith is possible only because sincerity is conscious of missing its goal inevitably, due to its very nature. I can try to apprehend myself as "*not being cowardly*," when I *am so*, only on condition that the "being cowardly" is itself "in question" at the very moment when it exists, on condition that it is itself *one* question, that at the very moment when I wish to apprehend it, it escapes me on all sides and annihilates itself. The condition under which I can attempt an effort in bad faith is that in one sense, I *am not* this coward which I do not wish to be. But if I *were* not cowardly in the simple mode of not-being-what-one-is-not, I would be "in good faith" by declaring that I am not cowardly. Thus this inapprehensible coward is evanescent; in order for me not to be cowardly, I must in some way also be cowardly. That does not mean that I must be "a little" cowardly, in the sense that "a little" signifies "to a certain degree cowardly—and not cowardly to a certain degree." No. I must at once both be and not be totally and in all respects a coward. Thus in this case bad faith requires that I should not be what I am; that is, that there be an imponderable difference separating being from non-being in the mode of being of human reality.

But bad faith is not restricted to denying the qualities which I possess, to not seeing the being which I am. It attempts also to constitute myself as being what I am not. It apprehends me positively as courageous when I am not so. And that is possible, once again, only if I am what I am not; that is, if non-being in me does not have being even as non-being. Of course necessarily I *am not* courageous; otherwise bad faith would not be *bad* faith. But in addition my effort in bad faith must include the ontological comprehension that even in my usual being what I *am*, I am not it really and that there is no such difference between the being of "being-sad," for example—which I *am* in the mode of not being what I am—and the "non-being" of not-being-courageous which I wish to hide from myself. Moreover it is particularly requisite that the very negation of being should be itself the object of a perpetual nihilation, that the very meaning of "non-being" be perpetually in question in human reality. If I *were not* courageous in the way in which this inkwell is not a table; that is, if I were isolated in my cowardice, propped firmly against it, incapable of putting it in relation to its opposite, if I were not capable of *determining* myself as cowardly—that is, to deny courage to myself and thereby to escape my cowardice in the very moment that I posit it—if it were not on principle *impossible* for me to coincide with my *not-being-courageous* as well as with my being-courageous—then any project of bad faith would be prohibited me. Thus in order for bad faith to be possible, sincerity itself must be in bad faith. The condition of the possibility for bad faith is that human reality, in its most immediate being, in the intrastructure of the pre-reflective *cogito,* must be what it is not and not be what it is.

6. THE "FAITH" OF BAD FAITH

We have indicated for the moment only those conditions which render bad faith conceivable, the structures of being which permit us to form concepts of bad faith. We cannot limit ourselves to these considerations; we have not yet distinguished bad faith from falsehood. The two-faced concepts which we have described would without a doubt be utilized by a liar to discountenance his questioner, although their two-faced quality being established on the being of man and not on some empirical circumstance, can and ought to be evident to all. The true problem of bad faith stems evidently from the fact that bad faith is *faith*. It cannot be either a cynical lie or certainty—if certainty is the intuitive possession of the object. But if we take belief as meaning the adherence of being to its object when the object is not given or is given indistinctly, then bad faith is belief; and the essential problem of bad faith is a problem of belief.

How can we believe by bad faith in the concepts which we forge expressly to persuade ourselves? We must note in fact that the project of bad faith must be itself in bad faith. I am not only in bad faith at the end of my effort when I have constructed my two-faced concepts and when I have persuaded myself. In truth, I have not persuaded myself; to the extent that I could be so persuaded, I have always been so. And at the very moment when I was disposed to put myself in bad faith, I of necessity was in bad faith with respect to this same disposition. For me to have represented it to myself as bad faith would have been cynicism; to believe it sincerely innocent would have been in good faith. The decision to be in bad faith does not dare to speak its name; it believes itself and does not believe itself in bad faith; it believes itself and does not believe itself in good faith. It is this which from the upsurge of bad faith, determines the later attitude and, as it were, the *Weltanschauung* of bad faith.

Bad faith does not hold the norms and criteria of truth as they are accepted by the critical thought of good faith. What it decides first, in fact, is the nature of truth. With bad faith a truth appears, a method of thinking, a type of being which is like that of objects; the ontological characteristic of the world of bad faith with which the subject suddenly surrounds himself is this: that here being is what it is not, and is not what it is. Consequently a peculiar type of evidence appears; *non-persuasive* evidence. Bad faith apprehends evidence but it is resigned in advance to not being fulfilled by this evidence, to not being persuaded and transformed into good faith. It makes itself humble and modest; it is not ignorant, it says, that faith is decision and that after each intuition, it must decide and *will what it is*. Thus bad faith in its primitive project and in its coming into the world decides on the exact nature of its requirements. It stands forth in the firm resolution *not to demand too much*, to count itself satisfied when it is barely persuaded, to force itself in decisions to adhere to uncertain truths. This original project and bad faith is a decision in bad faith on the nature of faith. Let us understand clearly that there is no question of a reflective, voluntary decision, but of a spontaneous determination of our being. One *puts oneself* in bad faith as one goes to sleep and one is in bad faith as one dreams. Once this mode of being has been realized, it is as difficult to get out of it as to wake oneself up; bad faith is a type of being in the world, like waking or dreaming, which by itself tends to perpetuate itself, although its structure is of the *metastable* type. But bad faith is conscious of its structure, and it has taken precautions by deciding that the metastable structure is the structure of being and that non-persuasion is the structure of all convictions. It follows that if bad faith is faith and if it includes in its original project its own negation (it determines itself to be not quite convinced in order to convince itself that I am what I am not), then to start with, a faith which wishes itself to be not quite convinced must be possible. What are the conditions for the possibility of such a faith?

I believe that my friend Pierre feels friendship for me. I believe it *in good faith*. I believe it but I do not have for it any self-evident intuition, for the nature of the object does not lend itself to intuition. I *believe it*; that is, I allow myself to give in to all impulses to trust it; I decide to believe in it, and to maintain myself in this decision; I conduct myself, finally, as if I were certain of it—and all this in the synthetic unity of one and the same attitude. This which I define as good faith is what Hegel would call the *immediate*. It is simple faith. Hegel would demonstrate at once that the immediate calls for mediation and that belief by becoming *belief for itself,* passes to the state of non-belief. If I *believe* that my friend Pierre likes me, this means that his friendship appears to me as the meaning of all his acts. Belief is a particular consciousness of *the meaning* of Pierre's acts. But if I know that I believe, the belief appears to me as pure subjective determination without external correlative. This is what makes the very word "to believe" a term utilized indifferently to indicate the unwavering firmness of belief ("My God, I believe in you") and its character as disarmed and strictly subjective. ("Is Pierre my friend? I do not know; I believe so.") But the nature of consciousness is such that in it the mediate and the immediate are one and the same being. To believe is to know that one believes, and to know that one believes is no longer to believe. Thus to believe is not to believe any longer because that is only to believe—this in the unity of one and the same non-thetic self-consciousness. To be sure, we have here forced the description of the phenomenon by designating it with the word *to know*; non-thetic consciousness is not to *know*. But it is in its very translucency at the origin of all knowing. Thus the non-thetic consciousness (of) believing is destructive of belief. But at the same time the very law of the pre-reflective *cogito* implies that the being of believing ought to be the consciousness of believing.

Thus belief is a being which questions its own being, which can realize itself only in its destruction, which can manifest itself to itself only by denying itself. It is a being for which to be is to appear and to appear is to deny itself. To believe is not-to-believe. We see the reason for it; the being of consciousness is to exist by itself, then to make itself be and thereby to pass beyond itself. In this sense consciousness is perpetually escaping itself, belief becomes non-belief, the immediate becomes mediation, the absolute becomes relative, and the relative becomes absolute. The ideal of good faith (to believe what one believes) is, like that of sincerity (to be what one is), an ideal of being-in-itself. Every belief is a belief that falls short; one never wholly believes that one believes. Consequently the primitive project of bad faith is only the utilization of this self-destruction of the fact of consciousness. If every belief in good faith is an impossible belief, then there is a place for every impossible belief. My inability to *believe* that I am courageous will not discourage me since every belief involves not quite believing. I shall define this impossible belief as *my* belief. To be sure, I shall not be able to hide from myself that I believe in order not to believe and that I do not believe *in order to* believe. But the subtle, total annihilation of bad faith by itself cannot surprise me; it exists at the basis of all faith. What is it then? At the moment when I wish to believe myself courageous I *know* that I am a coward. And this certainly would come to destroy my belief. But *first*, I am not any more courageous than cowardly, if we are to understand this in the mode of being of the-in-itself. In the second place, I do not know that I am courageous; such a view of myself can be accompanied only by *belief*, for it surpasses pure reflective certitude. In the third place, it is very true that bad faith does not succeed in believing what it wishes to believe. But it is precisely as the acceptance of not believing what it believes that it is bad faith. Good faith wishes to flee the "not-believing-what-one-believes" by finding refuge in being. Bad faith flees being by taking refuge in "not-believing-what-one-believes." It has disarmed all beliefs in advance—those which it would like to take hold of and, by the same stroke, the others, those which it wishes to flee. In *willing* this self-destruction of belief, from which science escapes by searching for evidence, it ruins the beliefs which are opposed to it, which reveal themselves as *being only* belief. Thus we can better understand the original phenomenon of bad faith.

In bad faith there is no cynical lie nor knowing preparation for deceitful concepts. But the first act of bad faith is to flee what it cannot flee, to flee what it is. The very project of flight reveals to bad faith an inner disintegration in the heart of being, and it is this disintegration which bad faith wishes to be. In truth, the two immediate attitudes which we can take in the face of our being are conditioned by the very nature of this being and its immediate relation with the in-itself. Good faith seeks to flee the inner disintegration of my being in the direction of the in-itself which it should be and is not. Bad faith seeks to flee the in-itself by means of the inner disintegration of my being. But it denies this very disintegration as it denies that it is itself bad faith. Bad faith seeks by means of "not-being-what-one-is" to escape from the in-itself which I am not in the mode of being what one is not. It denies itself as bad faith and aims at the in-itself which I am not in the mode of "not-being-what-one-is-not."[12] If bad faith is possible, it is because it is an immediate, permanent threat to every project of the human being; it is because consciousness conceals in its being a permanent risk of bad faith. The origin of this risk is the fact that the nature of consciousness simultaneously is to be what it is not and not to be what it is. In the light of these remarks we can now approach the ontological study of consciousness, not as the totality of the human being, but as the instantaneous nucleus of this being. . . .

7. THE EXISTENCE OF OTHERS

Let us imagine that moved by jealousy, curiosity, or vice I have just glued my ear to the door and looked through a keyhole. I am alone and on the level of a non-thetic self-consciousness. This means first of all that there is no self to inhabit my consciousness, nothing therefore to which I can refer my acts in order to qualify them. They are in no way *known; I am my acts* and hence they carry in themselves their whole justification. I am pure consciousness *of* things, and things, caught up in the circuit of my selfness, offer to me their potentialities as the proof of my non-thetic consciousness (of) my own possibilities. This means that behind that door a spectacle is presented as "to be seen," a conversation as "to be heard." The door, the keyhole are at once both instruments and obstacles; they are presented as "to be handled with care"; the keyhole is given as "to be looked through close by and a little to one side," etc. Hence from this moment "I do what I have to do." No transcending view comes to confer upon my acts the character of a *given* on which a judgment can be brought to bear. My consciousness sticks to my acts, it *is* my acts; and my acts are commanded only by the ends to be attained and by the instruments to be employed. My attitude, for example, has no "outside"; it is a pure process of relating the instrument (the keyhole) to the end to be attained (the spectacle to be seen), a pure mode of losing myself in the world, of causing myself to be drunk in by things as ink is by a blotter in order that an instrumental-complex oriented toward an end may be synthetically detached on the ground of the world. The order is the reverse of causal order. It is the end to be attained which organizes all the moments which precede it. The end justifies the means; the means do not exist for themselves and outside the end.

Moreover the ensemble exists only in relation to a free project of my pos-

12. If it is indifferent whether one is in good or in bad faith, because bad faith reapprehends good faith and slides to the very origin of the project of good faith, that does not mean that we cannot radically escape bad faith. But this supposes a self-recovery of being which was previously corrupted. This self-recovery we shall call authenticity, the description of which has no place here.

sibilities. Jealousy, as the possibility which I *am*, organizes this instrumental complex by transcending it toward itself. But I *am* this jealousy; I do not *know* it. If I contemplated it instead of making it, then only the worldly complex of instrumentality could teach it to me. This ensemble in the world with its double and inverted determination (there is a spectacle to be seen behind the door only because I am jealous, but my jealousy is nothing except the simple objective fact that *there is* a sight *to be seen* behind the door)—this we shall call *situation*. This situation reflects to me at once both my facticity and my freedom; on the occasion of a certain objective structure of the world which surrounds me, it refers my freedom to me in the form of tasks to be freely done. There is no constraint here since my freedom eats into my possibles and since correlatively the potentialities of the world indicate and offer only themselves. Moreover I cannot truly define myself as *being* in a situation: first because I am not a positional consciousness of myself; second because I am my own nothingness. In this sense—and since I am what I am not and since I am not what I am—I cannot even define myself as truly *being* in the process of listening at doors. I escape this provisional definition of myself by means of all my transcendence. There as we have seen is the origin of bad faith. Thus not only am I unable to *know* myself, but my very being escapes—although I *am* that very escape from my being—and I am absolutely nothing. There is nothing *there* but a pure nothingness encircling a certain objective ensemble and throwing it into relief outlined upon the world, but this ensemble is a real system, a disposition of means in view of an end.

But all of a sudden I hear footsteps in the hall. Someone is looking at me! What does this mean? It means that I am suddenly affected in my being and that essential modifications appear in my structure—modifications which I can apprehend and fix conceptually by means of the reflective *cogito*.

First of all, I now exist as *myself* for my unreflective consciousness. It is this irruption of the self which has been most often described: I see *myself* because *somebody* sees me—as it is usually expressed. This way of putting it is not wholly exact. But let us look more carefully. So long as we considered the for-itself in its isolation, we were able to maintain that the unreflective consciousness cannot be inhabited by a self; the self was given in the form of an object and only for the reflective consciousness. But here the self comes to haunt the unreflective consciousness. Now the unreflective consciousness is a consciousness *of* the world. Therefore for the unreflective consciousness the self exists on the level of objects in the world; this role which devolved only on the reflective consciousness—the making-present of the self—belongs now to the unreflective consciousness. Only the reflective consciousness has the self directly for an object. The unreflective consciousness does not apprehend the *person* directly or as *its* object; the person is presented to consciousness *in so far as the person is an object for the Other.* This means that all of a sudden I am conscious of myself as escaping myself, not in that I am the foundation of my own nothingness but in that I have my foundation outside myself. I am for myself only as I am a pure reference to the Other.

Nevertheless we must not conclude here that the object is the Other and that the *Ego* present to my consciousness is a secondary structure or a meaning of the Other-as-object; the Other is not an object here and cannot be an object, as we have shown, unless by the same stroke *my* self ceases to be an object-for-the-Other and vanishes. Thus I do not aim at the Other as an object nor at my *Ego* as an object for myself; I do not even direct an empty intention toward that *Ego* as toward an object presently out of my reach. In fact it is separated from me by a nothingness which I cannot fill since I apprehend it as *not being for me* and since on principle it exists for the *Other.* Therefore I do not aim at it as if it could someday be given me but on the contrary in so far as it on principle flees from me and will never belong to me. Nevertheless I *am that Ego*; I do not reject it as a strange image, but it is present to me as a self which *I am* without *knowing* it; for I discover it in shame and, in other instances, in pride. It is shame or pride which reveals to me the Other's look and myself at the end of that look. It is the shame or pride which makes me *live*, not *know* the situation of being looked at.

Now, shame, as we noted at the beginning of this chapter, is shame of *self*; it is the *recognition* of the fact that I *am* indeed that object which the Other is looking at and judging. I can be ashamed only as my freedom escapes me in order to become a *given* object. Thus originally the bond between my unreflective consciousness and my *Ego*, which is being looked at, is a bond not of knowing but of being. Beyond any knowledge which I can have, I am this self which another knows. And this self which I am—this I am in a world which the Other has made alien to me, for the Other's look embraces my being and correlatively the walls, the door, the keyhole. All these instrumental-things in the midst of which I am, now turn toward the Other a face which on principle escapes me. Thus I am my *Ego* for the Other in the midst of a world which flows toward the Other. Earlier we were able to call this internal hemorrhage the flow of *my* world toward the Other-as-object. This was because the flow of blood was trapped and localized by the very fact that I fixed as an object in my world that Other toward which this world was bleeding. Thus not a drop of blood was lost; all was recovered, surrounded, localized although in a being which I could not penetrate. Here on the contrary the flight is without limit; it is lost externally; the world flows out of the world and I flow outside myself. The Other's look makes me be beyond my being in this world and puts me in the midst of the world which is at once *this world* and beyond this world. What sort of relations can I enter into with this being which I am and which shame reveals to me?

In the first place there is a relation of being. I *am* this being. I do not for an instant think of denying it; my shame is a confession. I shall be able later to use bad faith so as to hide it from myself, but bad faith is also a confession since it is an effort to flee the being which I am. But I am this being, neither in the mode of "having to be" nor in that of "was"; I do not found it in its being; I cannot produce it directly. But neither is it the indirect, strict effect of my acts as when my shadow on the ground or my reflection in the mirror is moved in correlation with the gestures which I make. This being which I am preserves a certain indetermination, a certain unpredictability. And these new characteristics do not come only from the fact that I cannot *know* the Other; they stem also and especially from the fact that the Other is free. Or to be exact and to reverse the terms, the Other's freedom is revealed to me across the uneasy indetermination of the being which I am for him. Thus this being is not my possible; it is not always in question at the heart of my freedom. On the contrary, it is the limit of my freedom, its "backstage" in the sense that we speak of "behind the scenes." It is given to me as a burden which I carry without ever being able to turn back to know it, without even being able to realize its weight. If it is comparable to my shadow, it is like a shadow which is projected on a moving and unpredictable material such that no table of reference can be provided for calculating the distortions resulting from these movements. Yet we still have to do with *my* being and not with an image of my being. We are dealing with my being as it is written in and by the Other's freedom. Everything takes place as if I had a dimension of being from which I was separated by a radical nothingness; and this nothingness is the Other's freedom. The Other has to make my being-for-him *be* in so far as he has to be his being. Thus each of my free conducts engages me in a new environment where the very stuff of my being is the unpredictable freedom of another. Yet by my very shame I claim as mine that freedom of another. I affirm a profound unity of consciousnesses, not that harmony of monads which has sometimes been taken as a guarantee of objectivity but a unity of being; for I accept and wish that others should confer upon me a being which I recognize.

Shame reveals to me that I *am* this being, not in the mode of "was" or of "having to be" but *in-itself.* When I am alone, I cannot realize my "being-seated"; at most it can be said that I simultaneously both am it and am not it. But in order for me to be what I am, it suffices merely that the Other look at me. It is not for myself, to be sure; I myself shall never succeed at realizing this being-seated which I grasp in the Other's look. I shall remain forever a consciousness. But it is for the Other. Once more the nihilating escape of the for-itself is fixed, once more the in-itself closes in upon the for-itself. But once more this metamorphosis is effected *at a distance.* For the Other *I am seated* as this inkwell *is on* the table; for the Other, *I am leaning over* the keyhole as this tree *is bent* by the wind. Thus for the Other I have stripped myself of my transcendence. This is because my transcendence becomes for whoever makes himself a witness of it (*i.e.*, determines himself as *not being* my transcendence) a purely established transcendence, a given-transcendence; that is, it acquires a nature by the sole fact that the *Other* confers on it an outside. This is accomplished, not by any distortion or by a refraction which the Other would impose on my transcendence through his categories, but by his very being. If there is an Other, whatever or whoever he may be, whatever may be his relations with me, and without his acting upon me in any way except by the pure upsurge of his being—then I have an outside, I have a *nature*. My original fall is the existence of the Other. Shame—like pride—is the apprehension of myself as a nature although that very nature escapes me and is unknowable as such. Strictly speaking, it is not that I perceive myself losing my freedom in order to become a *thing*, but my nature is—over there, outside my lived freedom—as a given attribute of this being which I am for the Other. . . .

8. FREEDOM AND RESPONSIBILITY

Although the considerations which are about to follow are of interest primarily to the ethicist, it may nevertheless be worthwhile after these descriptions and arguments to return to the freedom of the for-itself and to try to understand what the fact of this freedom represents for human destiny.

The essential consequence of our earlier remarks is that man being condemned to be free carries the weight of the whole world on his shoulders; he is responsible for the world and for himself as a way of being. We are taking the word "responsibility" in its ordinary sense as "consciousness (of) being the incontestable author of an event or of an object." In this sense the responsibility of the for-itself is overwhelming since he[13] is the one by whom it happens that *there is* a world; since he is also the one who makes himself be, then whatever may be the situation in which he finds himself, the for-itself must wholly assume this situation with its peculiar coefficient of adversity, even though it be insupportable. He must assume the situation with the proud consciousness of being the author of it, for the very worst disadvantages or the worst threats which can endanger my person have meaning only in and through my project; and it is on the ground of the engagement which I am that they appear. It is therefore senseless to think of complaining since nothing foreign has decided what we feel, what we live, or what we are.

13. I am shifting to the personal pronoun here since Sartre is describing the for-itself in concrete personal terms rather than as a metaphysical entity. Strictly speaking, of course, this is his position throughout, and the French "*il*" is indifferently "he" or "it." Tr.

Furthermore this absolute responsibility is not resignation; it is simply the logical requirement of the consequences of our freedom. What happens to me happens through me, and I can neither affect myself with it nor revolt against it nor resign myself to it. Moreover everything which happens to me is *mine*. By this we must understand first of all that I am always equal to what happens to me *qua* man, for what happens to a man through other men and through himself can be only human. The most terrible situations of war, the worst tortures do not create a non-human state of things; there is no non-human situation. It is only through fear, flight, and recourse to magical types of conduct that I shall decide on the non-human, but this decision is human, and I shall carry the entire responsibility for it. But in addition the situation is *mine* because it is the image of my free choice of myself, and everything which it presents to me is *mine* in that this represents me and symbolizes me. Is it not I who decide the coefficient of adversity in things and even their unpredictability by deciding myself?

Thus there are no *accidents* in a life; a community event which suddenly bursts forth and involves me in it does not come from the outside. If I am mobilized in a war, this war is *my* war; it is in my image and I deserve it. I deserve it first because I could always get out of it by suicide or by desertion; these ultimate possibles are those which must always be present for us when there is a question of envisaging a situation. For lack of getting out of it, I have *chosen* it. This can be due to inertia, to cowardice in the face of public opinion, or because I prefer certain other values to the value of the refusal to join in the war (the good opinion of my relatives, the honor of my family, etc.). Anyway you look at it, it is a matter of a choice. This choice will be repeated later on again and again without a break until the end of the war. Therefore we must agree with the statement by J. Romains, "In war there are no innocent victims."[14] If therefore I have preferred war to death or to dishonor, everything takes place as if I bore the entire responsibility for this war. Of course others have declared it, and one might be tempted perhaps to consider me as a simple accomplice. But this notion of complicity has only a juridical sense, and it does not hold here. For it depended on me that for me and by me this war should not exist, and I have decided that it does exist. There was no compulsion here, for the compulsion could have got no hold on a freedom. I did not have any excuse; for as we have said repeatedly in this book, the peculiar character of human-reality is that it is without excuse. Therefore it remains for me only to lay claim to this war.

But in addition the war is *mine* because by the sole fact that it arises in a situation which I cause to be and that I can discover it there only by engaging myself for or against it, I can no longer distinguish at present the choice

14. J. Romains: *Les hommes de bonne volonté*; "Prélude à Verdun."

which I make of myself from the choice which I make of the war. To live this war is to choose myself through it and to choose it through my choice of myself. There can be no question of considering it as "four years of vacation" or as a "reprieve," as a "recess," the essential part of my responsibilities being elsewhere in my married, family, or professional life. In this war which I have chosen I choose myself from day to day, and I make it mine by making myself. If it is going to be four empty years, then it is I who bear the responsibility for this.

Finally, as we pointed out earlier, each person is an absolute choice of self from the standpoint of a world of knowledges and of techniques which this choice both assumes and illumines; each person is an absolute upsurge at an absolute date and is perfectly unthinkable at another date. It is therefore a waste of time to ask what I should have been if this war had not broken out, for I have chosen myself as one of the possible meanings of the epoch which imperceptibly led to war. I am not distinct from this same epoch; I could not be transported to another epoch without contradiction. Thus *I am* this war which restricts and limits and makes comprehensible the period which preceded it. In this sense we may define more precisely the responsibility of the for-itself if to the earlier quoted statement, "There are no innocent victims," we add the words, "We have the war we deserve." Thus, totally free, undistinguishable from the period for which I have chosen to be the meaning, as profoundly responsible for the war as if I had myself declared it, unable to live without integrating it in *my* situation, engaging myself in it wholly and stamping it with my seal, I must be without remorse or regrets as I am without excuse; for from the instant of my upsurge into being, I carry the weight of the world by myself alone without anything or any person being able to lighten it.

Yet this responsibility is of a very particular type. Someone will say, "I did not ask to be born." This is a naive way of throwing greater emphasis on our facticity. I am responsible for everything, in fact, except for my very responsibility, for I am not the foundation of my being. Therefore everything takes place as if I were compelled to be responsible. I am *abandoned* in the world, not in the sense that I might remain abandoned and passive in a hostile universe like a board floating on the water, but rather in the sense that I find myself suddenly alone and without help, engaged in a world for which I bear the whole responsibility without being able, whatever I do, to tear myself away from this responsibility for an instant. For I am responsible for my very desire of fleeing responsibilities. To make myself passive in the world, to refuse to act upon things and upon Others is still to choose myself, and suicide is one mode among others of being-in-the-world. Yet I find an absolute responsibility for the fact that my facticity (here the fact of my birth) is directly inapprehensible and even inconceivable, for this fact of my birth never appears as a brute fact but always across a projective reconstruction of my for-itself. I am ashamed of being born or I am astonished at it or I rejoice over it, or in attempting to get rid of my life I affirm that I live and I assume this life as bad. Thus in a certain sense I *choose* being born. This choice itself is integrally affected with facticity since I am not able not to choose, but this facticity in turn will appear only in so far as I surpass it toward my ends. Thus facticity is everywhere but inapprehensible; I never encounter anything except my responsibility. That is why I cannot ask, "*Why* was I born?" or curse the day of my birth or declare that I did not ask to be born, for these various attitudes toward my birth—i.e., toward the *fact* that I realize a presence in the world—are absolutely nothing else but ways of assuming this birth in full responsibility and of making it *mine.* Here again I encounter only myself and my projects so that finally my abandonment—i.e., my facticity—consists simply in the fact that I am condemned to be wholly responsible for myself. I am the being which *is* in such a way that in its being its being is in question. And this "is" of my being *is* as present and inapprehensible.

Under these conditions since every event in the world can be revealed to me only as an *opportunity* (an opportunity made use of, lacked, neglected, etc.), or better yet since everything which happens to us can be considered as a *chance* (i.e., can appear to us only as a way of realizing this being which is in question in our being) and since others as transcendences-transcended are themselves only *opportunities* and *chances,* the responsibility of the for-itself extends to the entire world as a peopled-world. It is precisely thus that the for-itself apprehends itself in anguish; that is, as a being which is neither the foundation of its own being nor of the Other's being nor of the in-itselfs which form the world, but a being which is compelled to decide the meaning of being—within it and everywhere outside of it. The one who realizes in anguish his condition as *being* thrown into a responsibility which extends to his very abandonment has no longer either remorse or regret or excuse; he is no longer anything but a freedom which perfectly reveals itself and whose being resides in this very revelation. But as we pointed out at the beginning of this work, most of the time we flee anguish in bad faith. . . .

9. EXISTENTIAL PSYCHOANALYSIS

The problem poses itself in approximately these terms: If we admit that the person is a totality, we cannot hope to reconstruct him by an addition or by an organization of the diverse tendencies which we have empirically discovered in him. On the contrary, in each inclination, in each tendency the person expresses himself completely, although from a different angle, a little as Spinoza's substance expresses itself completely in each of its attributes.

But if this is so, we should discover in each tendency, in each attitude of the subject, a meaning which transcends it. A jealousy of a particular date in which a subject historicizes himself in relation to a certain woman, signifies for the one who knows how to interpret it, the total relation to the world by which the subject constitutes himself as a self. In other words this *empirical* attitude is by itself the expression of the "choice of an intelligible character." There is no mystery about this. We no longer have to do with an intelligible pattern which can be present in our thought only, while we apprehend and conceptualize the unique pattern of the subject's empirical existence. If the empirical attitude signifies the choice of the intelligible character, it is because it is itself this choice. Indeed the distinguishing characteristic of the intelligible choice, as we shall see later, is that it can exist only as the transcendent meaning of each concrete, empirical choice. It is by no means first effected in some unconscious or on the noumenal level to be *subsequently* expressed in a particular observable attitude; there is not even an *ontological* pre-eminence over the empirical choice, but it is on principle that which must always detach itself from the empirical choice as its *beyond* and the infinity of its transcendence. Thus if I am rowing on the river, I am nothing—either here or in any other world—save this concrete project of rowing. But this project itself inasmuch as it is the totality of my being, expresses my original choice in particular circumstances; it is nothing other than the choice of myself as a totality in these circumstances. That is why a special method must aim at detaching the fundamental meaning which the project admits and which can be only the individual secret of the subject's being-in-the-world. It is then rather by a *comparison* of the various empirical drives of a subject that we try to discover and disengage the fundamental project which is common to them all—and not by a simple summation or reconstruction of these tendencies; each drive or tendency is the entire person.

There is naturally an infinity of possible projects as there is an infinity of possible human beings. Nevertheless, if we are to recognize certain common characteristics among them and if we are going to attempt to classify them in larger categories, it is best first to undertake individual investigations in the cases which we can study more easily. In our research, we will be guided by this principle: to stop only in the presence of evident irreducibility; that is, never to believe that we have reached the initial project until the projected end appears as *the very being* of the subject under consideration. This is why we cannot stop at those classifications of "authentic project" and "unauthentic project of the self" which Heidegger wishes to establish. In addition to the fact that such a classification, in spite of its author's intent, is tainted with an ethical concern shown by its very terminology, it is based on the attitude of the subject toward his own death. Now if death causes anguish, and if consequently we can either flee the anguish or throw ourselves resolutely into it, it is a truism to say that this is because we wish to hold on to life. Consequently anguish before death and resolute decision or flight into unauthenticity cannot be considered as fundamental projects of our being. On the contrary, they can be understood only on the foundation of an original project of *living* that is, on an original choice of our being. It is right then in each case to pass beyond the results of Heidegger's interpretation toward a still more fundamental project.

This fundamental project must not of course refer to any other and should be conceived by itself. It can be concerned neither with death nor life nor any particular characteristic of the human condition; the original project of a for-itself *can aim only at its being.* The project of being or desire of being or drive toward being does not originate in a physiological differentiation or in an empirical contingency; in fact it is not distinguished from the being of the for-itself. The for-itself is a being such that in its being, its being is in question in the form of a project of being. To the for-itself *being* means to make known to oneself what one is by means of a possibility appearing as a value. Possibility and value belong to the being of the for-itself. The for-itself is defined ontologically as a lack *of being,* and possibility belongs to the for-itself as that which it lacks, in the same way that value haunts the for-itself as the totality of being which is lacking. What we have expressed in Part Two in terms of lack can be just as well expressed in terms of *freedom.* The for-itself chooses because it is lack; freedom is really synonymous with lack. Freedom is the concrete mode of being of the lack of being. Ontologically then it amounts to the same thing to say that value and possibility exist as internal limits of a lack of being which can exist only as a lack of being—or that the upsurge of freedom determines its possibility and thereby circumscribes *its* value.

Thus we can advance no further but have encountered the self-evident irreducible when we have reached the *project of being*; for obviously it is impossible to advance further than *being*, and there is no difference between the project of being, possibility, value, on the one hand, and *being*, on the other. Fundamentally man is the *desire to be*, and the existence of this desire is not to be established by an empirical induction; it is the result of an a priori description of the being of the for-itself, since desire is a lack and since the for-itself is the being which is to itself its own lack of being. The original project which is expressed in each of our empirically observable tendencies is then the *project of being*; or, if you prefer, each empirical tendency exists with the original project of being, in a relation of expression and symbolic satisfaction just as conscious drives, with Freud, exist in relation to the complex and to the original libido. Moreover the desire to be by no means exists *first* in order to cause itself to be expressed subsequently by desires *a posteriori.* There is nothing outside of the symbolic expression which it finds in concrete desires. There is not first a single desire of being, then a thousand particular feelings, but the desire to be exists and manifests itself only in and through jealousy, greed, love of art, cowardice, courage, and a thousand contingent, empirical expressions which always cause human reality to appear to us only as *manifested* by a *particular man,* by a specific person.

As for the being which is the object of this desire, we know a priori what this is. The for-itself is the being which is to itself its own lack of being. The being which the for-itself lacks is the in-itself. The for-itself arises as the nihilation of the in-itself and this nihilation is defined as the project toward the in-itself. Between the nihilated in-itself and the projected in-itself the for-itself is nothingness. Thus the end and the goal of the nihilation which I am is the in-itself. Thus human reality is the desire of being-in-itself. But the in-itself which it desires cannot be pure contingent, absurd in-itself, comparable at every point to that which it encounters and which it nihilates. The nihilation, as we have seen, is in fact like a revolt of the in-itself, which nihilates itself against its contingency. To say that the for-itself lives its facticity, as we have seen in the chapter concerning the body, amounts to saying that the nihilation is the vain effort of a being to found its own being and that it is the withdrawal to found being which provokes the minute displacement by which nothingness enters into being. The being which forms the object of the desire of the for-itself is then an in-itself which would be to itself its own foundation; that is, which would be to its facticity in the same relation as the for-itself is to its motivations. In addition the for-itself, being the negation of the in-itself, could not desire the pure and simple return to the in-itself. Here as with Hegel, the negation of the negation cannot bring us back to our point of departure. Quite the contrary, what the for-itself demands of the in-itself is precisely the totality detotalized—"In-itself nihilated in for-itself." In other words the for-itself projects *being as for-itself,* a being which is what it is. It is as being which is what it is not, and which is not what it is, that the for-itself projects being what it is. It is as consciousness that it wishes to have the impermeability and infinite density of the in-itself. It is as the nihilation of the in-itself and a perpetual evasion of contingency and of facticity that it wishes to be its own foundation. This is why the possible is projected in general as what the for-itself lacks in order to become in-itself-for-itself. The fundamental value which presides over this project is exactly the in-itself-for-itself; that is, the ideal of a consciousness which would be the foundation of its own being-in-itself by the pure consciousness which it would have of itself. It is this ideal which can be called God. Thus the best way to conceive of the fundamental project of human reality is to say that man is the being whose project is to be God. Whatever may be the myths and rites of the religion considered, God is first "sensible to the heart" of man as the one who identifies and defines him in his ultimate and fundamental project. If man possesses a pre-ontological comprehension of the being of God, it is not the great wonders of nature nor the power of society which have conferred it upon him. God, value and supreme end of transcendence, represents the permanent limit in terms of which man makes known to himself what he is. To be man means to reach toward being God. Or if you prefer, man fundamentally is the desire to be God.

It may be asked, if man on coming into the world is borne toward God as toward his limit, if he can choose only to be God, what becomes for freedom? For freedom is nothing other than a choice which creates for itself its own possibilities, but it appears here that the initial project of being God, which "defines" man, comes close to being the same as a human "nature" or an "essence." The answer is that while the *meaning* of the desire is ultimately the project of being God, the desire is never *constituted* by this meaning; on the contrary, it always represents a particular discovery of its ends. These ends in fact are pursued in terms of a particular empirical situation, and it is this very pursuit which constitutes the surroundings *as a situation*. The desire of being is always realized as the desire of a mode of being. And this desire of a mode of being expresses itself in turn as the meaning of the myriads of concrete desires which constitute the web of our conscious life. Thus we find ourselves before very complex symbolic structures which have *at least* three stories. In empirical desire I can discern a symbolization of a fundamental concrete desire which is the person himself and which represents the mode in which he has decided that being would be in question in his being. This fundamental desire in turn expresses concretely in the world within the particular situation enveloping the individual, an abstract meaningful structure which is the desire of being in general; it must be considered as human reality in the person, and it brings about his community with others, thus making it possible to state that there is a truth concerning man and not only concerning individuals who cannot be compared. Absolute concreteness, completion, existence as a totality belong then to the free and fundamental desire which is the unique person. Empirical desire is only a symbolization of this; it refers to this and derives its meaning from it while remaining partial and reducible, for the empirical desire cannot be conceived in isolation. On the other hand, the desire of being in its abstract purity is the *truth* of the concrete fundamental desire, but it does not exist by virtue of reality. Thus the fundamental project, the person, the free realization of human truth is everywhere in all desires. . . .

10. ETHICAL IMPLICATIONS

Ontology itself cannot formulate ethical precepts. It is concerned solely with what is, and we cannot possibly derive imperatives from ontology's indicatives. It does, however, allow us to catch a glimpse of what sort of ethics will assume its responsibilities when confronted with a *human reality in situation*. Ontology has revealed to us, in fact, the origin and the nature of *value*; we have seen that value is the *lack* in relation to which the for-itself determines its being as a *lack*. By the very fact that the for-itself *exists*, as we have seen, value arises to haunt its being-for-itself. It follows that the various tasks of the for-itself can be made the object of an existential psychoanalysis, for they all aim at producing the missing synthesis of consciousness and being in the form of value or self-cause. Thus existential psychoanalysis is *moral description*, for it releases to us the ethical meaning of various human projects. It indicates to us the necessity of abandoning the psychology of interest along with any utilitarian interpretation of human conduct—by revealing to us the *ideal* meaning of all human attitudes. These meanings are beyond egoism and altruism, beyond also any behavior which is called *disinterested*. Man makes himself man in order to be God, and selfness considered from this point of view can appear to be an egoism; but precisely because there is no common measure between human reality and the self-cause which it wants to be, one could just as well say that man loses himself in order that the self-cause may exist. We will consider then that all human existence is a passion, the famous *self-interest* being only one way freely chosen among others to realize this passion.

But the principal result of existential psychoanalysis must be to make us repudiate the *spirit of seriousness*. The spirit of seriousness has two characteristics: it considers values as transcendent givens independent of human subjectivity, and it transfers the quality of "desirable" from the ontological structure of things to their simple material constitution. For the spirit of seriousness, for example, *bread* is desirable because it is *necessary* to live (a value written in an intelligible heaven) and because bread *is* nourishing. The result of the serious attitude, which as we know rules the world, is to cause the symbolic values of things to be drunk in by their empirical idiosyncrasy as ink by a blotter; it puts forward the opacity of the desired object and posits it in itself as a desirable irreducible. Thus we are already on the moral plane but concurrently on that of bad faith, for it is an ethics which is ashamed of itself and does not dare speak its name. It has obscured all its goals in order to free itself from anguish. Man pursues being blindly by hiding from himself the free project which is this pursuit. He makes himself such that he is *waited for* by all the tasks placed along his way. Objects are mute demands, and he is nothing in himself but the passive obedience to these demands.

Existential psychoanalysis is going to reveal to man the real goal of his pursuit, which is being as a synthetic fusion of the in-itself with the for-itself; existential psychoanalysis is going to acquaint man with his passion. In truth there are many men who have practiced this psychoanalysis on themselves and who have not waited to learn its principles in order to make use of them as a means of deliverance and salvation. Many men, in fact, know that the goal of their pursuit is being; and to the extent that they possess this knowledge, they refrain from appropriating things for their own sake and try to realize the symbolic appropriation of their being-in-itself. But to the extent that this attempt still shares in the spirit of seriousness and that these men can still believe that their mission of effecting the existence of the in-itself-for-itself is written in things, they are condemned to despair; for they discover at the same time that all human activities are equivalent (for they all tend to sacrifice man in order that the self-cause may arise) and that all are on principle doomed to failure. Thus it amounts to the same thing whether one gets drunk alone or is a leader of nations. If one of these activities takes precedence over the other, this will not be because of its real goal but because of the degree of consciousness which it possesses of its ideal goal; and in this case it will be the quietism of the solitary drunkard which will take precedence over the vain agitation of the leader of nations.

But ontology and existential psychoanalysis (or the spontaneous and empirical application which men have always made of these disciplines) must reveal to the moral agent that he *is the being by whom values exist*. It is then that his freedom will become conscious of itself and will reveal itself in anguish as the unique source of value and the nothingness by which the *world* exists. As soon as freedom discovers the quest for being and the appropriation of the in-itself as *its own possibles*, it will apprehend by and in anguish that they are possibles only on the ground of the possibility of other possibles. But hitherto although possibles could be chosen and rejected *ad libitum*, the theme which made the unity of all choices of possibles was the value or the ideal presence of the *ens causa sui*. What will become of freedom if it turns its back upon this value? Will freedom carry this value along with it whatever it does and even in its very turning back upon the in-itself-for-itself? Will freedom be reapprehended from behind by the value which it wishes to contemplate? Or will freedom by the very fact that it apprehends itself as a freedom in relation to itself, be able to put an end to the reign of this value? In particular is it possible for freedom to take itself for a value as the source of all value, or must it necessarily be defined in relation to a transcendent value which haunts it? And in case it could will itself as its own possible and its determining value, what would this mean? A freedom which wills itself freedom is in fact a being-which-is-not-what-it-is and which-is-what-it-is-not, and which chooses as the ideal of being, being-what-it-is-not and not-being-what-it-is.

This freedom chooses then not to *recover* itself but to flee itself, not to coincide with itself but to be always at a distance *from* itself. What are we to understand by this being which wills to hold itself in awe, to be at a distance from itself? Is it a question of bad faith or of another fundamental attitude? And can one *live* this new aspect of being? In particular will freedom by taking itself for an end escape all *situation?* Or on the contrary, will it remain situated? Or will it situate itself so much the more precisely and the more individually as it projects itself further in anguish as a conditioned freedom and accepts more fully its responsibility as an existent by whom the world comes into being? All these questions, which refer us to a pure and not an accessory reflection, can find their reply only on the ethical plane. We shall devote to them a future work.